THE AMERICAN PIETISM
OF COTTON MATHER

Alas, The *Vanity* which attends Humane Affairs!
As there are many Men and Things that are scarce
mentioned in *True History*, which deserve a mention
more than some that are universally celebrated; What
Hero's are buried among those who lived before the
Days of *Agmemnon?* And *Walter Plettenberg* is less
known than a Turkish Pyrate: What has been *ponderous*
has (as my Lord *Bacon* expresses it) been sunk to the
Bottom in the Stream of *Time,* while we have *Straw*
and *Stubble* swimming a top: So, 'tis a thing, that may
be too truly, but can't be too *sadly,* complained of;
That the Instances wherein *False History* has been
imposed upon the World, are what *cannot be numbred.*
Historians have generally taken after their Father
Herodotus: And even *One of themselves,* Vopiscus by
Name, has expressly said of them, They are all of them
Lyars: This Witness is True!

—Cotton Mather, *Manuductio ad Ministerium*
(Boston, 1726), p. 60.

You must have a Name *reviled on Earth,* 'tis so you
may be the fitter to find a Name *written in Heaven.*
There will be a Resurrection of *Names,* as well as of
Bodies, in the Day when God shall Raise the Dead. All
the *Good that you have done,* all your *Prayers,* all your
Alms, and the *Steps* of your watchful *Walk with God,* all
the brave Efforts of your *Self-Denial,* all the continual
Contrivances to serve Christ and his People, and your
Neighbours, in which you have been swallowed up
every Day, not one Day without them for many, many
years together; they, being *Sprinkled with the Blood of
the Lamb,* shall be found in the Lord's Book of Remembrance; they shall be proclaimed in the Golden Streets
of the City of God.

—Cotton Mather, *The Right Way to Shake Off a Viper*
(Boston, 1720), p. 12.

THE AMERICAN PIETISM OF COTTON MATHER

Origins of American Evangelicalism

by
Richard F. Lovelace

CHRISTIAN
UNIVERSITY
PRESS

A Subsidiary of Christian College Consortium
and Wm. B. Eerdmans Publishing Company
Grand Rapids, Michigan

This book is for Betty Lee.

Order from:
Wm. B. Eerdmans Publishing Company
255 Jefferson Ave., S.E., Grand Rapids, Mich. 49503

Library of Congress Cataloging in Publication Data

Lovelace, Richard F.
  The American pietism of Cotton Mather.

  A revision of the author's thesis, Princeton, 1968.
  Includes bibliographical references.
  1. Mather, Cotton, 1663-1728.   2. Evangelicalism—
United States—History.   I. Title.
F67.M43L68 1979   973.2'092'4 [B]   79-10023
ISBN 0-8028-1750-5

Contents

Preface

THIS WORK BEGAN AS AN EFFORT TO PROBE THE AMERIcan origins of the Great Awakening. Previous studies of the
roots of this phenomenon have quite naturally sought to
distinguish its message and techniques from those of the
Puritanism of the period of "spiritual decline" in New England, either emphasizing the influence of European
Pietism, or positing that a "personalization" of Calvinism by
Edwards and the Tennents was responsible for the remarkable popular response in the 1730s and 1740s. Some have
detected a kind of pre-revivalism in Solomon Stoddard's five
"harvests" of converts during his ministry in Northampton.
But the study of Mather and his period have led me to
conclude that the Puritan experiential tradition, which
Mather called an "American Pietism," constituted the main
root system of the Awakening in its American phase. The
form of existential Calvinism which Mather shared with
most of the other Boston ministry—and with Stoddard—was
substantially similar to the message at the core of the revivals
of the next several decades. The new pastoral strategies that
galvanized the old message to spark the Awakening and the
other factors (some of them obscure to historical investigation) that turned decline into renewal are outside the scope of
this inquiry. But this work revises the ordinary historical
image of Cotton Mather by placing him in the center of the

genetic line that leads from the colonial Puritans to the later evangelicals.

What follows is not a work of intellectual history, although it involves a good deal of analysis based on the history of theology. Rather it is an essay in what Roman Catholics call "spiritual theology": the history and theology of Christian experience. Because of the nature of Cotton Mather's religious expression and commitment, he is an ideal subject for this kind of study, and perhaps this approach can best apprehend his significance. Both the scope and the focus of this study have limited my inquiry into Mather's social, political, and economic environment; for the most part I have presupposed the reader's acquaintance with the work that has been done in those areas by Perry Miller, Edmund Morgan, Carl Bridenbaugh, and others. The spiritual-theological approach needs to be carefully integrated with other historical techniques, but it calls attention to one formative factor that is too little recognized in the writing of church history: the force of ordinary Christian experience. The existential details of the Christian's daily life held an overwhelming importance for Puritans, especially Puritan pastors, and we cannot understand the motives behind their theology and their behavior unless we have penetrated their understanding of the Christian life. While much of the analysis and evaluation in what follows is theological rather than historical in nature, I believe that a careful study of Mather's central experiential concerns sheds significant new light on many historical and cultural problems that until recently have been usually approached from other directions.

The reader should take note of two terms that are used in this book with a significance slightly different from their ordinary meaning. *Theocratic* is a term designating the establishment of religion and the civil enforcement of its beliefs and mores in the pattern dominating Western Christianity from Augustine through Calvin's Geneva and early colonial New England. It is used here as a code word for the inappropriate application of Old Testament principles and mission strategy under a New Testament regime. *Hyper-Calvinism* is used here for any rational manipulation of Calvinist doctrine which pushes its implications beyond the teaching and practice of Calvin himself, particularly when this involves moving the concepts of election and inability into the foreground of evangelism.

F. E. Stoeffler and George Marsden have cautioned me that the title of this work may lead some readers to confuse Mather's indigenous Puritan piety and the Lutheran Pietism with which he so deeply sympathized. But I believe the thrust of this book on Mather's theology of Christian experience is clear. He found his own Puritan concerns mirrored in those of his Lutheran correspondents, and was more confirmed than influenced by continental Pietism. This simply demonstrates the truth of Dr. Stoeffler's thesis that Puritanism and Pietism are kindred experiential movements with differing theological foundations.

* * * * *

This book originated as a doctoral dissertation at Princeton Theological Seminary under the direction of Professor Lefferts A. Loetscher. I owe a great debt of gratitude to Dr. Loetscher for his sensitive guidance in my pursuit of an interest in religious awakenings in America; his help has influenced not only this work but many related academic concerns. I am specifically grateful for his direction toward the study of English Puritan practical theology, the problem of "spiritual decline" in New England, and the introduction he gave me to Mather's *Diary* and the *Manuductio ad Ministerium*. For further help at Princeton I am indebted to Professors James Hastings Nichols and Edward A. Dowey. For additional comments, encouragement, and direction I must thank Clifford Shipton, James Smylie, Franklin Coyle, Sydney Ahlstrom, Martin Marty, and several colleagues in the study of Mather: Joyce Ransome, David Levin, and Robert Middlekauff. I am particularly grateful to Professor Middlekauff for his willingness to read this work in dissertation form and his help in revising it for publication. For my initial entrance into Puritan studies I am indebted to Calvin

Malefyt and Paul Woolley. For many practical insights incorporated here I am thankful to Susan Beers and Donald Mostrom.

I am grateful also for the courtesies extended to me at a number of libraries and research institutions, particularly the Rare Book divisions of the New York Public Library and the Boston Public Library; the Massachusetts Historical Society and the American Antiquarian Society; the Staatsbibliothek der Preussischer Kulturbesitz in West Berlin; and the Archiv der Franckeschen Stiftungen der Universitats-und-Landesbibliothek Sachsen-Anhalt in Halle. I must express special appreciation to Archivleiter J. Storz of the Franckesche Stiftung, and to Mr. Urs Dur, who has given me considerable help in connection with the Mather-Francke correspondence.

For the time needed to digest the Mather canon and write and revise this work, I am indebted to Julian Alexander and the Willow Grove Presbyterian Church in Scotch Plains, New Jersey, and to the administration of Gordon-Conwell Seminary. I am grateful to the small corps of typists who have labored over this work in its various incarnations. For support and sacrificial aid in completing this work over the years I owe a great deal to my wife, Betty Lee Agar Lovelace, and to my family.

CHAPTER ONE

Reinterpreting Mather: An Introduction

EVEN MORE THAN MOST PURITANS, COTTON MATHER retains a dark image in the popular mind. What W. F. Poole said in 1869 is unfortunately still true: "The present generation of youth is taught that nineteen persons were hanged, and one was pressed to death, to gratify the vanity, ambition, and stolid credulity of Mr. Cotton Mather."[1]

Among serious scholars, Mather's portrait has brightened a little with the revival of sympathetic and objective Puritan scholarship in the last half-century. He has been largely exonerated in the matter of the witchcraft scandal, the worst blot on his name. But he continues to be handled with a lingering distaste even by those who present themselves as the champions of Puritanism. One of the main sources of this distaste is the apparent mixture of qualitites in Mather's character. Since the early nineteenth century, even critical historians who were not simply in a rage against Mather have been baffled by their inability to understand him. This is reflected in one of the latest full treatments of Mather, that of Perry Miller, who finds him "in a hundred respects . . . the most intransigent and impervious mind of his period, not to say the most nauseous human being, yet in others . . . the most sensitive and perceptive, the clearest and most resolute."[2]

This kind of puzzled judgment has a long lineage of

precursors from the early nineteenth century down to the present. Probably the first to express it in print was Henry Ware, Jr., who in 1831 struggled to reconcile Mather's reputation at Harvard for instability and poor judgment with the apparent intelligence, liberality, and zeal for the public good of this admittedly "most wonderful man."[3] After the appearance of Charles W. Upham's *Lectures on Witchcraft* (1831), the first decisive attack on Mather since Robert Calef's in 1700, other writers labored to harmonize his alleged agency in the Salem affair with his own contrary testimony and the evidence of integrity in his own writings and those of his contemporaries. These strands of ambiguity, surrounded by other testimonies more positively denouncing or acquitting Mather, had accumulated into a bewildering, scarcely penetrable thicket of contrary opinions by the beginning of this century, so that even a defender of Mather was forced to conclude that "it is impossible now to estimate finally either his character or the quality of his accomplishment."[4]

This estimate is too pessimistic. We should be able to understand Mather as well as any historical figure can be understood. We know more about him—his inner and outward life and his ideas—than we do about any other figure in American church history, simply from the mass of documents which he left: the great diary covering most of his adult life, the longest listing of published writings produced by any American, and a wealth of unpublished letters and manuscripts. But the very bulk of this material has only contributed to the problem of understanding Mather. Few of his critics have been able to bring themselves to read him whole. Consequently, from those who have explored part of the territory we have reports variously describing him as a reactionary and a progressive; as a self-centered neurotic and a sublime mystic; as the last gasp of theocratic Puritanism and the earliest harbinger of the Enlightenment in America.

It is true that Mather was a complex personality; though he was probably no more so than any other human being, few other human beings have revealed themselves to us as fully as he did. Despite this complexity, however, and the inconsistencies produced by growth and change in the course of a long life, there is much more integrity in his character and work than he has been given credit for. But there is a quality in Mather that affects historians like the ink-blots in the Rorschach test: it draws up angelic or demonic archetypes from the unconscious and projects them inexorably on the helpless subject. David Levin says:

> For our society Mather represents a type toward which neutrality is almost inconceivable. . . . He has been a remarkably useful emblem of puritanical meddling, self-righteousness, bigotry, credulity, pedantry, and reaction, and the efforts of several commentators during the last century to sketch a more complex, more accurate figure have little effect on prevailing opinion either in the scholarly community or in popular lore. We seem almost bound to adopt a judicial attitude in the very act of imagining Mather's character and naming its traits. . . . We cannot be sure that he was *not* the perfect model for the hateful image of our national demonology, but it should be salutary to remind ourselves, every century or so, of how persistently we fit very meagre evidence to assumptions that are astonishingly simple-minded.[5]

This work is an attempt to move beyond the confusion, unjustified criticism, and unbalanced adulation of most previous accounts of Cotton Mather to find an integrated picture of the man and his work. It proceeds on the thesis that the key to his character and achievements is his theology, and that this in turn is most easily understood in terms of its emphasis on Christian experience. Mather claimed to be an American Pietist, and the analysis of that claim against the background of our expanding knowledge of the nature of European Pietism dissolves some of the apparent contradictions scholars have found in him and leaves us with a clearer sense of his identity and integrity. Most previous accounts of Mather have been negative either because they were generated in an atmosphere of religious warfare directed against Mather's theological position and tradition—in the struggles between orthodoxy and Unitarianism in nineteenth-century Boston—or because they have sought to comprehend Mather without careful analysis of his theology and his role in the development of the international Protestant consensus which became the Evangelical Movement at the time of the Great Awakening.

My purpose in this analysis is not to prepare a case for him as a great and good man, although such a study will inevitably dispel some of the unfounded popular and even scholarly prejudices against him. I find many of the same faults in Mather that are listed by the worst of his critics, but I do find him to be a coherent personality when understood in the context of the Puritan synthesis of Christian experience, and I find him to be a figure of major importance. "When a Boston preacher who died almost two hundred years ago can still divide our local republic of letters into hostile camps at a moment's notice," says Kittredge, "the presumption is that he amounted to something."[6] I suspect that the main difficulty people have had in grasping Mather is somewhat similar to that which has hampered many in attaining a unified scholarly view of such figures as Calvin and Edwards. Like these men, Mather strongly epitomizes a sharply defined theological position, a position that makes some wince and others rejoice. Like them, also, he cannot be interpreted as an isolated, freakish example of religious eccentricity; he must be understood as a member of a long and rather ample tradition of Christian thought and experience.

I do not mean to suggest that Mather is a star of that same order. He is better understood as the lesser member of a triad including two other men whom he loved and deeply respected, Richard Baxter and August Hermann Francke. Like them, he represents not the tired end of an outworn intellectual fashion but a new mutation in an old tradition within Christendom, a line that was centered on the development of Christian experience in the believing community. That mutation was by no means a sterile product doomed to perish because it could not adapt to the Enlightenment, or to disappear because it adapted too well. It simply continued and modified in important incidental details but not in essence. During the Great Awakening and the Second Awakening it flourished and bore fruit again as it had in the early period of Puritan expansion in England and America.

Some interpreters of the first Awakening have set it over against the Puritanism of Cotton Mather's period in distinct contrast, assuming that Perry Miller is correct in identifying Mather as part of the problem in New England's "spiritual decline" rather than an initial agent in its solution. Miller seems to suggest that the Awakening resulted from a new ingredient springing from the genius and artistry of Jonathan Edwards, so that it is distinct both from the original Puritan "experimental divinity" and the evolved Puritanism of Mather's era. But in what follows I will argue that the Awakening arose in some measure independently in Europe and America from sources within Puritanism and Pietism, movements that have a "mysterious common root," as Ernst Benz observes.[7] The groundwork for this movement in the Boston area was carefully—if unconsciously—laid down during four decades by a group of ministers initially led by the Mathers. An examination of Mather's life and his own concept of his ministry shows that he was both the leading synthesist of the Puritan past in America and the most representative pre-Revivalist during his lifetime.

While Cotton Mather was, as Thomas J. Holmes says, "an orthodox Protestant 'Liberal,' " a study of the general structure of his theology shows almost no departure from Reformation theology in the direction of the Enlightenment.[8] Mather was in fact a passionate enemy of the new rationalism, although he was willing to use some of its terminology in order to reach and hold his audience. While there is a strong effort in his thinking to simplify Reformed orthodoxy and reduce it to biblical essentials, this is neither Enlightenment latitudinarianism nor a desperate effort to recapture the American mind through the presentation of fewer beliefs and more piety. It is rather an effort to follow the lead of English progressives like Baxter and Continental figures like Spener and Francke in distilling the essence of biblical faith out of the expanded intellectual systems of Lutheran and Reformed orthodoxy. But if Mather's theology was doctrinally simplified, it was made practically complex by its incorporation of elements from Christian traditions other than his own, in which his erudition made him a fascinated visitor: patristic, medieval, and counter-Reformation Catholicism, and Lutheran Pietism. This involved synthesis was energized by another component that was alien to much of scholastic orthodoxy, Mather's millennialism, which was a main source of his activism and his predominant mood of revivalist expectation.

Mather also made some attempt to simplify the Puritan theory of conversion. This was no evidence of an anthropocentric shift from Calvinism, as some have suggested, since a great part of the Puritan theory went far beyond both Calvin and the biblical evidence in extrapolating the practical implications of the sovereignty of God. The hyper-Calvinism which terrified potential converts and produced a recurrent paralysis even in those professing conversion may have made a large contribution to the "spiritual decline" of the old Puritanism in America. In dealing with this problem, however, the cautious side of Mather's progressive conservatism is more evident than his ability to be innovative, since he retained the prolonged "process of conversion," which fixed the convert's gaze on his own unworthiness and inability to turn and required experiential evidence from the Christian's inner and outward life in order to confirm assurance. His persistent application of this and other Puritan prescriptions to his own spiritual life has had much to do with his reputation for psychological imbalance among his critics.

We must examine carefully the extent to which the Puritan experiential theory of the spiritual life operated with a built-in pathology. Mather did, however, make an effort to "buffer" this approach with a frequent emphasis on the grace and mercy of God and a repeated invitation to all his hearers to make a trial at converting. On occasion he moved to the brink of Wesleyan Arminianism in an effort to comfort one sector of his audience, but he returned immediately to the hard Puritan line as he sought to convict the complacent. His approach foreshadowed, but did not fully duplicate, the conversion theory of the post-Edwardsian revivalism of the nineteenth century. But in the fullness of his stress on conversion, his "loading" of all the content of the Christian life into its initial experience, he was consistent with both the Puritan past and the revivalist future.

The proliferation of the means of grace in Mather's practice, in contrast to the simplicity of his theology, was the result of his effort to sustain the intensity of the initial mystical assurance of the convert. In Mather's affinity for the asceticism of the fathers, and his unconscious emulation of later Catholic devotional practice, is reflected the fact that a large part of the Puritan tradition of Christian experience was produced by the adaption of medieval and and patristic piety to a Reformed theological base. His zeal in practicing and promoting this methodism is one of the features which has most repelled the critics of the last two centuries; but it was normal within Puritanism, except that in Mather it aspired to heroism.

In his treatment of sanctification, Mather retained the typically deep Puritan understanding of normative spiritual health as "the power of godliness." He also had a much deeper vision of the depth and complexity of sin than many critics have seen in him. While he gave relatively less space to the problems of sanctification than he did to the struggles of conversion, his handling of the subject was firmly anchored in the tradition of Augustine, Calvin, and such Puritans as John Owen. His supposed moralism is hard to maintain in the face of the abundant evidence that he detested real Enlightenment moralists, and that he grounded his ethical urgency firmly on the doctrines of grace as interpreted by Puritan evangelicalism. His activisim was quite typical of the Puritan tradition and the Pietism of his friends at Halle, although few in these traditions worked as hard as Mather at organizing their activity and recording this effort.

Mather's understanding of the outworking of piety in the practical mission of the church is an epitome of Puritan theory on the subject; but it was enriched by his eager adoption of new strategies of mission from London and the Continent. Cellgroups similar to the Pietist collegia had been functioning in New England apparently from the beginning of the colonial period, and Mather was a fervent advocate of these, so that it was natural for him to assume the American leadership in the formation of the new reforming societies invented in London in the 1690s. While these proved to be a failure because of their repressive legalism, Mather found

inspiration in Halle for a more positive evangelical concern
for the spiritual and social well-being of Boston, and his mind
poured out a host of projects in the early 1700s. Some of these
died stillborn and others provoked intense hostility even
where they proved obviously beneficial; but many either
foreshadowed or helped establish the patterns of voluntary
ecumenical action that flourished in the Benevolent Empire
of the nineteenth century.

In all of this animation of projects Mather was not simply
fighting a desperate holding action. He was working consciously to help bring in the premillennial awakening which
his eschatology led him to expect in the 1730s; and his
prayers during the prime of his life are full of conviction that
the great spiritual revolution which will end in Christ's return was soon to occur, preceded by remarkable outpourings
of the Holy Spirit and ingatherings of souls. As a correlate of
this chiliastic expectation, Mather—like the other main figures in the Puritan/Pietist stream—was firmly dedicated to
the goal of ecumenical union among evangelical Protestants
and worked all his life to establish a climate and a doctrinal
basis within which reunion might be possible, since for him
it was an indispensable prerequisite for the parousia.
Another such prerequisite, in his understanding, was the
vigorous extension of the church's mission among those
peoples not yet fully reached by the gospel. His millennial
hopes led him to a special concern for the Jews, and he was
also the most active spokesman of his generation in New
England on behalf of the ministry to American blacks and
native Americans. He responded to Halle's pioneering East
Indian mission with contributions of money and publicity,
and he suggested that similar work be carried on by American
Christians. In few of these emphases was he absolutely original, but he had a knack for appreciating, correlating, and
collecting trends within the Christendom of his time that
would prove to be the heart of the future.

What follows is an attempt to document this picture of
Mather with the use of all of the published sources and the
most important of those that remain unpublished. Before
launching into this study, however, it may be helpful to

rehearse the main events of Mather's life, clarifying the main forces that shaped his thinking.

The substance of Mather's thinking and the structure of his character owe a great deal to his membership in the most important dynasty in colonial New England history. Richard Mather (1596-1669), the founder, came to Boston in 1635 and carried out a careful and studious ministry in the church at Dorchester until his death. He was the principal developer of Congregational polity in New England, and the Cambridge Platform, which is cast mainly in the language of his draft, shows him to have been an original and articulate thinker.[9] His son Increase (1639-1723) was converted to serious Christianity in 1654, two years before his graduation from Harvard College. Urged toward scholarly eminence by the example of his father and the encouragement of his mother, he acquired a Master of Arts degree at Trinity College in Dublin. After a year of ministry in England he was forced back to America by the Restoration, loyal to his father's Nonconformist principles; and in 1661 he began to alternate in preaching in Dorchester and at the new North Church in Boston, to which he was called permanently as teacher in 1664. In 1662 he married John Cotton's only daughter, thus uniting two of the main genetic streams of spiritual and intellectual leadership in the colony. The first offspring of this union, born on February 12, 1663, was Cotton Mather (1663-1727).

During Cotton's childhood his father's career was a constantly rising star in church and political circles in the Bay Colony. Increase accompanied Richard Mather to the Synod of 1662 as a second delegate from the Dorchester church, and he joined President Chauncy and John Davenport in opposing his father's advocacy of the Halfway Covenant, appearing in print for the first time in a preface to Davenport's protest against the result. In this instance Increase showed a strong vein of intellectual courage and independence and also a conservative bent which is in contrast to the progressive temper of his father and his son Cotton. But in the reversal of his position by 1668 he displayed that adaptability under the pressure of practical necessity that characterized all three of the principal Mathers. In 1664, Increase was formally installed as teacher of the North Church. In 1667 he began a long list of publications with a treatise on the millennial awakening, which would involve the conversion of the Jews.[10] In 1674 he was appointed by the general court to the board of censorship, which regulated the press in New England, and in the same year was made an overseer of Harvard College. In the meantime he pursued a rigid course of study and devotional exercise, which is significantly reflected in his son's portrayal of the ideal Christian life, and he accumulated the finest and most extensive library in the colonies, which started at nearly a thousand volumes in 1664 and to which he made constant additions over the years.[11]

Growing up in such a household, the young Cotton Mather was in ideal surroundings for the nurture of learning and of ambition toward leadership. He readily took to the process of education, partly because his mind was exceptionally quick, and partly because his relationship with his father was close and affectionate. He tells us that he counted among his chief blessings ". . . especially, the Life and Health of my dear Father, whom I may reckon among the richest of my Enjoyments."[12] As Barrett Wendell remarks, "Cotton Mather never observed any other law of God quite so faithfully as the Fifth Commandment,"[13] and this receptiveness to authority enabled him to drink in eagerly and rapidly the lessons of his father and the teachers at the Boston free school. Meanwhile, his spiritual life developed with that precocity which seems to have been common among Puritan children, if we can accept the account he wrote for his son near the end of his life:

> I desire to bewayl unto the very *end* of my Life, the early Ebullitions of *Original Sin,* which appeared at the very Beginning of it. Indeed your Grandfather . . . would . . . comfort himself with an Opinion of my being *Sanctified by the Holy Spirit of God in my very infancy.* But he knew not how vile I was. . . . However, there were *some good things* in my childhood. . . . I began to *pray,* even when I began to speak. I learned myself to *write* before my going to school for it. I used *secret prayer,* not confining myself to *Forms* in it; and yet I composed *Forms of*

prayer for my school-mates (I suppose when I was about seven or eight years old), and obliged them to *pray*. Before I could write *Sermons* in the public Assemblies I commonly *wrote* what I remembered when I came home. I rebuked my play mates for their wicked *words* and *ways;* and sometimes I suffered from them, the persecution of not only *Scoffs* but *Blows* also, for my Rebukes, when somebody told your Grandfather, I remember he seemed very *glad,* yea, almost *proud* of my Affronts, and I then wondered at it, tho' afterwards I better understood his Heavenly principles. [14]

The young Mather entered Harvard College in 1675 at the age of eleven, [15] having already read in Catullus, Terence, Ovid, Virgil, Plato, Homer, and the Greek New Testament, and having begun the study of Hebrew grammar. His progress was predictably rapid:

I composed *Systems* both of Logick and Physick, in *Catachisms* of my own, which have since been used by many others. . . . I made *Theses,* and Antitheses upon the main *Questions* that lay before me. For my *Declamations* I ordinarily took some Article of *Natural Philosophy* for my subject, by which contrivances I did Kill two birds with one Stone. Hundreds of books I read over, and I kept a Diary of my studies. *My son* I would not have mentioned these things, but that I may provoke *your* emulation. [16]

His spiritual life kept pace: at fourteen he was observing whole days of prayer and fasting, and at sixteen he had come to a firm enough assurance of his salvation to join the North Church as a communicant member. However, his life was not entirely untroubled during this period. He underwent a particularly severe hazing at the hands of the much older upperclassmen; he was prone to melancholy and hypochondria; and he developed a stammer. We can read these symptoms in various ways, depending on our own childhood experience, our theology, and our personal response to mental and spiritual prodigies. Morison rejoices that "that insufferable young prig Cotton Mather was being kicked about, as he so richly deserved," by stronger spirits, while he enlisted others of more feeble wit to pray with him. [17] "In order to resist the tyranny of our own secular stereotype," David Levin comments, "I prefer to believe that if he was abused it was the sturdy spirits who prayed with him and the feeble wits who tormented him." [18] Mather himself undoubtedly felt that he was just another instance of Joseph among the brethren, and that his problems with some other children, in certain extraordinary contexts, were only a foretaste of the inevitable conflict that would accompany the spiritual leadership of his later life. Certainly the leaders of the college played the part of doting Jacobs effectively, alienating a certain proportion of the students from Mather and not incidentally exposing him to tremendous temptations to pride and egoism. In the commencement oration, when Mather gained his bachelor's degree in 1678, President Urian Oakes proceeded to parse the elements of Mather's name, expecting that "in this youth Cotton and Mather shall, in fact as well as in name, join together and once more appear in life."[19]

Cotton Mather had been reared with the ministry in mind and had preached his first sermon to a gathering of young people when he was only sixteen;[20] but he hesitated to enter a pastoral career with a speech handicap, and he turned for a while to the study of medicine. Continuing to attend Harvard while working as a tutor, he obtained the Master of Arts degree in 1681. He had been preaching occasionally during this period in some of the more prestigious churches in the colony, and his stammer was clearing up thanks to the habit of deliberate speaking which he adopted at the advice of a schoolmaster. In November of 1681 he was invited to become the pastor of the church John Davenport had founded in New Haven, a considerable testimony to his ability and reputation at the age of nineteen. After some vying between the North Church brethren and the New Haven brethren and a series of "importunate votes" among the former to secure the young man for Boston, Cotton decided to remain as an unordained assistant to his father and continue his studies.

Cotton Mather had been unanimously called as pastor to the North Church in 1683, before the age of twenty, but had elected to remain on a less formal basis as his father's assistant because of his extreme youth and his hesitancy to take on what he felt were awesome responsibilities involved in the pastorate. But the call was reissued in 1684, and he accepted and was ordained in 1685. He continued and expanded a vigorous pastoral program in the neighborhood of the North Church, which included evangelism among the poor and criminals and the creation of a young men's religious society in the south of town, as well as the regular labors of preaching, calling, and studying. He was married on May 4, 1686, to Abigail Phillips. By the time of his father's departure for England he had become, at twenty-five, an experienced pastor and preacher, well able to keep the church in order while his father was abroad. Accessions to the church membership during Increase's absence—which included Cotton's wife Abigail in 1689—continued at the regular average of twenty-five per annum, and in 1691 there was something of a revival, with forty-nine added. In 1692, while Increase was still abroad, Cotton admitted the first person to membership in the North Church under the Halfway Covenant, a liberal innovation that aroused resistance among some conservatives in the congregation.

His published literary production, beginning in the early 1680s with some occasional poems and broadening out to include a fair number of sermons through the period of his father's absence, had begun to recommend Cotton Mather's gifts to the public even beyond Boston. Encouraged in self-esteem from his childhood, Mather had set his sights on greatness in the conduct of his life's work. A *Diary* entry from his twenty-third year, written in February 1685 under the heading *Res Mirabilis et Memoranda*, recounts a vision he had after prolonged fasting and prayer, in which an angel applied to him the words of Ezekiel 31:3-5, 7, 9:

> Behold hee was a Cedar in Lebanon with fair branches, and with a shadowing Shrowd, and of an high Stature, and his Top was among the thick Boughs. The Waters made him great, the Keep sett him up on high, with her Rivers running about his Plants. His Heighth was exalted above all the Trees of the Field, and his Boughs were multiplied, and his Branches became long, because of the Multitude of Waters, when hee shott forth. Thus was hee fair in his Greatness in the Length of his Branches for his Root was by the great Waters. Nor was any Tree in the Garden of God like unto him in his Beauty. I have made him fair by the multitude of his Branches so that all the Trees of Eden that were in the Garden of God envied him.

Mather goes on to develop the application of the passage rather cautiously (the whole text except the biblical quotation is in Latin, since the author knew it would expose him to the charge of enthusiasm).

> This Angel said that he was sent by the Lord Jesus to bear a clear answer to the prayers of a certain youth, and to bear back his words in reply. . . . And in particular this Angel spoke of the influence his branches should have, and of the books this youth should write and publish, not only in America, but in Europe. And he added certain special prophecies of the great works this youth should do for the church of Christ in the revolutions that are now in hand. Lord Jesus! What is the meaning of this marvel? From the wiles of the Devil, I beseech thee, deliver and defend Thy most unworthy servant.[21]

This is indeed a memorable prediction, if it actually does date from the time of the original entry and is not an enlargement performed in Mather's later copying of his diaries.

Despite his youth, Mather was recognized in his father's absence as an able leader in behalf of Puritan interests. On June 12, 1690, he was elected a Fellow of Harvard College, becoming at twenty-seven the youngest man ever so honored. When the revolution occurred in England and the Bostonians seized the reins from Andros in 1689, he had spoken out to the public shortly before the insurrection in an "affectionate and moving Speech" which pressed "Peace and Love and Submission unto a legal Government, tho' he suffered from some tumultuous People, by doing so."[22] The "tumultuous" faction did not fail later to accuse Mather of seeking to manage the revolution to suit his private ambitions.

Meanwhile, Increase Mather had been seeking unsuccessfully to interest King James in restoring the vacated charter and securing Puritan theocracy in New England again, and incidentally in procuring another charter for Harvard which would anchor it permanently to Calvinism. Gradually recognizing that James was unwilling to relinquish as much control over New England as the colonists desired, he determined to reach a practical compromise and accept a more liberal government. His close friendship with Baxter and other English moderates had moved him away from theocratic absolutism and toward the ideals of religious freedom that had been developing in England since the Revolutionary period. Indeed, he may have already been travelling in this direction before his arrival in London, since his ties with English life and thought had always been close and strong since his youth. Thus the new charter he helped obtain, adopted in October 1691, enlarged the franchise beyond the church membership, and admitted royal appointment of the governor, balanced by a popularly elected council. Increase Mather's diplomatic skill had gained him sufficient respect in London that he was permitted to name the chief officers who were to put this government into operation. While Cotton Mather rejoiced at home over the possibilities for doing good in this situation, other voices claimed that his father had sold out to the establishment in exchange for the right to control the New England government. The Mathers were encountering opposition now from religious conservatives who disliked the new charter and wanted to return to the theocracy, and from others among the merchant class who wanted looser connections with the home country for economic reasons.[23]

This undercurrent of conflict was shortly intensified by a new crisis, the witchcraft cases in Salem. Most of the civilized West at that time, including the educated classes and the clergy, believed firmly in both the existence and the powers of sorcerers. They thought they were supported in this belief by biblical data, the judgment of authorities in the main Christian traditions, and common knowledge of enchantments and preternatural phenomena. Puritan theologians such as Perkins, Bernard, and Gaule had sought to define carefully the methods of detecting and trying supposed witches, but had not contested the existence of real and operative sorcery. During the latter half of the seventeenth century, religious apologists of all persuasions, including a surprising proportion of the budding scientific community, made the unhappy mistake of seizing on the existence of witchcraft as a prime piece of evidence to use against deistic "Sadducees," who were calling in question the whole realm of the supernatural. There had been an unusual circulation of this apologetic literature in English-speaking circles before the Salem affair.[24]

The New England clergy were particularly vulnerable to credulity in the matter of witchcraft for several reasons. They felt that the colonists had invaded a territory that had been under the control of the devil, exercised through sorcerers among the natives, and they felt that his agency was particularly active in the New World to solicit traitors against the exemplary Christian state established there. And as a condition of spiritual decline became apparent in the second generation, the ministers were susceptible to the idea that New England deserved a plague of witches. It is not surprising, then, that Increase Mather, one of the main opponents of that spiritual decline and an avid scientific amateur—in a day when scientific interest was so omnivorous as to include supernatural occurrences among the data of its investigations —should publish in 1684 his *Illustrious Providences,* which devotes some space to the discussion of cases of witchcraft.

In 1689, Cotton Mather published a similar work devoted entirely to witchcraft, *Memorable Providences,* including in it the account of his own ministry to the Goodwin family in Boston during the seizure of their children by an apparent enchantment involving demonic possession. Mather's labors in this instance were strictly pastoral, involving concerted prayer and counseling with the children. A washerwoman was tried, convicted, and executed for the crime of witchcraft in that case, but Mather had no part in the judicial proceedings, though he sought to give the woman spiritual counseling. *Memorable Providences* was reprinted in 1691 in London, prefaced by numerous ministerial recommendations, including one by Richard Baxter which lauded it as incontrovertible proof of the reality of sorcery. Included in it is a sermon Mather preached in 1691 under the same title as his later book, "Wonders of the Invisible World," which among other things stresses that in the last times God may permit an extraordinary descent of demons as a punishment for apostasy and a prelude to the end.

Since the problems with the Parris family in 1692 had some external resemblance to those of the Goodwin family described by Cotton Mather, it is possible to see something in the assertion that his book, and his father's, were inflammatory and partly to blame for the Salem scandal. But this is stretching the evidence, considering the number of works on this subject then in circulation and the common occurrence of isolated instances of witchcraft.

The new government, having appointed a court of oyer and terminer—whether the ministers had a hand in this, we cannot tell—proceeded to try and execute one witch, and then ask the clergy for their advice about proceeding further to investigate the outbreak of witchcraft, which was reaching epidemic proportions. Even before this trial, on May 31, 1692, Cotton Mather had written to John Richards warning specifically against the use of spectral evidence,[25] and apparently recommending the release of confessing criminals, which is a stage more merciful than common English practice.[26] The advice of the ministers, which was drafted by Cotton Mather and signed by all the Boston clergy, is one of those protean documents that can be cited by each side to prove its point. It heavily emphasizes the need for caution in the methods of trial and especially discourages the use of spectral evidence, but it does recommend that the trials proceed. It is perhaps best viewed as a clear application of the principles of the Puritan theologians to the existing problem, and it is considerably more cautious than common English judicial procedure.

It is difficult to avoid conjecture in reconstructing the part the Mathers played in the rest of the Salem outbreak. In a letter to John Cotton written on August 5, 1692, Cotton expresses himself as one thoroughly convinced that the prosecution is an effective retaliation against the devil's plot against New England.[27] He was later present at the execution of George Burroughs, and according to both Calef and Sewall spoke out to the crowd after his death justifying the sentence at a point when some were inclined to waver because of the man's protestations of innocence. Increase Mather, who was also present at the trial of Burroughs, seconded his son's judgment of Burroughs' guilt.

But there is no evidence that either Mather attended the trials except on two occasions, and Cotton was severely ill during this year. The assumption must be that the main scope of their involvement in the trials was to follow the news of them. But the Mathers, as well as other clergy and enlightened laity, soon became uneasy with the progress of the trials. One of the Mather government appointees, Nathaniel Saltonstall, resigned from the court; Samuel Willard published a tract against spectral evidence; and Thomas Brattle, in a private letter on October 8, 1692, questioned the methods of the court and referred to the opposition of Increase Mather and other ministers to the procedure in the trials. Five days before this, Increase had read to the Cambridge Association of ministers the manuscript of his *Cases of Conscience* (1693), a searching but not accusatory critique of the methods of the court. Most of the ministers rallied fairly rapidly to the cause of halting the trials, although Stoughton and other judges remained unconvinced, and a majority of the public seemed to support them. By January of 1693, Governor Phips had seen the wisdom of the ministers' advice, and the fifty-three persons yet remaining to be tried were either acquitted or pardoned. At the request of the court, Cotton Mather wrote his *Wonders of the Invisible World,* which sets forth the traditional Puritan approach to the handling of witch trials and endeavors to demonstrate the reality of satanic agency in the affair, in which the Mathers and virtually all others in New England believed. The book also puts the best possible construction on the actions of the court in the trials. There were many who found it in contradiction to Increase Mather's *Cases of Conscience,* but Increase specifically endorsed its opinions in the preface to *Cases* when that book appeared in London.

It seems that the Mathers were in fair agreement about the trials: they believed that there had been real witchcraft, that there had been errors in the trials (perhaps also satanically energized), but that it was best to pull the mantle of charity over the errors of the magistracy. Neither of the Mathers can be represented as "whipping up" the affair as a stalking horse for his own political power. Their united efforts in all that occurred were directed toward moderating the principles of the court and fighting the descent of devils, partly by a just administration of penalties but principally by fasting and prayer. Cotton Mather especially gave himself to these remedies; he preached and counseled with the suspects in prison, and he took six of the energumens into his home to effect a spiritual cure, keeping notably silent on their conjectures about the identity of their human oppressors. While there was a limited popular stir against the Mathers and the other ministers instigated by Robert Calef at this time, there is absolutely no evidence of the massive popular uprising against the supposed Mather theocracy which the nineteenth-century critics have conjectured.[28]

Some of these have judged it to be especially incriminating that, unlike Judge Sewall, Cotton Mather never publicly confessed any errors in the handling of the witchcraft affair. But this is understandable if it is realized that he was relatively uninvolved in the control of the public proceedings. Even so, at the time Sewall made his public announcement, Mather noted in his *Diary* that he was afflicted with discouraging thoughts of divine displeasure, "for my not appearing with *Vigor* enough to stop the proceedings of the Judges, when the Inextricable Storm from the *Invisible World* assaulted the Countrey"; but he felt himself quieted by a divine assurance—apparently in some measure involving his confession and forgiveness.[29] But on the previous day he had read a set of Articles of Confession at a public fast day, a rather typical jeremiad which had enumerated in its list of sins this item: "*Wicked Sorceries* have been practiced in the Land, and yett in the Troubles from the Divels, thereby brought in among us, those Errors, on both Hands, were committed, which wee have Cause to bewayl with much Abasement of Soul before the Lord."[30] Sixteen years later, in 1713, he was still seeking in prayer to understand "the Meaning of the Descent from the Invisible World, which nineteen years ago produced in a Sermon from me, a good part of what is now published."[31]

With the recovery of a measure of his health and the dying down of the Salem outbreak, Cotton Mather began to grapple with a variety of literary labors during the summer of 1693, among them two major ones: the preparation of a history of New England and the compilation of a giant collection of comments on the whole Bible.

During the middle 1690s, specifically in the year 1696, Mather began to develop in his thoughts and prayers a considerable interest in world affairs. This was centered first of all on political concerns in the Protestant-Catholic vying between England and France; but it gradually developed into a concern for the reviving of the ecumenical church in preparation for the return of Christ, which he, like his father, felt was imminent. It was fortunate that he was sustained by such eschatological optimism during these years, because the spiritual interests of New England as the Mathers saw them were in for a series of painful shocks as the turn of the century drew on. For one thing, there was a gradual consolidation of political opposition to the Mathers under the leadership of Elisha Cooke, who had been one of Increase's dissatisfied companions in London and who wanted the colony independent both of the king and the Mathers. For another, there was a different party that opposed the Mathers for religious reasons. The tutors who had been managing Harvard College under Increase's presidency, William Brattle and John Leverett, had been quietly recommending to the students books by latitudinarian writers in the Church of England, presenting a kind of religion that was, as Benjamin Colman put it, "all calm and soft and melting."[32] Oddly enough, Increase apparently was not able to detect the drift of his tutors during most of his tenure as president of the college. Gradually the difference in viewpoint became apparent, however, and the Mathers found themselves facing a broad-church coalition within the Harvard Corporation, led by the Brattles, Leverett, and Rev. Ebenezer Pemberton.

At the beginning of 1698, Leverett and the Brattles quietly set about organizing a new church based on slightly looser principles than were typical in the Congregational Church. In November of 1699, the young Benjamin Colman, ordained in London by Presbyterian hands, arrived as pastor of the Brattle Street Church, and the founders published a manifesto to support their innovations. These included the omission of the required relating of spiritual experience for church membership, the introduction of some other practices that seemed to weaken the spiritual fabric of the church (such as admitting the children of any professing Christian to baptism and the election of ministers by all contributing to their support), and others which were sore points in the troubled history of Puritan-Anglican relations (liturgical use of the Lord's Prayer and the dumb reading of Scripture).

The Mathers were intensely disturbed by this public eruption of dissent. Nevertheless, they worked to compose the differences, halting a counter-manifesto in the presses while Cotton went to negotiate with the other party, convincing them to unite with the other Boston churches on the bases of the *Heads of Agreement* of the Presbyterian-Congregational merger that Increase Mather had assisted while he was in London. The Mathers held a day of fasting and prayer with the new church on January 31, 1700, with Increase preaching on "following Peace with Holiness," and Cotton concluding in prayer. Nevertheless, the Mathers felt that they had to go on record publicly against the innovations in polity, and Increase's *Order of the Gospel* (1700), which stuck fairly well to principles and avoided personalities, touched off a brief but vicious pamphlet warfare between the two parties.[33]

During the period of this controversy, the general court was exerting pressure to dislodge Increase Mather from the presidency of Harvard College by requiring—not unreasonably—his residence there. The motivation behind this pressure was partly pragmatic and partly political (on the part of Elisha Cooke and other conservative advocates of the old charter), and probably not for the most part connected with Mather's religious stance, according to Murdock.[34] When the court eventually appointed Samuel Willard to replace the elder Mather in the summer of 1701, the loss of the position was undoubtedly in some measure a relief to Increase, who was far more interested in preaching to the many hundreds in his church than in supervising the tutoring of forty or fifty boys. But Cotton took the matter hard, as if it involved a loss of his father's honor. In the meantime, in November 1700, Robert Calef's *More Wonders of the Invisible World* arrived from London. Calef, a Boston merchant about whom we know little except what is expressed in his book, had been gathering materials for this work since the witch-craft trials, and in its latter stages he had been assisted by the Brattles, according to Sibley.[35] The Mathers had known about the preparation of the book since June of 1698, and Cotton had been praying against its appearance:

> There is a sort of *Sadducee* in this Town; a man, who makes little Conscience of lying; and one whom no Reason will divert from his malicious Purposes. This man, out of Enmity to mee, for my public Asserting of such Truths, as the Scripture has taught us, about the Existence and Influence of the *Invisible World*, hath often abused mee, with venemous *Reproaches*, and most palpable *Injuries*. I have hitherto taken little Notice of his Libels and Slanders; but this Contempt enrages him. I under-stand, that hee apprehends the shortest way to deliver People, from the *Beleef* of the Doctrines which not I only, but all the Ministers of Christ in the World, have hitherto mentained, will bee, to show the World, what an *ill Man* I am. To this End, I understand, hee hath written a Volume of invented and notori-ous *Lies,* and also searched a large Part of the *Books* which I have published, and with false Quotations of little Scraps here and there from them, endeavoured for to cavil at them. . . . Wherefore, in my Supplications, I first of all declared unto the Lord, that I freely *Forgave* this miserable Man, all the Wrongs which hee did unto mee, and I pray'd the Lord also to *forgive* him, and to do him good even as to my own Soul. But then, I pleaded with the Lord, that the *Design* of this Man, was to hurt my precious *Opportunities* of glorifying my Glorious Lord Jesus Christ; and I could not but cry unto the Lord, that Hee would rescue my Opportunities of serving my Lord Jesus Christ, from the Attempts of this Man to damnify them.[36]

When the book appeared in Boston, Increase Mather burned a copy of it in the Harvard yard, according to Sibley—the traditional way of stigmatizing a libelous book.[37] Cotton Mather and six friends issued a defense of Increase Mather's character and conduct, and Increase had Calef arrested for libel; but he later dropped the suit after a conversation with him. Mather seems to have felt that there was little disposition in Boston to believe the man, since Willard and other objects of his attack had been able to rebuff Calef by simply ignoring him. He could not, of course, reckon on the use generations of future anti-Puritans would make of the book, carrying its implications far beyond what Calef dared to intimate openly.

On the subject of witchcraft, Calef's work is a far better book than Mather thought it was. It is an inarticulate, poorly organized, but telling attack, first, on the Puritan theory of the real agency of witches, and second, on the mismanagement of the trials in New England; and its final summary is particularly cogent. On the subject of the Mathers and the Puritan ministers in general, however, the book is either simply erroneous or openly guilty of misrepresentation, or both. In this area it is basically a political attack, dredging up all the old resentments against the handling of the charter and arguing that the clergy must be stopped from this kind of meddling. Its personal attack on the Mathers was accepted at the time only among the limited circle of their political and religious enemies, and it was revived by these people in the 1720s during the inoculation controversy. Cotton's ultimate comment on Calef's book is written on the flyleaf of the copy in his library: "Job XXXI. 35, 36. My desire is that mine adversary had written a Book. Surely I would take it upon my Shoulder, and bind it as a crown to me. Co: Mather."[38]

During the succeeding years of the first decade of the eighteenth century, the Mathers gradually withdrew from political activity. Neither of them made a practice of attending the meetings of the college corporation from that point on. When President Willard died in 1707, they had considerable hope that Cotton Mather would be elected, but the corporation chose Leverett instead, to their considerable chagrin.

Cotton's first wife died in 1702, and he married a widow, Elizabeth Hubbard, the following year. With his magnum opus, the *Magnalia*, finally off the press in London, he continued to pour out a host of minor writings in various forms. His literary output had projected his fame in Europe, which was influenced by none of the political shadows that darkened it at home. It had also gained him a list of correspondents abroad that may have numbered fifty at one time, among whom we find men of the highest stature among his contemporaries, including Defoe, Watts, Sir Richard Blackmore, William Whiston, Lord Chancellor King, and John Desaguliers. In 1710 the University of Glasgow conferred on him the title of Doctor of Divinity, and from that point Mather wore a ring embossed with his old life-symbol, a spreading tree, inscribed *Glascua Rigavit* ("Glasgow has watered it"), finding excuse for this in the constant exhortations for fruitfulness to which this emblem provoked him. In 1713, Mather was proposed and virtually inducted as a member of the Royal Society in London, although his enemies then and since have found occasion to contest the validity of his claim.[39]

Since the rest of this work is devoted to an examination of the principles and practice of Christian experience that were Cotton Mather's main concern during the last several decades of his life, a brief sketch of the events framing these years will suffice. In ecclesiastical affairs the Mathers were from the beginning in opposition to Solomon Stoddard's proposals for the centralization of the Congregational polity (as well as his sacramental theory), but in 1705 Cotton Mather joined with Colman, Wadsworth, and a number of others in recommending a closer synodical linkage between the churches as one means of checking the spiritual decline and promoting the health of the churches. The *Proposals* of 1705 were apparently too "liberal" for the majority of adherents to the old Congregational Way, however, and this particular cause simply subsided into silence after the effective attack John Wise made on it in 1713.[40] As Harvard College departed increasingly from the intellectual and spiritual standards that Cotton Mather desired for it, he gradually cut his ties and allegiance to it. He considered education an instrument primarily for the nurture of an intellectually advanced but biblically based world-outlook, to be informed by vital piety, and Harvard seemed to him at that point to be aiming neither to be biblical, nor pious, nor profound. Mather transferred his allegiance to the new college founded in 1700 in New Haven, and he secured for it an endowment and a name from a merchant named Elihu Yale.

A number of events in family and public life conspired

to make the last decade of Mather's life a rather gloomy one, as it was also for the interests of Puritanism in New England. His second marriage, like the first, was a happy one; but Elizabeth Mather died in 1713. It was not long after his third marriage to Mrs. Lydia George in 1715, that she began to show signs of serious mental illness, which produced in her occasional periods of violent hostility toward him and which continued intermittently during the rest of their life together. Of the fifteen children born to Mather in the first two of these unions, nine had died in infancy. Of the remaining six, his favorite daughter, Katy, died in 1716, probably in her twenties; Abigail died in 1721 at twenty-seven; and Elizabeth died in 1726, aged twenty-two. And though Samuel and Hannah Mather outlived their father and enjoyed productive lives, Mather's favorite son, Cressy, born in 1699, was a wastrel, publicly charged with bastardy in 1717, and lost at sea in 1724.

Apart from these problems in his immediate family, Mather had taken on the administration of an estate in his third wife's family, and was under terrible financial pressure from this himself until his congregation took a collection to assist him. Apart from these family troubles, Mather suffered a great deal of abuse and was almost assassinated as a result of his one action that has commended the favor of nearly all historians, advising the use of inoculation in the smallpox epidemic of 1721. In 1724, a year after his father's death, he was again disappointed in being passed over for the presidency of Harvard, though he did not expect it. The effect of those troubles on him is visible in a regression to the jeremiad mood in the 1720s and occasional outbreaks of irascibility. But in his diary he also speaks much of the sanctifying effects of this schooling of the cross, particularly in the mortification of pride, a problem he had been aware of since his youth. After a period of depression at the end of his life, he died in a state of calm and peaceful joy. Asked by his son Samuel for a word of counsel, he murmured the one word that had been his life's motto: *Fructuosus*.

Benjamin Colman, the pastor of the Brattle Street Church, whose position had sometimes brought him into conflict with Mather, considered him

> . . . the *first Minister in the Town,* the first in Age, in Gifts, and
> in grace; as all his Brethren very readily own. I might add . . .
> the *first* in the whole *Province* and *Provinces* of *New England,* for
> universal Literature, and extensive Services. Yea it may be
> among all the *Fathers* in these Churches, from the beginning of
> the *Country* to this day . . . none of them amassed together so
> vast a *Treasure* of Learning, and made so much *use* of it, to a
> variety of pious Intentions, as this our Rev. Brother and Father,
> Dr. COTTON MATHER. . . . His *Works* will indeed inform all
> that read them of his great Knowledge, and singular Piety, his
> zeal for God, and Holiness and Truth; and his desire of the
> Salvation of precious Souls; but it was *Conversation* and Ac-
> quaintance with him, in his familiar and occasional Discourses
> and in private Communications, that discovered the vast com-
> pass of his Knowledge and the Projections of his Piety; more I
> have sometimes thought than all *his Pulpit* Exercises. Here he
> excell'd, here he shone; being exceeding communicative, and
> bringing out of his *Treasury* things new and old, without mea-
> sure. Here it was seen how his Wit, and Fancy, his Invention,
> his Quickness of thought and ready Apprehension were all
> consecrated to God, as well as his Heart, Will and Affections.[41]

This encomium is, of course, in the context of a funeral
eulogy; but Colman was an honest man not given to hyper-
bole, and he adds that Mather was not without faults. His
estimate of the central thrust of Mather's character is in the
body of the funeral sermon, which deals with Enoch's walking
with God. Thomas Prince compares Mather with Elijah; like
that prophet, he intimates, Mather was a man with passions
like other men—specifically with a fiery spirit on some
occasions—but with a deep zeal for true religion. He remem-
bers Mather as "a strenuous Asserter of Liberty both civil and
sacred: and of extensive Charity. . . . He seem'd to have an
inexhaustible Source of *divine Flame and Vigour.* . . ." And
yet, contrary to the later caricatures of Mather as nervous and
impulsive, Prince says that "He enjoyed a perpetual Calm"
through his private devotions.[42] Joshua Gee portrays Mather
in the role of Aaron, perhaps as the literary spokesman for
the Puritan movement in New England of which his father
was the Moses, and Gee observes that like Aaron he endured
some hard things from the flock, of which they later would
find occasion to repent. Gee, who was Mather's assistant

during his last four years, found his co-worker to be "pious, but not affected. . . . He was peaceable in his temper: but zealous against sin. . . . He was a vigorous defender of the reformed doctrines of grace, and of the mysteries of revealed religion. . . . And yet he was catholick in his charity to all good men, tho' differing from him in circumstantials and modalities."[43] While it is true that funeral sermons are designed to accentuate the positive, it is unlikely that Mather's eulogists would emphasize virtues that did not exist. The nineteenth-century Unitarian W. B. O. Peabody, a careful though severe critic of Mather, felt that the eulogies were more reliable estimates of the man than much of what was said of him during his lifetime by those disaffected from Puritanism.[44]

Judged by the range of his activity and the quantity of his writing, Mather was indeed a fruitful tree. His literary production included four hundred forty-four published works and fifteeen unpublished manuscripts. The great bulk of this material is composed of sermon collections and individual sermons, often published at the request of members of his audience and underwritten by them. Much of the rest of his production, like his sermons, was directed toward the practical spiritual needs of his people and other Christians within range of his concern: tracts, manuals of piety and catechetical aids for distribution during ministerial visits, and pastoral letters aimed at situations throughout Western Christendom. In the realm of scholarship, his medical and scientific writings are abreast and sometimes ahead of their time, despite the fascination with the supernormal that has been scored as extraordinary credulity by historians unfamiliar with the mind of the period; and his historiography is invaluable despite its flaws. He is at his weakest in his poetry and his exegetical thesauri, which are collations of allegorical minutiae from patristic, rabbinical, and philosophical sources. In the field of apologetics he wrote relatively little, despite the painful controversies in which the Mathers found themselves from time to time; and in the field of systematic theology, significantly, there is nothing, unless we count the unpublished eschatological works.

A comprehensive reading of Mather amounts to a condensed theological education, for Mather was not an indiscriminate collector of data; he was a magnet for important loci of experimental divinity in the patristic, medieval, Reformation, and Puritan eras. He seems to have had an immensely retentive memory for what he had read, and he developed a facility for getting to the heart of books by scanning through them quite rapidly until he came to something new to his knowledge, and then attaching it indelibly to his store of knowledge. Charles Chauncy observed: "There were scarcely any books written but he had somehow or other got a sight of them. He was the greatest redeemer of time I ever knew."[45]

In what follows I have sought, as much as possible, to present Mather's ideas in his own words. Thus the density of quotation approaches the structure of a compend of theology. I have done this partly because Mather's literary personality is so vivid and distinct that to summarize his best strokes does him an injustice and conveys only a faint image of the incisiveness of his perceptions, such as one would get in a faded photograph. And there is another reason: it is my purpose to offset the common opinion that he writes badly. Mather could write prose in any one of several contemporary styles, including the lean urbanity that was becoming the mode in England; but his favorite form of expression was the thick fabric of the allusive essay, jewelled with quotations, which he adopted from Thomas Fuller and Burton's *Anatomy of Melancholy*. The style was natural to him for two reasons: first, because he always regarded himself primarily as an editor and synthesist of other's opinions; and second, because there were many times when he plainly enjoyed showing off his learning. Moses Coit Tyler reconstructs his writing method in a passage that is probably quite accurate:

> The mind of Cotton Mather was so possessed by books he had read, that his most common thought had to force its way into utterance through dense hedges and jungles of quotation. . . .
> It is quite evident, too that, just as the poet often shapes his idea to his rhymes and is helped to an idea by his rhyme, so

Mather's mind acquired the knack of steering his thought so as to take in his quotations, from which in turn perhaps, he reaped another thought.[46]

Mather's allusiveness is unquestionably pedantry; but a generation accustomed to Eliot and Pound, with an interest rekindled in the seventeenth-century metaphysical poets, may find values in the symbolic richness of Mather's allusions and the quaintness of his conceits, which were so clearly out of fashion in the nineteenth century. Tyler finds in Mather's historical writing "an insuperable fondness for tumultuous swelling, and flabby declamation, and for edifying remarks, in place of a statement of the exact facts in the case. . . ."[47] This points, however, to the goal at which Mather aimed in most of his writings: spiritual edification. In the *Magnalia*, for example, his goal was history taught as a stimulus to Christian experience, and what he has provided as a result is a rather mixed bag of historical data surrounding a marvelous series of character-portraits that bring to life with considerable individuality the spiritual leaders of New England and speak volumes about the nature of Puritan piety. To the contemporary reader who has no taste for Puritan piety, this material seems vacuous because of its carelessness for facts and structures unrelated to the Kingdom of God as Mather saw it. But Mather would only rebuke such critics for throwing away the kernel of his creations and trying to eat the shell.

Edward Farley has observed that every theology implies a corollary piety, a set of practical applications within the existential requirements of daily life.[48] It would be more accurate to say that every theology *should* have a practical expression that is consistent with its core of meaning, since people's thoughts often point in one direction and their lives in another. It is even possible to maintain with a good conscience a piety that is essentially unconnected with one's theology—or perhaps even contradicts it. And there are, of course, systems so abstract that they have little possible connection with daily existence, such as the philosophy of Hegel, if we accept Kierkegaard's estimate. In such cases the theologian perhaps "borrows" his piety from another source, and then we have the problem of analyzing which source is his "real" ideology.

For some reason, the study of the interrelationship between theology and piety in a person or a movement is a neglected area. There are many older works centering on institutional history and many more recent ones engaging in intellectual, sociological, and even psychological analysis. But very few historical works attempt to relate concrete Christian experience to its source—or, on occasion, its result—in theology. The history of Christian experience is a genre that at this writing contains very few examples of scholarly theological exposition. The few works extant in this field specialize in one or another of the three experiential strands within Western Christendom: the Roman Catholic, the Quaker, and the Puritan-Pietist traditions. There is at present no work that gives an overview of the history of Christian experience, operating within a framework of acquaintance with all three of the main traditions, let alone some of the more recent pieties which Farley examines.

This work is a beginning essay in that direction. It is an effort to analyze Puritan theology as exemplified in Cotton Mather's thought and experience, with a necessarily modest attempt to relate Mather's experiential adaptation of Reformed orthodoxy to similar morphologies in patristic, medieval, and Counter-Reformation Catholicism, and in Continental Pietism. Since Puritanism has both a creative theological force and a profound existential concern, and also a logical drive to keep these two poles related, it is an ideal subject for such analysis. Despite his apparent idiosyncrasies, Mather himself is an almost perfect exemplar by which to study the practical outworkings of Puritanism, since he is undoubtedly the most thoroughly documented case study we have to show what Puritan theology does to a person's daily existence. He sought to construct an apotheosis of Puritan practical theology, and he revealed with relentless clarity of detail its effect on his own life.

The ensuing study will attempt to explore in its course the following questions concerning Mather's theology of Christian experience:

1. To what degree is Mather's "abnormality" (in the eyes of many secular analysts) due to his accurate exemplification of Puritan spiritual life? Has he acquired a reputation for eccentricity simply because he has shown us more of normal Puritan experience than others of his period and persuasion?

2. On the other hand, are the stresses and psychological imbalances that critics have seen in Mather the real and inevitable expression of pathological forces built into the Puritan theory of the spiritual life?

3. To what extent is Mather's Puritanism an accurate existential expression of Reformation theology? Puritanism sought to adapt patristic and medieval patterns of piety and to attach these to a Reformed theological foundation, but can we see in Mather areas where the old fabric imperfectly matched the new intellectual basis?

4. To what extent was there a shift in Mather's thought and experience from the old theocratic mood toward a renovated Puritan piety that prefigured later forms of revivalism?

The exposition that follows develops Mather's theology of Christian experience according to the Puritan conceptualization of "the rise and progress of religion in the soul," beginning with the rebirth of the Christian in conversion, and progressing through his nurture by the means of grace, his growth in sanctification, and his expression of renewed life in the activity of mission. Most of the inconsistencies other students have found in Mather's thinking can be resolved—or at least more fully comprehended—from this perspective. It is, after all, the stance from which Mather himself viewed his efforts as a proponent of the "true American pietism."

CHAPTER TWO

The Sources and Structure of Mather's Theology

A BRIEF EXAMINATION OF THOMAS HOLMES' THREE-volume bibliography will convince the reader that Mather's main interest was centered on literature that is practically useful in the nurture of spiritual life. Even when he seemed to be writing primarily to display his erudition, he did not write systematic theology but preferred allegorical exegesis of biblical texts interwoven with quotations from patristic, rabbinical, and Puritan sources. He went to any length to read something spiritually "edifying" out of a text, some-thing that carried a challenging or comforting application of the doctrines of grace to the believer's life. But he was wholly uninterested in the intricate probing of the thought pro-cesses of the deity sometimes attempted by the system-builders of Reformed orthodoxy. We might conclude that this reduction of theology to the practically useful was an effect of Mather's intercourse with German Pietism, which accorded importance to doctrines on the basis of their value in promot-ing godliness.

Mather came into contact with Halle Pietism sometime in the early 1700s through his connection with the Anglican Society for the Propagation of Christian Knowledge, estab-lished by his friend Edward Bromfield in London.[1] Ernst Benz has shown that Mather sent his *Magnalia Christi Americana* to Francke immediately upon its publication in

1702, and that he corresponded with Francke from 1709 throughout the remainder of his life.[2] Mather also wrote frequently to Anthony William Boehm, the brilliant and vigorous German expatriate who was the principal agent and exponent of Halle Pietism in London,[3] and to Bartholomew Ziegenbalg, the Pietist missionary in Malabar.[4] In 1709, referring to the newly published *Dust and Ashes* and *The Heavenly Conversation,* Mather said, "I represented the Methods of piety proposed in these Essayes, as being the true American Pietism."[5] It is clear that from this point onward he identified his own labors in America as an expression of the same spirit and aims embodied in the Pietism of Halle.[6]

One question that must be raised at this point, however, is whether Mather's identification of his own later ministry with Pietism was the result of Pietist influence on his thinking or simply an expression of the affinity he recognized between Halle and his own formulation of Puritanism. There is clear evidence that the latter is the case, and that Mather's already established direction was only reinforced by his contact with Halle. Writing to Boehm in 1717, Mather remarks: "I rejoice to find the *Magnalia Christi Americana,* fallen into your hands; and I verily beleeve, the *American Puritanism,* to be so much of a Peece with the Frederician Pietism, that if it were possible for the Book to be transferr'd unto our Friends in the Lower *Saxony,* it would find some Acceptance, and be a little serviceable to their glorious Intentions."[7] In a long letter to Francke in 1717, Mather observed that "the generality of the churches of New England are seeking that reformation for which all who can discern the times are longing, when the Kingdom of God will fully arrive; they are looking toward this with the most intense desire. And principally that Piety, in which the Eternal Gospel shall come to fruition, and we shall possess and see the substance of the Gospel."[8] Writing to Ziegenbalg, Mather summed up his understanding of the essence of Pietism in words that paraphrase the Puritan theologian William Ames: "It is most certain, that the Christian religion is nothing other than the doctrine of living unto God through Christ; and further, that it is more a practical than a theoretical science, of which the goal is the animation of real, solid, living piety, and the calling forth of men who are dead in sin unto a pious, sober, and righteous life."⁹

In all of Mather's Pietist correspondence the most extensive exchange involves Francke's letter of December 19, 1714, which was more than seventy pages long and which Mather summarized in his *Nuncia Bona e Terra Longinqua* (1715), and Mather's long answering letter of 1717. The content of this correspondence is significant. Francke's letter is not at all theological in nature; it is mainly an extensive summary of the benevolent activities at Halle during the period between 1708 and 1714: the growth of the orphanhouse and the various schools and the establishment of the infirmary, the apothecary's shop, the widows' quarters, and the bookstore and printing presses involved in the preparation of tracts. The conclusion of the letter gives an account of Pietist mission activities in East India. Mather's responding letter in 1717, on the other hand, is almost entirely theological in its thrust, expressing Mather's hopes that godly evangelicals in all the major confessional traditions will be able to join in promoting the essence of the gospel, and offering a fourteen-point summary of credenda which Mather had distilled and identified as that essence.¹⁰ Mather appeared to find his own basic interests mirrored in those of the Pietists, but he was concerned to communicate to them his own theological reflections on the ecumenical significance of the Pietist awakening.

From this exchange and from other indications in Mather's correspondence and published writings, we can conclude that one main effect of his contact with Pietism was the remarkable challenge of its practical achievements, which stimulated his own understanding of mission in the direction represented by *Bonifacius* (1710), the *Pia Desideria* of the "true American Pietism." It is possible to draw the ironic conclusion that the quality of Mather's Christianity that scholars have found most uniquely American and Matherian, its moral activism, was actually in part an effect of the combined influence of Continental Pietism and the English reforming societies.

A second major effect was the shock of deparochialization, as Mather suddenly became aware that something spiritually vital could flourish outside the tight structure of Calvinistic Puritanism and could in fact be the center of the only religious revival currently observable in Christendom, the revival for which he had been praying since the 1690s. The impact of this understanding certainly helped crystallize Mather's own pietist synthesis, with its components of stress on spiritual renewal, cultural transformation through voluntary societies, ecumenical union among the churches, and concern for world mission. But Mather seems to have found most of his own germinal ideas mirrored in Continental Pietism, so that he and his Pietist colleagues reinforced one another's concerns instead of radically redirecting these.

But was Mather's pietism really a new invention, as one of his remarks about it seems to imply? It was certainly not unique to his ministry: all of his colleagues, including the more theologically minded Stoddard and Willard, shared his practical emphasis on Christian experience.[11] Perry Miller has suggested that the Puritanism of the third generation was intellectually muted and experientialized because the ministers were searching for practical remedies for New England's spiritual decline: "Of course, all these preachers were loyal to *The Westminster Confession,* nor did they in any explicit particular renounce the intellectual architecture that formed the first part of this study: they simply stopped talking about it, while concentrating upon getting results. They would not understand what I mean, but actually in this fashion they were becoming Americanized—all the more speedily because, not obtaining the results they desired, they had to redouble their endeavors."[12]

This generalization, however, fails to grasp the unity of American Pietism with similar movements in Europe. There were plenty of pastors and theologians outside America who showed the same drift toward practical piety toward the end of the seventeenth century. Miller himself cites the example of one of Mather's favorite European theologians, Mastricht, who in his *Theoretici-Practica Theologia* (1699) "puts so much more emphasis upon the *Practica* than upon the *Theoretico* as to reverse the entire direction of seventeenth-century theology."[13] But Mastricht alone was not responsible for this "reversal." Seventeenth-century Puritanism had been moving in this direction for a long time before Mastricht and Mather; in fact, there had been a strong current of practical pietism in Puritanism from the very beginning. Recent scholarship has increasingly concluded that throughout most of its history English Puritanism can best be understood by examining its predominating stress on Christian experience, rather than by analyzing its institutional emphases, as an older school of interpreters did, or dissecting its doctrinal structure, as intellectual historians have done.[14]

Some authorities, in fact, have gone so far as to assert that English Puritanism and Continental Pietism were essentially the same movement.[15] This interpretation is not without its difficulties. For example, the two movements had different immediate roots: German Pietism traced back through Johann Arndt through the young Luther and behind him to Tauler, while Puritanism probably flowed from Bucer and Bullinger through English pastors until it began to find theological expression in Perkins and a series of later divines, including the Dutch Precisianists. It is also true that there is a difference in theological flavor between the movements, since they developed out of two different attitudes toward predestination. But both may ultimately be rooted in popular evangelical mysticism of the same species as the *Devotio Moderna,* penetrating into the orthodox Reformation in Germany and the Rhineland. Both were efforts to construct a new Protestant piety, a practical Christian lifestyle on Lutheran or Reformed theological bases, adapting or replacing the piety of Counter Reformation mysticism and asceticism. Both were reactions against forms of Christianity perceived as "having a form of godliness, but denying the power thereof."[16] In the case of Pietism, the reaction was against the kind of lifeless Lutheran confessional orthodoxy that seemed to fall so readily into "cheap grace"[17] and unsanctified wrangling over doctrinal details; in the case of Puritanism, it was against heterodox elements ranging from Catholic remnants to "Arminian" innovations, and also against all forms of orthodoxy that were merely "notional."

Both Pietism and Puritanism, therefore, were attempts to construct a theology that might be called "live orthodoxy," which affirmed the importance of assent to creedal propositions drawn from Scripture but sought to balance this emphasis on the Word and words by an equal stress on the illuminating and transforming work of the Holy Spirit and the resulting human response of faith and holy living. And the movements were essentially alike in their peculiar stress on the importance of initial regeneration (*Wiedergeburth* or "conversion"), in their balancing of a one-sided doctrine of justification by a thrust toward sanctification, in their emphasis on the development of interior godliness, and in their essential biblicism in contrast to more rational and systematic approaches.

After the simultaneous appearance of German pre-Pietism (Johann Arndt) and English Puritanism in the late sixteenth century, there was a considerable amount of borrowing, cross-pollination, and symbiosis between the English-Dutch and German forms of Puritanism/Pietism. One of the main formative influences on Spener's Pietism was the English in devotional literature translation (Lewis Bayly, Daniel Dyke, and Richard Baxter), which Spener found in his father's library and used for his early spiritual nurture. The English influence is even more pronounced in Francke, who was fascinated by Puritanism both in its English and American forms.[18] During the course of the seventeenth century this exchange of genetic material brought the English and German strains so close in their basic practice and devotional attitude that Mather and Francke found themselves on identical ground at the outset of the eighteenth century.[19]

In his study of Halle Pietism, Klaus Deppermann offers an intriguing list of elements shared by the two movements, due either to conscious borrowing or to independent invention: a focus on the methodical development of individual holiness, somewhat legalistic in its flavor; evidence of good works as a means of assurance of a state of grace; belief in providence, final perseverance, and striving for high spiritual goals; the ideal of work as the best ascetic means;

the use of diaries for spiritual growth; and the fostering of responsibility to God through the abolition of private confession.[20] James Hastings Nichols notes the presence in both movements of the use of conventicles and prayer meetings as a means of spiritual nurture.[21] And we might add that both movements share a strong drive to produce devotional literature and a significant affinity for one another's productions in this line.

If German Pietism evolved in the direction of Puritanism during the seventeenth century, it is also true that there is a complementary and converging revolution in that complex of movements and emphases we call Puritanism. We can observe what might be called a gradual "pietization" of Puritanism during the seventeenth century. It began as a loose collection of movements, all stressing the completion of what was felt to be a half-effected Reformation. The purity that was sought was for some mainly a matter of purging the worship of the English church; for others, a matter of altering the polity; for others, the defense of pure theological "Calvinism" or Reformed orthodoxy; and for still others, mainly a matter of the transformation of lives among the pastorate and laity.[22] Though called by the same epithet, these vectors were not always mutually compatible. The separatists, for example, were censured by most Puritans for ecclesiastical extremism. On the other hand, a given leader might combine many or all of these concepts of reformation in his own emphasis. Logically, it is possible to combine all of them under the ideal of "precision," as does the Dutch Puritan/ Pietist Gisbert Voetius: "We define 'precision' as the exact or perfect human action conforming to the law of God as taught by God."[23] This definition of the Puritan ideal, which fundamentally assumes the validity of a Zwinglian biblicist legalism and probably traces back to that source historically, can be applied equally well to purity of doctrine, worship, polity, and practical piety.

In English Puritanism, however, historical events and conditions interacted to form a distillation system that gradually subsumed the more external and legalistic elements, leaving a predominant stress on inner piety by the end of the seventeenth century. The condition of restraint and powerlessness in which Puritans developed at its outset was more favorable to the growth of the strain emphasizing internal piety than to any of the others. After the Revolution, when the reformers finally had a free rein to purify the English church, the cleavages in the reforming parties gradually led people to suspect that the New Testament did not speak with "precision" about polity, methods of worship, and even some high strains of doctrinal orthodoxy. But the two things that it did seem to stress loudly and clearly were *faith* and *repentance:* the Reformed doctrine of God's grace in salvation and the reformation of the lives of believers. Thus, as later Puritans like Baxter and Mather might put it, English Puritanism was hammered against the template of Scripture by the blows of history, and those elements within it that were not incontestably demonstrable among Christian people of good will were gradually either beaten off or quietly bent into the background of belief. By the last decades of the century men of the caliber of Baxter, and those with whom Increase Mather labored in the formation of the United Brethren, were striving toward union on doctrinal bases using many of the same criteria that Spener devised for the testing of credenda: the overwhelming biblical clarity of a doctrine and its vital necessity for the nurture of piety.[24]

In this evolutionary process, however, the pietistic strain of Puritanism was always the strongest, so it is no surprise that it was fittest to survive in the seventeenth century.[25] For we must remember that while Puritanism "surfaces" in history in the writings of a few theological systematizers, its main strength lay from the beginning among a host of practicing pastors, beginning in the last decades of the sixteenth century with men like Richard Greenham, Richard Rogers, and John Dod, who formulated the details of Puritan piety in their local parishes.[26] William Perkins took this popular biblicism and forged it into union with the elements of Calvinist scholastic orthodoxy, and from him it passed to Ames and the other Puritan or Precisionist theologians.[27] But even in Perkins, theology is defined not as a theoretical discipline but as "the science of

living blessedly forever";[28] and Ames defines it as "the doctrine of living unto God" and holds that faith is "a resting of
the heart in God."[29] Ames had disturbed and enlivened the
Dutch theological scene in the 1620s by the practicality of his
theological approach and his introduction of a biblical
casuistry of daily conduct into the theological curriculum.[30]
Considering, then, the pastoral origins of English Puritanism
and the continuing freight of practical theology even in its
systematizers, it is not surprising that Cotton Mather, who
was by calling not a theologian but a pastor and evangelist,
would revert to the pure practicality of the original
Puritanism, subject as he was to an undeniable pull toward
what was pastorally marketable, what was useful for the
edification of his people.[31]

Mather's "true American Pietism," however, was not
radical enough to discard all the historic Puritan structural
and intellectual distinctives for sheer invertebrate indulgence in Christian experience. Mather was a progressive,
but he was also part of a dynasty that had virtually built New
England Congregationalism and was therefore by inheri-
tance the caretaker of its tradition. And American Puritanism
was from the beginning more conservative than its
seventeenth-century equivalent in England, where certain
historical catalysts speeded up the process of distillation toward a more freely structured pietism. Mather could go so far
as to say in 1717 that all institutions within the church are
valuable only as they assist the development of piety, and
with amazing prescience he could advise missionaries to
propagate only the basic elements of the gospel and not "the
little *Peculiarities of a Party.*"[32] And yet he would build a
case in 1726 for the New England Way as the structure that
was most truly biblical and hence best suited to nurture
Christian experience.[33] He was still legalistic enough to preserve all the Puritan behavioral precision and to complain
against the introduction of "uninstituted worship" as a violation of *"the Religion of the Second Commandment"* until the
end of his life.[34] How he could maintain such continuing
stress on Puritan peculiarities and still propose union with
all other Christian parties on the basis of vital piety and a

very minimal creed is hard to comprehend, unless we suppose that there was some continuing oscillation within Mather between the progressive and conservative poles.

Scholars have speculated that another liberalizing influence on Mather's theology may have been the onset of Enlightenment rationalism. A number of authorities, most of them rather friendly to Mather in their own way, have sought to demonstrate that he was a theological innovator who "dabbled in deism."[35] It has become the common assumption that Mather's emphasis on Christian activism in the *Bonifacius,* and his handling of reason in a number of works, are supportive of one another, and that these are direct kin to the later rationalist moralism of men like Benjamin Franklin. This view connects Mather to those who resisted the subsequent Great Awakening rather than to its proponents. As Perry Miller puts it, "In the *Manuductio* . . . the Puritan manual of pastoral care first shows signs of disintegration: the element of Humanism originally combined with the theology is beginning to crowd it out, in spite of Mather's care for orthodoxy. His pronouncements show how far he had travelled with that segment of Puritanism that was journeying toward Arminianism, morality, and Unitarianism, that segment of which Benjamin Franklin himself was an offshoot, and against which Jonathan Edwards fought in his endeavor to revivify the seventeenth-century spirit."[36]

This view of Mather seems plausible at first, since there is a very real historical connection between Franklin's common-sense moralism and Mather's *Bonifacius.* When we take into account the entire body of Mather's writing, however, it becomes apparent that what Franklin and others did was break down a rather delicate synthesis of rational, orthodox piety which Mather and other Puritans had carefully put together in a state of balance and tension. Rationalistic moralism can be distilled out of Mather, but the product is something entirely distinct from Mather's own position. In the last decades of his life Mather uniformly supported reason, orthodoxy, and affective piety, assuming that when these terms are properly defined there is no opposition among them. It is difficult for us today to conceive of the existence of a position which is neither pure orthodox reaction nor rationalism, nor something in transit between these two poles. We do not allow for the possibility of a third force consistent with both reason and orthodoxy. There is the same conceptual defect here that we encounter occasionally in popular reactionary political theory: any deviation from laissez-faire capitalism must be "on the way to Communism." But the fact remains that Mather, the Continental Pietists, and the leaders of the Great Awakening represent such a third force, a movement essentially opposed both to rationalist forms of scholastic orthodoxy and to Enlightenment rationalism.

We can easily document the fact that Mather's rejection of the Enlightenment was unambiguous. Around August 1699, Mather became disturbed at the reported incursions of rationalism in England,[37] and he wrote a pastoral letter warning English nonconformists of "*Socinian Haeresies* and . . . *Atheistical Deism*. . . . And, alas, the strange care taken to fabricate a *Christian Religion* without a *Christ,* or the most Vital parts of *Christianity*."[38] At this point, the peril was still overseas: in his election sermon for 1700, Mather attacked "a nation full of Preachers, that will contrive to make Harangues upon Moral Vertues, but banish Christ," and rejoiced that there was not a single Socinian, nor even an Arminian, in New England.[39] Later in the same year he complained that

> there seems to be a Conspiracy in much of the *English Nation,* to fabricate a *Christian Religion* . . . without a *Christ;* not only are those *Deists* prodigiously multiplied, who are infinitely worse than *Mohametans,* and *Socinians,* which are but a sort of *Baptized Mohametans* . . . but also, if you search the Sermons and the Writings of the *Clergy,* you shall often find, Nomen Christi non est ibi, it may be there is not Christ, *name* or *Thing,* in more than *Seven Sermons* together: And there are Books Written, to prove, *That there is nothing requisite unto a Good Christian, or a Church Member, but only to Believe That Jesus of Nazareth is the Messiah;* whereas *that* Thing is many times over Confessed and Asserted even in the *Alcoran* of *Mohamed.*[40]

But in June 1702, Mather was concerned that the corruption of "the glorious Doctrines of Grace" in the Reformed churches of Europe would contaminate the younger clergy of

New England, who were being "poisoned by vile *Pelagian* Books, that from beyond-sea, are vended among us."[41] The books were apparently Arminian tracts being distributed by what Mather called the "Society for the Molestation of the Gospel in foreign Parts" (the Anglican Society for the Propagation of the Gospel),[42] which threatened to "obtrude a very defective Christianity on the nation."[43] Mather was also concerned at this point about the unguarded recommendation of this type of literature to ministerial students at Harvard.[44] In 1703 he lamented the common and open utterance in England of "Arian, Socinian, deistical blasphemies," and it was evidently still English Nonconformism that concerned him when he complained in 1706 of "a very Numerous party of men . . . who own no Grace necessary to bring a Sinner into a State of Salvation, but only that which they call *Moral Grace,* or, *Moral Suasion;* and which amounts to no more than a *Rational Proposal* of our Duty, *To turn from Sin to God in Christ,* with *Reasonable Considerations,* to Excite men unto the doing of this their Duty."[45] Again in 1706 he noted that "the *Pelagian Opinions* being introduced into the *English Nation,* have introduced an horrid *Corruption of Manners* with them; That no men do show less of a *Free-will* to all Spiritual *Good,* than the men who have been the great Asserters, & Admirers, of mans *Free-will.*"[46] In the same year he published his *Man of God Furnished* to protect New England from falling prey to seven heresies, among them Socinianism and Pelagianism.[47]

The second decade of the eighteenth century found Mather complaining to John Maxwell, at the University of Glasgow, of the "*Tarantula* with which this Age of Infidelity is poysened."[48] Mather was horrified to find that he himself could be bitten:

> My learned Friend *Whiston* (from whom I have this week received an Account of his Proceedings,) is likely to raise a prodigious Dust in the world; by reviving the *Arian* Opinions. He revives them with more than ordinary Advantages, and I am likely to have my own Mind shock'd with more than ordinary Temptations on this Occasion. Wherefore, I cry most ardently unto the glorious Lord, that He would graciously enlighten me; cause me to take up right Thoughts of my dear Jesus, and of His Holy Spirit; lead me into all Truth, and keep

me from Error, and show my Duty, and never leave me to hurt
any Interest of His Kingdome in the World.[49]

Within the week Mather had determined to become a cham-
pion of Trinitarianism against his friend,[50] and a year and a
half later he was busy writing "an Antidote against the
wretched Poison, wherewith *Whiston* is endeavouring to corrupt the Church of God; and particularly to defend the Students in our Colledge from the Corruption."[51] This was not
simply a matter of Mather's espousing his own part in a pet
cause célèbre; a little later we find him attempting to enlist the
blind but brilliant church historian at the University of Glasgow, William Jameson, in attacking Whiston.[52] Mather was
sufficiently intelligent to be susceptible to Whiston's arguments, but also sufficiently suspicious of his own reason and
that of other learned men to remain anchored in a traditional—and suprarational—scheme of Christian doctrine.

If Mather were to move away from the antirationalist
and antimoralist position he had developed up to this point,
it would necessarily be in that low period for his own interests and those of Puritanism, the 1720s, after his *Christian
Philosopher* was published (1721). But by far the most numerous and most vigorous protests against rationalism that he
composed were written in this period. The aftermath of the
Salter's Hall Conference in 1717 prompted Mather to draw
the line quite firmly at the boundary of his pietist
ecumenism.

> It surprizes [New England Congregationalists] to see that the
> Vomit of a *Valentinus* . . . spued out . . . in the *English* tongue,
> should be so greedily imbibed by Multitudes, who are loth to
> herd with the grosser *Arians.* . . .
>
> They *who dwell in the wilderness, are afraid at the Tokens* . . . that
> a fearful Decay of real and vital Religion, and of Love to a
> Glorious JESUS, may have introduced that *easy Disposition.* . . .
> And its astonishes them to see what *Stars* the Tail of the
> *Dragon* has reached in this *Apostasy.* They mightily approve
> and pursue the Design of making the *Terms of Communion*
> to be no other than the *Terms of Salvation;* and of all good
> Men coming . . . to unite on the Basis of that PIETY, on which
> all the Children of God are indeed forever united. But yet . . .
> they are at a loss how they shall suppose the *Terms of Salvation*

duly complied withal, where ONE GOD in THREE PERSONS is not prayed unto; and where a *Baptism* into the Name of ONE GOD, and of *Two Creatures,* is made the *Budge of Christianity:* or how they shall suppose, that Men come up to that PIETY, which will oblige us to acknowledge them as our Brethren in CHRIST, while they do not acknowledge any CHRIST, but a Son of God who is not *One in Essence* with His Father, but one infinitely inferiour to the most High God; infinitely different from him, whose Name alone is JEHOVAH . . . They cannot comprehend, what our Brethren mean, when they require no *Confession of Faith* . . . other than what they know all the Hereticks upon the face of the Earth, as well as the Socinians, will readily come into.[53]

In 1724, Mather noted the concern of his father about Arian intrusions into the United Brethren,[54] and there is no doubt that the two Mathers stabilized one another in the face of the growing rationalism of English theology.[55] In the *Manuductio ad Ministerium* (1726) he advises ministerial students against "a *Set of Books* which of late Years have brought in a *Fashionable Divinity.*"[56] It might be supposed that Mather's reaction was against a set of doctrines that were unfashionable and unorthodox in Boston at the moment, rather than rationalism as a theological method. But in another late work he exposed the root of the problem with the new divinity:

What ails the *Baptized* Enemies of our GOD, that they will not let us quietly enjoy our *BAPTISM;* Foolishly pretending their *Idaea's;* and their *Idaea's,* and it is, forsooth, an Age of *Idaea's;* and they have no *Idaea* of such a *Trinity:* — As if nothing were to be received upon a *Divine Revelation,* concerning an Incomprehensible GOD, but what a sinful and a shallow Mortal will please to say, he has an *Idaea* of. . . . An *Idaea* of *Three Persons in one GOD,* is altogether as easy to be comprehended, as an *Idaea* of an INFINITE or an ETERNAL Being.[57]

In Mather's later years, then, he was a vigorous opponent of English Unitarianism. In 1721 he spoke of his being at considerable expense in diffusing a tract on the Godhead of Christ throughout New England.[58] In 1725 he wrote to Bradbury of his "Insupportable Grief" at the "pretended Irenicums" of the United Brethren in England, which "do purposely and perpetually Leave out the Faith of our Lords

Eternal Deity, when they pretend unto an Enumeration of our Fundamental Articles."[59] In one of the last letters he wrote before his death, to Thomas Prince, he expressed himself on the liberalizing tendencies of Isaac Watts, whose poetry and piety he had formerly held in the highest admiration.

> I take him, to be a very Disqualified person, for the Managing of the Vast Subject he has undertaken; He is not only too shallow for it; but also Led away with a Spurious and Criminal Charity, for those Abominable IDOLATERS, the *Arians*. . . . For my own part, I Look on the part which our Brethren . . . have taken in Countenancing the Conspiracy to dethrone and degrade and ungod the Eternal SON of GOD, as having a deep share in preparing the world for that *Catastrophe*, which my, *Diluvium Ignis* warns you of. . . . As for you, *My Son*, . . . I will say one Thing to *you*. *Take heed unto your Spirit*. The Candour, or Humour, in the Spirit of our Friend on the other side the water, has betray'd him into a most mischievous Treachery to the Faith of the Gospel and unhappy Disservice to the Best Cause in the world. I highly approve and admire the Goodness of your Spirit, and the Equanimity with which you Look upon Displeasing Things. But yett, watch over it, Lest you admitt of an *Indolence*, where an Holy Zeal shall be called for; and where a John himself would be a *Boanerges*, with zealous Testimonies. . . .[60]

Although there was a steady growth of charity and tolerance in Mather's position as he grew older, we should remember that there were always distinct limits to this, a line beyond which he would not move in accommodating to differing views.

One of the strongest anti-Enlightenment features of Cotton Mather's work, which has escaped the notice of most of his commentators, is the Christocentric thrust of his preaching. This was a heritage from Increase Mather, who told his son to fill his sermons not with his own learning or moral precepts but with Christ if he wanted "His Holy SPIRIT Powerfully and Marvellously Breathing" in his ministry.[61] Mather repeatedly emphasized his father's counsel to ministerial candidates, most eloquently perhaps in the supposedly rationalistic *Manuductio*.

> Among all the Subjects, with which you *Feed* the People of GOD, I beseech you, Let not the true *Bread of Life* be forgotten;

but exhibit as much as you can of a Glorious CHRIST unto them: Yea; Let the *Motto* upon your whole Ministry, be CHRIST IS ALL. It has been among the *Grievous Things,* which I have seen in the Days of my Pilgrimage, that not only in some of the most celebrated *Sermons,* which we have seen published on the most Illustrious and Memorable Occasions, a CHRIST is . . . not so much as *once* mentioned; but also some of your Great Men have it related of them as an Instance of their *Wisdom,* that they gave it as their Advice unto Ministers, *That they should not Preach much about the Person of CHRIST.* I have thought, Would A blessed PAUL have *uttered* such a Word! A PAUL, who said, *I determined to know nothing among you, save JESUS CHRIST, and Him Crucified.* It is reported by some Travellers, That in the *Mohametan Moschs,* there are sometimes *whole Sermons* on the Glories of a JESUS. And shall they who call themselves *Christians,* and would be honoured as *Ministers of the Christian Religion,* preach as if they were *ashamed* of making the *Glories* of a JESUS, the *Subject* of their *Sermons;* and so rarely introduce Him, as if it were an *Indecent Stoup* to speak of Him! GOD forbid! I make no Doubt of it, That the almost Epidemical Extinction of True *Christianity,* or what is little short of it, in the Nations that profess it, is very much owing to the inexcusable *Impiety* of overlooking a Glorious CHRIST, so much in the Empty *Harangues,* which often pass for *Sermons.* [62]

It is significant that Mather here recognizes spiritual decline as a condition afflicting not only New England but the entire world, and diagnoses Arian rationalism as one of its ingredients.[63] Although Mather's Christocentrism was especially pronounced after the Salter's Hall Conference, when English Arianism became acutely visible, it was present at the very beginning of his preaching career and continued to pervade his work in this medium as the dominant principle of his exegesis of Scripture. As he put it, "The *Name* of our Lord *JESUS CHRIST,* in the Oracles of the Sacred Scripture, is, *the Face of God;* and in that one Hint, you have a Golden Key, to open a thousand passages."[64]

In his advice to young ministers Mather does not recommend a sentimental devotion to the human Jesus as was characteristic of some weaker strains of European Pietism, but he calls for sharp theological definition of the Savior's person and work as presented in Scripture and in the intellectual structure of Reformed doctrine.

What I wish for and urge to, is This; That your *Knowledge of the Mystery of CHRIST,* may Conspicuously shine in your *Sermons;* and that it may be esteemed by you, as a Matchless *Grace given you,* if you may *Preach the Unsearchable Riches of CHRIST* unto the WORLD. The *Heavens do Praise that Wonder;* the *Angels* in the *Heavens* are swallowed up in the Praises of that *Wondrous ONE!* Be, like *Them,* never so much in your Element, as when the *Person,* the *Offices,* the *Benefits,* the *Example,* the *Abasement,* and *Advancement* of a Glorious CHRIST, are the *Subjects* of your *Sermons.* . . . In every *Article* of the *Treatises* which you bring into the *Assemblies of Zion,* ponder upon This; What *Aspect* a Glorious CHRIST has upon the *Truth* now before you, and let your Hearers be made sensible of it. . . . If you Preach on the *Evil of Sin,* and the *Misery* Man fallen by *Sin,* still carry your Hearers to their mighty and only SAVIOUR: When you Preach on the *Duties* of a *Godly,* and *Sober,* and *Righteous Life,* still carry your Hearers to their SAVIOUR, as not only affording a *Pattern* for all those things, but also as Offering to *live,* and act, and work in them, as a *Principle of Life,* by which alone they can live unto GOD.[65]

This is not only totally removed from the contemporary English rationalism; it is a goal that is more Christologically centered—and less rationalistic—than much Puritan preaching before Mather.[66]

Along with this Christocentric stress, Mather preserved throughout his life the rest of the distinctive emphases of Reformed orthodoxy. In 1702, Mather drafted for the General Convention of Ministers at Boston a comprehensive defense of Calvinistic orthodoxy. Issued as an attack on English Arminianism and citing the Thirty-Nine Articles against it, this defense asserted man's total depravity through original sin, unconditional election by God's sovereign mercy, the effectual calling of the elect through irresistible grace, the bondage of the unregenerate will, and justification by faith through the imputation of Christ's righteousness.[67] Mather's two sermons on *Free-Grace* (1706) are a vigorous assertion of the value of the doctrine of election for practical piety, for comforting believers, and for breaking the back of their resistance to the divine Lordship:

Indeed the Doctrine of PREDESTINATION hath its Mysteries, its Abstruse Difficulties, and Soaring Sublimities. But for men to pretend therefore, that it should be Silenced and Smothered

> & Shut out of Sermons, is for them to be . . . more *Nice* than
> *Wise,* more Cautious than they need to be; and there is usually,
> *A Snake in the Grass,* when such a *Doctrine of Godliness* is much
> *hissed* at. We find, the Doctrine of PREDESTINATION Pro-
> posed by our Lord, and His Apostles, with a very frequent
> Inculcation; We find, that it hath a wondrous Tendency to the
> *Edification* of the Faithful.[68]

Mather's Calvinism here is thoroughly integrated with his
pietism. It is mainly the practical expression of faith in God's
sovereignty and its effect on the spiritual life that interests
him, not the theoretical formulation of the doctrine. Mather
continued to be outspokenly tough-minded in his Augus-
tinianism, and in the last year of his life he warned that the
decay of morals in Britain was due to the decline of Calvinism there.

A number of scholars have interpreted Mather's activistic pietism as a movement away from Calvinism into a more
anthropocentric outlook. But from the beginning of his
ministry Mather put the traditional Puritan emphasis on
theocentric piety. One of his earlier published sermons is
based on the doctrine that *"While we pray to* live, *we should
account the* Praises *of God to be the Cheef End of our* Life, *in
which the* Judgments *of God are to be sought and used as our*
Help," gracefully submitting to losses and punishments,
since these detach us from self-concern and lead us into a
God-centered life, where his will is all that matters.[69]
Elsewhere he tells those under hard circumstances that "The
Sovereignty of God, must be our *Song in the Night*";[70] and he
can even encourage those fearful of reprobation to "adore the
uncontroulable *Sovereignty* of God which may make you a
Vessel of Dishonour."[71] In *A Short Life* (1714) he makes clear
that the satisfaction of God himself is the chief concern of
true piety: "'Tis Enough, that be our *Time* never so *Short,*
the Infinite God, has had the Pleasure of *Beholding* the Man,
whereof He is the *Maker.* . . . This is *End* Enough to be
assign'd for the whole Creation."[72] These expressions were
not simply lip service to a doctrine; Mather fell into them
with an ease indicating that they were of the essence of his
way of looking at the world. His activism was not based on
some new and high value set on mankind, but was, like

Francke's social concern, merely the expression of a rigorous effort to be obedient to God, who remained firmly at the center of his thought. In later years his own spiritual experience led him more and more into a piety of "resignation" or yielding of self-interest in the presence of the divine sovereignty, showing some affinities for Jansenism and Quietism, movements that are antithetical to anthropocentric humanism.[73]

Mather had an equally firm grip on another Reformation doctrine that was ignored by the rationalizing divines: justification by grace through faith in Christ, on the basis of the imputation of Christ's righteousness. This is particularly noteworthy since Mather's Puritan pietism, like all movements attempting to forward "practical godliness," risked obscuring justification by its stress on sanctification, or even absorbing the former into the latter. In his early tract *Little Flocks Guarded* (1691), Mather attacks the Quakers and Rome together for doing just this, confusing justification with sanctification in holding that people are justified by infused righteousness.[74] His *Everlasting Gospel* (1700), a work specifically directed to defending the Reformed doctrine of justification, develops its thesis, "The righteousness of God is by faith in Jesus Christ," with a clear statement that this is an imputed righteousness apprehended by faith. Mather negotiates all the problems involved with ease: "God never gives the *Righteousness* of the Lord Jesus Christ unto any man, without giving him *Faith* to Take the Gift of *Righteousness*. . . . *Faith is the Instrument of our Justification*. . . . *Faith* does not *justify* us, as it is a *Work*; No, 'Tis *Instrumentally*, and *Relatively*, and because it carries us unto the *Righteousness* of our Lord Jesus Christ alone, for our *Justification*."[75]

Mather was careful to preserve an indissoluble connection between justification and sanctification, as preceding orthodoxies had not always done, maintaining that "The *Faith* which does Receive the *Righteousness* of the Lord Jesus Christ, will *Purify the Heart*."[76] One of his later writings, *The Marrow of the Gospel* (1727), identifies the central doctrine of Christianity as the *unio Christi*, since we are justified through an imputed identity with Christ in his obedience, sacrifice, and total work on earth, and sanctified through the transforming presence of his Spirit within us, uniting us to him.[77] There are innumerable treatments of this doctrine in Mather's work. It is alluded to in every applicatory section that deals with regeneration, and that means virtually every sermon Mather preached. The absence of the doctrine of justification by faith in the English rationalists was one factor that moved Mather to be concerned about their apostasy. If there was any rationalism involved in Mather's handling of this and the other Reformation emphases mentioned above, it was orthodox rationalism rather than Enlightenment heterodoxy.

But it has been asserted that there was enough scholastic rationalism in Mather's tradition to move him unconsciously toward the Enlightenment—at least enough so that the soil he cultivated became receptive to the seeds of the new emphasis on reason. We must, therefore, consider Mather's own positive evaluation of the place of reason in theology and in the Christian life.

Along with Reformed orthodoxy in general, Mather allowed both for a certain kind of knowledge of God obtainable by the natural man through reason and a valid use of reason by the regenerate personality. The Westminster Confession had stated that there was sufficient knowledge of God available through natural revelation to leave people inexcusable in their rebellion against God.[78] And in fact this seems to have been the position of Calvin himself, following Romans 1:18-21 and 2:14-16.[79] Mather is not really going beyond Reformed orthodoxy when he says in 1709:

> There is in every Man . . . a Faculty called Reason. 'Tis that Faculty which is called, Prov. 21:27 . . . *the Candle of the Lord.* By the Light of this precious and wondrous *Candle* it is, that we discern the *Connection & Relation* of Things to one another. There are certain *Idea's* imprinted on the Spirit of Man, by . . . GOD . . . a rich cluster of *Idea's* which we are born withal, and which are only awakened, and brought into Exercise by Observation. . . . *Reason* Judges of what is *Mathematically True* or *False*. But this is not all; It Judges as often, and as clearly, what is morally *Good*, or what is *morally Evil*.[80]

In this passage, as in several others in his work, Mather opposes not only the moral relativism of Hobbes but also the Lockean rejection of innate ideas, a trademark of Socinianism. In the ensuing context Mather seems to ascribe a godlike eminence to the rational faculty, but the orthodox concept of reason securing mankind's inexcusable guilt in rebelling against God is still his basic point:

> We have to do with GOD, as often as we have *Right Reason* calling upon us. . . . And I will now say, We never *Transgress* any *Law of Reason,* but we do at the same time, *Transgress* the *Law of GOD.* . . . God sets up *Reason* in Man. If we do not keep *Reason* in the *Throne,* we go to *Dethrone* the Infinite GOD Himself. The voice of *Reason,* is the *Voice of GOD.*[81]

This is perhaps the strongest statement of apparent rationalism in Mather. But he is not speaking here of the trustworthiness of human reason as it normally operates in the unredeemed mind, but of what Tillich calls the "depth of reason," the kind of consciousness in which the mind, awakened by the Spirit, perceives truth and goodness theonomously, at a level beneath its rebellious rationalizations against God. For Mather was thoroughly convinced that the normal rationality of the race has been corrupted by the Fall:

> *There is hardly any one thing in the World, the Essence whereof we can perfectly comprehend.* But then to the *natural Imbecility* of REASON, and the *moral Depravations* of it, by our Fall from God, and the Ascendant which a corrupt and vicious *Will* has obtained over it, how much ought this Consideration to warn us against the Conduct of an *unhumbled Understanding* in things relating to the *Kingdom of God?*[82]

Besides recognizing the corruption of the mind, Mather also strongly contends—against the English rationalists—that there are many important elements of biblical revelation that are beyond the capacity even of the enlightened and corrected reason to grasp.

> There are *Mysteries* in *Religion,* which we *know not now,* but we may *know hereafter.* Those Men are strangers to *Christianity,* who are so Vain, as to write, *Christianity not Mysterious.* . . . 'Tis true, there is nothing in the *Christian Religion,* that is *against Reason.* . . . God, who makes *all Truths,* will make no Rules of Reason, that shall give any Contradiction to them. Neverthe-

less, there are *Truths* that go *beyond Reason;* Truths, that soar *above Reason; Truths* which the faculties of our feeble *Reason* cannot see into, especially as our Fall from God has enfeebled, and impaired our Faculties.[83]

This is an explicit attack on the Toland style of English Deism. Mather feels that there is a covert linkage between Quaker enthusiasm and Deistic rationalism and that both are guilty of idolizing human reason: "*Reason* is *Idolized,* When Men will set *Reason* above *Revelation* . . . When the *Light Within,* becomes unto us, a CHRIST, and a GOD; When the *Natural Conscience* is advanced unto all the Offices of our only SAVIOUR. A *Creature,* and one too that is darkned and wounded by Sin, must not be *Deified.*"[84]

A study of the total context of Mather's statements about the use of reason must lead us to the conclusion that he was not a rationalist in the eighteenth-century sense. Because Mather frequently dealt with the subject of reason after 1700, it has been suggested that he must have wanted to jump on the Enlightenment bandwagon—or, more exactly, to "capture the Enlightenment," to seize the reins of the wagon and steer it in a conservative direction.[85] But Mather was doing what every Christian leader of stature attempts: he was relating himself to the *Zeitgeist* and witnessing to it in its own language, even while rejecting its basic presuppositions. This is always a delicate maneuver. When one seeks to speak the language of the cultured despisers of biblical Christianity, it is easy to lose one's footing and come over to their ground. But Mather did not accept the rationalists' presuppositions and methodology.[86] Rather, he criticized them for being irrational in the deepest sense of reason:

Many Hearers do much admire, that which they call, *Rational Preaching;* but when they have opposed it unto *Scriptural Preaching,* they have but betrayed a sufficient want of *Reason.* The most shallow *Divines,* and the most empty *Harangues,* have most unjustly been sometimes distinguished by the name of *Rational.* Whereas, the more of *Gospel* there is in our *Preaching,* the more of *Reason* there is in it. *Scripture* is *Reason,* in its highest elevation.[87]

Mather does not say, "Reason is scripture," but the reverse, and with a qualification. He allows that there is much in revelation that is suprarational. He only insists that the self-styled rationalists are actually talking culpable nonsense; that inwardly they are suppressing the witness of "true reason" and building a false theology that insults God, in a universe which, even in the imperfect natural revelation, shouts against its validity. "The Greek word, KATEXEIN, used [in Rom. 1:18], carries an *Imprisonment,* in the Signification of it. There are men that have the *Truth,* in their *Understandings,* in their *Consciences,* in their *Memories;* but there they *Hold* it. They do, by a Violence upon it, *withold* it, and *Fetter* it, from having that Impression, which it would Reasonably go on to hold, upon their *Affections,* and *Conversations.*"[88]

It may be objected that this is orthodox rationalism of the sort that can very easily cross the bridge to the eighteenth-century side. Perhaps it is, although our own location in a century that has reacted against reason makes it difficult for us to judge. It must at least be admitted that Mather does not sufficiently indicate the difference in *kind* between the knowledge the mind can have of God apart from personal encounter and illumination by the Holy Spirit and the knowledge given by the convicting witness of the natural conscience and reason. He represents the difference as a matter merely of degree.

> More of the *Thing that is Right,* is to many People declared by *Revelation. Reason* alone, will tell us what is *Right,* as far as concerns meer *Natural Religion,* and the Peace of *Humane Society.* But *Reason* alone, without further and Special Instruction from God, will not carry us on to all the *Right Things* that are to bring us unto the Fruition of God. Our *Light within,* especially since our Soul has been wounded by our Fall from God, is an Insufficient Guide unto everlasting Happiness. Wherefore, our God has helped us by Revelation.[89]

This is substantially the position of Aquinas. But we must remember that a Thomistic concept of the relation between natural and revealed religion is typical of Reformed orthodoxy and common among Puritans up through Edwards, who continued to use this conceptual framework although his religious epistemology transcended it.[90] Even if we grant the fact that there is a degree of orthodox rationalism in Mather, it cannot be demonstrated that this seminal amount has gone to seed in him. On the contrary, he seems to lean over backwards in reaction to the logic-spinning of scholasticism. This accounts for his supposed double attitude toward reason, in which he seems to be both an anti-intellectual and a proponent of some of the new uses of reason. Mather had Luther's contempt for the schoolmen, for their "Metaphysicks; which a learned Man too justly calls, *Disciplinarum Omnium Excrementum,* tho' she would set up for the *Queen of Sciences.* . . . A *Suarez,* than whom you cannot easily find a greater dealer in *Metaphysicks,* after all declared, The *Hours* which he took in Studying and Examining and Rectifying his *own Heart,* were of infinitely more Use and Worth to him than all his *Metaphysical* and Voluminous Lucubrations."[91] Mather was especially critical of Aristotle, that "Muddy-headed Pagan . . . Who after the prodigious Cartloads of Stuff, that has been Written to explain him . . . he yet remains in many other Things besides his *Entelechia* sufficiently *Unintelligible,* and forever in almost all things *Unprofitable.*"[92] Although his father had learned his aversion to Aristotle from Peter Ramus, Cotton was dubious of the value of all systems of logic including the Ramaean:

> What is there usually got by the *Vulgar Logic,* but only to be furnished with a Parcel of *Terms,* which instead of leading the Mind into the *Truth,* enables one rather to carry on *Altercations,* and *Logomachies,* by which the Force of *Truth* may be at Pleasure, and by some little *Trick,* evaded. The Power and Process of *Reason* is *Natural* to the Soul of Man; And those *Masters of Reason,* who argue the most Rationally, and make the most *Rational Researches* into the true State of Things and . . . arrive to the most notable Discoveries, I pray, what sort of Logicians are they? Either they never once read a Page of any *Burgesdicius,* or else they have unlearnt and forgot all their *Vulgar Logic.* To exhibit in the pompous Form of an *Art,* what every One does by meer *Nature* and *Custom* . . . appears as impertinent, as if one should with much Formality teach the *Art* of *Eating* or *Drinking* or *Walking.* And it might with equal Solemnity be shown, what Points of *Regular Management* are exemplified by the Boys playing at their Marbles.[93]

Much of the American future is in this statement. Mather turned from scholasticism to equate true reason with New England common sense. He also showed that he strongly preferred the inductive logic of the Scientific Method, which he goes on to praise unrestrainedly: "As thorough an Insight as you can get into the *Principles* of our *Perpetual Dictator,* the Incomparable Sr. *Isaac Newton,* is what I mightily commend unto you. Be sure, the *Experimental Philosophy* is that, in which alone your Mind can be at all established."[94]

But if Mather sounds "modern" in these passages, it does not follow that he is in transit *theologically* toward the Enlightenment. He found some kinds of "reason" overly complex, those involved in systems of deductive logic and scholastic metaphysics, and these he sought to simplify. Other kinds he found basically irrational because of their false presuppositions, as with religious rationalism, and here he sought to uncover and refute the underlying foundations. In both these reactions there is really a movement contrary to orthodox rationalism. For while the latter sought to extrapolate a "theology of glory" from a tenuous basis in biblical evidence, Mather strove constantly to arrive at indubitable biblical fundamentals. The anti-intellectualism some find in him is really the same Protestant biblicism exhibited by Spener and Francke, which is always critically in tension with confessional orthodoxies.

It has also been suggested that Mather's pietism, with its simplification of theology, was itself susceptible to transformations leading toward Enlightenment rationalism.[95] This argument also appears plausible, for we have grown used to thinking of Pietism as a theological solvent—an ingredient in German theology, for instance, which could lead Halle to embrace the rationalism of Thomasius and Christian Wolff by the middle of the eighteenth century, and produce the subjectivism of Schleiermacher by the beginning of the nineteenth.[96]

Unless we start with Pietism at its worst and weakest, however, it is difficult to draw a straight line from its teachings to those variant theologies that surrounded and occasionally supplanted it. Whatever "rationalism" may be, its antithesis is certainly a profound dependence on objective revelation, and this is paramount in the biblicism of Spener, Francke, and Mather. Classical Pietism held that wherever theological authority is anchored on something other than biblical data illuminated by the Holy Spirit—whether the alternative be the Inner Light, or a set of orthodox rational constructs supposedly rooted in revelation, or clear and evident truths of reason—there is a bridge established that leads to rationalist thought-systems. No "system" or "strategy" adopted by a Pietist leader could prevent his followers from building illicit bridges after him, often by removing elements of his thought from their context and dismantling structures that were in tension. But it is unfair to bring these leaders to account for the mutations in their followers. We cannot hold Edwards responsible for the New England Theology; much less should we hold Mather accountable for American rationalism. He anticipated some of its better features, but he vigorously repudiated both its method and its content as he saw these beginning to operate in English and American theology.

Mather's theology is, then, essentially Reformed Orthodoxy stripped back to biblical essentials. But there are many scholastic remnants still present, and an ornamental crust with "spiritually edifying" fragments broken from an amazing variety of traditions. For Mather was quite eclectic in the sources of his theology. The authorities most cited in his work are the fathers of the early church: Augustine above all, and then (in descending order of frequency) Chrysostom, Origen, Tertullian, Cyprian, Jerome, Justin Martyr, Nazianzen, Clement of Alexandria, Basil, Ambrose, Ignatius, Irenaeus. There is little mention of medieval authorities, only scattered references to Aquinas, Bernard, and Hugh of St. Victor. A considerable number of allusions to "the incomparable" Calvin and to Luther are present, and other Reformation figures such as Bucer, Peter Martyr, and Ursinus are occasionally cited. Among orthodox writers, Voetius is mentioned fairly often and referred to as "very great," along with Witsius, Alsted, and Cocceius; and there are fleeting references to Beza, Scaliger, Zanchy, Heidegger, Chemnitz, Alting, Keckermann, Brentius, Bartholinus, and Amyraut. Puritan and Pietist authors are much more heavily cited than these. Among the former, Baxter rivals Augustine in frequency of citation; and Mather also gives much attention to Watts, Owen, Goodwin, Perkins, Ames, and a host of practical divines such as Matthew Henry, Flavel, Poole, Bayly, Downame, Scudder, Sibbes, Baynes, and Caryl. Pietist authorities cited with frequency are first of all the "incomparable" Francke, the "great" Arndt, Spener, Gerhard, and the Moravian Comenius. Mather was acquainted with conforming divines attractive to Puritan taste, among them Usher, Latimer, Andrewes, and Herbert. He was impressed with the intelligence of Grotius and was quite frequently involved either in refuting him or enlisting his aid. He also had an unusual acquaintance with and respect for Counter Reformation theology, citing Bellarmine and De Sales on occasion. His unusually wide knowledge of rabbinical writings has already been mentioned. He showed little acquaintance with philosophy but had a good knowledge of physical scientists such as Newton and Copernicus. Among literary artists he was familiar with Euripides, Propertius, Lucretius, Cicero, Seneca, Plutarch, Sallust, and Dryden, among others.

At the end of his life, in the section of his manual for ministerial students devoted to theological study, Mather recommends careful study of the Bible itself as the primary source of the minister's theology, aided by the consultation of practical commentaries like those of Poole and especially Matthew Henry, whose work "has Out-done most that we have yet had, in this Regard: The SPIRIT which dictated the *Sacred Scriptures*, operating on the Mind of the Commentator, in the Dispositions and Observations of *Experimental Piety*."[97] Mather also recommends the use of individual commentaries, rich in experiential observation, by English Puritans. It is only at this point that he goes on to recommend systematic theologians: "Let the Men who *Corrupt the Earth . . . Sit in the Seat of the Scorner,* and *Laugh,* and *Scoff,* at all *Systematical Divines* as long as they please, there are SYSTEMS OF DIVINITY, which I most seriously advise you, to be most intimately acquainted with."[98] He recommends Wollebius, Ames, Witsius, Marckius' *Compendium Theologiae,* Usher's *Body of Divinity,* John Edwards' *Theologia Reformata,* and a host of less familiar writers, among them Prideaux,

Tuckney, Hemingius, Aretius, and Pearson. He reserves special praise for Calvin's *Institutes*, but also for the works of Alting and Mastricht because of their experiential vitality; and he notes that those who would like a small but complete theological library would need only the works of Johann Gerhard and Voetius. Among polemicists Mather recommends Alsted and a host of minor writers on particular controversies; and in the field of casuistical divinity, Ames, Alsted, Baxter, and Baldwin.[99]

Despite the unusual variety of his sources, Mather's basic theology is neither extensive nor complex. As I have noted, he spent most of his life trying to boil down the Christian faith to its absolute doctrinal essentials. It has been suggested that part of the reason for this was a desire to sharpen up the tools of Puritanism by paring away scholastic excrescences, in order to penetrate the increasingly dulled religious sensibility of New Englanders.[100] But there are two other strong motives that led to his experiments in doctrinal simplification: his obvious evident pastoral desire to communicate the essence of Christian faith to children, "*Negro's,* and others like them, of the Dullest and Lowest Capacity";[101] and his later consuming interest in closing the ranks of evangelical Protestants in some form of ecumenical union.

Mather's "Very Short Catechism" of 1708, like much of his writing in this genre, is strongly oriented to experience and self-examination rather than to bare doctrinal statement. It simply asks three questions: "Who made you?"—followed by a short definition of God and man's purpose as his servant; "Who saves men?"—with a definition of Christ as both God and man; and "What will become of you when you die?"—promising heaven to those obedient to Christ and hell to those persisting in wickedness.[102] This, however, is Mather speaking to the most elementary level of intelligence, to the child or the mentally or culturally retarded. His "Abridgement of the *Shorter Catechism*," contained in the same catechetical manual, is a fairly artful condensation of the Assembly's work, preserving both its rudimentary Calvinism and its admixture of covenant theology. Mather's main work here was not to modify the structure of the *Catechism*, which may be identified as the basic framework for his thinking throughout his life, but simply to condense its major theses by eliminating bridge passages. There is, however, a considerable simplification of the subject of sin, in questions 14-19: Mather does not here insist on the minutiae of our federal connection with Adam's sin, and does not distinguish original and actual sin, or amplify the results and misery of sin in fallen humanity.

A somewhat earlier formulary is also an abbreviation of the *Shorter Catechism* into thirty-three articles, but it has less direct emphasis on election and covenant theology.[103] *Le Vrai Patron des Saines Paroles* (1704), on the other hand, is a fourteen-point creed contained in a tract appealing to French Catholics, and Mather appropriately but pugnaciously stresses such Reformation distinctives as predestination and justification through the imputation of Christ's righteousness.[104] *Pastoral Desires* (1712) contains, along with longer summaries of doctrine, a short creed of seven points oriented to practical spiritual needs: God as infinite creator and governor, man's fall, Christ as divine/human redeemer born of a virgin, justification by faith and sanctification through the Spirit, the duty of repentance, the value of the sacraments, and the final destiny of people in heaven or hell. But by and large Mather was happiest with the *Westminster Shorter Catechism* as a basic theological summary. In the *Manuductio* he does not propose simplifying this, but amplifying it with a few distinctive Matherian emphases: the active obedience of Christ securing our justification and the ministry of good angels on our behalf.[105]

The other main motive for Mather's theological simplification, concern for ecumenical union, appeared during the last twenty years of his life when he was especially involved in contacts with Francke and other Pietists. Mather was here engaged in much more radical condensation than he had been in his catechetical reductions. His first sketch of the "Maxims of the Everlasting Gospel," upon which all evangelical Protestants are to unite, is in fourteen points, but most of these are challenges to personal piety rather than doctrinal articles. The points are these: One God in triune form, Christ as the eternal Son of God, the Bible as the rule of faith, repentance unto life, the acknowledgment of God in all one's life, becoming a new creature, conformity to the example of Jesus, benignity to men, the observation of the Golden Rule, careful stewardship of temporal goods, care in scriptural worship of God but also charity toward differing forms, the use of public office for good, contempt for worldly glory, and longing for piety on the whole earth.[106] This odd mixture of creed and exhortation is substantially repeated in *The Stone Cut Out of the Mountain* (1716), but by 1717 Mather had reduced its doctrinal core to three elements: faith in God, belief in Christ, and commitment to the Golden Rule as the guide to evangelical obedience.[107] This schema reappears as a touchstone of self-examination for regenerate piety in *The Tryed Professor* (1719),[108] and again in *India Christiana* (1721)[109] and the *Manuductio* (1726), from which I quote its full expression:

> I. The ONE most High GOD, who is the FATHER, and the SON, and the Holy SPIRIT, must be my GOD: And I must make it the *main Intention* of my Life to *Serve* and *Please* Him, in all Holy *Obedience* and *Submission* to Him, Remembring that His Eye is always upon me; and be afraid of *every Thing*, which His *Light* in my Soul shall condemn as an *Evil Thing*.
>
> II. A Glorious CHRIST who is the Eternal SON of GOD, Incarnate and enthroned in the Blessed JESUS, is the REDEEMER, on whose great *Sacrifice* I must Rely for my *Reconciliation* to GOD, looking to Him, at the same time, that I may live unto GOD by Him *Living in me:* And under His Conduct I am now to expect a Blessedness in a *Future State*, for my *Immortal Soul;* to which He will restore my *Body*, when He shall come to *Judge the World*.
>
> III. Out of Respect unto GOD and His CHRIST, I must heartily *Love my Neighbor*, and forever do unto *Other Men*, as I must own it Reasonable for them to do unto *myself*.

Mather goes on to add two other codicils which he represents as understood in the three principal maxims: adherence to Scripture as the rule of faith and practice, and freedom of conscience with full civil rights for all "Faithful *Subjects* and Honest *Neighbors*."[110] This simplified and "experimentalized" creed still has compressed into its second article a rejection of Arianism, a statement of justification by faith, sanctification through the *unio Christi,* and the bodily resurrection of believers. Its third article seems anthropocentric in that it restricts the rule of obedience to the second table of the Law, but this is guarded by the opening clause and by the emphasis on the primacy of obedience to God in the first article.

Even so, this is a radical reduction of the theological curriculum articulated in the ample dimensions of the Westminster Confession. In the pursuit of his minimal creed, Mather foreshadowed two major tendencies of a later time: he was in a sense the first "fundamentalist" and the first major ecumenist in American church history.

This does not mean, however, that Mather gradually came to abandon as unimportant the theological distinctives of his tradition. When he was not speaking in the simplicity of ecumenical or catechetical discourse, or the heat of revivalist zeal, he exhibits many of the insignia of orthodoxy. Most of these occur in his treatment of the doctrine of God. God is defined in remarkably Aristotelian terminology: "There must be a *First Cause.* This *First Cause* must be *Independent;* must be *Everlasting;* must have the *Perfections* of all *other Beings* in Him, and be *Unlimited* in His Perfections. . . . 'Tis impossible, there should be *Two Infinite Beings.*"[111] God is *"pure Act,* and when we call Him so *pure* a Thing as a *Spirit,* it is too *Gross* a Name to be taken without a Figure."[112] Throughout his life Mather conjoined to his Christocentric piety a devotion to the Godhead thus philosophically defined, and often analyzed into His various attributes.[113] The divine sovereignty as conceived by Beza and Perkins he defends in vigorously rational arguments in early works such as *The Principle of the Protestant Religion Maintained* (1690), which chooses to attack George Keith's Quakerism by asserting double predestination,[114] and another anti-Quaker tract, *Little Flocks Guarded Against Grievous Wolves* (1691), which flaunts its logic in the faces of enthusiasts: "*There is an eternal reprobation.* . . . If there were an *Eternal Election* of some, ask them whether it be not pure Non-sense to say, that some were *Chosen,* and others were not *left Unchosen?*"[115] The logical connection of election and reprobation remained axiomatic with Mather during the rest of his life.[116] But Mather nowhere entered into the subject of the order of the decrees. He did not explicitly condemn this form of theological speculation, but he quietly ignored it as if he were unconscious that such issues could be raised. And unlike Jonathan Edwards, he would not speculate about the resolution of the tension between election and free will: "Who can reconcile *Divine Prescience* with Humane Liberty?"[117]

> If you ask me, *How tis done?* I am not altogether Ignorant, how the Schoolmen have expressed their Thoughts of the matter: They tell us, (& very truly,) there is that *Power & Wisdom* in the Divine Providence, that no *Liberty* of the Humane *Will* can Resist the Efficacy thereof; and yet it so Cooperates with all causes, *Ut suaviter moveat*, All is most *Sweetly* carried on. . . . But I wave Their Speculations; I have plain People to deal withal. And for them, I will make as Learned an Answer to it, as any that I have met withal. My Answer is, *I cannot tell;* I say, *I cannot tell.* The best Flight of our Learning, in such a Point as this, is a Confession of our Ignorance.[118]

Here an echo of Calvin combines with a premonition of American pastoral skill in the next century, which also "waived speculations" in order to deal with plain people.

The covenant theology, which provided a conceptual framework for William Perkins and almost all subsequent theologians in the Puritan line, is present in the background in most of Mather's writings. It recurs so frequently because it is essential to Mather's technology of regeneration, his handling of the process of "closing with Christ" which it was his main concern to propagate among his people. Mather was content to carry over from his tradition the drama of the intra-Trinitarian covenant of redemption, resting on a slender biblical basis, because it furnished a fine counterpoint for his insistence that a covenant of response must now be made between the people and their God, for a conversion involves laying hold of a covenant.[119] God offers himself in all his Trinitarian perfection, all his attributes, the mediator of the new covenant, the very kingdom of heaven itself, but there must be reciprocation: we must subscribe to a "covenant of reconciliation" with God for these benefits to be effective.[120] Mather rarely entered into detailed handling of the double covenant and its implications, but he simply stuck to his appeals for a quid-pro-quo response to God's action in the covenant of grace. I have located only one reference in his published opus in which he really gives a detailed handling of the federal headship of Adam and our implication in his sin through representative guilt and actual pollution, although this is a late reference and thoroughly orthodox.[121]

Mather's eclectic spirituality occasionally led him to decorate his system with ornaments from outside the Reformed tradition. Most of his interest in patristic and medieval spirituality was centered on mystical and ascetic techniques, but he was occasionally fascinated by a theological concept also. One such recurrent idea is the Augustinian analogy of the structure of the Trinity to the activity of human thought, which is outside the mainstream of Reformed orthodoxy.[122]

> God cannot be Infinitely and Absolutely *Perfect,* without the *Perception of Himself,* and an Immense *Joy* and *Love* resulting therefrom, in finding Himself, *The Alsufficient Good;* and this *Perception,* and this *Joy* and *Love* must also be of the most *Perfect Kind* . . . far more Excellent than that which is *Modal,* such as Creatures have: whose Perceptions and Operations are with Images, which are not the Soul it self. This is the Prerogative of the *Deity;* God has a *Substantial* Representation of Himself within Himself, and a *Substantial* Satisfaction thereupon. The *Father* is the *Fountain* of the Deity; The *Son* is the *Express Image* of the Father's Person, or God Essentially Representing of God, or the Eradiation of His Glorious Riches and Fulness; therefore also from all Eternity containing in Him the *Idea* of all that was to be made in Time; The *Holy Ghost* is that wonderful *Joy* and *Love,* which God has in Himself by the Grateful *Perception* which the Father and Son eternally have of one another.[123]

Mather is impressed by the devotional power of this representation of the interior commerce within the Godhead, and he recommends meditation on it to infuse God's love and joy into the believer's heart. While he repudiated Platonic mysticism, he had a sweet tooth for its products that is frequently evident in all his work.

But perhaps the most important novelty Mather fused into his orthodox theological groundwork was his eschatology. Chiliasm is one of the most frequently recurring motifs in Cotton Mather's writing, and it is one major root of the revivalist and ecumenist goals he shared with German Pietism.[124] In his earliest lengthy publication he speaks of himself as an eager chiliast with "impatient longings for the revolution of a golden age, wherein there shall be . . . a general peace or truce, throughout the whole world."[125] In two sermons preached in 1691 he set aside the conventional jeremiad to present a view of the "wonderful state of Peace" toward which he felt the church moving, defined as a thousand-year earthly reign of Christ after his return, with a restoration of the Davidic kingdom to the Jewish people. The destruction of Roman Catholic power had to precede this, and Mather concluded that this might at least begin within twenty-five years.

Following the earlier premillennial speculations of Joseph Mede, Mather reasoned that the "hindrance" to the appearance of Antichrist mentioned in II Thessalonians 2:7 was the presence of the Roman Empire, and that this hindrance was removed about A.D. 456 with the destruction of the old empire, leading to the rise of the papal Antichrist, the "deadly wound" given to the "fourth kingdom" of Daniel having thus been healed through the reappearance of the Beast in religious guise. Since the period of antichristian power was generally agreed by millennial theorists to be 1260 years (Daniel's "time, times, and half a time" [Dan. 7:25] considered as 3½ years, and interpreted as 1260 day-years), the first decisive blows against Antichrist would begin to be struck 1260 years after A.D. 456 or 1716. Mather felt confirmed in this date by the general presumption that the end of history might occur at the end of the earth's sixth chiliad; according to the Usher chronology, the year 6000 would arrive in 1716. In the meantime, he was looking for the end of the Turkish "second woe," the waning of Moslem power—the third and last woe, the destruction of Antichrist, would begin in 1716—and for the plentiful effusion of the Holy Spirit that would be necessary for the conversion of the Jews and a great ingathering of other converts. He felt that this fulfillment of Joel's prophecy of the Spirit's outpouring (Joel 2:28-32) might well begin "half a time" (180 years) after the first Reformation in 1517 (which Pierre Jurieu had identified with the "harvest" of Revelation 14) or around 1697, inaugurating a "New Reformation" (the "vintage" mentioned in the same passage).[126]

During the next three decades Mather's eschatological outlook remained essentially intact, although he entertained minor variations in response to the unfolding of history and the publications of other theorists. His unpublished "Problema Theologica" of 1703 attempts to prove the thesis that the "Happy State of the Church" predicted by Old Testament prophecy must be identified with the concept of a literal millennium drawn from Revelation 20:4-10, and that this must begin after the personal return of Christ. The millennium will follow a national conversion of the Jews (possibly effected by Christ's return), the destruction of the papal Antichrist, the resurrection of the righteous, and a great conflagration of the present world succeeded by the creation of "a New Heavens and a New Earth." Two groups of saints will survive the conflagration: the "Raised Saints" who will dwell with Christ in the New Jerusalem, which will remain suspended in the heavens, and the "Changed Saints," those alive at Christ's return, who will dwell on the new earth. While the changed saints will continue to engage in marriage and procreation and the subduing of the earth, the raised saints will be transformed into a heavenly condition beyond marriage and will occasionally descend to serve as teachers of those remaining on earth. At the conclusion of the thousand years the hostile antichristian powers Gog and Magog will rise up from a source we cannot now foresee, and the millennium will conclude with Christ's destruction of them and the Final Judgment.

We can see that Mather's eschatological timetable had changed only slightly over this period. He still held that a decisive movement toward the end began in 1697 with the passing of the Turkish "Second Woe," but he did not mention the year 1716. He had recalculated the date for the inception of the seventh chiliad of world history and now held this to be 1736; and he also offered a different timing for the end of the power of Antichrist, which is now assumed to begin around A.D. 440 or 445, continue for 1260 years, and wane during a 75-year period of the "Cleansing of the Temple." This would have placed the end of world history around 1775 or 1780, although Mather felt that it could come sooner, and in fact might come immediately.[127]

In 1706, Mather began writing his great unpublished Bible commentary, the "Biblia Americana," and by 1713 he had reached the last book of the Bible. His commentary on Revelation is immense compared to the other New Testament sections, partly because he occasionally presents the reader with a smorgasbord of diverging theories on disputed points, such as the order and identity of the different judgments that are to conclude the present age, including the opinions of Thomas Goodwin, Pierre Jurieu, and many other theorists. In the body of the commentary Mather is extremely cautious about dates, tentatively repeating Jurieu's schema involving 1697 and 1716 but offering several alternatives. The section on Revelation 20 presents a very complex millennial scenario adopted from William Torrey, calling for two conflagrations (one at the beginning and one at the end) and two different confederacies typified by the biblical Gog and Magog (the first attacking the Jews on their way to Palestine, and the second rising against all the saints at the end). The body of the Revelation commentary is extremely tentative and speculative in its tone, but in an appendix ("Coronis") Mather reports the new light he has gained on the subject from William Whiston's *Essay on Revelation* (1706), which offers not merely "*Conjectures,* but irrefragable and incontrovertible *Demonstrations*" of many things that have been dubious up to now. The major certainty Mather seems to have drawn from Whiston is that 1716 would indeed be a crucial year, one which would involve "Great Mutations," including the breaking of the persecuting power of Rome and the cleansing of the sanctuary. Soon after this, Mather says, we can expect the Seventh Angel to sound the great trumpet for the outpouring of the vials that contain the last plagues, which will destroy the Kingdom of the Beast.[128]

The details of Mather's eschatology shifted slightly toward the end of his life, after his hopes for a decisive movement toward the millennium in 1716 seemed to be unrealized. In June 1724 he recorded in the *Diary* that God had convinced him that all the events preliminary to the millennium had already occurred in history, so that there was no need to watch for further signals before the return of Christ.[129] By 1726 Mather had incorporated this insight into the unpublished manuscript of "Tri-Paradisus," a treatise prepared sometime before 1720 which sums up his eschatological thinking. "Tri-Paradisus" contains a remarkable divergence from most millennial thinking of the sixteenth century: Mather has rejected the notion of the conversion of the Jewish nation at the end of history, returning to the Augustinian interpretation of Old Testament prophecies and Romans 11:25-29 as either already fulfilled or symbolic of the Israel of God.[130] Until his father's death Mather had firmly concurred with him in expecting that the coming "revolution" would involve an ingathering of the Jewish people, and consequently he was constantly alert during this time for harbingers of the conversion of Israel. He labored himself to convert Jewish individuals, relayed every transatlantic report of successful conversions, and mentioned the subject frequently in his writings.[131] But despite the evidence of the outpouring of the Spirit in Halle Pietism, there did not seem to be any mass movement of Jews toward Christ during this period. Finally, Mather seems to have abandoned hope for the whole complex of desired events prior to the millennium, including the New Reformation, unity on the basis of true piety, extension of the gospel, and conversion of the Jews. He did not, however, press for an immediate *parousia*, allowing that this might occur as late as A.D. 2000, although he still held out the possibility that 1735 or 1736 might be a crucial date.[132]

At first glance, it may seem impossible for Mather to have been an ardent chiliast and at the same time a prophet of ecumenical renewal and activist reform of church and society who helped lay the groundwork for the Great Awakening. We are not used to premillennial optimists. From our standpoint in history we tend to associate all premillennialism with the Darbyite subtype which temporarily came to dominate the Evangelical Movement after D. L. Moody: it was individualistic, socially quietistic, and pessimistic about the prospects for renewing or uniting with presumed apostate denominational structures. Our tendency is to assume that Jonathan Edwards' postmillennialism was an essential ingredient in his concept of revival which dynamically transformed Puritanism into a culture-conquering renewal movement.

But several important recent studies have shown that the postmillennial thrust in Puritanism considerably antedated Edwards, and that it was able to work in harmony with "classical premillennialism" in the seventeenth century to promote reformation and renewal in the church. In fact, it may not be inaccurate to say that most of the component movements within the Puritan coalition were from the beginning attuned to the Edwardsian understanding of revival, or at least evolving toward it. [133] A theology of hope for better times in the church and in the world had already emerged in the work of Theodor Bibliander, Heinrich Bullinger, Martin Bucer, and Peter Martyr Vermigli, and their early influence in England can be seen in the thinking of John Foxe and John Jewel. These and other continental influences helped to produce four major varieties of millennial thought in seventeenth-century Puritanism:

1. What might be called positive amillennialism did not believe in a literal thousand-year period of prosperity but held this to be symbolic of a time of progress for the church and expansion of the gospel in the future. This school is represented by the strongest consensus of Puritan leadership, including William Perkins, Richard Sibbes, John Owen, Thomas Manton, Samuel Rutherford, David Dickson, John Eliot, the Westminster Standards, and the Savoy Declaration. On the continent the Pietists Spener and Francke entertained the same "hope of better times."[134]

2. Literal postmillennialism looked for a triumphant expansion of a reforming church prior to a literal thousand years under the personal reign of Christ. This strand was inaugurated by Thomas Brightman's *Apocalypsis Apocalypseos* (1609) and later echoed by John Cotton, Daniel Whitby,

and Jonathan Edwards.

3. Classical premillennialism held to a literal thousand years of peace inaugurated by the return of Christ, advocated in England in 1642 by the translation of J. A. Alsted's *Diatribe de mille annis Apocalypticis* (1627), and further developed by Joseph Mede, Thomas Goodwin, Thomas Beverley, Thomas Burnet, Isaac Newton, and by Increase Mather and Samuel Sewall in America.

4. Radical millenarians such as the Fifth Monarchy Men were generally characterized as "fanatical chiliasts" by mainstream Puritanism.

In one way or another, therefore, nearly all Puritanism was motivated by millenarian expectations during the seventeenth century. The only major figure to adhere to a more neutral amillenarianism, one that did not look forward to a predicted Golden Age for the church, was Richard Baxter. The positive amillennial and postmillennial strains were driven toward an Edwardsian concept of revival because their understanding of the church's perseverance in the future had to depend not on the bodily return of Christ but on his spiritual rule through the outpouring of the Holy Spirit. It might be assumed that literal chiliasts would lack this dynamic and would be indifferent to the cause of reformation and the extension of the gospel, particularly those who felt that Christ's coming was imminent. But the fact is that we find premillennialists like the Mathers and Sewall solidly connected to the work and the sentiments of Eliot and other positive amillennialists, and harmonizing with their concerns. The solution to this apparent contradiction lies in a shared conviction that united the two groups: the necessity to press for a national conversion of the Jews, which was normally viewed as the outcome of a mighty purification and extension of the Gentile churches, according to Romans 11:25-29. Originating in Martin Bucer, this article of faith was picked up by Perkins, Alsted, Mede, and Brightman, and communicated to all the major millennial streams through their work. The ultimate source of the Edwardsian tradition was thus the author of *De Regno Christi:* for before the Jews could be gathered the church had to be revived.[135]

The function of this principle in Mather's eschatology, turning it into an active rather than a passive premillennialism, is apparent during most of his lifetime. Mather went on record in 1706 against setting a definite date for Christ's return, in a sermon on a very pointed text, Matthew 24:44:

> The Time of our Lords *Appearing in His Kingdom,* is a Perfect *Secret;* an Utter *Secret;* no man alive may without Presumption go to fix the Time for it. Some *Fanatical People* have done so, and have had nothing but an *Infamous Nickname* for the Reward of their Folly. . . . Perhaps the rash confidence of many Students in *Apocalyptical* matters, carrying in their *Computations* may contribute unto the scornful and slothful *Security,* that shall then grow so Epidemical.[136]

There is thus a strong presumption that Mather was predicting a preparatory revival of indefinite extent, and not the return of Christ, both in 1697 and 1716, and this is borne out by his earliest description of what he was expecting in 1697: "A REFORMATION more Glorious, more Heavenly, more Universal far away than what was in the former Century. . . . We are got into the very *Dawn* of the Day, when God will vouchsafe a marvellous Effusion of His own Spirit upon many Nations, and REFORMATION, with all *Piety,* and *Charity,* shall gain the Ascendent, over those Men and Things, that for many Ages have been the Oppressors of it."[137] In another place Mather admits that the fullness of the millennial kingdom can only come with Christ's return, but he advocates an activist strategy that parallels his position on the role of preparation in conversion. He admits that no human energy can bring in the kingdom an hour sooner than God intends, but he urges that people anticipate the works of the kingdom by making "some fair Indications [imitations?] of it" beforehand, particularly in efforts at peace and union among the churches, in the missionary extension of the gospel, and in prayer for the conversion of the Jews, which will lead to the millennium.[138]

In the exhausted and perhaps angry mood of his later years, when he faced personal tragedy and rejection in his own neighborhood and saw the interests of the church at home and abroad afflicted with the dead calm of spiritual decline that preceded the Great Awakening, Mather shifted to a position that was more pessimistic and passive. Oddly enough, he seems to have rejected the Jewish national conversion because he considered it "an error, calculated for, and contributing to, the *Faulty Sleep of the Latter Times*";[139] for what could be used among vital Christians as a spur to awaken the church to its mission could be turned by the rebellious into a drug-producing carnal security. Mather surrendered this instrument for awakening the church's sense of mission just at the point when others were about to use it most successfully in renewing the church. But throughout most of his life his public utterances and published exhortations were almost indistinguishable from the general urgency for reform found among positive amillennialists, and the vigor and quantity of these made them a powerful force in creating a hunger for awakening in New England.

CHAPTER THREE

The Experience of Rebirth

ONE OF THE IDENTIFYING MARKS OF THE EVANGELICAL tradition descending from the eighteenth-century awakenings has been the insistence on spiritual rebirth as an indispensable first experience of all genuine believers. An emphasis on conversion and regeneration was central in the work of Frelinghuysen and the Middle Colony evangelists, Edwards, Whitefield, the Wesleys, and Zinzendorf; and the same is true of the later work of Timothy Dwight and Lyman Beecher, William Wilberforce and Charles Simeon, Charles Finney, D. L. Moody, Billy Sunday, and Billy Graham.

Most of these figures are in one way or another connected with English and American Puritanism, even those whose Arminian theology is a mutation from the Puritan stock, and this explains their common stress on the importance of being "born again." The foundations for this emphasis were laid by the theologies of live orthodoxy constructed by the English Puritans and Continental Pietists. In any treatment of Puritan theology of Christian experience the subject of rebirth should be handled at the outset, not only because this experience was for Puritans the inception of piety but also because in their tradition this first awakening to God received a distinctive and exaggerated stress, enlarging it to the point of hypertrophy.[1] Conversion, for Puritans, was not just a prologue to the Christian life; sometimes it seems to have been more like a climactic drama to which the rest of spiritual development was only a long, quiet epilogue. The resulting imbalance might be called a "loading" of the conversion experience, which forces it to bear an extremely heavy freight: all the developed content of the most refined and matured Christian sensibility, the fruit of years of growth as defined in other experiential systems, is here poured into the mold of the soul's first dealings with God.

This is why Cotton Mather, standing at the end of the Puritan movement in its theocratic phase, returned to the theme of conversion with hypnotic regularity, making it the first and principal application of nearly all his sermons. For Mather, the "one thing needful" in his early treatise *Unum Necessarium* is, predictably, not the listening nurture of the reborn disciple mentioned in the biblical text but the experience of saving grace through the conversion process.[2] Mather was typically Puritan in his reliance on conversion as the main tool in spiritual awakening and pastoral care. The appeal to "go through a process of repentance" is the central point of application in almost every Mather sermon; it is the Puritan counterpart to the twentieth-century evangelist's appeal to "come forward."

We might assume that this peculiar emphasis on the inception of the spiritual life is a correlate of the Puritan ecclesiology, which strives toward a pure church of regenerate members. It is true that there is a supportive interaction between the theory of church membership and the theory of conversion. Nevertheless, as Edmund S. Morgan has pointed out, the ecclesiological motive was secondary. The main energy behind the Puritan preoccupation with the morphology of conversion was the same one that drove Luther in his definition of justification *sola fide*—a passionate desire for assurance of salvation.[3] But why were the Puritans dissatisfied with Luther's answer, and why did they persist in probing the nature of initial saving faith?

It was undoubtedly because they sensed a certain weakness and one-sidedness in Luther's approach as it was developed by his successors, as did the Pietists and such later critics as Kierkegaard and Bonhoeffer. Bonhoeffer has unforgettably characterized this weakness as the offer of "cheap grace," justification through the imputation of the "wholly alien righteousness" of Christ, held in an artificial separation from sanctification, so that it can rest on the believer like a clean garment covering a basically uncleansed life. Almost any system of experiential Christianity is involved in the attempt to build into itself safeguards against cheap grace. In medieval Catholicism the safeguards were a semi-Pelagian theology combined with the institution of the confessional.[4] The experiential balance between presumption and despair was here achieved, of course, at the cost of an injection of legalism. The Reformation reaction against legalism could sometimes be twisted into a practicing antinomianism by subsequent generations of Protestants. In reaction to this imbalance, the Continental pre-Pietists and the English Puritans, influenced by New Testament sources and by the same currents of pre-Reformation mysticism that affected Anabaptist teaching on Christian experience, turned from the medieval solution to the motif of rebirth.[5]

Continental Pietism may have avoided loading the experience of conversion in quite the same way as did Puritanism, because the Lutheran doctrine of baptismal regeneration led to a greater stress on the development of the Christian life begun in baptism, and because Pietists did not make the deductions from the concept of election which tormented the Puritan with the necessity of being assured at the outset. In Arndt, and in the subsequent Continental tradition through Spener and Francke, there is a balancing stress on the continuous process of sanctification which follows regeneration. Arndt was concerned to emphasize repentance as well as the creedal faith of the orthodox, but he remembered well the first of Luther's theses, that evangelical repentance is not a single act but a lifelong attitude.[6] Even Francke, with his Puritan-influenced stress on the definite conversion experience, had a full treatment of Christian growth as a continuing process.[7]

In the Puritan tradition, however, a strongly predestinarian theology thrust upon the event of rebirth an especially heavy content of spiritual experience, which was required to ease the crisis of assurance in the believer's mind. Hence the loading of this experience is particularly a Puritan phenomenon, and it is the trademark of this tradition in all its subsequent historical incarnations. We cannot say, of course, that a movement which produced works like Owen's treatises on indwelling sin entirely ignored sanctification in its preoccupation with initial regeneration. The fact remains, however, that the believers who could pass the entrance requirements in most Puritan churches were so thoroughly searched out that they scarcely needed Owen's guidebooks to remaining depravity. Puritan converts were virtually presanctified; like fine watches, they were subjected to so many tests in the assembly process that they could almost be guaranteed against breakdown in future backsliding.

Part of the depth obtained in Puritan conversions results from this analysis of the experience into a *process*, a series of preparatory stages. This was something of an innovation on the Reformers, for they gave little attention to the psychological analysis of conversion. Evidently they considered the heart as being taken by storm in regeneration, with the divine sovereignty enlightening the mind and rectifying the will without much conscious seeking or cooperation on the human side. Calvin and Bullinger, however, allowed that the Law could constrain the unregenerate heart toward repentance, and the English Puritans moved from these embryonic hints into a developed psychology of conversion. However, there is an immense and fascinating variety in their teaching. The founding theologian of Puritanism, William Perkins, discerned eight distinct stages in the process, four of them prior to regeneration (hearing the Word, recognizing the Law, realizing particular sins, and legal terrors) and four that could only occur in the regenerate (considering the promises, faith, evangelical sorrow, and new obedience).[8] Perkins' great pupil, William Ames, reduced these to four: hearing the Law, conviction, despair, and evangelical humiliation. On the other hand, the great pastor and eloquent preacher of grace and the Spirit's working, Richard Sibbes, reacted against the spelling out of stages of conversion and the introspective searching of the heart for assurance, though he did believe in preparation. He felt that the special operations of the Spirit were too subtle to be accurately discerned and argued that common-grace workings in the unregenerate could often seem deeper and more spectacular than the quiet work of the Spirit in the converted. Disdaining "law-work" and legal terrors as unworthy of the gospel dispensation, he simply urged an earnest striving toward repentance and a believing dependence on grace until assurance was reached, leaving the exact point of regeneration uncertain. The equally influential John Preston followed along similar lines, except that he felt that effective preparation could only take place in those already regenerate, so that preparation for grace was already a sign of its presence.[9]

Among the New England Puritans there was a continuing dichotomy between the strict preparationists and those who were made uneasy by this kind of close analysis and preferred to concentrate more simply on repentance and dependence on divine grace for salvation. Among the former were Thomas Hooker and, most influentially, Thomas Shepard, who re-emphasized the importance of legal terrors. On the other side, Peter Bulkely agreed with Preston that preparation is already a sign of conversion; and John Cotton, consciously striving to return to a position closer to that of Calvin, reverted to the image of the heart taken by storm and rejected any idea of conversion through preparatory stages. In the outcome of the Hutchinson trial in the 1630s, however, the concept of conscious striving in the preparation of the heart won the day over Cotton's more Calvinistic approach, and preparationism was established as the reigning orthodoxy in New England experientialism.

Thus, while the Puritan tradition was generally united in the loading of the conversion experience, it was diverse in its treatment of the exact details of conversion. The diversity was principally the result of the earnest efforts of the pastor-theologians in the movement to apply the gospel to the variety of spiritual conditions in the local congregation. Puritan pastors had to keep an uneasy balance between comforting the afflicted and afflicting the comfortable. They had to make their sermons sharp enough to convict those who were complacently resting in a common-grace self-righteousness, and yet they had to have balm enough to apply to those wounded by the mishandling of their instruments of conviction. As a result, they not only contradicted one another in their schemas of conversion; they often contradicted themselves. We cannot read and understand any of their statements on conversion without envisioning the target at which it was aimed, the spiritual condition in a part of the congregation which they were seeking to move and change; and only thus can we comprehend how sections even within a single sermon can run counter to one another.

It is thus not surprising that Cotton Mather, standing at the end of a heterogeneous development of conversion theory in the seventeenth century, was remarkably equivocal in his own treatment of regeneration. He stood above all the figures in the previous century, allowing some value to each peculiar emphasis and choosing among these according to the immediate needs of his audience. Like his hero Baxter, he was much inclined to suspect that all sides of the question had something of value to offer and that many divergences sprang from semantic problems.[10] He was not concerned to set forth a consistent system of teaching on conversion, but he aimed simply to convert his audience using whatever stress was necessary.

Several statements Mather made throughout his career anticipate the reaction of later revivalists against complex schemes of preparation. He says that it is dangerous to doubt our conversion just because we have not consciously touched all the bases of the standard conversion schemes.

> Many of the *Elect* undergo fearful *Troubles,* hideous *Terrors,* in their conversion to God and Piety. But some that have had a *Religious Education,* and been Restrained all their Days from the more Scandalous Abominations; These are Converted unto God, after a more *Insensible manner.* . . . They know not *Where* it was, nor *How* it was, that they were first brought into an *Union* with their Saviour. . . . The *Preparatory Contritions, &* *Consternations,* are not alike in all that come with *Labouring* and *Heavy-laden* Souls unto our Saviour. Is the *End* of all *Preparations* attain'd upon you; and a CHRIST so Endear'd unto you, that you cannot bear or dare to *neglect His Great Salvation?*

Then, Don't make *Ill Signs* of those that are none. Don't make a CHRIST of the Things, whereof all the End and Use is to Prepare you for Him.[11]

Mather himself was one of those who was converted "insensibly" in his religious upbringing, and so it is not surprising to find him here foreshadowing Bushnell. In another place he says of the insistence on a standardized conversion model, "This is to bring the *Covenant of Work* into the *Covenant of Grace*,"[12] which was his grandfather Cotton's objection to preparationism. But he hesitates to abandon preparation entirely: "It is not to be supposed, that we may not lay hold on Christ by Faith, till we find such and such remarkable *degrees* of *Humiliation* in us. Those Books which tell us we *presume* if we *believe*, before we have arrived unto certain *high strains* of Contrition in us, will not bring us to *sincere Conversion*, but *sorrowful Desperation. . . .* But let no Pillows be thereby sown under the Arms of them, *whom the Lord says, there is no peace unto*. Let every Man despair of ever *seeing the Kingdom of God*, unless he be *born again*."[13] While administering balm to the wounded, Mather here gives a quick glance at the large mass in his audience who are resting in stolid complacency, and he gives them the goad. He does not really reject preparationism but merely seeks to confine it within safe and healthy practical limits.

> There is a *Variety* in that *Preparatory work*, . . . and *Converts* do sometimes needlessly *Distress* themselves, and even Deceive themselves, by insisting too much on the *Measure* of this *Preparation*. But *so much* of this Work, as will render us *Restless* without a CHRIST; *so much* of this Work, as will render a whole CHRIST *Precious* to us; Be sure there must be *so much* in our Experience, if we would be *Saved*.[14]

Mather insists throughout his writings that repentance is ordinarily a *process*, a preparatory work over an extended period of time, though he differs from other preparationists in not precisely defining the stages of that process. Motivated by the fear that some member of the congregation would slip off the hook, using the rationale of the deathbed repentance, Mather goes to the length of insisting that the thief on the cross had been preparing his heart before his interview with Christ!

> Every thing looks as if he came thither *Prepared*. . . . We have not the least Intimation of any *Pains* taken there to *Enlighten* him, and *Admonish* him. . . . And yet the *Grace* Exercised by this Penitent, was of so Various and Marvellous an Application, that one may say, He does in a *few Hours* the work of *some Years*. . . . It looks as if he *came thither armed* with a Zealous and Intense Desire to Propagate a Sense of God in the Hearts of others. . . . One does not *Per Saltum* come to this degree.[15]

The significant item here is the denial of immediate conversion. However insensibly it might come, conversion, for Mather, took time—often a long time. He notes approvingly that his cousin Thomas Walter, who had preached the gospel for years and yet died in despair, spent months at the end of his life going over and over the "process of repentance."[16] He advises his unregenerate hearers to set aside a half-hour each day to go through the process.[17] He even tells of a group of condemned pirates who broke prison in order to gain sufficient time to go through the process before their execution.[18]

Mather regarded the process of repentance as work of the most strenuous and exacting sort: "An *Old Nature*, is like an *Old Devil*; it goes not out, without much Prayer to God."[19] Those who wish to be justified by faith in Christ "will have to *Wrestle* for it, with Importunate Supplications," with "Agonies of Importunity."[20] So arduous is this work that it cannot be delayed until the brink of death: "Have you never heard a *Sick* Person among them that have been *wise unto Salvation*, declare; *Oh! if my Grand Work were now to do, I were beyond all Imagination Miserable!* . . . When you have your *Head sick*, and your *heart faint*, and all the *Powers* of Soul and Body *shaking*, is it now a Time to do a *Work*, that calls for the uttermost of all your *Powers*? The *Work of Repentance* will do so."[21]

Conversion is represented as an arduous ploughing of the soul with continuous repetitions of the process of repentance, for "The *Fallow Ground* will not be thoroughly *broke up* . . . except the *Plow* do over and over again go over it."[22] This process is to be as detailed and as rigorous as the whole life's confession of a new Catholic penitent. "It is not enough, to *come* unto the Lord JESUS CHRIST, only that we may be brought into his *Righteousness,"* Mather says. "We must also ponder on all the *Maladies* of our Souls, and Specify them *All,* and Mention them *All,* and Long for the Relief of them *All."*[23] But when the Puritan had finished the process he did not receive an objective and authoritative human declaration of absolution, but only a "perhaps"; and Mather took it for granted that once through the process might not be enough to achieve a sense of pardon.

In a very late work Mather summarizes the preparatory process in four steps: 1) admission of inability to repent and unworthiness of redemption, and confession of dependence on divine grace; 2) specific confession of areas of sin in the life—according to the decalogue—and of original sin; 3) pleading the blood of Christ for cleansing of these, until assured of pardon; 4) consecration of the life to a walk of holiness.[24] This simplified model is not often explicitly spelled out in Mather's work; he simply refers continually to the "process of repentance," taking for granted that his audience is acquainted with the details of this, as well they might be. While he relies on this formula in his pastoral work, even leading condemned prisoners through a routine of prayer based on it,[25] he does not seem to consider it an archetypal pattern to be followed in every case, except that it is a convenient expansion of the two elements acknowledged by the Reformation to be basic to salvation: repentance and evangelical faith.

In his later ecumenical writings Mather never refers to this pattern as important for safeguarding the regenerate membership of the church, but he simply focuses on the necessity of repentant faith. It seems fair to say, then, that his simplified conversion-model was a piece of methodology that he used in his own pastoral work, a convenient structure through which to process the work of evangelism, but without deep theoretical roots in his theology. It is above all a process of *repentance,* an attempt to ensure that initial commitment to the Christian life would involve more than the shallow emotional or volitional "going through the motions" that later revivalism might induce, so that there would be a real transformation in the convert's life, a searching out of the contours of rebellion expressed in his particular character, and a conquest of these provinces under the government of Christ. Like the Ignatian spirituality of the Catholic Counter Reformation, Mather insisted on the value of lengthy meditation, consideration of the spiritual facts of the soul's situation, to motivate a deep and lasting redirection of the life's energies in the service of God. In so doing he was poles apart from the Arminian revivalist's easy invitation to faith, for he was still seeking to presanctify the potential convert.

It is frequently claimed by scholars that Mather's use of preparation was a departure from Calvinist piety toward Enlightenment moralism, since it focused attention on the need for human effort and response along with dependence on sovereign grace. It is apparent from the foregoing that Mather was no more vulnerable to this critique than any other Calvinist who seeks to do evangelism. Like all Calvinists endeavoring to preach biblically, he was striving to lay hold of both ends of a paradox and call his hearers to work out their salvation with fear and trembling without forgetting that it was God within them who was working both to will and to do.[26] It could be claimed with greater justice that the real problem with Cotton Mather's evangelism was that it retained too much Calvinism—not the Calvinism of the Reformer himself, but that of the English Puritans. While the Puritans are sometimes charged with attentuating the grandeur of Calvin's vision of the divine glory and sovereignty, Puritan evangelism sometimes went far beyond the Reformer in austerity by isolating the doctrines of election and total depravity and building logical constructs on these apart from the controlling direction of biblical revelation. In this sense many Puritans were hyper-Calvinistic. They felt obliged to announce to unbelievers truths that Calvin would have kept for the faithful: the belief that the unregenerate were unable to respond to the gospel unless released to do so by divine grace, and that God was under no compulsion to save any except his own elect.

Mather retained in his process of repentance one of the

oldest components of the Puritan model of conversion, which could be traced back to Richard Greenham: confession of inability to repent. This humbling admission of the sovereignty of God, usually followed by a trembling period of waiting in which the prospective convert wondered whether or not God was going to grant the needed ability to turn, was in part the cause of the length of the conversion process as Mather conceived it. It was also the source of a paralyzing blight of passivity that may have been a cause of spiritual decline in New England.[27]

Mather was aware that the doctrine of inability was a tool that was subject to easy and dangerous misuse in two opposing ways: either to excuse the rebellious from immediate repentance or to oppress the regenerate with scruples. In a number of places in his writings he comments on the small number of practicing communicants in his audience, and he seeks to encourage the faint-hearted and to spur the negligent on to the action of repentance.[28] He remains too cautious to abandon the emphasis on inability in his evangelism and simply press for immediate commitment in the more biblical style of later revivalists. But from the beginning of his ministry he introduced a significant and increasing stress on the necessity of beginning the process of repentance without delay and "making a trial" of one's ability to repent with divine enablement, with a good prospect of success. In later years especially, he stressed the responsibility of the sinner to begin the process of repentance immediately on hearing the summons of the evangelist, without the delay introduced by a passive waiting on God.[29]

Recent historians have interpreted this emphasis on volitional response in Mather's preaching as a shift toward Arminianism. Perry Miller suggests that the preparation formulas the early Puritans used to safeguard divine sovereignty were turned by the Mathers into a bridge toward the expansion of the limits of human ability.[30] It is certainly true that Cotton Mather is at times indistinguishable in tone from Arminian evangelism. He uses the analogy of Christ's healing the man with the withered hand in the way still regularly used by modern revivalists—to encourage the hearer to try to "stretch out his hand" in exercising the will to repentance.[31] He invites potential converts to "open the door of their hearts" on the basis of Revelation 3:20, another favorite text of post-Finney revivalism.[32] The speaking of a single word, he says, is all that is needed to close the contract between the soul and Christ.[33] Mather plainly seeks to combine the teaching of inability with exhortations to action. "You cannot Repent, you cannot Believe, of your selves; yet make some *essay* to *Repent* and *Believe* in hopes that the Pity of the Most High may help you go through with it."[34] "You may make a Tryal. There can be no hurt in trying, whether you can *turn and live,* or no. There is at least, a *who knoweth?* There is a, *who can tell?* of Salvation for you."[35]

But the encouragement to "make a Tryal" is not an effort to retain nominal orthodoxy while shifting to practical Arminianism; it is a perfectly consistent, if paradoxical, approach exactly like that of the early Puritan preparationists. Mather repeatedly stresses the bare paradox of the Calvinist understanding of freedom and responsibility: "'Tis very true, That GOD *Commands* us to *Turn* unto Himself . . . but it is also True, that we are *unable* to *Turn* ourselves."[36] The structure of the points in *The Quickened Soul* (1720), which seeks to establish the doctrine that *"Those unable to fulfill God's commands should yet try,"* is a good summary of Mather's thinking on the matter: 1) God commands the impossible (conversion); 2) until He enables, we are impotent and should realize this; 3) however, our inability is no excuse; and 4) therefore we ought to try to turn.[37] Inability is moral in nature: the sinner's *"Cannot* is a *Will not,"*[38] an inevitable but willful refusal to turn. But though inability is a voluntary loss of power, it involves the unregenerate in an absolute bondage of the will: "Indeed, the Natural and Essential *Freedome of our Will,* remains unto us; it wills *freely,* whenever it *Wills* at all: but alas, 'tis no better than, *Free among the Dead:* only Dead Works are grateful to the Will of the Unregenerated."[39]

Nevertheless, Mather felt it was both rational and biblical to encourage his audience to "make a Tryal" at repentance and faith, for several reasons. Part of the design of his approach was to leave the unconverted without excuse, since the latter is responsible to turn and culpable if he does not try. But Mather also encouraged efforts at conversion in order to discourage that passivity which he considered an improper logical deduction from the doctrine of inability: "You may rest Satisfied; There is no such *Decree* as This; That the *Elect* shall be *Saved*, whether they *Work about their own Salvation;* or no. . . . The *Decree* of the *End*, always includes a *Decree* of the *Means.*"[40] Mather occasionally expresses a conviction, also, that an active seeking of salvation on the part of the inquirer may indicate that regeneration has already taken place, for "*Faith* is actually *Begun*, in The Soul, that is made Sincerely *Willing* to Believe."[41] Here he seeks to counterbalance the effect of the doctrine of inability for the segment of his congregation that was already regenerate but fearful and scrupulous. Whenever he has this audience in mind, he speaks with the voice of Sibbes, Preston, and John Cotton, encouraging believers to rest content with their mustard seeds of repentant faith; but when he turns to address the apathetic majority, he thunders with the voice of Shepard, insisting on a thorough and arduous ploughing of the soul.[42]

In addressing this other group in his audience, which misused the doctrine of inability—those who excused themselves from the necessity of repentance because they were unable—Mather moves very close to a congruent grace solution: "If men did in Religion, more than they do, & *All* that they could by a *Natural Power* do, there would be a greater Likelihood, (I say not, a *Certainty*, but a *Likelihood*,) that God would grant them the *Higher Power;* they would be much more in the likely way, of *Coming to a Savior.*"[43] But elsewhere he explicitly repudiates congruent grace as a theoretical position: "A sinner can indeed so little *Convert* himself, that he can't so far *Dispose* himself to *Conversion*, as that God should be obliged, by his well-improving of *Common Grace*, to bestow *Saving Grace* upon him."[44]

Taken in context, Mather's statements on this issue are not those of a crypto-Arminian clinging to technical orthodoxy by a thread. He firmly believed in inability, and he placed the soul's realization of this truth near the center of the conversion experience, for *"The Gospel Reveals to me, His Grace in dying for Sinners, and my sin in my not Believing on Him, and my inability to believe."*[45] A person who included as part of the Good News the knowledge that one cannot respond to it without divine assistance surely can be marked as a whole-hearted believer in the doctrine of inability! It is thus not true that Mather was moving toward a theoretical expansion of the limits of human ability; his only departures from orthodoxy are made in the interests of his pastoral concerns and his desire to be biblical rather than systematically consistent. We can conclude that many analysts have misread Mather as an Arminian because they do not take into account the problem of Puritan hyper-Calvinism which he was unconsciously seeking to counterbalance.

But the potential for dangerous side effects in Puritan evangelism was not localized merely in the doctrine of inability. Perhaps even more perilous in the long run was the systematic insistence on exhibiting predestination to the potential convert. Most Puritans acknowledged that God was under no obligation to accept any applicant for his mercy, and that he might justly turn away some as reprobates. In a purposeful loyalty to Calvin, however, many went far beyond him: in order to magnify divine grace, they constantly reminded seekers that they might be rejected, that their strivings might be the result of mere common grace. Consequently, it required more than the general promises of the gospel to assure converts of acceptance. They needed either strong behavioral proof of their sanctification or a powerfully infused conviction of their election, given through an emotional or mystical assurance of God's mercy.

There is no doubt that converts who could weather the agonizing uncertainties of the period of application, during which they cried out for such direct assurance, would emerge with a considerable depth of faith, convinced of the graciousness of divine mercy and kindled to an extraordinary degree of experiential consciousness of God. On the other hand, the quicksands of subjectivity involved in this practice swallowed up many a soul in despair. The Puritan formula of conversion here seized on a severe spiritual illness, the *ten-*

tatio praedestinationis, which had effected a deepening of certain lives—Luther's, for example—and made it a standardized process through which every Puritan convert must pass. But many constitutions could not bear it. Two of the great Puritan pastors, Paul Baynes and Richard Greenham, died despairing of their salvation after productive lives in the ministry.[46]

Though he admired the sufferers of despair as spiritual heroes, Cotton Mather was aware that the Puritan handling of election could on occasion be the cause of their illness. He was critical of the wounding quality of *The Sincere Convert,* attributed to Thomas Shepard, though he admired Shepard's *The Sound Believer.*[47] His own approach was again a matter of retaining the traditional doctrine but striving to ameliorate its difficulties. His *Free-Grace* (1706) is an apologia for the retention of the received tradition. Mather here conceives of himself as defending Calvin against Arminius.

> The Illustrious Doctrine of PREDESTINATION, Some that Profess the Belief of it, very Sinfully *Pervert* it, as if it were a Doctrine Calculated either for the *Security,* or for the *Discouragement,* of them who should be brought unto *Repentance;* to make Sinful Men, either *Presumptuous* or *Desperate,* Whereupon the Doctrine is decried . . . as if it were an *Useless,* yea, and an *Hurtful* Doctrine, and as if it were best of all never at all to meddle with it. A Glorious Doctrine of Christianity, has been *Crucifyed* between Two Thieves.[48]

Mather admits that misuse of this doctrine has reached epidemic proportions in New England, for "It is a Folly, which we daily see Raging among us; it Stabs the Souls of Multitudes who . . . accuse the PREDESTINATION of God, as the cause of their Impenitent Unbelief."[49] A good number in Mather's audience were using election to excuse their passive apathy. Mather counters with the common answer that the decree of election always involves a decree of active striving for salvation.[50] Turning to the other side of the problem, despair among serious believers, Mather does not mention the possibility that such individuals might already be converted but merely tells the disturbed soul to look on the positive side: "*Sinner,* Thou dost not know, but that there are *Thoughts of Mercy,* yet in the Heart of the Blessed GOD concerning thee. . . . *Many* of the *Elect* of God, have been left unto all the horrid *Abominations*, that have made thy Soul so *Desolate*. . . . *Who can tell?* No man alive can tell, but *Thou* . . . O worst in all the Black Tribe of Sinners, *Thou* mayest by One of These."[51]

This falls short of the ringing evangelical declaration which a later Arminian revivalist could make. Similarly, when Mather deals with the temptation to believe that one has committed the "unpardonable sin," he merely states that to conclude oneself reprobate is itself a great sin, for we can be sure in this life that we are elect but never that we are reprobate.[52] This is a gesture of help to the agonized convert, but again it offers comfort only from a possibility. But Mather does contrive to neutralize the doctrine of Limited Atonement with the general offer of the gospel: "How *Limited* soever the *Efficacy* of our Lords Blood may be, in the *Secret Purpose* of God . . . There is in the *Blood* of our Lord Redeemer, such a *Sufficiency*, as to *Cleanse* every one of us all *from all our Sin*, if we come unto it."[53] He then proceeds to a statement that plunges to the limits of Calvinism: "Nothing shall hinder thy Salvation by the Blood of the Lord JESUS CHRIST, O Sinner, but thy wilful Refusing of it."[54] And then, like any later Arminian evangelist, he brings in a great text from John, "Him that cometh to me I will in no wise cast out" (John 6:37 KJV), noting that this was an antidote much employed in Puritan evangelism before his time.[55]

Mather made obvious attempts in other writings to alleviate the emphasis on election by accenting the mercy of God. He tells a convicted pirate at the gallows, "You have not Sinned beyond the *Bounds* of a *Mercy* that has no *Bounds*."[56] On the other hand, in urging people to begin the process of repentance without delay, Mather teaches that there is for everyone a *terminus gratiae*, a point beyond which his petitions will not be heard by God because he has "used up" his supply of grace.[57] Elsewhere, however, he observes that those who are worried that their day of grace is past are most certainly those who still have a prospect of mercy.[58] Here again pastoral necessities have brought him into apparent self-contradiction: he felt he had to stress the *terminus gratiae* to rouse procrastinators to action, but this necessitated a constant administration of comfort to the scrupulous who wrongly appropriated this emphasis to themselves.

The greatest answer to the problem of despair is the consideration of the work of Christ, and Mather's Christo-centrism was employed to particular advantage in meeting this problem.

> The discouraged Soul may go on; *But if I come unto my Saviour, what a wretched and rueful Thing must I bring unto Him? A Mind full of Errors; an Heart that is Deceitful above all things, and desperately Wicked; a Soul over-run with the most filthy Leprosy; all sorts of Maladies and Abominations.* A Merciful SAVIOUR still says, *Come to me, and I will not cast thee out.* Oh! let it revive all the discouraged Souls, in the Congregation of God. . . . Satan may tell you, The *Day of Grace* is over with you. Yet, Oh! *Despair* not . . . Satan may tell you, You have *Sinned Unpardonably,* Yet, Oh! *Despair not.*"[59]

This passage gives us a revealing glimpse of the amount and the kinds of spiritual illness Puritan medicine produced even while it healed many. The passage does, however, promise mercy through Christ, and the same promise of mercy is extended in *Zalmonah,* where Mather makes use of the image of the brass serpent on the pole, promising the seeker that only a look of faith at the Christ, who has been lifted up as the Savior of all people, is sufficient for redemption.[60] But then he goes on to indicate that this look is not to be the single quick glance of insight into justification; it is to be a prolonged looking, a meditation on Christ.

There is a tendency here for the *sola fide* of the Reformers to slip over into works quite like those prescribed by Ignatius Loyola. Mather elsewhere draws fine distinctions between works-righteousness and the effort necessary to appropriate salvation, and he reduces the latter to a vanishing minimum.[61] Yet there is a persistent intrusion of *doing* in the form of some kind of semimeritorious action, even where the grace of God is most magnified:

> Indeed there is Nothing to be done by us, to merit our Salvation, But something must be done to secure our Salvation. Indeed there is Nothing to be done by us, in our own strength. But something must be done by us, thro' Christ who

strengthens us. More plainly. Our Blessedness now cometh not unto us, on the Terms of a Covenant of works, 'Tis not properly our doings, that is the Condition of our Blessedness. We are to be Saved, by Taking rather than by Doing. The Condition is receive and be saved. It is, approve, and be Saved. Or, Be willing to be Saved. We speak of Doing, in the Largest sense of the word; and we still say, Something must be done, that we may be Saved.[62]

Mather can define justification in perfectly classical Reformation terminology: "'Tis a Receiving of, and a Relying on, the Gift of Righteousness from God, by our Lord Jesus Christ."[63] However, it is obvious that the believer's dependence is not univocally fixed on the perfect righteousness of Christ received by imputation through faith, but is involved with a strong element of infused righteousness, upon which his conscience is painfully fixed as he seeks to measure whether the belief he feels in his heart is merely a common-grace production of his own efforts and not that special grace, infused from above, which alone can lead to redemption. It is not surprising, therefore, that in a list of qualifications for entering heaven, an early work of Mather lists belief in the name of Christ as fourth, following *"Regeneration, subscription to God's Covenant,* and *interest in the Bible,"* all works of infused grace.[64] Seeking to maintain the balance between justification and sanctification, striving to avoid a dead orthodoxy that would substitute mental assent for faith and bare imputation for sanctification, Mather imperceptibly reverts to medieval criteria for justification when he deals with the unawakened; but in other instances, with another audience, he speaks in the language of Paul and Luther.

Ralph Bronkema has argued rather persuasively that the Puritan handling of the application of redemption confused regeneration with conversion. He states that whereas for Calvin and classical Reformed theology regeneration is God's re-creation of the depths of the soul which he performs on a passive object, followed by living faith involving active, conscious conversion as the fruit of this rebirth, Puritans located conversion—or preparatory strivings toward it—before faith in the order of salvation and failed to distinguish regeneration from either.[65]

These strictures do seem to apply to many Puritan writers, but not to all. Mather was clearer on these distinctions than were many of his colleagues. He insisted on the priority of regeneration as a work of prevenient grace in the depths of the soul, which inclines a person to hear the gospel and respond in repentance and faith.[66] It would seem that the problem here arises not merely from confusing terminology or lack of technical distinctions but from the Puritan's extreme suspicion of psychological operations within himself that appeared to be faith and repentance but that he could not trust as evidences of a real regeneration. The problem is better defined by Peter De Jong as an exaggerated separation of the realms of nature and grace, so that ordinary moral and mental operations were relegated to the realm of common-grace strivings unless detectably infused with the Spirit's presence.[67]

While Mather did not always precisely designate the initial transformation of the soul under the term "regeneration," he often defines what he means by the rebirth of the soul: the implanting of "a Principle inclining the Soul, to Fear God, and Prize *Christ,* and hate all *Sin,* and sleight this *World,* and do all the *Good* we can to all about us, and Look and Long for the Glories of the *Heavenly World.*"[68] In its inception the regenerate principle may be only a seed of life, infused with the origination of faith; but "if the *Grace* to *Believe* on the Lord JESUS CHRIST, be infused into the Soul, the *Habit* of every *other Grace* is at the same Instant infused."[69] It thus involves a total reconstruction of human nature, predisposing the soul to respond in conversion.[70]

The new person thus created draws his life from a supernatural union with Christ, for regeneration involves the entrance of the Holy Spirit into the life, who will *"Renew a right Spirit* in them; will *Purify their Heart* by a *Faith* of His Working there; will make them the *Temples* of GOD. The Holy SPIRIT will *write his Laws* in their Heart, and *Rectify* all Disorders there, & bring all things to rights within them."[71] Mather allows for an expression of the regenerate nature that

is less full and perfect than this, in which the regenerate soul
is slumbering or backslidden:

> They that have Everlasting Life begun in their Souls, yet may
> have it ly, as if their Souls were in a Swoon. The *Habits of Grace*
> are there; and the *Acts* would soon appear upon a due Excita-
> tion: But they are not exercised as they ought to be. It is true,
> when the *Children of GOD* are at the Worst, and the truly Pious
> are most Asleep, still their Souls *cleave unto God.* Still their
> Deliberate Choice is this; *Thou art my Portion, O Lord; I have
> said, That I* will keep thy words. 'Tis this; *A Glorious* CHRIST, *is
> my Life, and my All; and my spirit rejoyces in God my Saviour.* Still
> they deliberately chuse *Eternal* Blessings before *Temporal* ones,
> *Heavenly* Blessings before *Terrestrial* ones. A Course of sin still
> appears to them Dangerous and Odious; but a *Godly* and a
> *Sober* and a *Righteous* Life infinitely Reasonable: Infinitely pref-
> erable. Nevertheless, There is an unhappy *Sleep*, whereto the
> *Children of GOD* are Liable.[72]

Such conditions at their worst seem to the modern reader
astronomically advanced beyond the spiritual acuity of the
average church member. But like the Anabaptists and the
modern fundamentalists, Mather does not hesitate to brand
the majority of professing Christians as counterfeit. "'Tis a
Similitude that hath been sometimes used; The Souldiers
took the Coat of Christ, & *Four* of them cast *Lots* for it, but
onely one of the Four, did obtain it. So, says One, scarce
One in Four, of those are called Christians, do obtain that
Spiritual and Illustrious Garment, the *Righteousness* of
Christ, for their own; and then, they have none at all."[73] The
harsh appearance of this is mitigated, however, when we
recognize that Mather is summoning his audience to a de-
tectable degree of genuine and humble sainthood, for he had
little use for common standards of goodness resting in self-
righteousness: "I know we have a sort of *Good People,* that
have no *Goodness* in them. We flatter them, that they are to
Live with us in Heaven, tho' none cou'd *Live near* them on
earth. I can be none of their Flatterers."[74]

Mather, in company with most Puritans, did not regard
the grace of regeneration as inevitably tied to the sacrament
of baptism. The waters of baptism convey only a promise of
heaven to those dying in infancy and of a gracious environment in which covenant faith can be exercised in those who

survive to rationality. He describes regeneration (again under the term "conversion") as normally wrought through the instrumentality of the Word by the Spirit:

> It is the Good Pleasure of God, that in the *Moral Work* of the *Spirit*, for the *Conversion* of a Sinner, the *Gospel* should be His *Instrument*. So, for the Dividing of the Red-Sea, *Moses's* Rod must be lifted up. . . . When the *Spirit* of God *Converts* us, He deals not with us, as with *Stocks* and *Stones*, that have no *Reason* in them. He deals with us as with *Men; Drawes* us with the *Cords of a Man. Reasons* with us by His *Gospel*, and sets before us the *Great Things* thereof in the highest Light of *Reason* imaginable. Tis true, Tis not enough to Enlighten our *Understandings:* Our *Wills* must be Rectified, as well as our *Understandings* Enlightened. Yet the *Spirit* of God accommodates Himself to our *Nature*, when He brings us into a State of *Grace*.[75]

On the other hand, Mather did conceive of regeneration coming in some instances without the "moral efficiency" of the Word, in the case of deaf and dumb persons, and elect infants dying before the age of rationality.[76] In a sense, this case might even be considered normative, since Mather felt that "no doubt, there are more *Spirits* of *Infants* in *Heaven*, than *Saints* of any other Age."[77] He also leaned toward the possibility that most elect children of covenant lines are regenerated quite early in their experience, perhaps before the time they might rationally comprehend the Word.

> I have observed the Children of our Faithful, when they grow up, to prove, many of them, Serious, gracious, devout Children. And tho' they may when they come to be a dozen years old, or so, backslide from God into many Vanities, and Levities, yet a great part of them Return to God. . . . There is cause to think, That very many of the Children which grow up to maturity, were *Sanctified* in their *Infancy*. A principle of *Godliness* as well as a principle of *Reason*, may be infused into the Souls of *Infants*, before their Age render them capable of Exercizing or Discovering it.[78]

In one instance, Mather again sounds rather strikingly like Horace Bushnell:

> Would *Parents* thus conscienciously do their *Duty* to their *Children* . . . the *Children* belonging to the *Election of Grace*, would be so brought home to GOD by the *Parental Ministry*, and have

the Fear of GOD so gradually and effectually insinuated into them, that your *Pastors* would have little to do, but *Instruct,* and *Confirm,* and *Edify* such as have already been Converted unto serious PIETY, and as it were *suck'd it in with their Mothers Milk,* and in a way that would leave them unable to tell the *Time* of their *First Conversion.*[79]

It is quite evident, then, that Mather had a clear distinction in his mind between regeneration and conscious conversion, whatever his terminological confusion may have been. But if the ideal to be aimed at was an insensible regeneration occurring in infancy, how can we reconcile this goal with the Puritan insistence on a conscious process of repentance?[80] The answer that suggests itself is this: that while Puritans acknowledged that Christians could be regenerated by God without any of the particular searchings and strivings they prescribed, they held to preparation because it was to them inescapably an adjunct of assurance of salvation. The covenant seed might indeed be regenerate from their earliest years, but the only way this regeneracy could be tested and known to themselves and the rest of the covenant community was through their eventual entrance into wrestlings with God, followed by the comfortable persuasion of their election.

Thus we return to what we have already designated as the most important cause of the Puritan loading of conversion: the desire for assurance of salvation. In emerging from his own agony of doubt, Luther had powerfully contradicted the medieval semi-Pelagian system by asserting that assurance was the birthright of a healthy Christian. He had grounded that assurance solely on a simple faith in the atoning work of Christ, although he did make the balancing thrust that this must be a living faith active in love. Calvin, concerned about the generation of presumption, had cautioned against trying to determine one's election too strictly, and yet he had hazarded a few clues by which we might guess at our regeneracy: faith in the justifying work of Christ, followed by sanctification.[81] Part of the essential dynamic of Puritan spirituality lay in its returning to Luther's insistence on achieved assurance, while developing

Calvin's criteria into an involved casuistry.

The Hutchinson conflict in the 1630s which was a watershed for the issue of preparation, was also determinative for the later New England views on assurance. Richard Sibbes had leaned away from the Puritan casuistry of assurance and had sought to direct the convert's attention away from the problem of his election and to fix it on the Redeemer, as Staupitz had counseled Luther to find release from his despair in the wounds of Christ.[82] John Cotton, following Sibbes, felt that reliance on internal "marks of regeneration" for assurance was presumptuous and untrustworthy and tended toward the establishment of a "covenant of works." He did not, however, propose to replace these only with a bare faith apprehending the grace of Christ through faith but stressed above all the direct assurance available to the believer through the interior witness of the Spirit.[83] The opposition was fearful of the possibility of antinomian abuse of this subjective approach and insisted on the retention of objective criteria as counterbalances, chiefly the inspection of biblically determined marks of regeneration in the inner and outward life. Subsequent positions made uneasy efforts to recombine those components, with some objectivists taking the extreme position that denied not only the witness of the Spirit but also his personal indwelling in the believer.[84]

Standing near the end of this development, Mather continued to place a heavy emphasis on assurance, since he felt that "a true Child of GOD can be at no Peace, till he has found out whether he be indeed a Child of GOD."[85] He considered assurance to be an essential incentive to godliness rather than an occasion for licentiousness,[86] and he believed that God may allow trials and accusations of insincerity until the uncertain believer is actually forced to press through to a settled confidence.[87] Reading between the lines of Mather's work, however, we can get a definite intimation that while a state of assurance was considered normative for New England Christians, it was by no means normal. Mather remarks in his writings that in many cases a full assurance was not given until saints were on their deathbeds.[88] Also he indicates that assurance is a somewhat perishable commodity, that those who have it should keep on earnestly praying that it will continue to be with them.[89] There is an extensive literature both in Mather and in earlier Puritanism designed to cure despair and despondency. It was not only the laity who were afflicted; many spiritual leaders endured recurrent bouts of despair because they could find neither works of grace nor the Spirit's presence in their souls. Mather himself, in the *Magnalia*, mentions the gifts Hooker had for handling such cases, and he points to afflicted members of the clergy such as Nathanael Rogers, Richard Mather, and Nathanael Mather.[90]

But an examination of Mather's teaching on assurance indicates that although he was aware of the drawbacks inherent in all the Puritan theories of assurance, and sought to compensate for these, he hesitated to move away from introspection as an essential technique. Mather's treatment of this issue falls in the main tradition of New England, mediating between direct assurance by the Spirit (the so-called *syllogismus mysticus*) and indirect assurance through inspection of marks of grace (the *syllogismus practicus*). However, he does seem to give especially clear treatment to Cotton's side of the case, and the stress on the Spirit's direct assurance may predominate somewhat, especially in his later writings.

In his treatment of the Hutchinson case in the *Magnalia*, he repudiates the position of the sectaries, especially in its extreme form in which assurance was by immediate revelation apart from the Word. He does, however, give a qualified approval to the milder statement of Cotton that "the Spirit of God by a powerful application of a promise" assures us, if it is taken in conjunction with objective evidences in sanctification: "The truth might easily have united *both* of these perswasions."[91] A harmony of these approaches is seen in an anti-Quaker tract drafted principally by Mather and signed by the other Boston ministers, which denies the reliability of a totally subjective "witness of the Spirit," but insists that the Holy Spirit uses the Scripture in assuring us and that his witness coinheres with ours as we examine ourselves on the basis of biblical marks of grace.[92] But Mather seems to have the same kind of distrust of reliance on logical conclusion from objective evidence that his grandfather Cotton had had; he says that "when we set ourselves to argue our *justification*, from the marks of our *sanctification* that we can find upon ourselves, we do *well*. . . . But yet we cannot well see our sanctification, except a special operation of the spirit of God help our sight."[93]

In a late work devoted specifically to the subject of assurance, Mather analyzes the phrase in Romans 8:16, "The Spirit itself beareth witness with our spirit," and breaks down the ground of assurance into a double witness: the testimony of our own self-examination and the testimony of the Holy Spirit, reinforcing our reasoning, giving a direct light to the mind, bringing peace and joy, and leaving a bias toward holiness in the heart.[94] Mather frequently emphasizes that without the second testimony the first will be worth little to us. The confirming "seal" of the Holy Spirit's operation in assurance is described in the most exalted mystical encounter with God:

> There is a *Discursive Assurance* . . . And then there is a more *Intuitive Assurance* of it; In which the Holy SPIRIT, more Immediately, and most Irresistably, and with a *Mighty Light*, bears in upon the Mind of the Beleever a powerful perswasion of it, That he is a *Child* of GOD, and his GOD and *Father* will one day bring him to *Inherit all things*. The Soul of the Beleever is now wonderfully moved and melted and overpowered with such Thoughts as these; *God is my Father, CHRIST is my Saviour, and I have an Inheritance in the Heavens reserved for me*. . . . The Holy SPIRIT now mightily *Irradiates* our Minds, and causing us to dissolve into Tears of Gladness at the Tidings, He says unto us, *Be comforted, Thy sins are forgiven thee!* . . . Inexpressible is the *Peace* and *Joy* and Satisfaction of the beleever, when the *Testimony* of the Holy SPIRIT comes in to satisfy him.[95]

It is not surprising that this kind of assurance is relatively infrequent. Mather admits that "there are very *Few*, very *Few*, among us, that enjoy a strong Testimony of the Holy SPIRIT unto their *Adoption* of God, or have an undoubting *Assurance* that though GOD was *Angry* with them, His *Anger* is *turned away* from them."[96] This is why there are so few who partake in communion, Mather notes; and of those who do, "How many can come no otherwise, than *Trembling*,

like the poor Woman that came to touch the *Fringe* of our
SAVIOUR'S Mantle? . . . How few have a Soul *Rejoicing in the
Hope of the Glory of GOD?* In what *Bondage* are they still kept
by the *Fear of Death?*"[97] Mather asks himself the reason for
this endemic sickness and concludes that it is due to a general neglect of the Puritan casuistry of assurance! But the
fusion of John Cotton's direct assurance with the inspection
of internal marks has hardly alleviated the burden of the
seeker; it has rather set a heavier weight of dubious subjectivism on his shoulders, as he is compelled to regard as
normative for his own case the "inexpressible irradiations"
which Mather experienced in his ecstasies.

The objective marks which Mather instructs believers to
look for are generally located deep in the wellsprings of
human motivation. In *Menachem* (1716) he lists four signs: a
turning in the soul's bias from idols to God, a universal zeal
for Christ's work, a sense of being always under the eye of
God and so in fear of him, and a willingness to take up the
cross.[98] Elsewhere he speaks of a disposition to sacrifice all
earthly goals for that of glorifying God;[99] a total commitment
to sanctification in every realm of life;[100] or a total control of
the thoughts in obedience to Christ. So central is the problem
of assurance to all Mather's preaching, however, that in dealing with almost any subject he is likely to throw out observations on various minor signs which may chime in to confirm
regeneration, such as engagement in secret prayer,[101] or
even singing hymns in the proper manner.[102] Contrary to
the Weber thesis, Mather never—in all the mass of his
preaching and writing—points to prosperity as a sign of
election; on the contrary, in one place he cites a proper
submission to poverty as a mark of assurance.[103] It is no
wonder that Mather says that assurance grows with sanctification; no one who had not advanced well into holiness
could get a clear sight of such graces in the cloudy caverns of
the soul.

To compound the problem, Mather (at least when speaking to one kind of audience) advises the seeker to assume
himself guilty of unregeneracy until issued a pardon directly
from the hand of God.

When you hear any Symptomes of *Hypocrisy* mentioned, Enquire, Lord, *Is it I? Is it I?* And when you hear any Symptomes
of *Integrity*, be extremely uneasy, if you cannot find your own
Souls affording of them. Yea, don't stay till these *Discominating
Symptomes* are brought unto you; but Go to them, Call for them;
Enquire after them. . . . Do not ordinarily go to Sleep at Night,
without some Serious Thoughts on this Question . . . *Am I
in Safety for Eternity?* . . . If you find any *Suspicious Marks* on
yourselves, be ready to suspect the worst of yourselves. . . . I
will not positively and peremptorily say, Every man is an
Hypocrite, who has these *Marks* found upon him; Yet . . .
'Twill be best for such a Man to judge himself an *Hypocrite* . . .
until he has got these Things cured in him.[104]

It is hard to understand how the author of this summons to
hypochondria could have been a critic of Thomas Shepard.
Particularly bad signs according to Mather were the complacent indulgence in any habitual gross sin or a continued
aversion to any one point of godliness.[105] On the other hand,
Mather could invert this dictum with the greatest ease to
assure those who had been thrown into a case of scruples. In
the *Companion for Communicants* (1690), an effort to activate
the majority of the congregation who were abstaining from
the Lord's Supper because of lack of assurance, he says that
those who are fearful have the most cause to assume their
salvation, for "these *Fears . . . are like Thistles, a Bad Weed, but
growing in Good Ground.* Indeed they commonly grow most in
that *ground*, where there is least *ground* for their Growth, and
it is because *Good Hearts* do too much Nourish and Indulge
them."[106] The timorous are to come to the table if they have
the least grain of faith, and "a *Grief* is a *Grain* . . . a *Groan* is a
Grain."[107] Mather comes within a hair's breadth of Stoddard's position, for "ASSURANCE is not Absolutely Necessary in order to a *worthy Coming* unto the Holy Supper. We
are to Examine ourselves, and if upon the *Examination* we do
not find full cause to pronounce ourselves *Unregenerate*, we
are to come, tho' we have many *Fears*, whether we be indeed
Regenerate or no."[108]

In the beautiful sermon called *An Heavenly Life: A Christian Taught How to Live in an Infallible & Comfortable Perswasion of the Divine Love*, Mather states that if the seeker's heart

rejoices at the thought that God loves him, then he is indeed elected by God.[109] Mather often goes back to the case of the person with weak faith, agreeing with Perkins and Sibbes that not the quantity of the faith present but its quality is the important factor. "This *Faith* is very *weak*, in many that have it begun in their Souls. . . . It is often so, that a *Spark* of Grace may lye and live, in a *Sea* of Corruption. . . . In some truly Regenerate souls, the struggles between the *Spirit* and the *Flesh* are so dubiously managed, that one will have much ado to say, which overcomes."[110] Mather often makes the point that no one who is concerned about his spiritual state can be outside the pale of God's mercy; for it is "a Golden Sentence of Antiquity . . . If God give the *Grace* of *Desire*, He will also give the *Desired* Grace."[111]

But in common with the early Puritans and even such non-Puritans as Andrewes,[112] Mather was still quite concerned to focus microscopically on the difference between common-grace "marks" and those evidences of regeneracy that are unmistakable fruits of special grace, in the manner of Shepard and Edwards' *Treatise on the Affections:*

> There may be many savory *Frames* in an Unregenerate man, and mighty pangs of Mourning and Fearing, and Joying, and Hoping, about the Affairs of the Eternal World; yea, and he may continue in these Frames all his days, and be in some sort of a *Religious* man, to his Dying Day. All this may a man do, and be but a Pharisee after all.[113]

This case is no rare monstrosity, since "there is nothing more Common under the Means of Grace, than for *Common works* of Grace to be, through the Mysterious working of the Devil, mistaken for *Saving works.*"[114] The matter is complicated by the possibility of unconscious self-deception, for "an *Hypocrite*, he may seem to Embrace CHRIST: And yet something of CHRIST he has an Aversion for; and he is not Aware of it."[115] The theological rationale for this stress is, of course, partly to harmonize the emphasis on permanent regeneration with the observed fact of apostasy, which is explained by the concept of common-grace gifts; for "a man may be furnished with *Miraculous Gifts,* and yet the SPIRIT of God may afterwards totally withdraw from him. A man may *taste of these*

Powers of the World to come, and may finally *fall away* after all."[116] The only way we can explain the juxtapositon of passages of such hair-raising ominousness with those of such gracious condescension is, once again, to consider the differing condition of the patients for whom Mather was prescribing. But what a perilous medicine chest the Puritan pastor used! It was the sort that had better be administered by the physician personally, for it could be deadly in the patient's hands.

The two means of assurance that the pastors recognized, inspection of works and the witness of the Spirit, were useful tools in stirring up believers who were passive or inattentive to the presence of God. They could appeal to biblical precedent, and for sluggish and insensitive Christians they seemed to be the right medicine. For the sensitive and the scrupulous, however, they could be poisonous. It is remarkable that the Puritans could so easily overlook a third biblical path to assurance that Luther had uncovered: naked reliance on the work of Christ; for it was the ideal cure for the discouragements of the "finer mold of Christians" who made up the Puritan ministry, who recorded in their diaries the periodic agonies of despair induced by the standard Puritan teaching on assurance.

An indispensable aid for Mather in his efforts to encourage conversion and assurance was the motivating use of "hellfire and damnation" imagery. The evangelistic technique of many Puritans and some later revivalists has left a deep allergy in the American spirit to this practice. Christian educators have particularly complained about the psychological effect of this method on young children,[117] but other critics have observed that this was a desperate and ineffective technique even when used among adults in an effort to halt spiritual decline.[118] While Jonathan Edwards is the figure most associated with this tendency in the popular mind, the use of negative eschatology in Mather's sermons is much more frequent than in his later colleague and almost as prevalent as his appeals to go through the process of repentance.

His use of these devices is part of an old homiletical tradition common to many other spiritual streams within the history of the church, especially in patristic, medieval, and Ignatian piety. In all these contexts the contemplation of "the four last things" was employed to create an existential "limit-situation" in the mind of the hearer, urging him on in sanctification. As Mather says, "The Direction of Old has been, *To keep the* Four Last Things *much in our Eye*," and then he quotes a couplet:

> *By what Good Thoughts may men Temptation* quell?
> *On* Death & Judgment, *Think, on* Heav'n & Hell.[119]

The aim of this approach was to create a serious state of mind which would be conducive to conversion or sanctification. Mather found support for this emphasis in a number of Old Testament passages encouraging people to number their days and apply their hearts to wisdom. He returned to this theme with a frequency that suggests morbid preoccupation, but the modern reader must remember that Mather lived in an age that always faced the possibility of imminent death. Mather himself observed that 60 percent of the children born in New England died by the age of seventeen, and 90 percent of the people by the age of forty-six.[120] Whereas it might be an unnatural and forced ploy today to warn the average congregation of impending death—despite the danger of nuclear war—in Mather's day it was only existential realism. Mather notes, however, that although people theoretically allow for the fact that they will die, they still live as though they did not really believe this in their hearts, for "men seem to make their *Own Death*, as Difficult an Article of Belief, as the *Resurrection of the Dead*."[121]

Since the fact of death is a powerful reminder of sin and a summons to redemption, Mather's effort was to get people to concentrate on this hard fact until it sank in, even reading it in the constitution of nature: "We are *from all Quarters* invited unto the *Meditation*. . . . Our very *Diet* is on *Dead* Creatures. Our very *Cloathing* is from *Dead* Creatures. From *them* there is that Loud Voice unto us all; *Remember, you are your selves to Die*."[122] Some of these passages in Mather are set in contexts of dust and gloom; others breathe a sense of the joy and glory of reality beyond the grave for the Christian. Most often, however, death is the terminal limit that warns us of the shortness of our days, the urgency of repentance, the brevity of time within which our work can count for Christ. The possibility of death is most strongly inculcated in little children because of the probability of their early passing: "*Children,* go unto the *Buryingplace;* There you will see many a *Grave* shorter than your selves."[123]

Death, in the seventeenth century, had as its principal terror the possibility of hell; and Mather does not hesitate to go into this subject quite graphically.

> Remember, The Wrath of God, like a Formidable Fire, will at last, with Exquisite Agonies, and Anguishes, Torture the Souls of them, that shall *Dy* in their *Unregeneracy*. One that felt some flashes of that *Fire,* in the Troubles of his Conscience, hearing of some speaking about *Burning to Death,* cry'd out, *O! That is but a metaphor to what I Endure!* And another that was broiling in the Fire of such Troubles, Roared in this manner, *O might I have this mitigation of my Torments, to ly as a Backlog in the Fire on the Hearth, for a thousand Ages!* I urge this, when you are by the *Fireside,* this *Winter,* think seriously with your selves, *Could I bear to Roast in this Fire? Alas, this is but a painted Fire, to that wherein God shall take vengeance on those that Know Him not, and that Obey not His Gospel? And if I can't bear the Metaphor, no, not so much as for a minute, How can yet I bear to remain under the Wrath of God in Hell for infinitely more millions of Ages, than all the Fires on Earth have made ashes in the world!* [124]

Mather appears to commit himself to belief in a literal physical hell, "a Dark Dungeon, where the horrid Rattle Snakes of Hell, are crawling and coiling about him. . . . Be sure, the *Torments* of that *Hell* cannot be less, than those of the Fires, & Racks, and Wheels, which the Persecutors have here inflicted on the Servants of GOD, and which must be Retaliated there."[125] And yet the frequently recurring phrase used in connection with fiery emblems of hell—that these "are but a Metaphor" for what the damned feel—is significant. Mather's full understanding of the meaning of hell is certainly more sophisticated, for " 'Tis a *Pain of Loss,* that is the Hell of Hell it self."[126] At any rate, Mather never speaks to children or young people without some graphic allusion to hell's pains. "Ah, Children; Be afraid of your going *Prayer-*

less to Bed, lest the *Devil* be your *Bed-fellow*. Be afraid of *Playing* on the *Lord's-Day*, lest the *Devil* be your *Play-fellow*. Be afraid of Telling *Lies*, or speaking Wickedly, lest that *Evil Tongue* be one Day tormented in the Flames, where, *A drop of water to cool the Tongue*, will be roared for."[127] Mather does not shrink from verbal pictures of demons grabbing infants and freckled adders crawling over them in hell.[128] In *Perswasions from the Terror of the Lord*, a sermon at the funeral of a child crushed by a cart, Mather not only makes explicit use of the horrible accident as a warning, but also describes the final judgment in the words of the *Dies Irae!*[129]

Mather retained these incentives because they were a means of psychological compression through which the terrors and ecstasies necessary to assurance might be generated, and by which the congregation might be more sensibly awakened and arrested in its spiritual decline. This illustration of his worst excesses does little justice to him in its failure to indicate the predominant stress on God's grace and love in his preaching. It is remarkable, however, that he failed to recognize the implications of his own faith in God's sovereignty in the regeneration of infants. His practice was undoubtedly aimed at forcing regenerate covenant seed from a condition of potential holiness into a state of actual spiritual vigor. It apparently succeeded in doing this in many instances; but once again, it was harsh medicine.

In all the problems outlined above, Cotton Mather was struggling half-unconsciously with the defects of his tradition. He was dimly aware that he was trapped in a theology of conversion that was inherently self-contradictory with respect to faith, and which, following the biblical precept that we should examine ourselves to determine whether we are in the faith, had somehow overshot the mark and wandered into a dangerous climate where spiritual sickness was inevitable, where the majority of those in the congregation were numbed and fearful bystanders while a few of a more volatile temperament were able to achieve a fitful stability of assurance. In the gradual evolution of his pastoral approach there is certainly a mitigation of the harsh logic of some of the original Puritan theories of conversion. It is true that his thinking did not really break free from his tradition; what he offered, rather, is a sort of buffered Puritanism—the Puritan theory of conversion with an assortment of neutralizing medicines to safeguard against pathological side effects.

Critics in the Reformed tradition have complained that the Puritan concept of conversion presupposed too great a chasm between nature and grace in the "before" and "after" of the convert's experience.[130] In Puritanism a state of "cold faith" accompanied by strenuous and sacrificial activity of the will in obedience to God and love to others could be labeled as unregeneracy because it had no sensible emotional epiphenomena, or extraordinary outward graces.

Of course, this very separation between nature and grace was a main theological factor in the American phase of the Great Awakening. It was a sharp-edged scalpel that divided between a dead and a living orthodoxy, and was thus a powerful instrument of awakening in the church. Kierkegaard, in his *Attack on Christendom*, notes that it is easy to fire at heretics and scoundrels with the artillery of the New Testament, but that it is "hard to punch a blow at real life, at the actual world in which we live, where for one certified hypocrite there are 100,000 twaddlers, for one heretic, 100,000 nincompoops."[131] What the Puritans had invented was a way to make the New Testament get at the twaddlers and the nincompoops, the people outwardly conformed to the conventions of Christendom but empty of inner commitment.

But there is another way of phrasing the nature/grace problem which indicts Mather's tradition in a way that is almost unanswerable. This is to recognize that the Puritans implicitly assumed that every Christian was to be a mystic. They felt that all believers are called to what Catholics would describe as a contemplative vocation, a life of strong devotion to meditation and prayer, and they gave the impression that every Christian will attain the heights of what a Catholic spiritual director would call "infused contemplation"—a direct and sensible outpouring of divine comforts within the heart, independently initiated by God and unacquired by effort or merit. The Puritan position virtually demanded that every person attain infused contemplation before he or she could be called a Christian. To the Catholic spiritual director this would be to command the sovereign grace of God to work outside its chosen limits; for by far the more normal way of contemplatives lies in the foothills of "acquired contemplation," in which a normal use of the faculties, and faith which "hopes for what it does not see," combine for the purification of the soul.[132]

In the Puritan process of preparation for conversion, a theology is at work that is far less "Calvinistic" than this, one that shows less reverent respect for the autonomy of God.[133] The logic of the impossible demand for infused contemplation as a ground for assurance pushed the Puritans toward the assumption that acquired contemplation might eventually *require* God to give a direct infusion of assurance, and the very un-Reformed notion of congruent merit began to reappear, as it always must when assurance is grounded on scrutinized experience rather than an outward-directed and dependent faith in the Savior. The spiritual result of this doctrinal imbalance was, as Alan Simpson says, that "the whole history of Puritanism is a commentary on its failure to satisfy the cravings which its preaching had aroused. It was forever producing rebellions."[134]

But this invention was not without a certain cost, in the pathological side effects it produced. The Puritans in their evangelism were using nets which would catch big fish— mystics and lay spiritual leaders—but which would lose the great majority of lesser disciples. Long before Mather's time, English Protestants were showing concern over this deficiency. H. C. Porter notes that already in the 1590s there were people at Cambridge in states of depression induced by Puritan hyper-Calvinism, unable to believe that Christ had died for them, and that some of these were turning to Arminianism to solve their problem. He adds that the necessity of dealing with problems of assurance was making Calvinists turn Arminian in the pulpit, as Mather often seemed to do.[135] Such a committed Puritan theologian as Thomas Goodwin almost became an Arminian because of spiritual depression induced by the fear that he was not elect.[136]

Near Mather's time, Richard Baxter was critical of the dangers of unhealthy introspection and overnarrow qualifications of church membership in Puritanism, and he felt that the Antinomians might be putting a needed emphasis on free grace in Christ against an excessive weight in Puritan experimentalism.[137] Continuing in the stream of Baxter's irenic moderation, Philip Doddridge, in the early eighteenth century, had proceeded quietly to drop the "highest points of Calvinism," such as reprobation and irresistible grace, as unworkable elements to place in the foreground of Christian experience, and had moved into a rather fluid Arminian evangelicalism.[138] According to C. J. Stranks, the phenomenal popularity of the Pelagian *Whole Duty of Man* during the eighteenth century was due not only to its accessible common-sense legalism and the popular drift toward "Socinian moonlight," but because—contrary to predestinarian extremism—it said that believers can influence their eternal destinies by their response to divine grace.[139] English Protestantism was searching for a way out of the mind-blocking impasses of hyper-Calvinism, and the great stream of English experimentalism was consequently shifting from a Calvinist toward an Arminian basis.

In the simultaneously developing Lutheran Pietism in Germany, criticisms similar to these had been voiced from the outset, as was almost inevitable in the environment of anti-Calvinist Lutheran orthodoxy, and Halle Pietism was true to this theological base in carefully avoiding most of the excesses of hyper-Calvinist Puritanism and adopting practical approaches to conversion which approximate Arminianism. In the continental phase of the Great Awakening under Zinzendorf, beginning in 1727, an even more pronounced *solafideism* is present, returning to Luther's practice and directing the attention of the convert outward in dependence on the objective work of Christ rather than inward toward character or emotional states. The semi-Augustinianism of the Wesleys leaned in the other direction in placing a greater emphasis on works, but it unloaded the conversion experience of much of its Puritan content and called for immediate repentance. The Awakening in America was still Puritan to the heart, both in the Middle Colonies and in Edwards' chronicles of the work in Northampton; but throughout its long repercussions during the eighteenth century in America there seems to have been a growing underground reaction against the Puritan use of Calvinism in its doctrine of conversion. Early in the nineteenth century Lyman Beecher abandoned the Puritan conversion model.

> For cases like mine, Brainerd's Life is a most undesirable thing. It gave me a tinge for years. So Edwards on the Affections—a most overwhelming thing, and to common minds the most entangling. The impressions left by such books were not spiritual, but a state of permanent hypochondria—the horrors of a mind without guidance, motive, or ability to do any thing. They are a bad generation of books, on the whole. Divine sovereignty does the whole in spite of them. I was converted in spite of such books. I wish I could give you my clinical theology. I have used my evangelical philosophy all my lifetime, and relieved people without number out of the sloughs of high Calvinism.[140]

Here is one major root of the rising dominance of Arminianism in the revivalism of the nineteenth century. While this doctrinal shift was undoubtedly partly due to the growing rationalism of the later New England theologians, much of it was motivated by pastoral concern. Puritans, from the standpoint of Reformation Calvinism, were doing the wrong things for the right reasons in their evangelism, and wounding and alienating many souls in the process. Arminians such as Finney, for all the crudeness of their intellectual systems, were doing the right things for the wrong reasons: they were calling for simple and immediate repentant faith in harmony with the New Testament. In their theoretical rationale, however, they paid for this freedom by losing a Pauline and Augustinian profoundness, which was grounded in the paradox of divine sovereignty and human responsibility.

Subsequent revivalists would retain the Puritan stress on initial conversion, eviscerating it of its inappropriately complex loading of advanced Christian experience. They would then neglect the reinsertion of this content in the development of the Christian life through progressive sanctification, except in the form of second or third crisis experiences in the models proposed by John Wesley, Finney, and the early Pentecostal movement. The result would be the comparative spiritual poverty of some later Evangelicalism, with a two-dimensional portrait of the Christian life embracing a shallow conversion at the outset, followed by a life of interior emotionalism and exterior verbal "witnessing." The "second work of grace" model of sanctification, or the fullness of the Spirit, could recapture something of the deeply spiritual activism of the Puritan life, but not enough to satisfy the liberal tradition leading from Bushnell through Gladden and Rauschenbusch into the twentieth century. Ironically enough, the very stress on regeneration established by the Puritans as a guard against "cheap grace" became an instrument of cheap grace when conversion was unloaded and sanctification neglected. The various types of modern liberalism, suspicious of the multitudes of "born-again" believers relaxing in a complacent moralism thoroughly conformed to the world in its social attitudes, sought to rebalance the theology of Christian experience by insisting on costly obedience as the sign of genuine Christianity. If obedience is divorced from a clear theology of redemption and lacks any deeper Christological connection than the attempt to imitate Jesus, however, it can easily lapse into sociopolitical moralism. Despite its pathogenic side effects, the Puritan approach in searching out and purging sin through the process of conversion may have produced a deeper level of repentant faith than many subsequent approaches, and it is not surprising that both Mather and Edwards were reluctant to abandon it.[141]

CHAPTER FOUR

The Machinery of Piety

FROM THE SUBJECT OF THE INCEPTION OF THE spiritual life, it is appropriate to move on to the methodology of its nurture. This is especially true in the case of Cotton Mather, for one of the salient features of his piety is its fascination with the machinery through which grace enters the soul.

Mather's work incorporates a baroque embellishment of the means of grace which at first glance seems a little suspicious. The modern reader can easily get the impression that Mather was more dedicated to the promotion of these channels of grace than he was to the Giver. His teaching and his personal habits constitute a jackdaw's nest of methodology for the cultivation of growth in Christian experience.

This is an aspect of Mather's piety that fairly leaps out at the casual reader of his works, especially the *Diary*, and it is probably one of the main reasons for his reputation for superficiality. At times Mather almost seems to define godliness as the operation of a set of devotional gadgets. This was especially true in his youth. When he was twenty he wrote of "the welcome Entertainment which I would give, *all the Day long*, unto *Methods* that may occur for my Serving of God . . . and reserve many written Memorials, of my Conclusions and Contrivances" (*Diary*, I, 60).[1] Just how comprehensively he felt the methodology of nurture is to be applied to life is shown in an ensuing passage: "And especially, the little Parcels, Fragments, and Intervals of Time, wherein the Generalitie of People, do suffer their minds to ly like the Field of the Sluggard, *overgrown with Weeds*, I would have to bee so well-husbanded by mee, as that at all Places of Diversion, I would be at my spiritual Alchymie" (I, 61-62). This "spiritual Alchymie" was so important to him that during this period of his life he would penalize himself by a fine if he neglected any part of the daily machinery of religious duties (I, 71,100). He was so involved in ascetic disciplines at times that he "*over-did,* in these Mortifications. I broke the sixth Commandment, I wasted my Strength, I wounded my Health, very sinfully, in the Excesses of my Devotions. I doubt, I have shortened my Dayes, by this Over-doing; I feel that I have thereby brought upon myself splenetic Maladies" (I, 81). Spiritual growing pains of this sort were common in the youth of many eminent Puritans, including the great Jonathan Edwards. But Mather never ceased to tinker with the "instrumentation of piety," to use Herbert Perluck's apt phrase.[2] In middle life, fending off a proposal of marriage by a young lady, he "mention'd my way of living, in continual Prayers, Tears, Fasts, and macerating Devotions and Reservations, to divert her from her Proposal."[3] In his son's biography of him, the longest single chapter is devoted wholly to Mather's "methods of piety."

When Mather is viewed against the background of the whole history of Christian experience, however, his handling of the means of grace appears much less eccentric. We do not normally associate such a development of religious methodology with Protestantism, but many of Mather's emphases were rooted in his own tradition. What is unusual is his importation of elements from other religious backgrounds. Other Puritans shared this omnivorous approach to piety, but few were as catholic in their taste as was Mather.

Otho Beall and Richard Shryock comment that Mather thought of himself mainly as a digester and compiler of the discoveries of others rather than as an innovator.[4] This is true in all areas of learning and action: Mather excelled as observer and implementer rather than as creator, although these talents were so well developed in him that he actually anticipated the future by extrapolating trends that were contemporary with him. But nowhere were his talents as collector more fully exercised than in the field of spiritual methodology.

He was, first of all, a terminal figure in a century characterized by this kind of collecting within the Puritan tradition itself. Just as Bach summed up the style and techniques of the Baroque era, while thoroughly out of fashion in the period in which he lived, so Mather was the apotheosis of Puritan methodology. At the beginning of the seventeenth century, the devotional manuals of the English Puritans were filled with this methodism, used as an aid to their innerworldly monasticism. This emphasis crossed the Atlantic and became normative in New England.

The Puritan tradition itself was not innovative in most of its devotional practice; it was merely concentrating and reformulating on a Reformed basis practices that were already common in the Catholic tradition. Pourrat points out that regulated "spiritual exercises" date from the beginning of the mendicant and preaching orders, which broke out of the monasteries to bring the "higher life" of developed piety to the masses. The Renaissance, in turn, challenged the vitality of the whole church and drove it into methodology as into a set of protective walls.[5] Counter Reformation Catholicism, under the dual pressure of a secularizing society and the example of Protestant efforts to make monastic piety breathe the outside air, elaborated its own disciplines of "religious life within the world";[6] and there was considerable cross-pollination between Reformed and Counter Reformed methodologies. But most of these postmedieval forms of spiritual method were evolutionary adaptations of traditions already alive in the earlier periods of the church. As a scholar, Mather was interested in pushing behind the Puritan models of devotion, as well as the medieval or Counter Reformation forms, to the original devotional practices of the patristic period. Later in his life he considered assembling "an Extract of such things as peculiarly belong to the Christian *Asceticks*,"[7] as he called the fathers. It is interesting to find Mather harking back to these sources for authority in his methodology, just as Reformed theologians habitually resorted to patristic sources to buttress their doctrinal interpretations.

Most of Mather's devotional practice can be summarized under the double rubric of meditation and prayer, and this is characteristic both of Puritan piety and earlier devotional models. Nearly all experiential traditions recognize faith as the heart of the spiritual life, and they recognize exposure to what is believed as the natural method of reinforcing and enlarging faith. In the medieval tradition, particularly, meditation—and not programmed austerities—became the primary tool of ordinary spiritual growth.[8] Bernard of Clairvaux states that meditation and prayer are the two feet by which men ascend to God.[9] Hugh of St. Victor made reading and prayer the first two stages of mystical ascent, and subsequent mystical disciplines followed his approach.[10] At the end of the Middle Ages and in the early Renaissance those who were concerned about spiritual awakening in the church stressed meditation as the key to this.[11] The Puritans in their own form of spirituality placed meditation very close to the core of what is vital in Christian nurture;[12] and, in fact, the content of all their methodology can really be reduced to the two basic techniques of meditation (on heard, read, or observed revelation) and prayer—a two-way communication of the soul with God.

Among the postmedieval Catholic and Protestant traditions, the *content* of meditation became a point of intense controversy. There was, first of all, the question of whether meditation should have an intellectual object at all or whether it should simply reach out for the being of God in mental and sensory darkness. While St. Teresa and John of the Cross both insist on a superintellectual contemplation of the divine nature, the ordinary teaching of the church emphasized meditation on the life of Christ and the basic core of Catholic doctrine as the safer path. Thus doctrinal and Christological meditation make up the core of that great instrument of Counter Reformation piety, the *Spiritual Exercises* of Ignatius Loyola.[13] The Devotio Moderna and other schools among the northern Christian humanists gravitated toward Scripture as the content of meditation, rather than the doctrinal formulations of the scholastics. Gerard Groote, for example, recommends meditation on the Gospels as of first importance, second the Old Testament, and last the saints and doctors of the church.[14]

Reformation piety insisted even more stringently on a form of meditation that concentrated on the text of Scripture. Both the Puritans and their opponents in the Counter Reformation were basically relying on the same devotional machinery for the energy and direction of their faith and action; but the engine of meditation was powered by different fuels. The Ignatian piety is sensual in its approach to the Gospels, endeavoring to reproduce in "compositions" of biblical events in the imagination the experience of kissing the footprints in the Nativity, seeing the biblical scene in the mind's eye, and even smelling its accompanying odors, and thus awakening motivation for the Christian life. Puritans rejected this approach as a fleshly effort to counterfeit the infusions of the Spirit by manipulating natural human emotions. Their own meditation aimed at a deeper stimulation that would affect the mind and heart at the roots of the personality, through the application of biblical truth by the Spirit.

Despite his extensive extrabiblical scholarship, Mather gave considerable time daily to meditation on Scripture in the original tongue. Before his twentieth year he had formed the regular habit of reading fifteen chapters of the Bible every morning and meditating on these.[15] For the average Christian he recommends establishing communion with God immediately upon rising by fixing the mind on him in meditation, and entering as soon as possible into a time of scripture reading and "closet-prayer," followed by public reading and prayer with the rest of the family and the servants. No precise directions on the amount of Scripture to be read are included; other occasions of reading and meditation might recur during the day. In a tract for sailors Mather even recommends the reading of Scripture twice a day, combined with many occasions of prayer.[16]

The process of meditation on the truth obtained through these times of reading was, like all of Mather's methodology, arduous. Early in his own life he began *"reading the Scriptures*, with such a devout Attention, as to fetch at least one *Observation*, and one *Supplication*, a *Note* and a *Wish*, out of every Verse in all the Bible. . . . The Method, which I thus used in *Reading*, I also took up for Singing."[17] Later in his life he adopted an even more ambitious technique of making Scripture real in his experience, which he called the "porismatic method":

> The Holy Spirit of GOD who inspired His Chosen Servants to write the Oracles He has given us in the Scriptures, made heavenly Impressions on the Minds of the Writers, which raised Heavenly Affections in them. When I take a Passage of the Bible under my Consideration, I will nicely observe, what Affection of Piety appears in the Passage, and press after the raising of the same Affection in myself, and not count that I have the full Meaning of the Text until I have done.[18]

While his earlier practice had been a sort of utilitarian processing of verses to mine their doctrinal and practical implications, this new technique sought the re-creation in his own soul of the emotional or affective state of the author. It was as though the heart of the reader were like the phonograph needle which must vibrate in the same tones present in the engraving stylus in order to reproduce the original music. Mather implies that both in his earlier and later methodology he obtained his teaching from no man, but directly from the Spirit; but his whole approach in the porismatic method is redolent of European Pietism, and the second *Diary* passage is almost a copy of a passage in Francke that speaks of the difference between a living and a dead orthodoxy in their approach to Scripture.[19] In a work published in the same year as the second *Diary* entry, Mather notes that he concurs with Francke in the use of the porismatic method, and four years later he connects it with an emphasis of Spener.[20] We might conclude that Mather adopted the porismatic method, and a new and more deeply affectional outlook, from the

Continental Pietists, except that he remarked on the same emphasis in Matthew Henry.[21] The affective piety of Spener and Francke was latent in the New England tradition, as Edwards later demonstrated by his *Treatise on Gracious Affections,* and Mather occupied identical ground, for in his *Psalterium Americanum* he holds that "all True PIETY is begun by the Enkindling of these *Affections* in the Soul. It proceeds, it prospers, it improves, as these Affections gain strength and vigour there."[22]

In his treatment of the object of meditation, Mather oscillates between medieval and Reformation styles. While he occasionally proposes meditation on such "absolute" doctrinal truths as the Trinity or the Four Last Things, he generally recommends the use of passages of Scripture. His own treatment of these, however, is often extravagantly allegorical, abounding in eschatological and Christological interpretation of difficult passages. Like Thomas à Kempis and the Devotio Moderna, he emphasizes meditation on Christ for the purpose of imitating the life of Christ, but he also recommends above all other objects of consideration the person and work of Christ on our behalf.

> I have read, that *five* devout persons being together, there was this question started among them: how, in what ways, by what means, "they strengthened themselves in abstaining from sin against the God of heaven?" The first answered, "I frequently meditate on the vileness and filthiness and loathsomeness of sin, and the excellency of grace, which is contrary unto so vile a every day as my last."
>
> The second answered, "I frequently meditate on the strict account of sin that I am to give at the day of Judgment, and the everlasting torments in hell, to be inflicted on them that can give no good account." The third answered, "I frequently meditate on the vileness of filthiness and loathsomeness of sin, and the excellency of grace, which is contrary unto so vile a thing." The fourth answered, "I frequently meditate on the eternal rewards and pleasures reserved in heaven for them that avoid the pleasures of sin, which are but for a moment." The fifth answered, "I frequently meditate on the Lord JESUS CHRIST, and his wondrous love to miserable sinners, in dying a cursed and bitter death for our sin; and this helps me to abstain from sin, more than any other consideration what-

soever;" and the answer of this last was indeed the greatest of all.[23]

It is hard to say which is more remarkable here, the persistence of patterns that are fundamentally incompatible with the Reformation or Mather's ability to transcend these and cleave to an evangelical and Christocentric stance.

In the Puritan development of "worldly asceticism," the believer's daily contact with invisible realities through the medium of biblical revelation was designed to neutralize the effect of the layman's journey among the distracting spiritual disorder of daily business. But meditation was also expected to reach out and embrace the common occurrences of life and extract nurture also from natural revelation. Apart from its importance as therapeutic nurture, this meditation on natural theology was assumed to be one of the normal expressions of the healthy Christian life, an inevitable concomitant of "heavenly-mindedness," for "a Man that is *full of God*, beholds God in every *thing*, sees the *Face* of God in every *Work* of God. This man sticks not in *any Creatures*, stays not at *Second Causes;* with a spiritualized Soul, he soars up to God in all."[24] While Mather makes no more than ordinary orthodox use of natural theology in his theoretical substructure, he returns to this source habitually as a devotional aid. On rare occasions he follows this into something deceptively close to deistic piety, as he seeks to penetrate behind natural causes to the glory and immensity of the original creative mind. But even in his physico-theological works there is a determined movement away from bare natural theology toward a devotional understanding of the universe that can only emerge as the fruit of special revelation. Again, his piety is basically Christocentric: "I will assert, that a glorious CHRIST is more to be considered in the *Works of Nature* than the *Philosopher* is generally aware of; and my *CHRISTIAN Philosopher* has not fully done his Part, till He who is the *Firstborn of every Creature* be come into Consideration with him."

> One says upon it, "If this be so, we need not break the Glasses of *Galileo*, the Spots may be washed out of the *Sun*, and *total Nature* sanctified to God that made it!" O CHRISTIAN, *lift up*

> *now thine Eyes, and look from the place where thou art* to all
> Points of the Compass, and concerning *whatever thou seest,*
> allow that all these things are formed for the Sake of that
> Glorious-One, who is now *God manifest in the Flesh* of our
> JESUS. . . . He is that WORD of *GOD by whom all things were
> made, and without whom was not anything made that was made.*
> . . . *The infinite Wisdom which formed all these things is peculiarly*
> seated *in the Son of God;* He is that *reflexive Wisdom* of the
> eternal *Father,* and that *Image of the invisible God, by whom all
> things were created;* in Him there is after a peculiar manner the
> original *Idea* and *Archetype* of every thing that offers the infi-
> nite *Wisdom* of God to our Admiration. . . . Then 'tis impossible
> to stop without adding, *How glorious, how wondrous, how
> lovely art thou, O our Saviour!*[25]

This is not the literal Aristotelianism of the deistic
natural theologians, but a neoplatonic vision of Christ as the
logos-pattern, in whom are hidden all the archetypes of
beauty and excellence that are separated and refracted in the
material creation, the personal and original blueprint of all
goodness in the divine mind. Mather's meditation on nature
is not a mere reading of the natural evidences to catch glimpses
of the "power and godhead" of God, but rather a symbolic or allegorical reading of typology in nature. Just as he
constantly pushed beyond the propositional substance of
Scripture to find typological references to Christ, so he reads
the universe allegorically, fixing on symbolic references to
biblical realities that he finds woven into the structure of
reality.

The origins of this approach lie in the Victorine piety of
the twelfth century. Richard and Hugh of St. Victor, influenced perhaps by the allegorical exegesis of Scripture in the
Alexandrian school, had used the natural world not only as a
ladder to climb toward the vision of God through contemplation of his wisdom and grandeur displayed in the creatures,
but also had viewed it as a richly detailed mirror image of
invisible things of God. The universe was for them a vast
cathedral in which both the whole architecture and the
smallest details of decoration were designed with hidden
theological referents.[26] The Victorine concept of a sacramental universe was picked up in the Counter Reformation by
Ludovicus Vives as an aid to innerworldly mysticism; and

from Vives it slipped over into the English Protestant tradition, where it became closely identified with Puritanism.[27] By Mather's time the enterprise of cracking the code of nature through meditation on its parabolic detail, which he calls "occasional reflections," had become a standard tool in Puritan methodology.[28] Mather was not alone in this practice; his master was the English Puritan John Flavel, and all the ministers in Boston joined him in it.[29]

The method of occasional reflection is woven through almost everything Cotton Mather wrote. His first published sermon, a series of such reflections, states that *"it would be an incredible benefit to the Church of God,* for men to have their houses furnished with Treatises *which shall teach them* how to Spiritualize *the outward occurrents of their* Occupations, and set Pulpits, and faithful Preachers *for them in every* Business *that they have to meddle with."*[30] Almost every subsequent publication has at least one example of occasional reflection and often a reference to the practice; and several larger works are wholly composed of such reflections. Part of the reason for this obsession with this form is its usefulness as a medium for easy communication to his listeners. The agricultural metaphors of *Agricola* are addressed to his home congregation, which included many husbandmen.[31] He uses nautical reflections in tracts for fishermen and sailors and obstetrical metaphors in a tract for women in their confinement.[32] But the compelling motive behind much of his use of this method in his literary craft was in his own daily immersion in the practice of occasional reflections.

It has been suggested that Mather's practice in this area seems to indicate a compulsive religiosity or a desperate seeking for interior stimulation in the wake of the Puritans' political disinheritance. There are other times when its products are, to say the least, homely.

> I was once emptying the *Cistern of Nature,* and making *Water* at the Wall. At the same Time, there came a Dog, who did so too, before me. Thought I; "What mean, and vile Things are the Children of Men, in this mortal State! How much do our *natural Necessities* abase us, and place us in some regard, on the same Level with the very Dogs!"[33]

> There are with me . . . the usual Evacuations of Nature. . . . I
> would improve the Time which these call for, to form some
> Thoughts of Piety. . . . The Actions themselves carry Humilia-
> tions in them; and a Christian ought alwayes to think humbly
> of himself, and be full of self-abasing and self-abhoring Reflec-
> tions.[34]

Mather's choice of symbols could sometimes be trivial
and tasteless. Occasional reflections, however, were designed by the Puritans to speak to people through the most
ordinary actions of daily life, such as rising in the morning
(resurrection), disrobing and reclothing (justification), and
washing (sanctification). The Puritans found justification for
their practice in the parabolic teachings of Jesus, who seems
to have found the ordinary events of daily life heavy with
this kind of significance, either bearing the lineaments of a
planned symbolism in the Creator's mind or else malleable
for allegorical purposes in the human imagination. Many of
the parables have the richness, allusiveness, and content
density of a kind of folk poetry, not a poetry of nightingales
and stars and other easily refinable "poetic" coinage, but one
that deals in common, ordinary objects such as we moderns
find in W. H. Auden's poems. The everyday mysticism of
the Puritan was closely allied to this strain of sensibility,
continually jumping the gaps of experiences and situations
with sparks of parabolic insight. A flawed poetic imagination (which Mather's most assuredly was) would often
emerge with similes and tropes that were unconsciously
grotesque, while Edwards' "Images or Shadows of Divine
Things" were the result of the same religious sensibility
heightened to the point of poetic genius.

One form of occasional reflection that exposes Mather
at his most questionable—both theologically and stylistically
—is what might be called the "symbolic judgment." One
characteristic of the Puritans frequently noted by their critics
was their propensity to interpret events as "providences,"
rewards, and (more often) punishments directly and dis-
cernibly meted out by the divine hand. Both Mather and
his father adopted the habit of connecting uncomfortable
events in their own lives with the displeasure of God,[35]

expressed as if the purpose of the Deity were, like that of the Lord High Executioner, to make the punishment fit the crime. Thus, on the corporate level, Mather connects the accidental burning of the meetinghouse in Boston with various "fiery sins" preceding the fire, including lust and contention.[36] The least dignified and most unintentionally humorous of Mather's interpretations along this line, however, have to do with symbolic providential judgments on individuals, such as when he threatens insomnia to those who sleep in church.[37] He worries in the *Diary* about his own maladies and their cryptic meaning:

> About the Middle of this Month, I lost abundance of precious Time, thro' tormenting Pains in my *Teeth* and *Jawes*; which kind of Pains have indeed produced mee many a sad Hour, in my short Pilgrimage. . . . I sett myself, as well as I could for my Pains, to *search and try my Wayes.* I considered, I. Have I not sinned with my Teeth? How? By sinful, graceless excessive *Eating.* And by evil Speeches, for there are *Literae dentales* in them?[38]

In January of 1697, suffering from "a Time of much Calamity to mee" due to "Epidemical and Pestilential *Colds,*" he reminds himself: "I must enquire, whether, a malignant Cold, bee not the very distemper of my Soul; a cold Indisposition to Religion, accompanied with sinful Malignity" (*Diary*, I, 248). Somewhat later we find him contemplating his navel: "I would anatomically and particularly consider, every Part of my Body, and with as explicit an Ingenuity as may be, consider the several Actions, and Uses thereof; and then go on to consider, on what Methods I may serve my glorious Lord with them. . . . Thus I would occasionally be awakened . . . when I suffer any Pain or Disorder in any Parts of my Body" (*Diary*, II, 75). One is tempted to suspect that the mind that found time for this kind of activity did not have sufficient practical business to occupy its talents—not because its political ambitions had been thwarted, but because it was polishing its piety instead of caring for the work of the kingdom. This is neither sound mysticism nor sanctification but a kind of busywork of the soul designed to kill time in a spiritually respectable manner.

Prayer, the "broadcasting" component of the cycle of communication with God, was fully as important to Mather as meditation. Mather was typical of Puritan spirituality in the high value he set on "Secret Prayer," "the very Vital Breath of Christianity; the Glory, the Comfort, the Armour of the Christian."[39] Prayer is both the main barometer of a soul's spiritual health and the principal means of securing a healthy state. It is a specific to insure spiritual prosperity, for "a *Praying* Soul, will be a *Thriving Soul. Much Prayer*, as it were keeps the Soul in a breathing *Sweat*, which by Degrees does consume all the Distempers of it. In our *Prayers*, all our *Graces* come to be Exercised, and so to be Strengthened, so to be perfected."[40] Prayer is a primary weapon in spiritual conflict against the powers of darkness:

> You cannot contrive a more effectual preservative from the Hurts of Temptation than Prayer; daily, wrestling, Restless *Prayer*, The infamous Day of *Origen's* foul Apostasy, was a day whereon he had been *remiss* in his morning Prayers. I will not tell you Nazianzen's Story of what a Devil was forced to own unto Cyprian, about his inability to work upon a *praying* Soul, in his dayes: But this I am sure of; the Trumpets of Gideon did not more fright the Midianites, than the Prayers of the Faithful do all the Devils in the dark Regions.[41]

Prayer is the gateway to regeneration for ourselves and can prevail upon God to regenerate others.[42] ". . . the principle aid in a daily walk with God is to *Walk* much with Him."[43] Beyond this, the prayers of believers can result in the institution of reformation in the church and can affect even national destinies.[44]

All of this concentration on what we may call the instrumental necessity of prayer—its potency as a tool and a weapon in the spiritual life—might seem to impersonalize the exercise, to turn it into an instrument of enlisting God's help and binding him to our goals instead of an intimate communion with him. And it is true that Mather sometimes defines prayer as if it were pure request, as in "the *Presentation of our Desires unto the Glorious GOD*."[45] Like most Puritans, he advises keeping what is very nearly a bookkeeping account of answers to prayer.[46] And yet even here his principal concern is for the appreciation of God's love disclosed in such answers: "The Children of God having their *Prayers answered,* have the *Love of God* shining upon them, in the Answers. . . . When our good Things come to us, with such a Mark as this upon them there is a Whisper of Heaven accompanies them; *Here, take this, as a Token that I am thy Father, and that I have loved thee!*"[47] His concept of petition can sound almost magical: "Make use of [the name of Jesus] and you have what you ask for!" But this is countered by his Calvinistic emphasis on submission to God's will: "There is that which has been of old called, *The Hinge of Prayer.* All turns upon that Hinge; That *wherein our God shall be most Glorified.* This will infallibly be done."[48]

He elsewhere states that the goals of prayer are not primarily to obtain our request or even to inform God of our need, but to realize his attributes, to rehearse and penetrate the meaning of Christian doctrine about him, to profess our dependence on him, to nourish our communion with him, to preserve the good order of our souls, and to support the heart under griefs.[49] Unlike mystical prayer in the medieval and Counter Reformation traditions, which often calls for a quietistic suspension of the faculties, Puritan prayer engages all of these in hard effort: "True *Prayer* is *Heart-Work,* and *Soul-Work.*"[50] But it is not a mere multiplication of words, for "a Broken *Heart,* a Flaming *Heart,* a Gracious *Heart,* is of more Account with God, than all the *Flourishing Expressions* imaginable."[51]

Such prayer is only possible for the regenerate, for "men have the *Grace* to be much in *Supplication* when that *Spirit* has once Renewed them, and possessed them; they have then a *Spirit for Prayer* continually."[52] Although Mather was convinced that only a live relationship with the Holy Spirit can lead to vital prayer, and urged that the first step in any prayer be the invoking of the Spirit's help, unlike some earlier Puritans he did not discourage the use of forms and models of prayer for those novices who need these;[53] he even offered some models of his own.[54] Still, he was convinced that continued reliance on forms could become a dangerous crutch that would stifle spiritual growth, for "after all, a *Soul* touched with a sense of your Condition, and fired with the Sight of what you are, and what you *want;* and what your SAVIOR is willing to do for you, will cause you to *Pray* beyond what any *Forms* in the World can do."[55] He was also inclined to recommend the Lord's Prayer, as well as a sort of prayer-trellis made of segments obtained from Scripture through meditation, as the best structural guides for prayer.[56]

The monastic regimens of medieval piety, with their tradition extending back into the early centuries of the church, had observed a structured pattern of daily prayers at stated intervals—the canonical hours. While some forms of Anglican devotion, such as that used at Little Gidding, continued to make use of the canonical hours, most of English Protestantism considered them too close to Old Testament legalism and countered with the notion that all hours of the day were to be considered holy.[57] This led to an emphasis on unstructured shorter prayers during the course of the day. But they still felt a need for the daily structure of stated prayers, based on biblical example. A triple pattern of daily prayer was drawn from the examples of David (Ps. 55:17), Daniel (Dan. 6:10), and Psalm 110:64, which suggests a sevenfold pattern of prayer. It seems to have been the practice to commend the shorter regimen to the laity and reserve the "perfect number" for the clergy; and Mather apparently prayed at seven stated intervals during the day, though his son was under the impression that it was the very heterodox number of six.[58] In the *Manuductio* he does not dare to recommend more than the number of three for ministerial candidates,[59] and he recommends twice or thrice daily for the average layman, with special emphasis on prayer at the beginning and close of the day.[60] Mather himself seemed to take delight in those occasions when his duties led him to exceed the regular number of stated prayers and pray ten times in an afternoon or an evening, rather like a runner clocking his speed or a golfer counting his strokes.[61]

The practice of offering short spontaneous prayers in times of special need or stress during the day was well established in the Puritan tradition, as it was also in the preceding history of Christian spirituality.[62] Mather picked up the practice of such "ejaculations" directly from his father, who, he says, kept up a constant stream of such arrows launched toward the throne of grace like Homer's heroes.[63] Mather's rationale for the practice was twofold: it was a means of remaining constantly in the presence of God during the day,[64] and it was necessary as a constant acknowledgment of dependence on God in the face of special stresses or crises, such as the meeting of heavy responsibilities or the repulsion of satanic injections and temptations.[65] Mather was also in the habit of listening to sermons with ejaculatory applications, and he tried to manage the more difficult feat of preaching with interwoven silent interjections for his congregation, as he records in the *Diary* (I, 108-109). Very early in his life he established a habit of praying in this manner for individuals he encountered in the course of his daily conversation:

> It has been a frequent Thing with mee, to redeem the *silent,* and otherwise, *thoughtless,* Minutes of my Time, in shaping Thousands of *ejaculatory Prayers* for my Neighbours. And by reciting a Few of them, the Way of my shaping the Rest, may bee conjectured. . . . In passing along the *Street,* I have sett myself to *bless* thousands of persons, who never knew that I did it; with *secret Wishes,* after this manner sent unto Heaven for them (*Diary,* I, 81, 83).

Very often these ejaculations are cast in the form of occasional reflections on the persons prayed for, as when Mather prays for a tall man passing by, "Lord, give that Man, *High Attainments* in Christianity: lett him fear God, *above many*" (I, 81, 83). Here again we are in the presence of a sentiment that verges on the ridiculous. We must remember that Mather was only twenty when he wrote these notes. But he persisted in this laborious dedication all his life, with a relentless determination to make every gully and hillock in the acreage of his life bear fruit for God.

In a tract on the necessity of "being brief" in conversations about and with the Lord, *Grata Brevitas* (1712), Mather remarks that Christ and other authorities inclined to favor ejaculatory prayer over long sessions of more formal prayer, for the early Christians "thought it best, to *Pray Briefly;* but *Very Often, Very Often,* to be engaged in it."[66] Nevertheless, one of the most noticeable features of Mather's own prayer life, and one of which he himself was proudest, was the great number of days and nights of secret prayer he clocked in his lifetime, which amounted to some four hundred and fifty.[67] Here again he adopted the practice directly from his father, who held a monthly day of prayer "even with *Rigid Fasting.*"[68] This method of devotion was firmly established among Puritans, especially the clergy, from the time of the earliest Puritan pastors.[69] Mather's son notes that he began the practice of whole days of fasting and prayer at fourteen, directed by the example of his father and by Scudder's *Christian Daily Walk.*[70] Mather himself observes that the practice ultimately traces back to the early church fathers, quoting Cyprian and Tertullian to justify it.[71] In March of 1702, under the influence of his patristic reading, Mather began a new practice related to these days of prayer, which is recorded in the *Diary.*

> I called now to Mind, that The primitive Christians . . . in Obedience to that Commandment of *Watching unto Prayer,* sometimes had their *Vigils.* . . . To spend a good Part of a *Night* sometimes in Prayer, and so take the Advantage of a nocturnal Solitude, and abridge themselves of their usual Rest, for the sake of a devout Conversation with Heaven; they found God often rewarding the Devotions of such Vigils, with a more than ordinary Degree of heavenly Consolation. Accordingly, I resolved, that I would this Night, make some Essay towards a *Vigil.* . . . I dismissed my dear Consort unto her own Repose; and In the Dead of the Night, I retired into my Study; and there casting myself into the Dust, prostrate on my Study-floor before the Lord, I was rewarded with Communications from Heaven, that cannot be uttered (I, 421-422).

This was not the only instance in which Mather showed a remarkably disciplined inventive zeal in his approach to marathon prayer. When he was eighteen, the *Diary* observes: "As the last Week, I kept a Day of Supplication, so I was desirous this Week to keep a Day of *Thanksgiving,* in secret Places before the Lord. I never knew of any person, or heard of more than one Person [*margin:* My Grandfather *Cotton*],

who did accustome themselves unto such an Exercise"
(I, 18). A few years later he set out the plan of an ordinary fast
day of supplication, involving a mixture of biblical reading
"largely turned into *Prayers,*" meditation on his sin, singing
of hymns and psalms, meditation with occasional reflections,
and supplications for his own spiritual growth and the pros-
pering of his ministry (I, 56-59). The content of the day is not
properly intercession, since it is almost wholly centered on
spiritual self-improvement. The same is true of the substance
of the vigil of June 23/24, 1711 (II, 83), and in the triple-
header series of prayer days Mather held on April 13-15,
1703, in which he spent a day confessing his sins, a day
resigning himself to God's will, and a day asking for angelic
support in his ministry and protection from spiritual assaults
(II, 477-480). But though Mather considered his days of
prayer primary instruments in his own spiritual growth,
most of these were also heavily involved with pastoral concerns, reaching from his immediate parish to the boundaries of the Protestant cause overseas.

The mechanism of the day of prayer is first of all commended by Mather to pastors, as indispensable to their effective ministry;[72] but he also frequently recommends the practice to the laity. In *Bonifacius* he notes that days of public and
private thanksgiving should be kept by Christians "of the
Finer Mould";[73] and in *The Religion of the Closet* (1705) he
gives instructions on how to manage a day of humiliation
and supplication and a day of thanksgiving (pp. 16ff.).[74] He
even hesitantly recommends the practice of vigils to lay
leaders:

> I will not proceed in *Describing,* much less in *Prescribing,* the
> Asceticks of the *Ancient Christians;* they were not always free
> from *Superstition.* Yet will I prevail with my self, to mention
> one of *their* Noble Exercises. . . . To spend a good part of a
> Night sometimes in *Prayer.* . . . I would not carry this Affair
> too far. However, if such things are by any thought not fit to be
> *practised,* yet there may be a Profanity in Deriding of them
> (pp. 30, 31).

There is some consciousness here on Mather's part of the fact
that he is asking a great deal of laymen. One wonders where

they would have found the time, but Mather apparently assumed that everyone had a flexible schedule such as his own. There is also a marginal awareness of the problematic side of the "Ascetick" approach to the Christian life, and an indication that Mather himself was criticized in his own time for advocating it. But his overall position seems to have been that clergy and laity alike should practice these daily retreats as often as once a month, which was his general practice, together with a day of prayer on one's birthday; for "we can't have our Desires, without *whole Days of Prayer*, to ripen us for the Desired Enjoyments."[75]

The duplex mechanism of meditation on the Word combined with prayer was used by the Puritans in two main public applications, along with its private use as described above. The first was in those modified and abbreviated worship services that were held in "the church in the home," the Puritan family devotions. The early Puritan conforming ministers, according to one opinion, chose to construct a model of the perfect church in the worship of the Christian home when they were frustrated in their projected reformation of the external church.[76] William Perkins, a moderate yet consistent conforming Puritan, defines the family unit as if it were a small church; the spiritual importance he gives it is almost patriarchal and is in sharp contrast to the devaluation of family life in the medieval ethic, with its emphasis on virginity as a condition of perfection.[77] Perkins' position was normative for the subsequent Puritan tradition, and Richard Baxter thought that a large part of his "Reformation" of the Kidderminster parish—which looks suspiciously like what later terminology would call a "revival"—was due to the firm establishment of family religion.[78] Francke, again perhaps under Puritan influence, made the institution of family worship part of his reformation in the community at Halle.[79]

Mather was especially concerned to energize family piety within his church, and he wrote a number of sermons and tracts on the subject. He approached his people with an airtight sociological and theological rationale for the practice. There are three kinds of societies instituted among people, he notes: the domestic, the ecclesiastical, and the political; of these, the domestic is the first instituted and in some ways the most pivotally important.[80] Each of these societies owes some acknowledgment to God for its conduct, and so the domestic society should have some periods of corporate worship involving the husband and wife, the children, and the servants together.[81] Following Baxter's *Christian Directory* and general Puritan tradition,[82] Mather recommends in *Family Sacrifice* two daily periods of joint family worship, morning and evening, along with table graces at every meal—in short, "let no *Season,* for *Family prayer* go without it" (p. 27). He notes that family worship can be a bore if it is not discreetly managed, for "on the one side, *Family-Prayer* should not be *Tedious;* but on the other side, it should not be hastily Slubbered over" (p. 30). The content of the family service should include the reading of Scripture, the singing of hymns or psalms, family instruction, and prayer (pp. 30-38). Apart from Scripture, material for meditation in the service may include published sermons (or, on a sabbath, the sermon of the day), catechisms, and devotional writings.[83] Every member of the family should be encouraged to take part in prayer; there may even be set prayers, but these are to be reasonably informal.[84] Instruction of the family should ideally include a genuine pastoral probing of their spiritual condition by the *pater familias,* inquiring into their current spiritual experience, reproving sin, encouraging prayer, and even evangelizing those not professing conversion.[85]

It is not hard to discern—between the lines of Mather's writing—that this kind of semipastoral supervision in the home was not being realized in the daily experience of his parishioners. He remarks on a multitude of excuses that were used to beg off the duty of family exercises. The most frequent of these was lack of oratorical skill in prayer. Mather advises the use of form prayers or the adaptation of psalms or other Scripture passages, and he notes that it takes little talent to cry to God out of a real and desperate sense of one's need, which is what family prayer must be if it is to be more than an aesthetic exercise.[86] Against the objection that family worship as managed by most can only aspire to a dead form inherited from tradition, he remarks in *Family-Religion*

Urged: "May not a good as well as a bad Conversation be received by Tradition from our Fathers? . . . Will not Families that issue from godly Families, retain at least a Form of Godliness? And will not a Form of Godliness, often by the grace of God, prove a Vehicle for the power of Godliness?" (p. 9). Mather simply brushes aside the complaint of lack of time or the intractability of the family as rationalizations for a lack of heart for God and for prayer. As incentives for the half-hearted, Mather lays on a heavy barrage of typically Puritan warnings for prayerless households. Such homes are particularly subject to the plague, and should, like quarantined houses, have an inscription of "Lord Have Mercy" written over the lintel because of their blighting influence in a community (*Family-Religion Urged*, p. 9), for he says in *Small Offers*, "If your *Houses* be not Warmed with your *Prayers*, the fierce Wrath of God abideth on them" (p. 29).

> The *Curse* of God is the Sauce in every *Dish,* the *Curse* of God is the Cover to every *Bed,* in that lamentable *Family.* Houses molested with Devils, are not more miserable, than Houses destitute of *Prayers.* I have seen it in an house, when the *Devils* have had Possession of a child, that when *Family-Prayer* began, the Devils would make Hideous Roarings and Noises in the Room, as being under a Vexation thereat, which was intolerable to them. Truly, The Devils have *No* Disturbance in Houses where *Family-Prayer* is not maintained; prayerless houses are *haunted* houses, and the Fiends of Darkness reign, and ramp, there without controul (p. 41).

A strict keeping of the first day of the week as a spiritual retreat had been normative since the outset of the Puritan movement. The exact historical origins of Puritan Sabbatarianism are not precisely determinable, but the careful observance of "the Lord's day," in opposition to the looser policy of the Reformers and the antilegalistic Anabaptists, is probably traceable to the influence of the Rhenish Reformers Bucer and Bullinger.[87] In British church history it appears in the north with John Knox's *First Book of Discipline,*[88] and in England with the activity of the legalistic and anticeremonial Puritan John Hooper and his successor, John Bradford.[89] The much more stringent and extreme emphasis of Nicholas Bowndes in the 1590s established the strict sabbath as a

universally recognized distinctive of Puritanism, as cere-
monialism yielded to Sabbatarianism as the *cause célèbre* and
point of contention between the Puritan party and Laud.[90]
Spread popularly by the Puritan devotional manuals, and
entrenched in their major theological systems, the Puritan
sabbath survived Laud and the Restoration and very nearly
conquered the field by the end of the seventeenth century, as
Anglican practice in some quarters capitulated and embraced
the stricter view.[91]

Undoubtedly a main part of the reason for this conquest
was not theological in nature but pragmatic. In spite of the
drawbacks of its legalism, the Puritan sabbath *worked* as an
instrument for the development of piety, for it was, in essence, a miniature weekly Protestant "retreat." Both
Catholics and Protestants in the postmedieval period found
that if the monastic solution to the problem of spiritual culture was transcended by moving the church into an innerworldly stance, some new methodology of intensive spiritual
nurture had to be developed to prevent the church from
dissolving into the world. In the Catholic Counter Reformation, Ignatius Loyola and his order developed the methodology of the prolonged retreat followed by re-entry into the
common world, with the retreatant inspired by enlarged
knowledge and an awakened sense of vocation. The retreat
became for Catholics a sort of portable monastery; and in the
seventeenth, eighteenth, and nineteenth centuries it was one
of the primary engines for energizing the church spiritually.[92]

On the Reformed side, Bucer in Strassbourg, the early
Puritans with their prophesying sessions, and the later
Pietism with its conventicles developed the "small group
meeting methodology." Later Evangelicalism emerged with
the protracted revival meeting, and in the nineteenth century
it adopted from Catholicism the retreat methodology and
applied it to summer "spiritual life conferences." The element all these methods shared is prolonged and intensive
study of doctrinal truth in an atmosphere of prayerful response. The later Puritans of Mather's period did not use the
prophesying sessions (which were originally a stopgap substitute for the muzzled pulpit), nor did they have prolonged

retreats; but they did have a miniature, day-long retreat each week—the strict Sabbath.[93] The weekly discharge of accumulated pastoral potential in the long sermons and the ministers' marathon prayers, absorbed by the people with an appetite (or at least a tolerance) that amazes modern observers, was a powerful instrument for the transformation of the English and American character.[94]

Cotton Mather placed a particularly high value on the strict Puritan sabbath. His concern was a blend of pragmatic pietism with ceremonial legalism. He felt that the sabbath worked as an instrument of nurture, since "If you look through the World, you shall see that Men's *Religion* is as their *Sabbath* is. The *Sabbath* is the *engine* by which, by the *Bible*, true Remembrance of God is kept alive."[95] Beyond its significance in nurture, however, Mather felt that the sabbath was also "a *Seal* to the whole *Covenant of Grace: a Seal* common to both Testaments," the violation of which would bring spiritual desolation.[96] It was not just that a strict Sabbatarian would be healthy and a loose one would suffer malnutrition; God would reward the first and curse the second.[97]

Mather's whole view of the sabbath is concisely summarized in *The Day Which the Lord Hath Made* (1707), a tract he reprinted in an Indian translation, apparently judging this to be one of the weightier points of the faith without which Christian Indians could not survive spiritually. He sets out two propositions: first, there is to be a day in each week holy to the Lord (initially, the seventh day, to point to God's grace in Creation); and second, in these times God has appointed the day of resurrection to supplant the seventh day, to point to redemption, and to prepare people for a better world. He appeals to the fathers (Justin Martyr, Tertullian, Augustine, Ambrose, and Origen) to prove that in primitive times a careful observation of the day was the mark of a Christian. (Mather here and elsewhere deplores the use of "Sunday" as a designation for the Lord's Day and laments the fact that the fathers fell into this habit, which he explains as a device of theirs to bridge the cultural gap in their witness to paganism.) As for how the day is to be kept, he denies that it is in any sense a fast day but asserts that it is a time when people should cease from all tedious works that are the curse of sin, works other than those in some way directly related to God's service. Note that the Lord's Day is to be occupied by *work*, not primarily by rest: we are to cease from our own work, but not from "God's works." Following Origen, Mather advises that the day be wholly given over to observing God's works, and not polluted by idleness, profaneness, by *"Sins of Omission;* By *Sleeping immoderately;* by *Walking* only to take the Air; by Leaving undone, what we ought to do" (pp. 19-20). If leisure is inappropriate, so is mere amusement, for "if our *Labours* are prohibited on the *Lords-day*, methinks our *Pleasures* must be so too. It was no mistake in *Austin*, That it were better to Plough, than to *Dance* on the *Lords-day*. 'Tis *Gods Time*, and will not admit any *Pastime*" (p. 18). To fill the painful emptiness left by the evacuation of ordinary pursuits and pleasures, Mather recommends *"Heart-melting Meditations* on the *Words* and *Works* of God, and especially on those points whereto the *Lords-day* has a special Reference" (p. 21). Public and private worship of God are also part of the pattern of godly labors. Mather nowhere mentions works of corporal mercy as part of the sabbath regimen, perhaps because the average layman had all he could do to fit in all the prayer and meditation that the ministers advised and structured into the day.

Legal ceremonial and pragmatic pietistic motives are closely interwoven in another refinement of Mather's position on the use of the first day: the question of whether Saturday or Sunday evening ought to be considered part of the twenty-four-hour period which was strictly "the Sabbath." This had long been a point of contest between Puritan rabbis, and the New Englanders differed freely about the matter. Increase Mather evidently held with John Cotton that Sunday evening was part of the holy day, allowing that most other ministers held otherwise and that Christians may differ in love on such matters.[98] Cotton Mather was tolerant about the problem (*Day*, p. 25) but arrived at a solution typical of his omnivorous piety: both evenings are to be kept holy.[99] It would be inappropriate not to make a fit preparation for the sabbath on Saturday evening (*Day*, pp. 34-35); but it would also be harmfully inefficient to allow the piety of a well-spent sabbath to be dissipated in an ill-spent evening:

> Christians, Why should we lose the *Heat* of the Day, (as one aptly Expresses) it, in the cool of the Evening? Why should we let useless Discourses, hurtful Distractions, carnal Excursions, in the Evening, Extinguish the Frame which the Devotions of the *Day* had Enkindled in us? . . . *Bells,* and *Saints,* of a good Metal, will keep the *Sounds,* when the *Strokes* are over (pp. 26-27).

Mather recommends using the sabbath evening for "Savoury Conferences" if visiting is absolutely necessary, meditation, prayer, family worship or catechizing, or perhaps attending the young people's meetings he inaugurated partly to cure the misuse of this time. The Mathers were particularly concerned about the increasing occurrence of ungoverned "night-walking" by the unoccupied youth of Boston, which was occasioning a "Danger that among many People, the *Dies Dominicus,* will conclude, in a, *Vespera Daemoniaca;* It will be, *The Lords Day,* but it will be, *Satans Evening.*"[100] Mather comments that it even looked as though New Englanders were weary of the sabbath.[101]

Those who were spiritually alert and willing undoubtedly thrived under the Puritan system of a weekly day-long retreat. There are certain features about this technique of short weekly retreats that recommend it over the pattern of brief (and often nominal) Sunday attendance, combined with widely separated retreat or conference experiences, which is the rule in many Protestant and Catholic churches today. The average Puritan obtained more "training in Christianity" in one month, through the sabbath ministries, than many Protestants do in a year, even with midweek discussion sessions and small group meetings.

We have long been aware of the unpleasant features on the other side of the ledger. The ritual observance of recurrent holy days was a part of the Old Testament legal pattern which the Puritans themselves repudiated; and yet it is ironic that they really substituted fifty-two holy days in the year for the few they abolished. Mather observes that "The

(New England) Churches make a Difference between *Taking* a *Time* to *Do* a *Sacred Work*, and the *Doing* a *Work* to *keep* a *Sacred Time*."[102] But we have already shown that there is an indissoluble mixture of pragmatic spiritual strategy and ritual asceticism in the Puritan and Matherian definition of the sabbath. The fact is that the New England ministers were constantly having to tell their people what to do to fill up the time, rather than seizing, adapting, and molding time to provide room for an organic spirituality springing up among the people. An approach to the sabbath that was centered on nurture instead of ritual observance would have relaxed its discipline to meet the children, the neophytes, and the unconverted where they were, instead of presenting them with a legal demand for the full measure of mature godliness.

The fact that the sabbath was a ritual holy day was further complicated by the Puritan definition of it as a day of holy work rather than a day of rest. Whereas the Old Testament use of holy days and of the sabbath in particular was anti-ascetic—feasting was prescribed more often than fasting, there was no prohibition of games or recreation, and the response toward God was defined in terms of worship, reflection on God's works, and gratitude—the Puritan doctrine of vocation spilled over into the use of Sunday, making it just another day of strenuous labor, albeit of a more spiritual sort. Here we touch on something symbolic of the whole problem of Puritanism. The Puritan sabbath takes a day which for Calvin was to be one of pure response to God's grace and insists that this grace be worked into the soul by hard labor. It is thus no accident that the sabbath question assumed so large a place in the Puritan movement.[103]

Other components of the Puritan/Pietist experientialist movement generally sought to ameliorate the strict Sabbatarianism of the English Puritans. Baxter, as usual, held a moderate position on this issue.[104] Among certain Pietists of the Dutch school, for example, Cocceius and Labadie, adopted a nonceremonial usage of the day, somewhat looser than the Puritans, mainly for the expediencies of piety.[105] Spener and Francke adopted a mitigated Puritan sabbath, but placed their main emphasis on nurture rather than legal

obligation, in characteristic Lutheran fashion.[106] Wesley retained the Puritan sabbath as consistent with his own kind of
"methodism," as Nagler indicates.[107]

It is appropriate here to consider Mather's treatment of
the sacraments as means of grace. Critics of the sacramental
practice of nineteenth-century revivalism, such as the Mer-
cersberg theologian John Nevin, have correctly indicated that
some movements that evolved from Puritan stock declined
considerably from the high regard for the sacraments characteristic of the Reformers.[108] The low-church, almost Anabaptist practice of the later revivalism made this inevitable. But
the Puritanism of the seventeenth and early eighteenth centuries did not share this deficiency. In the matter of the
Lord's Supper, the Puritans believed in frequent but careful
communion, preceded and accompanied by lengthy and
serious meditation and self-examination. The importance of
this sacrament for Puritans is indicated by the proliferation
of guides and manuals for communicants in their literature of
piety. The number and extensiveness of these suggest a
sacramental concern the modern Protestant would expect
only in Anglican or Roman Catholic authors.[109]

Mather himself was the author of several such manuals,
and his *Diary* reveals that he took the Lord's Supper with the
utmost seriousness as a means of strengthening his own
spiritual life.[110] His concern for the numbers of scrupulous
persons withdrawing from the sacrament testifies to his belief in its spiritual efficacy.[111]

When we examine the reasons for Mather's appreciation
of the Supper, however, we discover that he was more interested in it as a means of "leverage" for spiritual self-
improvement than as a declaration, or a means, of grace.
While many Puritans were closer to Calvin than to Zwingli
on the doctrine of the real presence of Christ in the sacrament, and did not conceive of the elements as mere signs or
memorials,[112] Mather nowhere refers to the direct presence
of Christ in the Supper. He does admit and emphasize the
infusion of supernatural grace and illumination through the
working of the Holy Spirit in his writings, but he does not

directly connect this with the presence of the Second Person of the Trinity or with the reception of the elements. He was far more interested in the "improvement" of the sacrament through extensive preparation before it and meditation on biblical and doctrinal truth during it than he was in the actual consummation of the sacrament.

Under the term "preparation," Mather includes, first of all, what he calls "habitual preparation" for the Lord's Table, which appears to be simply the work of preparation involved in initial conversion, embracing three things: a consideration and personal ratification of the covenant of grace, a contemplation of the crucified Savior, and the urgent seeking of a sensible work of grace in the heart. Persons who have done this, however, must come to each new communion with a work of "actual preparation" in which they review the points of their habitual preparation and also engage in extensive self-examination.[113] If persons are willing to go through this kind of preparation, Mather is ready to receive them at the table of the Lord, for "Tho' you are not *fully sure*, of your *Sincerity*, yet you may come, and you may *do it in Faith:* Inasmuch as you have no *plain Evidence* remaining, to determine a *Predominant* Hypocrisy."[114]

Thus, as we have seen, he practices a modified Stoddardeanism, in which the sacrament is basically used as a tool for conversion if not as a converting ordinance; the difference is that Mather will not simply invite all those who would receive grace to the Supper, but invites instead all those who are willing to prepare to receive it.[115] For the regenerate, on the other hand, he uses the Supper as a lever to advance their sanctification through the demand for self-examination and increasing surrender of the life to the Holy Spirit. He finds biblical justification for all of this in that favorite Puritan text, I Corinthians 11:28: "But let a man examine himself, and so let him eat of that bread and drink of that cup." Having made his or her preparation, the communicant is to come to the table ready to meditate on the significance of the elements and also to think of special designs of piety during pauses,[116] or meditate on the weak spots in the armor of his or her sanctification.[117] Everything in the sacrament thus becomes, through the machinery of meditation, grist for the mill of sanctification.

Mather's concentration on preparation and improvement in the sacrament, however, combined with the theory of regeneration we have already discussed, made it inevitable that great numbers of the congregation would develop scruples and abstain from the sacrament. Another effect of this treatment of the sacrament was that it accentuated the atomic individualism which Puritanism retained as a heritage of monastic perfectionism. There is no mention in any of Mather's writings on the Supper of the corporate inclusion of all believers in the body of Christ, symbolized in their joint participation in the sacrament. In his celebration of the sacrament, believers do not so much eat together as a body; rather, each concentrates his attention wholly toward God in spiritual self-concern, as if the members were isolated points on a wheel's hub connected to the center by spokes.

Mather dealt rather less frequently with the subject of baptism. Apart from the usual comments on the complexities of the "New England Way" in the administration of this sacrament, most of his remarks point again to its instrumental value in testing and assuring the regeneracy of those requesting or observing the ritual.[118] In the case of those who are already assured, Mather recommends other improvements of the sacrament. Speaking of the early fathers, he says, "How awful, how useful to them, was the Remembrance of their *Baptism* all their Dayes! If after their Baptism, they were Tempted unto any *known Sin*, they would Reply, *No, I have been Baptised, and I durst not pollute myself by Sinning after it.*"[119] Mather concurs with Luther in this use of baptism:

> Those Temptations which are peculiarly called, *The Fiery darts of Satan:* Why should we not bring our Baptism to quench those Fiery darts . . . by thus arguing, *Baptisata Sum.* . . . And thus, if we are hurried at any time to question the Truth of the *Christian Faith* . . . (to) argue so: Is there not a *God!* Yes, I was Baptised for Him. Is there not a *Christ!* Yes, I was *Baptised* into His Name. Is there not a *Future State of Glory* for the Righteous? Yes, I was Baptised into the *Belief* of it. I can tell you, that Satan will not be able to stand before such *Thoughts* as these; And

Sanctity will be advanced by such *Thoughts* unto Astonishment![120]

While certain New England Puritans did hold to baptismal regeneration, and the whole covenant theology and the conception of New England as Israel tended to move in this direction,[121] Mather did not allow of any certainty of assurance on this ground, as we have seen above. His occasional willingness to use baptism as a comforting reminder of God's grace was therefore a medieval remnant ill-suited to the base of his theology. But these occasions were rare; the main significance of baptism for Mather was that it is a great engine which when rightly improved can bring holiness.[122]

Besides the principal means of grace, Mather was drawn to a bewildering profusion of lesser instruments for the development of spirituality, most of these of medieval or patristic derivation. One of these, the regular practice of introspection, has already been viewed as a component in meditation and in preparation for communion; but it is so important and so ubiquitous in Mather's methodology that we should consider it separately as a devotional method. Mather again appeals to early patristic piety for a warrant for the practice: "SELF EXAMINATION is a Duty in the Christian *Asceticks*, than which there is none of greater Consequence."[123] He employed it, however, in forms that were distinctly Puritan evolutionary products—the spiritual diary and the use of manuals of self-examination.

The development of the use of diaries for self-examination in the earliest Puritan leaders, such as Rogers and Perkins, was a methodological substitute for the Catholic confession.[124] But much of the effort poured into the diaries was directed toward the detection of the marks of regeneration rather than the nurture of sanctification. This is the sense in which Increase Mather understood the work of self-examination.[125] Cotton Mather's "manual for self-examination," *The Tryed Professor* (1719), is one of those instruments for the detection of hypocrisy and common-grace spirituality of which Daniel Dykes' *Mystery of Self-Deceiving* (1614) was the progenitor[126] and Edwards' *Treatise on the Affections* the apotheosis. Here Mather advises his readers to prize a ministry that searches them out and to take time besides to search themselves for such dangerous signs of unregeneracy as regular indulgence in known sin, allergy to secret prayer and exceptional holiness in others, habitual unfairness in business, and fanatical religious zeal. He urges the examiners to penetrate behind the common-grace virtues in their lives until they reach the "things that accompany salvation."[127]

Two other devotional techniques Mather mentions from time to time are "vows" and "acts," or "intentions of piety." The latter, which Mather was very fond of, he began to practice at the age of eighteen, resolving in that New Year "To act as much as may bee, for God, every Action" (*Diary*, I, 73-75). His recommendations of the practice in sermons are frequent and uniform over the whole period of his ministry.[128] In several cases he almost seems to define the process of sanctification as a continual engaging in intentions of piety, "Those *Thoughts,* with which the *Life of God* is to be carried on" (*Diary*, II, 335):

> The Holy *Dr. Usher* being desired to write about *Sanctification,* with Tears lamenting the defect of it in himself, gave this Description of it,—*It is for a Man to be in the offering up of his Soul continually, in the flames of Love, as a whole burnt-offering to God in Jesus Christ.*[129]

Thus, although Mather claims to have discovered this method uninfluenced by his tradition, the basic elements of it were not unknown to English Puritan piety. The flavor of this practice is, of course, much more redolent of the Catholic piety of the Counter Reformation, and specifically Ignatius Loyola's vigorous emphasis on the will.

Among other minor means of edification to which Mather briefly refers is "religious conference"—conversation with friends on spiritual subjects—and the reading of devotional literature. Even friendship was methodized for Mather: the title of his tract on religious conference, *The Rules of a Visit* (1705), is indicative. Mather himself aimed to steer the subject of every conversation to something edifying, and he recommends the same strategy to his parishioners. His manual on how to visit profitably states that the primary aim should always be kept in mind: to contradict atheism in bad times and "*Encourage* one another in the wayes of Deserted, Despised, Derided Godliness" (p. 7).[130] At the least, the aim should be to avoid subjects of conversation that are spiritually harmful to oneself or others; at best, there should be a striving toward that which is spiritually edifying. Not that religion should be the only subject of conversation—Mather himself is a little horrified by that thought—but there is to be a sober preparation of head and heart for whatever the discourse is, an economy in speaking, an avoiding of the speculative or disputatious, and an attempt to do some spiritual good in the company before leaving. At times a religious question can be asked to turn the conversation in a "profitable" direction. But Mather is concerned not to propagate an unnatural religiosity (p. 35). He is not against an admixture of humor in conversations:

> An *Innocent Pleasancy* may sometimes be humored in our Visits. You remember, that I said, *Innocent*. I meant an Intercourse of *Doves*, not an Intercourse of Serpents. . . . We may very *Serviceably* bring in *Sauce* as well as *Meat*, unto them whom we are Entertaining. Only then It must not be *All* nothing but *Sauce*; and we must beware lest it go so far, as to leave a Tincture of *Carnality* on our minds (p. 30).

It is clear that Mather is describing here his own habitual practice, as it has been reported by his colleagues. If even Benjamin Franklin was charmed by his discourse, this method may not have been entirely without success as he managed it.

In both the Puritan and Pietist developments of Protestant Christian experience there was a profuse development of devotional literature during the seventeenth century.[131] Mather heartily recommends that the chinks in his people's spiritual armor (and in their schedules) be filled in with the reading of such works. In *Honesta Parsimonia*, which might be described as a tract on how to become a miser with time, Mather notes that one way surplus spare time can be filled up is by the use of such literature.[132] Mather's own colossal literary production is attributable not only to his drive for recognition but to his concern to flood New England households with such products. He even advises himself to read his own books! (*Diary*, II, 28). But he is equally interested in recommending the whole store of Puritan writings to his people, as well as the new productions of German Pietism.[133]

Viewed from one perspective, Mather's lifelong fascination with the machinery for supporting the spiritual life hints at a rather fragile, hothouse quality in his own spirituality. The gardener who is preoccupied with fertilizers and trellises may be laboring with a sick rose. The epithet Luther applied to the Anabaptists, "New Monachism," is at times appropriate for Mather's Puritanism. The monastic and anchoritic heroes of his patristic sources separated themselves from the world by walls and deserts, and they narrowed the focus of their concept of mission to their own religious self-improvement. While this could be understood as a vocation contributing to the kingdom through prayer and witness, it could also very easily turn to sanctified egocentricity. Disengaged from active mission within the world, they could easily devote themselves to the elaboration of devotional machinery. This may have been partly the case with Mather also. A Log College pastor might wonder where Mather got the time for so much cultivation of his own spirit in the midst of a parish of so many souls. And it is probable that many of these souls were not helped, but only intimidated, by the Jacob's ladder of methodology through which Mather sought to bring down spiritual gifts from heaven.

Only too often Mather's ladder was reversed: unlike Jacob's, in which angels descended with gifts, Mather's had to be climbed by the recipient. Though it was presented not as a counsel of perfection but as normative Christian godliness, the Puritan devotional machinery must have seemed to many New Englanders not an aid to natural spiritual growth but "a yoke upon the neck of the disciples which neither our fathers nor we have been able to bear" (Acts 15:10 RSV).

We have already commented on the "instrumentalization" of piety in Mather, in which the purpose is not the celebration of God's grace *for* the believer but rather the different methods of obtaining spiritual graces *in* the believer;

godliness is almost defined as a system of methods, rather than method being defined as an aid to the attainment of organic spiritual growth. One effect of this instrumentalization may be to divert interest away from God, the object of piety, and to fix the attention on the manipulation of the channels of grace. What results is a secularization of piety, in which the spiritual life which is normally centered on God and on mission is structured instead in an orbit revolving around the self. The goal of the pious individual becomes spiritual self-aggrandizement, the polishing of an image of devotional heroism, with God regarded as a kind of celestial parts department supplying the elements of a renewed nature, as the believer constructs the idol of his own sanctity.

But the typical Puritan preoccupation with devotional machinery that Mather exhibited is not simply the spiritual equivalent of the complacency of the body-builder. The sources of motivation here are much more complex. There is also an underlying element of anxiety that the Puritans shared with patristic spirituality, which made it natural for them to connect ascetic devices with Reformation *sola-fideism*, despite the historical and logical incongruities involved. Both for the desert fathers and the Puritans, the search for the way to find a gracious God that occupied Luther was always an open question; neither could maintain an assurance of God's favor without striving for heroic piety. Puritans could not permit themselves to relax in the honest confession that they were both sinners and believers in Christ, the essence of the fresh breeze of spiritual liberty that blows through Luther's *Galatians*. That way led to "antinomianism" and "cheap grace." Instead, they had to turn their attention away from Christ and the atonement and look inward, either for the witness of the Spirit or the marks of a gracious character.

Since there was always an element of subjectivity and uncertainty possible in these methods of assurance, the cultivation of rigorous spiritual discipline and heroic sanctity was necessary to quiet the conscience and calm anxiety. The ideal of sainthood exalted in Puritanism was that of the spiritual athlete, not the forgiven sinner released from sin and religious compulsion to be merely—but truly—human. The pressure toward exceptional sanctity was not wholly eased once believers attained assurance of their initial conversion since the question of God's immediate attitude toward them was not settled on the grounds of dependent faith but on the grounds of current spiritual performance and achievement. The Puritan whose sanctification was not making exceptional progress could anticipate providential judgments. In eighteenth-century life, the incidence of tragedy was frequent enough to keep Christians alert and anxious to become visible saints.

The goal of religious methodology should logically be either to strengthen or to express faith, which most Christian theology recognizes as the heart of piety. Some Puritan methodology was instead an expression of lack of faith, at least a lack of the kind of faith that might bring assurance of justification. An over-elaborated prayer life can indicate a lack of confidence in God, as Jesus indicated. And when the Puritan ideal of heroic sainthood was presented to a church of distracted laity as the norm of religious behavior, the result might have been not to challenge faith but to encourage despair. The ideal of superhuman piety that energized the founders of New England may have intimidated later generations and contributed to the decline.

On the other hand, there is a great deal in Mather's methodology that springs from a healthier piety and leaves modern readers who carefully examine him surprised and respectful. If the style of his meditations made Mather's spirituality baroque, it also made his thinking uniquely rich in apt quotations and solid theological perspective. His use of ejaculatory prayer is a simple expression of faith focused outward in very real concern for others. Even his more elaborated days and nights of prayer were often centered on intercession for world events that required lengthy consideration and prayer; in tackling these concerns Mather placed himself in the line of later leaders like Edwards and Wesley, whose natural pastoral sense embraced an ecumenical parish. The Puritan adaptation of the monastic regimen of prayer to the private devotions of individuals and families was just as vital an expression of organic piety in Mather's parish as it was later in Susannah Wesley's household.

Later Evangelical tradition altered the Puritan machinery in the same way that it transformed the pattern of conversion, keeping the essential structure of prayer and meditation but pruning and simplifying the luxuriant overgrowth of method. Even where Mather may have erred in accumulating such a complex methodology out of the whole tradition of Christendom, he is still an interesting and instructive model of catholicity; for his taste for piety almost led him beyond the wall separating Protestants and Catholics in his era and pointed the way toward the larger ecumenical sympathies of the future.

CHAPTER FIVE

The Godly Life

IN APPRAISING MATHER'S SPIRITUALITY AFTER EXAMIN-
ing his extensive methodology, we might be tempted to
summarize it with the phrase "Reformed orthodox asceticism": a form of Christianity in which medieval and patristic
devotional exercises have been imposed on a framework of
Protestant scholasticism. This characterization furnishes an
easy explanation for the intermittent periods of decline in the
Puritan experiential tradition, since it posits a built-in
catabolism in the movement that is bound to erode its vigor
periodically, whenever its orthodoxy and methodology
poison its mystical vitality. A number of interpreters have
adopted this theory, asserting that American Puritanism ultimately withered because, unlike Calvin, it did not have an
existential and personal definition of faith, but settled instead for a noetic and conceptual definition with the "testimony of the Holy Spirit" added as an afterthought.[1]

Although this theory is suggestive and illuminating, it
ignores the difference between the goals of Protestant experientialism and those of mere confessional orthodoxy. The
contrast is clearly visible in the intense conflict generated by
the Lutheran Pietist awakening, in which the orthodox
theologians bitterly attacked Spener and Francke because of
their efforts to make biblical truth subjectively real to the
common laity, while the Pietists in turn reacted with accusa-

tions of deadness and Pharisaism toward those who differed only minutely from them in conceptual doctrine. While the Puritans of Mather's generation had no dead orthodoxy to contend with other than that embodied in their own laity, and so spent their polemical energies against various forms of heterodoxy, the leaders of the Great Awakening had to contend both against Enlightenment erosion and orthodox brethren who were alarmed by their emphasis on Christian experience.[2] The Puritanism which inspired the Awakening in this country was, as we have said, neither mere orthodoxy nor rationalism, nor was it a compromise; it was a *tertium quid*.

And yet, doctrinally, the Puritan/Pietist movement had an orthodox bone structure.[3] How then did the spiritual goals of orthodoxy and Puritanism differ? Scholastic orthodoxy—both in Reformed and Lutheran circles—would have called persons spiritually healthy if their thinking was conceptually sound and biblical (or perhaps confessional) on the main point of justification and a great number of lesser ones, while their wills were fixed in some fairly consistent pattern of Christian morality, and their emotions were experiencing a combination of gratitude and the sense of dependence. Most Puritans would characterize this level of piety as at best minimal and quite possibly as an unregenerate state tempered by common grace.

The Puritan standard of piety and spiritual health differed in two respects: it was more existentially focused—it demanded a constant and pervasive practical reformation of a person's life—and it had a pneumatic element, a dimension of spiritual and supernatural vitality that lifted it out of the flat plane of the orthodox faculty psychology. Puritanism insisted that the spiritual life was distinctly supernatural, both in origin and in conscious experience. Individual saints were to be aware of exchanges between their own lives and that of the risen Christ, of communications and operations of the Spirit within the moving tides of their mental and motivational lives. Thus "devotion" or "piety" for the Puritan was not a sort of incidental glaze of emotional warmth which might be spread over the thinking and will of an individual, as it seemed to the orthodox. "Emotions" for the Puritans were merely epiphenomena. The important thing was the existential condition of the whole life: the grounding of mind, will, and feeling—and behind these, the heart, the central wellspring of consciousness—in a participation of the life of God. This supernatural enlivening was not merely an added enthusiasm, so that a healthy Puritanism would be defined simply as an energetic orthodoxy; it was a quality that not only motivated but also transformed and redirected thought and action, so that the mind actually thought differently using the same truths. The Puritans complained in their diaries of a "dead frame of spirit," even at times when the mind and will were straining to serve God; for "the power of godliness" was indissolubly connected with a sense of the divine presence.[4]

The precedence of "live orthodoxy" over "mere orthodoxy," and even over ascetic method, is clearly stated in Mather:

> What is true *Holiness?* Many mistakes have there been about that glorious thing: A man may be *Orthodox* in his *Perswasions,* and yet not be *Holy:* You may say of a Man, *That he has a Righteousness equal to that of the Scribes and Pharisees,* and yet the Man may be a stranger to true *Holiness* after all. O but when once it can be said of a Man, *He walks with God!* then, then *Holiness* is to be seen upon him.[5]

Here true holiness is not defined merely as a spiritually energized orthodoxy or orthopraxy. It is delineated as taking place in a context of personal confrontation with God and practical obedience to him. In a sermon on III John 4 ("I have no greater joy than to hear that my children walk in truth"), he places a very rich Johannine and nonpropositional content on the word "truth":

> To Walk in Truth, is to Lead such a Life, as we must and shall, when the Truth has a Lively Power on us. . . . To Walk in Truth, is to Walk under a Powerful Impression and Efficacy of the Truth. . . . To Walk in Truth, is, to Love this JESUS, and Receive Him, and put ourselves under His Conduct, in all our Walk. . . . Our blessed JESUS has told us; John XIV. 6. I am the truth. So then, To Walk in Him, is to Walk in the Truth.[6]

On the other hand, Mather is convinced of the necessity of a kind of orthodoxy, and his concept of sanctification makes extensive use of propositional truth. This truth, however, must be extracted from the text of Scripture, so that Mather, like the German Pietists but perhaps to a lesser degree, advocates a Bible-orthodoxy rather than a dogma-orthodoxy, as Brunner would say.[7] He regards biblical doctrine to be the backbone of genuine piety for two reasons.

First, he is convinced that biblically orthodox thinking is a touchstone of authentic spirituality. If the Spirit of truth has done any work of grace in human hearts, if their inward set of will is toward God, they will gravitate toward correct intellectual expressions of biblical truth and finally anchor upon these. "The more of *Godliness* there is in any Man, the more is the *CHRISTIAN RELIGION* without Controversy to him. . . . Yea, A WORK OF GRACE brings a Man Experimentally to *feel* the *Main Truths* which the CHRISTIAN RELIGION is composed of."[8] On the other hand, the converse is also true: an ungracious disposition of heart is at the root of departures from biblical faith, for *"Vice* does beget *Infidelity."*[9] But Mather does allow that a dead orthodoxy, in which biblical concepts held in the mind may be short-circuited by a vicious will and a Spiritless frame of heart, will also inevitably lead to ultimate heresy: "People *hold the Truth in Unrighteousness;* They do not joyn Practice with their *Knowledge:* Were the Truth more *Practised,* it would be less *Disputed.* . . . This provokes the Justice of Heaven to give them up unto *Strong Delusions.* . . . *Light* without *Flame* is the Scandal of our *Reformation;* the Ruine of all *Religion."*[10]

In the second place, biblical orthodoxy was important for Mather because, in the Puritan view, the progress of the whole personality in holiness was basically dependent on the entrance of truth into the mind: "You can't come to *Goodness* without *Knowledge.* . . . For 'tis by *giving us the knowledge of Salvation,* that God brings us to it."[11] Although Mather allows that sanctifying grace can enter the souls of irrational infants in the covenant without an accompanying understanding of the gospel, in the normal course of this world, truth is in order to godliness.

> Indeed, *Knowledge* is the first Thing, that is necessary in order
> to *Salvation*. . . . 'Tis an Erroneous and Pernicious Principle,
> That a Man may be Saved in any Religion, *if he do but* Live
> according to it. The Unerring and infallible Gospel has ex-
> pressly told us otherwise 2 Cor. 4:3 *If our Gospel be hid, it is hid
> unto them that be lost.* . . . We have not the least Intimation in
> the Book of God, That an unknown Saviour will be ours.[12]

So essential is propositional knowledge for the regeneration
of adults that nations not receiving the gospel must perish
eternally, since *"the Sun of Righteousness* visits them not. . . .
They are *destroyed for the lack of the knowledge* of the only
SAVIOUR."[13] What is here applied only to regeneration
Mather held as true across the whole spectrum of sanctification. While it is Christ, through his Spirit, who alone can
infuse spiritual life by an independent "Vital Work" in the
soul, yet he also uses propositional truth as an instrument to
precipitate conscious conversion, through a "Moral Work."

> It is the Good Pleasure of God, that the *Moral Work* of the *Spirit,*
> should accompany the *Vital Work* . . . and . . . that in the *Moral*
> Work . . . the *Gospel* should be His *Instrument.* So, for the
> Dividing of the Red-Sea, *Moses's* Rod must be lifted up. If the
> Souls of Sinners are *Dead,* unto what purpose is it then to
> *Prophesy* over them? It seems a very odd Thing to Address the
> *Dead.* . . . Yet the *Gospel* of the Lord *JESUS CHRIST* . . . 'tis the
> *Vehicle* in which the Holy *Spirit* of God comes to give *Life* unto
> them. . . . There is indeed an *Aptness* in the Gospel for this
> Excellent work. . . . When the *Spirit* of GOD *Converts* us, He
> deals not with us, as with *Stocks* and *Stones* that have no *Reason*
> in them. He deals with us as with *Men* . . . *Reasons* with us
> by His *Gospel.* . . . Tis true, Tis not enough to Enlighten
> our *Understandings:* Our *Wills* must be Rectified, as well as
> our *Understanding* Enlightened. Yet the *Spirit* of God accom-
> modates Himself to our *Nature,* when He brings us into a
> State of Grace.[14]

But just as correct propositional truth can be the instrument through which (or accompanying which) the Spirit
brings life into the soul, lies, or incorrect propositions about
God, can be the instruments of destruction when the mind
and will do not resist them: "Heresies may be such, as to
Extinguish the *Life of* GOD in the Soul, and ruin the Dependence both on the SON of GOD, and on the SPIRIT of
God, which must *accompany Salvation.*"[15] So strong is

Mather's connection of spiritual life and correct propositions about God that he can refer to *homo-ousios* as "a Term which saved the Life of the Primitive Churches."[16]

For Mather then, and for others in the Puritan and Pietist traditions, it was truth that set men spiritually free. Biblical truth focused by the Holy Spirit on the spiritual condition of the unbeliever was the instrument of regeneration and conversion. It was also the precondition of further growth in sanctification; it was the atmosphere of the godly life.

We have seen that Mather and other Puritans magnified the importance of regeneration, the initial stage of sanctification. This does not, however, imply that they neglected the subsequent stages, for Puritan literature offers the most fully developed treatment of sanctification and the Christian life in the English language. Mather's handling of this teaching, or at least his own example, has been judged to be eccentric. But this may simply be because he was more catholic than later observers, who perhaps were unacquainted with the existence of Protestant mysticism. When his practice is set against the Puritan and Counter Reformation theologies of Christian experience, his piety seems less exceptional for a Christian leader of his era.

As in classical Reformation Protestantism, Mather approached sanctification as a double process involving the mortification of sin and the vivification of purified areas of the personality. While the desert fathers and the early monastic writers had interpreted mortification and self-denial in the sense of a superficial asceticism, Augustine, with his deeper insight into the corruption of human nature, emphasized once again the interior mortification of the roots of sin rather than exterior penance.[17] Theologians in the Augustinian tradition, such as Calvin,[18] Owen,[19] and the Counter Reformation school of Berulle,[20] emphasized that the fallen nature in the Christian should not be domesticated or reformed or driven underground in some form of sublimated respectability, but had to be put to death and resurrected in a new life, no longer autonomous but under the control of the Spirit. Some advised the Christian to follow the *via negativa*, following the trail of indwelling sin into the

sources of motivation—and this is the predominant approach in Puritanism, as any reader of Owen's treatises[21] can
readily see—while others stressed the *via positiva*, concentrating on the virtues aimed at rather than vices to be exter-
minated.[22] In either case, there was a common recognition
that the ground of this process of mortification/vivification
lay in the mystical union of the believer with Christ in his
death and resurrection. The cross and resurrection were not
considered merely metaphors for psychological processes of
death and rebirth; the believer was felt to have an ontological
share in what happened on the cross and afterward, so that
the process of sanctification was as Christocentric as the
work of justification and found its center in the same
locus—the atonement.[23]

Puritan treatments of sanctification, however, were
often better at tracing the problems of indwelling sin than
they were in providing the Christological answer. Mather's
analysis of the lingering effects of total depravity in the
believer is typically Calvinistic: "The very best of our *Perfor-
mances* are Defective, are Defiled; let us do our very Best,
some Sin will still cleave unto it."[24] He is aware of the fact
that many gracious souls are still caught in deep-rooted
bondages of sin, that "the Soul, which has been truly Renewed
by the *Grace* of God, may have *Indwelling* Sin, with so much
Strength oppressing of it, that the *better Principle* shall be
scarce discernible. In some truly Regenerate Souls, the
struggles between the *Spirit* and the *Flesh* are so dubiously
managed, that one will have much ado to say, which overcomes."[25] The path of the growing Christian is therefore
not a series of glittering achievements of saintliness. "Alas,
the Highest that we generally reach unto, is, to have the
Desires of what we should reach unto. *Austin* truly observed,
That the *Life of a Christian is Little other than a course of
Holy Desires.*"[26]

This does not mean that the Christian is bound in a course
of sinful actions in quite the same way as the unregenerate
man, for "there is a difference between the *Consent* which a
Godly Man yields unto Sin, and the *Consent* given by a *Wicked
Man.* When a *Godly Man* Sins, his Fault rather lies in this,

that he does not *Deny*, than that he does *Consent*. As when a thing is put unto the *Vote*, a Man who does not *oppose*, but only *suspend* his *Vote*, in some sort, yields his *Consent*."[27] But the godly soul cannot rest easy in the presence of its own indwelling sin, rationalizing that this is an inescapable condition of earthly life.[28] And there is even a kind of evangelical perfection toward which the aspiring soul should strive and in which it should ultimately rest, for "Arriving to *Sincerity*, O *Walker* with GOD, thou art arrived at what may be esteemed a *Perfection* in thy *Walk* with GOD."[29] Mather felt that in a developed state of sanctification it is even possible for a person "to be inspired with an *Antipathy* to every known *Sin*."[30] He was far from limiting our continuing sinfulness to such isolated atomic actions of the will, however, and in his writings he probes into states of alienation from God that lie beneath the surface of consciousness, considering these to be the most serious forms of indwelling sin.

> Some of you may *Go Mourning* . . . in *Odious Corruptions* from which you would fain be delivered. An *Hard Heart*, This pains you, afflicts you, affrights you! An *Earthly Mind;* the *Chains* of that are galling to you. *Impurities* vex your Souls, make you weary of your Lives. Your *Sloth*, your *Pride*, your *Froward Anger*, the Squinting and Evil Eye of *Envy* haunting of you: These are cruel *Burdens* on you.[31]

In common with other Puritans, Mather carried over from the Catholic heritage the notion of the "besetting sin."[32] While he considered every part of human nature unrenovated by the Spirit to be uncontrollably averse to God and his ways, he believed that the various branches of sin are organized around a central trunk that is the "master sin." The enemies of our souls would be able to do us little harm, he says, if there were not "some peculiar *Lust*, like a *Trojan Horse*, within us, assisting of all their Enterprizes."[33] In identifying the most dangerous besetting sins, however, Mather is not "puritanical" in the popular sense of the word. Although he felt that there is a peculiar danger of defilement in sensual sins such as drunkenness and unchasteness,[34] and in sins involving hostility, he believed that the great trunk of the tree of human sinfulness lies in such radical evils as idolatry, "the *Principal Crime of Mankind*,"[35] and pride, for "every *Sin* (as one says of every *man*) hath a *Pope* in the *Belly* of it; something that *Exalts it self against all that is called* GOD."[36] So radical is this evil that God may even allow the soul to fall into more gross displays of corruptions in order to dry up the roots of pride:

> Since we have not been *Withheld* from some very *Enormous Out-breakings of Sin,* by this very Thing, we may and should be *Withheld* from One Sin which is very offensive to the most High God; such an Offense, that He *knows* them, & throws them *afar off,* and makes Rejected Lepers of them that are under the power of it; PRIDE is that Sin. It may be, our *Pride* caused our *Fall;* And now our *Fall* may cure our *Pride.* . . . If a *proud Thought* begin to rise in our Minds, we should presently retund it, with such a Stroke upon it; *What! Such a wretch as I, ever be proud of any thing!* When we meet with any *Contemptuous Treatment* among our Neighbours, we should now bear it very patiently. . . . And, when we see others *Overtaken with a Fault,* with what Compassion, with what Levity, with what Clemency, should we now dulcify the *Reproofs,* which we must give unto them![37]

It is odd that Mather's work has no extended treatment of the subject of recovery for the backslidden soul, which is a point of eminent importance for Catholic piety and post-Finneyan revivalism, and not unknown among Puritans.[38] He does often describe the condition, especially in his jeremiads; but his diagnosis here is usually lack of conversion. He does speak of the somnolent Christian, who still can say, "*I sleep, but my heart waketh.*"[39] But Mather's usual complaint about his unresponsive hearers is not that they are asleep but that they are dead. Thus, in his usage, backsliding does not refer to those lengthy detours from the road to the Celestial City which non-Puritan pastors have resigned themselves to watching patiently in their parishioners. These Mather would attribute either to lack of definitive conversion or to decay and apostasy from "common grace convictions" which never went the whole course to achieve a sound conversion.[40] The initial convictions that Puritans expected were supposed to penetrate very deeply in the mortification of human sinfulness, even down to the very roots of pride itself;[41] as Mather puts it, "A man is never truly Converted, except he be Converted from *Self*, as well as from *Sin*."[42] Those who could clear this kind of hurdle would form a small cadre of extremely dedicated laypersons.

Mather understood the Pauline doctrine of the grounding of the process of mortification/vivification in the believer's union with Christ in his death and resurrection, though he mentions it rather infrequently. Defining the nature of the *unio Christi*, he notes that it is not so purely mental or metaphorical that we have no real ontological connection with the Savior, and yet not so literal that we become part of the Godhead. It is a union that is most intimate, so that Christ himself is in us as a vital principle through the presence of his Spirit; and yet the exact nature of it is quite mysterious, like the union of the persons within the Trinity or the relation between the two natures of Christ.[43] In a few places Mather closely connects the process of mortification with this union. In a sermon on Romans 6:3, 4, he notes:

> We are by our *Baptism* obliged unto a conformity unto the *Death* of our *Buried JESUS*, and unto His *Rising* again; unto His *Death* in our *dying* to Sin; unto His *Rising* again in our *living* to GOD. . . . O! that I may feel the Virtue of His *Death*, in a *Death* brought upon all my evil Appetites; O! that I may feel the Virtue of His *Life*, in my being brought unto the *Life* of God, and so quickened from Him, that it may be *no longer I that live, but* CHRIST *living in me.*[44]

But in the majority of those occasions when Mather refers to the event of the cross and its relationship to the believer he is making use of it as a devotional lever to motivate the pursuit of mortification, rather than referring to the atonement as the source of power for the freeing of the personality from the grip of sin. Sometimes this leverage is gained through meditation on the sufferings of Christ, for "it hath been said, *Crux pendantis est Cathedra Docentis,*—thus, while you Behold Him *hanging* on the *Cross*, let Him *Teach* you *how to War*, and to *Fight*, especially against the *Sin which doth most easily beset you.*"[45] At times there is a development of the obvious allegorical relationship between the believer's mortification of sin and Christ's death.

> Let your *Principle Corruption* be put unto such a *Death* as your
> Dying Savior has given a Semplar of. . . . Handle it with
> *Severities* analogous to those which Jesus Christ was crucified
> withal. . . . Did they withdraw all *Refreshment* from our Lord
> Jesus Christ in His rueful *Agonies*. . . ? Just so Do you withhold
> from your *Lust* that *Sustenance*. . . . Did they *Torture* our Lord
> Jesus Christ . . . ? Do you make your *Lust* undergo the *Pains* of
> an *evil and a bitter thing*. Let it Cost you those Prayers and those
> Tears, and manifold *Austerities*, which may *tire* it out and Dis-
> courage it from *haunting* of you.[46]

Mather does not reflect that his hearers might tire more
rapidly than their sins. The note of asceticism here comes out
again in Mather's discussion of John Eliot:

> Never did I see a person more mortified unto all the pleasures
> of this life. . . . The sleep that he allowed himself, cheated him
> not of his morning hours. . . . Rich varieties, costly viands,
> and poinant sauces, came not upon his *own* table, and when he
> found them on other men's, he rarely tasted of them. . . . And
> for a supper, he had learned of his loved and blessed patron,
> old Mr. Cotton, either wholly to omit it, or to make a small sup
> or two the utmost of it.[47]

There is a testimony here to the strong hold which medieval
and patristic models of sanctification had on Mather. The
covert antipathy to sensory pleasure that always peers
around the edge of the Puritan ethic comes out again in a
diary passage in which Mather equates mortification with
denial of normal enjoyments: "Breathing in the midst of so
many *Deaths*, what can there be so needful and so proper for
me, as for me to *Die Daily*, and become a Man dead unto this
World; crucified unto all worldly Enjoyments and Impressions! I resolve . . . to be restless until I find a very sensible
and powerful Mortification brought upon all my Inclinations
for this World, and every Thing that is in it."[48] In *The Good
Old Way*, Mather admires the fathers for looking on the pleasures of eating and drinking as poisons, fasting to the point
of emaciation, and many other austerities.

By far the majority of Mather's references to mortification, however, deal not with the inward "putting to death by
the Spirit" of the roots of sin but with outward afflictions
brought upon us by providence as "crosses" which mortify

our sinful natures to a depth that could seldom be managed by the interior work of the Spirit alone. This interpretation of "bearing the cross" and self-denial was, of course, a familiar part of the Protestant tradition, much emphasized by Luther, as Mather notes:

> Luther call'd Affliction, *Theologium Christianorum;* A Christians learning of *Divinity.* And, It was a Good Speech of Luthers vertuous Wife, *There are many sweet Psalms in the Bible, and I had never known the meaning of the sweetness of them, if God had not brought me unto some Affliction.* Truly, In the Frosty Nights of our Troubles, more of the *Stars* of Heaven shine upon us, than at other Times.[49]

Mather even goes so far as to say that the largest part of the work of sanctification in our lives is done in the way of passive obedience under afflictions.[50] There are some lessons that will never be learned unless they are written into the spirit by the iron pen of providence.

> There is a *Moral Death,* to be pursued and obtained; A *Death* upon our Vitious Appetites; a *Death* wherein we shall have our *Lusts Mortified;* a *Death* in which we shall be *Dead with CHRIST,* and have nothing but a CHRIST left *Alive* unto us, in regard of any strong Relish in our Souls. . . . Our Faithful SAVIOR sends *Killing things* upon us; perhaps they are without a *Metaphor* so. He *Loves* us, when He *Kills* us.[51]

Of course, it is true that people can grow spiritually in conditions of happiness, since these also are tests of faith:

> Indeed, all the Providences of God unto the Children of men are *Probations.* . . . When we are *praised* by our Neighbours; we are Tried in those *praises.* And thus, when we are *blessed* by our Maker, we are Tried in those *blessings. Honours* from below, they do, *Indicare virum,* or *Try* what mettal the man is made of. . . . So *Mercies* from above, do the like. . . . So does our God bring us to the Rivers of plenty, and says, *I will Try them there.*[52]

But Mather inclines to feel that the best climates for spiritual growth are those in which the darkness and cold of affliction predominate, for "The growth of *Thorns* in This, is wisely ordered by Heaven, to prepare a Good Man, for another and a better World. . . . As Holy *Baines* Expressed it; *God is fain, with many Trials, to Smoke us out of the World.*"[53]

There is a poignant ring of personal experience in his treatment of one form of affliction, the endurance of slander, which he finds a very searching instrument for the mortification of his own acknowledged besetting sin, pride.

> If God single out *you*, to be made an Object of numberless *Indignities* and *Malignities*, and satisfy himself in beholding what is done to you . . . *there is nothing to be murmured at.* . . . It will be but a due compliance with the *Righteousness* of God, for you to confess before him, *That He is infinitely just in the greatest Injustice that any reproaching Man, can offer you.* You know so much amiss by yourself, that if it were all known abroad in the World, they who now *falsely speak* what is ill of you, might very *truly speak* what is a good deal worse. . . . Humble yourself deeply before God, for this *Secret Sin.* . . . I am sure there will need no long Divination, to bring you unto this one, sensible stroke of Repentance.[54]

He can grow positively enthusiastic over the sanctifying possibilities of hardship: "The *Delights* in thus *parting with Delights*, I tell you truly, you will find them Wonderful, Wonderful, Wonderful!"[55] But there is no sign in him of the notion that souls of a saintly temper will actively crave afflictions as penance, which is fairly common in Counter Reformation piety.[56] Yet, as he grows older, an almost stoical note creeps into Mather's sermons, most notably in *Tela Praevisa* (1724), an essay on foreseen troubles, which states that we should "Live in continual Expectation of Troublesome Changes."[57] In *The Religion of the Cross* (1714), Mather advises the readers to "Be *Daily* Thinking, *This Day, May for ought I know, bring some New Cross upon Me.*"[58]

As Mather's own life began to come under the pressure of losses and afflictions, there is a growing interest in his writings in the concepts of sacrifice and resignation. The sermon *The High Attainment* (1703), the first major treatment of this subject, is based on the doctrinal statement that "Resignation to the Will of God is a mark of eminent sainthood." Resignation is defined not as stoical apathy or patiently putting up with the vagaries of providence, however, but as a welcoming of affliction as a sanctifying aid, discerning God's hand behind it, affirming his continued love and goodness, and suppressing the murmurs of our wills. Mather includes a form for an "Action of Retired Christianity," "which by being *often done,* every time we do it, we shall gain more and more ground upon our *will,* and at length gain the point of a most *Resigned Will.*"[59] This "gaining ground" he speaks of many times as an increasingly complete yielding of the entire personality to the possession and control of the Holy Spirit.[60]

Mather rarely connected the progress of resignation in the soul with the *unio Christi.*[61] Generally, resignation is the human side of sanctification, in which the ego cooperates with the Holy Spirit in the passive mortification of its old life. By the end of his life Mather regarded this early formulation of "Let go, and let God" as both the royal road to sanctification and the mark of the highest degree of piety. It is the highest "Pitch of Elevated Christianity . . . *To Delight in Sacrificing of Delights: To Delight* in doing the part of *Sacrificers.*"[62] He himself speaks of the frequency with which he used the concept of resignation,[63] and Colman in his funeral eulogy notes this as almost a trademark of Mather's later ministry.[64] There are strong resemblances here to the teachings of Catholic Quietism, which, through the writings of Molinos, had a great deal of influence on Francke and Halle Pietism.[65] Mather hints at some sympathies in this direction: "The Incomparable *Tallents,* would sometimes ingeniously say, *The Quietists are the best Christians.* This I will say, A *Quietism,* that lies in a *Soul cured of all Sadness, by being Poured out before the Lord,* is Excellent *Christianity.*"[66] He can even admire a Catholic's lack of assurance for its quality of resignation: "It was a sweet speech that fell from the Pen of the Renowned Chancellour of *Paris, I don't know what the Lord intends to do with me forever, but this I know . . . He is worthy that I should Love Him & Serve Him, and I will do so.*"[67] In one place he entertains the *resignatio ad infernum* as a possibility.

> If such a Thought should come into thy Soul; *What if the Glorious and Righteous and Sovereign GOD, should for ever cast me off?* 'Tis not a thought indeed that we are call'd unto. But if uncall'd it thrust itself in upon us, Dost thou come to This; *Yet will I adore Him, and for ever silence all Murmuring against Him!*

> *Yea, I will take part with Him against my self; and be satisfied that*
> *He is glorified!*—The Holy SPIRIT of GOD will now undoubt-
> edly come in upon thee with His *Testimony: No . . . I will not*
> *cast thee off. . . .* Could a soul be sent into *Hell* with such
> Things in it, it would carry *Heaven* thither with it.[68]

There is some reservation here, however, which Mather
spells out elsewhere: "There is a Sacred *Indifferency of will,*
which we should maintain towards every thing, but the
Spiritual Blessings, which 'tis a *Cursed* Thing to be without."[69]
It appears from this that Mather concurred with Catholic and
Protestant orthodoxy in condemning extreme Quietism.

Besides the "act of resignation," there are a great many
other spiritual strategies for the pursuit of mortification that
Mather recommends. There is a kind of instantaneous, on-
the-spot meditation or "consideration" of various sorts, centered on God's continuing surveillance of our lives;[70] the
nature of sin and the fact that we are being tempted by the
Devil;[71] the person of Christ;[72] or the last things.[73] There is
also a constant and strenuous mental hand-to-hand combat
which must be carried on in the center of the personality to
repel sinful thoughts and thus check the seeds of full-grown
corruption, for "there is that *Spirituality* in the *Law* of GOD,
that it lays injunctions on the very *Thoughts* of Men: It lays
Restraints on the *First Motions of Sin* in the *Thoughts;* and
even dashes out the Brains of the *Bratts,* in the very *First*
Conceptions of them."[74] Along with an instant mobilization
against the outbreakings of indwelling sin, there is to be a
constant mortification of its inner substance—and particularly where it has massed itself in "besetting sins"—through
continually enlarging our understanding of the nature of the
particular sin and a deepening repentance for it. This is the only
effective means of getting at the roots of such eruptions, for
as we have noted, Mather's understanding of sin went far beneath the conception of it as visible and isolated atomic acts.

Mather's proliferation of methods for exterminating sin,
drawn from patristic and medieval sources, was a far cry
from later teachings on the "victorious life" which, following
Wesley, would stress the exercise of faith in Christ's finished
work and dependence on the Spirit, and treat the laborious

Puritan remedies as an attempt to "make perfect in the flesh what was begun in the Spirit" (Gal. 3:3 RSV). It is interesting that Spener and Francke anticipated Wesley's later teaching that sanctification as well as justification was a fruit of faith, and held that Christians could reach a state in which sin was present in but not reigning over their lives. Mather's occasional exhortations to "act faith peculiarly upon the death, blood, and cross of Christ," as Owen puts it,[75] have been lost in a profusion of other prescriptions; and at times it seems that where sin might be dispatched cleanly with one Christologically centered bullet, Mather advises us how to torture it to death with a variety of racks, boots, and thumbscrews.

On the other hand, there is hardly a strategy or practice he favored that is not biblically grounded. Later Protestant approaches may not quite do justice to the difficulties of sanctification, as if a physician were to attempt to cure all illnesses with wonder drugs without recognizing the parallel importance of proper diet, rest, isolation, and careful nursing. The Puritan medicine chest was crowded with centuries of theological folk remedies; but it recognized at least the seriousness and tenacity of the disease of sin in human nature and endeavored to attack it from all directions. It is also true that most of the methods Mather recommends are united in a common assumption, which is that the most important aids in the mortification of sin come through the channels of knowledge and understanding, that light kills the roots of sin, so to speak—continued piercing scrutiny of one's own makeup and of God's nature and his gracious provision. There is a recognition that without the Spirit's power all the knowledge in the world will not avail much; but the main exhortations are to seek a more and more deeply ingrained understanding of the doctrines of grace and the self that is mirrored in the application of the Law by the Spirit.

The relatively complete reflection of the Puritan approach to sanctification that Mather inherited is scattered through a fairly small body of his writing, whereas his concern for regeneration comes out in nearly every separate work he wrote. This may be partly due to the hypertrophy of conversion in his tradition. But it is also true that Mather's own temperament leaned increasingly away from the *via negativa* as his life progressed. He continued to regularly examine the roots of corruption in his nature; but increasingly he also looked outward, in that fascination for positive projects of good will for which he is famous. After 1709 his *Diary* ceases to record the details of his soul struggles and becomes an account of his weekly cycle of "Good Devices," in which the whole territory of his life is mapped into seven regions, just as a farmer divides his land into fields, with a day given to some project of planting or harvest in each area. Moving in this direction, Mather opened himself to the charge of moralism. We must now move on to examine the validity of this and certain other charges that have been made against him.

There is no doubt that Mather was in theory—and very often in practice—a dynamic activist. His interest in "essays to do good" began long before the shift in 1709 that transformed his *Diary* into an anthology of good devices. Samuel Mather says that the concept of "doing good" as an expression of godliness was with his father from his teens.[76] A note dating from Mather's eighteenth year records his new resolution "to have my *sett Times* for Meditations on that Enquiry, what is there that I may do for the Interests of God,"[77] which is just a simplified form of his later weekly cycle of searching for projects.[78] The essence of his later emphasis is found in *The Serviceable Man* (1690), a jeremiad on the threatening decay of New England which notes the activism of the enemies of God and calls for opposing action on the part of "those who would do good."[79]

Following the publication of *Bonifacius* in 1710, Mather's references to benevolent action become much more numerous and almost thematic for his later writing. In 1722 he describes the whole course of the pastoral ministry as a mission of servanthood in doing good to the community, which will promote the fullness of the Spirit in those who practice it.[80] In later years he defines "walking with God" and even "asceticism" in terms of ethical activism:

Walking has a *Motion* in it. In a *Life* of PIETY we are to be full of *Motion*. A good Man is never to be at a *Stand*. He knows the meaning of a *Standing fast*, but he knows not the meaning of a *Standing still*. . . . Walking is an *Exercise*. A *Life* of PIETY was called, [*askesis*], or, an *Exercise*, in the Language of *Primitive Christianity*. It is a life of *Asceticks* . . . 'Tis a *Patient continuance in well-doing*.[81]

The proximate influence on Cotton Mather's activism was undoubtedly the temperament of his father.[82] But the same quality is observable in Baxter,[83] and in fact the Puritan tradition from early pastors onward was essentially activistic, motivated by a theocratic community concern and a doctrine of vocation that necessitated the crowding of every waking moment with fruitful activity.[84] Its correlative emphasis on contact with God and the development of the inner life may seem to harmonize poorly with this fact, until we realize that for the Puritan mysticism and activism are intimately and organically connected.[85] But the same activism was present in the hurricane of civic and spiritual action that was Francke's Halle.[86] It is visible also in most of the figures involved in the Great Awakening, and the cultural transformation left in the aftermath of this movement is well known. It begins to appear that it was not just Mather who was an activist, but everyone who had anything to do with the Puritan/Pietist experiential synthesis. It is no accident that a nineteenth-century American Sunday School tract could present Francke in terms reflecting the purest Matherian activism:

He was never willing to suffer opportunities for doing good, to pass by unimproved. . . . And what may we learn from his history? One plain lesson is, that the amount of good which we may do, is immense. There was nothing that Francke attempted, which is not practical at the present day. We may labour for the salvation of our fellow-men, for the education of the ignorant, for the relief of the distressed, and for the extension of the knowledge of the gospel among the heathen. We may, like him, preach the gospel and circulate Bibles and tracts; and we too may have that faith which overcomes the world.[87]

If Mather's activism was not peculiar to himself, however, it is still possible to assert that there was something peculiar about the intensity and the motivational roots of it.

But the "ceaseless, driven activist" of Wendell's biography and subsequent portrayals is only one of several possible projections from the sources—and not the most likely one. It is not difficult to make a case for Mather as primarily a contemplative who spent most of his time laying out on paper the possibilities for action. We have noted that after 1709 he followed a cyclical pattern of meditation during the days of the week to think up new projects of benevolence. The cycle was as follows:

> I. *Lord's day* Morning . . . *What Service to be done . . . in the FLOCK. . . ?*
> II. MONDAY Morning, *what to be done in MY FAMILY?*
> III. TUESDAY Morning . . . Two *Quaestions* alternately. On the First Week . . . *What Service to be done for Christ, and my* RELATIVES ABROAD? . . . Every other Week, instead of my *Relatives,* . . . I singled out my *personal Enemies* . . . and considered, *what good may I do unto them?*
> IV. WEDNESDAY Morning . . . *What Service to be done for Christ . . . in the Country, or among other People?*
> V. THURSDAY Morning; *what Service in and for the* [RELIGIOUS] *SOCIETIES?*
> VI. FRIDAY Morning, what particular Objects of Compassion have I to do good unto? Here, I fill'd my *List,* successively, with *afflicted* People. And, I did what I could for them.
> VII. . . . SATURDAY Morning . . . *What remains to be done for the Kingdome of God in* MY OWN HEART AND LIFE?[88]

The orderly care and the generous spirit here are praiseworthy. Mather wanted to sound like an heroic activist on paper; he ended up sounding like a neurotic activist to his critics. He probably was neither, but simply a typically conscientious Puritan with a somewhat overdeveloped interest in letting his right hand know what his left hand was doing.

It has been suggested that Mather's activism was infected with Enlightenment moralism, though he paid lip service to justifying and sanctifying grace.[89] Taken by itself, *Bonifacius* does have a definite propensity toward moralism in that "the good" is chosen as the regenerate man's ethical goal rather than "the will of God." Mather says we are to be humbled because we have done so little good in the world, not because we have sinned against God.[90] It is true, again, that Mather in certain places makes a great deal of the Golden

Rule, "the most Refined MORALITY that ever was introduced among the Children of Men: The most Complete *Rule*
that can be given, to *Regulate* our *Manners*, and make us
Happy in one another. . . . This One Word brought into Num-
berless Affairs, MAKE IT YOUR OWN CASE . . . This One
Ingenuous Word, how powerfully would it correct and prevent Irregularities."[91]

But we misread Mather if we project on him the image of
the modern Protestant who "keeps the Golden Rule, the
Sermon on the Mount, and the Ten Commandments." For
Mather, the Golden Rule was not only a teaching of his
Savior; it was also written on people's hearts through general
revelation, and he despaired to see that Christians who pretended to hear the Spirit speaking through special revelation
were blind even to the light of nature. The sentiment is not
unknown to churchmen today who reflect on the millions of
parishioners' failure to see how they should "make it their
own case" in issues of social justice.

It is true also that Mather puts occasional emphasis on
the actions of Christ as a moral rule, in the manner of *In His
Steps*.[92] He will go so far as to say that "It is not the *Recitation
of a Creed*, but the *Imitation of a Christ*, that will make a
Christian."[93] But the context of these statements is so qualified with doctrinal buttresses that only by ripping them out
in isolation can they be turned to prove moralism. Mather
was bound to bring Christ into his ethics as well as his
soteriology. He was a great admirer of Thomas à Kempis,
and he placed a full mystical content in the concept of imitating Christ, which was evacuated in later moralism. And he
was aware of the misuse of this approach by Enlightenment
ethics:

> A *Christian* must not imagine, that when our Lord Jesus Christ
> came among us, the *Sole design*, or indeed the *Chief design* of
> His coming was to set us an *Example*. . . . It has been a *Satanic
> Stratagem*, to press the *Imitation* of Christ, with an intent
> thereby, to draw off the minds of men from Faith in the *Satis-
> faction* and *Propitiation*, of Christ. That the *Guiltiness* of the *First
> Adam*, and the *Righteousness* of the *Second Adam*, is no other-
> wise ours, than by *Imitation*, are two *Damnable Haeresies*. . . .
> There are *Incommunicable perfections* of the Lord Jesus Christ,

> wherein a *Christian* may not propose to Imitate Him. . . . In our
> Lord Jesus Christ, there is a *Fullness* of those Things, whereof
> the best of us can have but a *Little*.[94]

The dominance of moralism in English church life,
which Horton Davies brackets between the Act of Toleration
and the early years of the Evangelical Awakening, was
coterminous with most of Mather's career.[95] The main
characteristic of Anglican preaching within this period, as
Leslie Stephen points out, was a divorce between theology
and morality, and a specialization in the latter,[96] with a quiet
undercover rebuilding of the whole structure of religious life
on theological foundations which were Deistic, Socinian, or
Pelagian. We have already shown that Mather had a clear
vision of the changes going on in the underlying theological
strata and would have nothing to do with these. But he is
equally suspicious of the surface morality being preached.
Thus he faced the change of climate at Harvard University
with a grimace of distaste, and in *Malachi* asserts the primacy
of pure theology and spiritual experience over the new fads
in ideas and morals.

> The *Languages* and the *Sciences* should be brought into a due
> subserviency unto PIETY. What is not subservient, but rather
> inimical to the MAXIMS OF PIETY should be laid aside. And
> the common *Ethicks* especially thrown into the Rubbish. All
> *Academical Erudition* is but a splendid, and a noisy Ignorance;
> The *Philosophy* is but a *Morosophy*, which does not help to
> Restore fallen Man.[97]

In *Benedictus* (1715), a definitive essay on the nature of "a
good man"—"The *Best* Thing that any Man can have Spoken
of Him!"[98]—Mather smashes head-on into the Enlightenment concept of goodness.

> First; the *Foundation* must be *Laid Low* enough. The *goodness* of
> One who is a *Good Man,* begins with a deep Apprehension and
> Acknowledgement of his *Badness*. . . . 'Tis a *Regeneration* that
> makes a Good Man. . . . Having dug this *Low* for the *Founda-
> tion,* we must then see to it that there be the *Rock* in the
> Foundation. What I mean is, *A Faith* which brings us into an
> *Union* with our SAVIOR. . . . Our Savior has told us, Jn. XV 5.
> *Without me, you can do nothing*.[99]

The same theological substructure for morality—repentance, regeneration, faith in Christ, the implantation of "good principles" by the Holy Spirit—is present in countless other sermons. In reality, Mather rarely mentions goodness without qualifying the term theologically and spiritually, as he does in *Bonifacius*. Believers are to do good in order that "the Great GOD and His CHRIST may be more Known and Serv'd in the World,"[100] and because the new nature inclines to the good (*Bonifacius*, p. 23). Our first action must therefore be conversion to Christ (p. 36), our first duty toward our family is to secure their regeneration (pp. 53ff.), and in doing good to neighbors we must above all consult their spiritual good (p. 77).

One of the primary concerns we should have for our neighborhood is the welfare of the religious societies, which are tested engines for the spiritual revival (pp. 83ff.). The final section of *Bonifacius*, dealing with the duties of ministers, is almost an effort to meet the moralists on their own ground and wrestle them over to Christian foundations. It certainly is an articulation of a post-theocratic strategy, but it is a deeply religious strategy and has little to do with morals or politics considered apart from Christ. It is simply one of the earliest formulations of a concept that is quite popular today: the church is in the world not to dominate it but to serve it as the agent of a servant Lord. It would not be difficult to demonstrate that Mather's vision of this service was considerably better grounded in transmoral theological principles than is much current activism. The Puritan/Pietist synthesis detested both a dead and inactive orthodoxy and a theologically empty moralism.[101] When the followers of the tradition decayed, the synthesis broke down into sterile orthodoxies and barren moralism.

If the goals of Mather's ethics were Christian rather than moralistic, the norms by which those goals were achieved may strike us as legalistic. Mather was clear that initial justification is wholly a matter of faith and grace. Nevertheless, in examining Mather (and nearly any other Puritan) the modern reader has a disquieting sense of being haunted by the Law, of its having been reintroduced at some subsequent point in the believer's journey. And in fact it has been brought in again in order to guard against the various forms of Antinomianism, and to make sure the believer pays enough heed to legal sanctions to maintain the fear of the Lord and remain on the right track ethically.

The common Puritan belief that God would punish nations that were in covenant with him but involved in disobedience or apostasy, that "national sins deserve national judgments,"[102] is not exactly what is in question here. One cannot speak of a nation as being justified by faith. But Puritans carried over this theocratic concept of divine sanctions into God's dealings with the individual Christian. They rejected furiously the notion of penance—Mather calls the separation between *reatus culpae* and *reatus poenae* "a vain distinction" and maintains that in justification both the punishment and the guilt of sin are remitted[103]—and yet in practice they found that it seemed necessary for the ethical health of the community to brandish the penal rod occasionally. The difference, of course, was that what they threatened as the result of sin was not eternal death but temporal loss. Here is Mather's late and considered utterance against the Antinomian position as he saw it in contemporary English Christianity and in the Hutchinson affair:

> Men may be *Justified* for the *Life to come,* and yet by their Miscarriages come into such Ill Terms with Heaven, that they may in *this Life,* be Exposed unto Tremendous *Judgments* of God. Certainly, it becomes the Believer to maintain this Temper and Terror alwayes in his Mind; *O Lord, My Flesh trembles for Fear of thee, and I am* afraid of thy *Judgments. . . .*

> Sirs, There *is* Poison in the *Box,* let what will be in the *Title,* when it shall be thence Insinuated into the Minds of them who profess themselves *Believers,* That there is *no Fear of their being Hurt by, or for their Sins. . . .* Will it be *no Hurt,* if the *Grieved Spirit* of God withdraw from you? . . . *No Hurt,* for Him to leave you in the Dark, without the joyful *Seals* and *Hopes* of your Salvation? *No Hurt,* for Him to grant a Permission, that Satan shall fall upon you, hurry you into fearful Disorders, distract you with Terrors, Persecute your Souls, do horrible Things upon you?[104]

Mather does not hesitate to differ with the Reformers themselves in this matter:

I wish, that the Renowned *Luther* himself had foreborn some Rhetorical, and Hyperbolical *Expressions.* What a *Violent Sound* is there, in his, *Fide homo sit Deus.* . . . . Unto *Rash Expressions* I would annumerate all those, that have a tendency, to Extinguish that *Sorrow for Sin,* and to Discourage and Enfeeble that care to *Work out our Salvation with Fear and Trembling,* which ought alwayes to be Cherished in the People of God. It is ill done, to Speak . . . as if *God could see no Sins in His people,* and, as if *their Sins could not ly under the Anger of God* . . . and, as if *nothing we do in Religion will conduce a jot unto any Good Ends* . . . Or, as if God were *never displeased with the Sins of Believers, nor pleased with their Graces or Duties.* These are *Unsanctified Expressions,* and inimical to *Sanctity.* [105]

Mather notes the *Mollification* and *Irenic* which Witsius had written to explain such statements, but he cannot understand why people use such expressions if they need such explanation after they have been spoken. [106]

In *Agricola* (1727) Mather says, "When we have *Repented* of our *Errors,* there will be the *Harrow* of *Affliction* oft drawn over us"; [107] and in the *Magnalia* he warns that parents may expect disasters to come upon their children because of old sins of uncleanness of which they have insufficiently repented. [108] He does not find the biblical example of David at all comforting in this respect, but only muses on the additional guilt David has incurred by emboldening countless others into uncleanness through the record of his sin with Bathsheba. [109] He was a firm believer in mortal sins, that is, "sins unto death," which draw down upon themselves the ultimate temporal punishment. [110]

On the other hand, there are occasions when Mather goes directly against the grain of this teaching when he is seeking to comfort bruised consciences. Though he constantly implies that God will judge us openly in such a way as to intimate the nature of our provoking sin—that if, for example, we slander, we shall find ourselves slandered, and if a child goes wrong, we have cause to test our own past dealings with it—Mather recognizes that there is something potentially dangerous in this counsel. "There is one thing in the 'judgments of God' whereof we should always be afraid; that is, lest we do make an injudicious interpretation of them. It is a caution given to us, in Psal. xxxvi. 6: 'Thy judgments are a great deep, O Lord,' and we should be very cautious, lest we drown our selves in such a *deep*, when we go to fathom it."[111] And in *Menachem:* "Some Things may have the *Appearance* of *Good Signs* upon them, which yet are not *Really* so. Some Things may to *Appearance* look like *Ill Signs*, and yet be *Tokens for Good*. Wherefore, when you Judge of *Signs*, beware of passing a *Rash Judgment* upon them."[112]

Speaking to those "fainting under trials," he denies the punitive nature of the misfortunes sent by providence: "Our *Adversity* now comes, not so much to *Revenge* our Sins, as to *Reform* our Sins."[113] Passing on to his congregation the comforts he has obtained from God in the aftermath of a series of deaths in his own family, he muses, "Why the Holy God, will bring a *Night of Affliction* upon any of His Children? . . . It is to give us Opportunity for our *Songs in the Night.*"[114] He goes on to add, *"Our GOD LOVES us too well, to hurt us in the worst that He shall do unto us."*[115] While he never abandoned the legal emphasis that sought to motivate godliness by the fear of divine retribution, often in later years he moved out into the sunlight of evangelical gratitude, admitting, " 'Tis impossible for *Piety* to have a greater Enkindler than this; a *Perswasion* of our share in the Love that our SAVIOR has unto His People."[116] In this context, adversity comes as gift and not as punishment: "Whatever does advance our PIETY, brings with it the *Love* of our SAVIOUR to us."[117]

It is interesting that Richard Baxter abhorred as a form of "counterfeit holiness" the "bondage of fear" produced by some forms of Puritanism.[118] Despite his affinity for most Puritan emphases, Francke shared the same caution about this matter and urged ministers to explain often

> the Difference betwixt a Legal and an Evangelical Frame and Principle of Religion; or betwixt that slavish Fear, by which alone it is that some Persons, even of a serious Turn of Mind, are forced and dragg'd as it were to their Duty, and that Evangelical Newness of Spirit, that filial Love to God and Delight in his Service, which usually grows and flourishes in the Soul where it is once planted, and which produces a free, unconstrained and acceptable Religion.[119]

The other sense in which the word legalism is often used is that which defines it as ethical guidance by biblical rules, issuing in the development of an involved casuistry. Parallel-ing the development of dogmatic, natural-law casuistry in the Counter Reformation, there was a wide growth of Protes-tant biblical casuistry, localized particularly in English Puritanism and Dutch Precisianism. This was the product of a confluence of two streams: the approach to the Bible that treated it as a codebook of law, tracing back to the Zwinglian Reformation in Zurich;[120] and the continued reliance on medieval casuistry among Anglicans and Puritans alike (the contemporary Jesuit work on this line was spurned).[121] Per-kins and Ames as the founders of Puritan casuistry and Baxter in his *Christian Directory* (the summation of their work and the most widely influential manual of its kind) took the earlier casuistry and sought to reground it on authority that was strictly biblical in nature. Thomas Wood contends that Puritan "cases of conscience" differed from their counter-parts in Counter Reformation moral theology because Puri-tan casuistry was seriously looking for the precise will of God in every situation and not perpetually running interfer-ence for the bound human will by searching for moral lowest common denominators.[122] The importance of casuistry for Puritans as an instrument for godliness is indicated by Wil-liam Ames' opinion that it was exactly what was needed to prod the stolid orthodoxy in the Netherlands into a state of revival.[123]

We have already referred to Mather's fondness for the casuistry of the early fathers and especially that of Origen, who is in a sense the godfather of Puritan legalism. Mather was just as fascinated by rules for right living as he was by rules of devotional growth, and he urges his hearers to "gov-ern the little that remains of your Lives, by the *Rules* of *Him that is from the Beginning.*"[124] The primary source of these rules is, of course, Scripture.[125] Mather entirely identifies the fulfillment of biblical commands with ethical completeness: "No Works are Good, but such as are contained in the *Two Tables* of the *Ten Commandments.*"[126] This is an application of Puritan divine-right legalism, normally directed toward the sphere of worship, to the whole of ethics. Any position softer than this he denounces as antinomian.

The Puritan legal approach to ethics is, of course, most famous for its legislation on apparently indifferent—or at least debatable—matters in the spheres of dress, mores, and recreation. What the Puritans did in this realm was simply to take a mass of scruples from the early fathers, which medieval Christianity had domesticated by transforming into "counsels of perfection," and let them loose again on the laity by establishing them as norms of ordinary Christian living. From the early eighteenth century on there was a ferocious reaction against this among disgruntled secular leaders of English culture, although Anglican authorities did not dare lose face morally by taking lower ground, and they adopted the alternate strategy of attacking the Puritans for Calvinistic indifference to the moral behavior of the elect.[127]

Puritans varied in the strictness with which they stuck to the guidelines of their precisionism. Mather's grandfather John Cotton, for instance, was quite mild on the subject.[128] Baxter was also moderate, and Doddridge, at the beginning of the eighteenth century, was extremely casual about legal minutiae.[129] However, the Continental Pietists, under Puritan influence, moved in the opposite direction. In the Dutch stream inaugurated by Ames—though Teellinck concentrated more on inner development and less on legal forms—Ames, Lodensteyn, Voetius, and Cocceius were quite strict.[130] Spener noted that one of the things that should characterize true Pietists was a willingness to give up their Christian freedom in some minor matters; but he was generally lenient, merely indicating that some forms of art and activity had been corrupted, though they were not intrinsically wrong.[131]

Francke and the early Halle Pietists, however, were more legalistic, perhaps more so than many Puritans.[132] Francke concluded that the common orthodox *"alla-modischen Christ-tenthum"* was willing to go along with political necessity in condemning gross sin that threatened the life of the community, but was too cowardly to attack refinements such as cursing, alcoholism, prostitution, the dance and the theater, because the wealthy nobility engaged in these and profited from them.[133] Some schools of later Pietism, however, such

as the healthy and moderate Württemburg group represented by Bengel, were more balanced.[134] Most commentators admit that the legalistic reaction of the later Pietists
was understandable in view of the corrosive moral drift of
the early eighteenth century: a legal response was as yet the
only kind Christians historically had known how to give.[135]

Like Francke, Mather was a full advocate of Puritan
"precision." The good Christian must be "singular," he says,
both because of the extreme depravity of the surrounding
non-Christian world and because Scripture commands the
believer to be "peculiar" (I Pet. 2:9).[136] In choosing which
side to take on some practice that is in question, he advises
abstaining even from practices that *might* be lawful, because
they may be *"Snares in Lawful Things."*[137] And then, of
course, the consistent disciple "will even abridge himself of
some liberties which he might lawfully take, if the *Liberties*
prove stumbling-blocks to a fellow-Christian."[138]

Mather did recognize that there is such a thing as
"Christian liberty."[139] But the "Mosaic yoke" from which we
are now released is apparently limited to the ceremonial law
of the Old Testament. He freely accepted the Puritan elaboration of a whole new legal apparatus of "clean and unclean
practices" through the use of casuistry. Among these there
were three matters that were absolutely prohibited: dancing,
the theater, and gambling. He launches out in *A Cloud of
Witnesses* against the first of these supported by an army of
authorities summoned up out of every party in the church's
history: the Westminster *Larger Catechism* under the treatment of the seventh commandment; the fathers (Chrysostom, Ambrose, Augustine); virtuous pagans (Scipio Af-
ricanus, Sallust, Cicero, Seneca, Plutarch); Reformed councils
in France, Poland, and the Netherlands (the Synod of Dort);
Church of England divines (Downame, Babington, Andrewes, Usher); and even a few "papists."[140] The severity of
Puritan casuistry was obviously not unique among Christians. Mather condemns the theater as another school of lust
condemned by many of the same authorities,[141] though he
does not refer to the original rationale for Puritan condemna-
tion of the theater, namely, the origin of this art form in the

worship ceremonies of the Greek idolaters. He objects to the use of cards, dice, and other games of chance not so much because of the social dangers of gambling but for a theological reason: they make a mockery of the sacred use of "the lot," and they violate the concept of divine providence either by bringing in a pagan concept of "fortune" or by recognizing God's control over the dice but involving his activity in an essentially trivial affair.[142]

There are a number of other items that Mather considered lawful but subject to very careful control and moderation. In the matter of apparel, it is well known that he found nothing inconsistent in following the current fashion and wearing a wig himself, to Judge Sewall's intense disgust.[143] But in most cases he carried on the Puritan tradition of severe modesty in clothing, especially female clothing.

> Now this is One Argument which the *vertuous woman* has against the *Painting* of her face or any part of it; *It is the Guise of an harlot.* An *Adulterate* Complexion, is but agreeable to an *Adulterous Condition.* A *Painted Face* is but a *Painted sign* hung out for advice to Strangers, that they shall find Entertainment there. Tis often the *Whours Forhead* which admits Paint upon it. Tis well, if you don't find a *Snake,* where you see a Painted Skin! . . . And alas, what a World of Time, is thus thrown away, by poor Creatures, who are so taken up with *Painting* of the *Sepulchres* in which their *Souls ly Dead;* as that they do Little or Nothing for the Beautifying of those *Black,* Forlorn, Forsaken souls![144]

There must also be careful self-control in monitoring one's own literary diet, for "*Play*-books, and *Jest*-books, and *Novels,* and *Romances,* the Volumns of *Satans Library,* will be none of the best *Companions* for you. . . . Your Appetite for the *Bible* will be notoriously palled; You will be seized with a sort of Loathing for the *Manna* of Heaven."[145] In one's own family, and regarding the household servants this control may go so far as an actual censorship of reading material.[146] Similarly, Mather advises Christians to "avoid ill companions" just as they shun corrupting literature.[147]

With regard to those shibboleths of the post-Finneyan revivalist tradition, tobacco and alcohol, Mather is, like most Puritans, cautious but moderate. He considers the use of tobacco a lawful thing,[148] but one in which the Christian should be "Excessively Moderate."[149] He is also tolerant of a controlled use of alcoholic beverages, for "the Great *Basil*, very justly declares, *That we cannot exactly prescribe unto all men, just what they shall Eat or Drink, because of their very different Constitutions.*"[150]

> I would be so understood, that the ABUSE and EXCESS of the Liquor, is all that is complained of. It is a *Creature of God*, that comes into the *Charter*, that we have in the first Epistle to *Timothy*. . . . *It is good, and not to be refused, if it be received with Thanksgiving.* One way of spoiling a *Reformation*, is by *Overdoing*. . . . Men may *receive with Thanksgiving* such *Refreshments* as the Compassion of Heaven has thus provided for them. Only, Let them do nothing that is contrary to *Thanksgiving*. . . . Certainly, Men don't express their *Thankfulness* to God, when they Debauch themselves."[151]

But he condemns the practice of drinking healths,[152] along with all indulgence that leads to actual drunkenness, for "the *High Feeding*, and the *Hard Drinking*, so common among the *Christians* of our Dayes, is fearfully condemned by the *Rules* of the *Christian Religion*."[153] He comments that "it may be, God will sooner give away the country to *Papists*, than let it be possessed by a Generation of *Drunken Protestants*."[154] Mather was not utterly set against the use of taverns, but he was concerned that they be run with what might be termed Christian responsibility.[155]

Mather became increasingly alarmed by the social consequences of the West Indian rum trade, which led him to utter a vigorous blast against hard liquor in a 1708 publication, appropriately called *Sober Considerations*. "Rhum," he says, is "a flood out of the dragon's mouth," since it wounds the soul, causes mental deterioration, brings poverty, destroys the family, and breaks down the whole fabric of society. Mather was especially concerned because the traders were peddling the liquor to the Indians, who, as he notes, were especially subject to a destructive addiction to it: "*Satan* had a *Strong Hold* of these doleful Tawnies before, but by the *Drunkenness* . . . there is no small Strength added." The worst thing about this situation was that it made the Indians averse to the gospel.[156] In the face of this threat, Mather begins to sound a little more like a nineteenth-century "temperance" crusader: "A branch of the *River of Death* is turning in upon us. . . . But, after what a *Contemptible Manner,* does our Grand Adversary propose to Ruine us, that a liquor of so diminutive, so dishonorable, so disreputable a Character, that a Minister even blushes to mention the *Name* of it, should be the *Instrument* of the Ruine!" (p. 3). And yet Mather was not a prohibitionist or even an advocate of total abstinence: "I should *Overdo,* if I should say, Let none be brought into the Country; or, Let no body taste a drop of it, if it be here. Tho' I am sufficiently a stranger to the use of it, my self; yet I can readily yet allow, its being of a manifold use, both as a *Medicine,* and a *Cordial*" (pp. 5, 18).

But the very integrity of the Puritan biblicistic legalism kept Mather from following the practice of nineteenth-century revivalism, which extended the list of forbidden adiaphora to cover all forms of alcohol, tobacco, and even (in Finney's case) coffee and tea. In their biblical casuistry, the Puritans were not just searching for points of behavior in which a Christian could be "separate" from the world and marked out as different; they were searching for biblical norms of behavior that would preserve Christians from the contemporary cultural decay. Later generations retained all of their strictures but quite often forgot the real theological rationales behind them and added new ones to produce a taboo-morality very similar to the Levitical code. Mather would have been aghast, as Hodge was, at the "temperance" movement's substitution of grape juice for the wine of the Lord's Supper, because this measure violated biblical casuistry and improved on the wisdom of the Bible by the introduction of a chain of human reasonings derived from current social need.

Even the more restrained casuistry of the Puritan fathers can easily strike the modern observer as a dry and forbidding Pharisaism. Beyond their rules, however, the Puritans were supremely interested in the experience of communion with God. The seventeenth-century Puritans acknowledged some kinship with the Catholic "Mistical Divines," who kept alive spiritual religion in the midst of papal darkness.[157] The con-

nection is even more clearly visible in the Continental
Pietists, who inherited from Johann Arndt a mystical emphasis conditioned and modified by the thought of Luther.
Francke defined the goal of the Christian life as "the closest
communion with God,"[158] to be reached in the process of
prayer, and referred to his own thinking as a true "Mystical
Theology."[159]

There are, however, distinct differences between most
Puritan/Pietist mysticism and normative Catholic mysticism.
Augustine, and later medieval mystics, conceived of union
with God as the product of a long process of ascent in which
the soul is gradually purified of carnal and sensual components and made fit for the vision of God. In the high Middle
Ages this process was codified by Bonaventura into a standard "triple way," consisting of successive purgative, il-
luminative, and unitive stages, accomplished by meditation,
prayer, and contemplation.[160] While there are slight traces of
the triple way in a few thinkers associated with Puritanism,
the main stream of Puritan thinking, in its treatment of
sanctification, either abandoned the three stages or else reversed the order of them, beginning with the *unio Christi* as a
basis for spiritual growth and proceeding through the illumination of faith to the mortification of sin.[161] It may, of
course, be argued that in its concept of regeneration
Puritanism simply reintroduced the triple way in a very
condensed form, leading not to mystical contemplation but
to assurance of salvation. Whether or not this is the case,
in its development of the concept of communion with God
subsequent to regeneration Puritanism tended to carry over
the mystical concept of communion with God as a "mountain-
top experience" which had to be achieved by hard human
labor, by ascending to God through meditation and prolonged prayer undertaken by the individual in comparative
isolation from the world. It is true that the pilgrim begins at
the foot of the mountain as a justified sinner forgiven by God.
Assuming that he has achieved assurance of salvation, he is
not working his way up to forgiveness, in the pre-Reformation pattern, but simply toward more sensible contact with
God. Catholic mysticism distinguishes between "acquired

contemplation," contemplative prayer produced by our own activity aided by grace, and "infused contemplation," the experience of God given directly by the Holy Spirit apart from our own devotional efforts; and these concepts are also useful in defining Puritan practice. Like the mystics of the Counter Reformation, Cotton Mather spent a good deal of time working his way toward communion with God, always recognizing that this acquired comtemplation might not result in the sovereign gift of infused comtemplation.

The hours Mather spent in secret prayer indicate that he shared the medieval concept that communion with God is best developed in isolation, in a condition of "retreat" from the world, although this is out of accord with his common image as a frenetic activist. What he claims to have experienced in his meditation and prayer closely resembles what is reported in Catholic mysticism:

> The *Joy* of the *Heavenly World*, a little of it, breaking into the Mind of a Beleever, while he is yet on *this side of Heaven*, Oh! It Ravishes him! It Amazes him! It even overcomes him! He is not able to subsist under it. It is unsupportable. It makes him cry out, *Lord, stay thy hand!* If the *Joy* be so Exuberant, when a *little* of it here *enters* the soul, what will thy *Joy* be, O *Faithful Servant*, when thou shalt *Enter into the Joy of thy Lord!*[162]

Mather thus agreed with most Catholic mystics that mystical experience involves a certain wear and tear on the psyche and even the physical health of the subject.[163] He also concurred with the older mystical tradition in describing the experience itself as literally unreportable, either because it is unlawful to do so or because the experience cannot be precisely recalled or put into human language.[164] "*What is that Fulness of God?* . . . This *filling*, truly it is a thing better *felt* than *spoke*. . . . It is one of the unutterable *things*, yea, it is one of the *unfathomable things*. . . . We may say, as in I Cor. 2:9, *Eye hath not seen it, nor Ear heard it*. . . . Not accurate Scholarship, but *experimental Christianity* alone will help us to conceive of these things."[165] These joys more than compensate in Mather's mind for the ascetic discipline of Puritanism: "The Great GOD has more Sublime, Celestial, Rapturous *Consolations* for us, than any of this World. . . .

Ah, my Young People; when you have thought, that the ways
of *Religion,* were Severe, Austere, Morose, and *Melancholy*
wayes; That you must never See a *cheerful Minute* more, after
you become *Seriously Religious;* It was a *Lying Devil* which
told you so."[166] The center of delight in all these experiences
is the vision of God himself, conveyed by the illumination of
the Holy Spirit:

> There are *Delightful Enjoyments* of the Blessed God . . . when
> His *Glory* appears unto us, glitters before us . . . His *good Spirit*
> . . . gives us strength through our Faculty to discern the *Glory*
> of that Object, *which no man hath seen at any time, or indeed can
> see.* . . . We have that privilege; Eph. 1:18, *The Eyes of your
> Understanding being enlightened.* . . . *Happy, Happy, O Glorious
> One, Happy are thy Servants, who stand before thee, and see thy
> Glory!* That Problem, *What, and where His Blessedness;* can have
> none but that Solution; Matt. 5:8, *Blessed are they that see God.*
> . . . *Truly the Light is sweet, and a pleasant thing it is for the Eyes
> to behold the Sun!* But how *sweet* is it then . . . for our *Eyes* to
> behold Him who made the Sun, who is the *Father of Lights,* and
> before whom the *Sun* it self is but a Lump of *Darkness!* A
> *Mathematical Demonstration;* So *Delightful* it is unto the Stu-
> dents of the Mathematics, that they are even transported with
> it. But what then is the *Contemplation* of the Blessed GOD,
> when He causes *His Goodness, and His glory* to pass before
> us![167]

The quality of awareness of communion with God in
Mather's experience is by no means eccentric within the
Puritan tradition. In commending this practical mysticism
to the laity, he was simply following the common teaching of
the early Puritan devotional manuals and the great writers on
the person and work of the Holy Spirit—Richard Sibbes and
John Owen. When Edwards defended the validity of the
Awakening experience in Northampton, he pointed to the
fact that the converts were moving from a dead conceptual
orthodoxy into this kind of Spirit-illuminated vision of God,
which had become a normative goal within Puritanism.
There was a distinctively Protestant flavor to this mysticism.
It was not supra-intellectual contemplation in the pseudo-
Dionysian tradition; it was based on the Reformation concept of the illuminating work of the Holy Spirit, "opening the
eyes of the heart" so that biblical truth became a transparent

medium revealing the glory of divine reality beyond the conceptual symbols. It was not aimed at stirring up "feelings" or "emotions" in the common sense but at the sudden exercise of a hidden faculty of the soul, in which the presence of God became intuitively known.

Nearly all of Mather's recorded mystical experiences contain a strong component of the personal assurance of God's love for him, and more specifically his purposes in Mather's ministry.[168] Mather was very conscious of his vocation as a writer and very earnest in seeking particular assurance from God on the success of this. It is interesting that in the middle and latter 1690s, when Mather's ministerial and writing careers were just beginning to open up into full stride and he was working on his acknowledged masterpiece, the *Magnalia*, he recorded an unusual number of experiences of assurance that God was going to make an extraordinarily broad use of his talents.[169] In many of these instances, as he indicates in the *Diary*, there is a high degree of outward-directed appreciation of God as he is in himself:

> This Day after my *public Labours,* retiring into My Study, at the Evening, I there cast myself prostrate in the Dust, on my Floor before the Lord. And there, a *wonderful Thought* with an *Heavenly Force,* came into my Mind; That *God loved my Lord Jesus Christ* infinitely, and had given Worlds unto Him, and made Him the Lord of all; and, that I had, thro' the Efficacy of His Grace upon mee, my Heart exceedingly sett *upon the glorifying of my* Lord Jesus Christ and was entirely devoted unto Him. Hereupon, an *unutterable Joy* fill'd my Mind, from *Assurance,* that God, for the Sake of my Lord Jesus Christ, had *great Things* to do for mee; that Hee would even *delight* in mee, and delight in *using* mee, and use mee in *eminent Services* for Him, who is dearer to mee, than all Things (I, 255).

But here again there is an almost indissoluble admixture of self-reference in the mystical experience. The last sentence might either be the extremely full expression of outgoing love or the extremely intricate transformation of *agape* into a form of self-interest. It is interesting that in later years, in the midst of a series of "killing things" in his family and in public life, Mather's ecstasies more and more take on a tone of sober reality, and their theme becomes self-emptiness.

> I behold myself in the Condition of one that is nailed unto a *Cross*. A Man that is *crucified,* endures very *uneasy Circumstances,* and has all possible Indignities heaped upon him, and finds himself stript of everything he had in the World. . . . My Spirit is reconciled unto this Condition; tis welcome to me, in regard of the glorious Designs which my SAVIOUR has, in ordering for me such a Conformity unto Himself (II, 476).

Mather is first brought to the point of willingness to sacrifice all the memorials of his earthly fame, such as his *Diary* (II, 514-515). Later he comes to the sacrifice even of the spiritual goals and rewards of his career: "I am content, that I see no Reward of PIETY in the whole Time of my Pilgrimage upon Earth; and that none of my Prayers have such Answers here given to them, as I could have wished for" (II, 641). It seems that Mather himself gradually became aware of some admixture of religious selfishness in all his previous life. The purging he describes is interestingly similar to the weaning process described by John of the Cross, in which the night of the senses mortifies the soul's attachment even to spiritual joys and blessings. And yet Mather did not ultimately destroy the diaries. A comment he made near the end of his life indicates that his experiences were not unknown to the public, and were even used in his enemies' attacks; but these he would not sacrifice: "A Man in black, may deride these Things, under the Name of, my *Extasies,* but, I bless GOD, I know the Meaning of them" (II, 774-775).

A special form of spiritual experience with which Mather was much preoccupied, and which often occurred to him in the ecstasies of his early years, was what he called the "particular faith." There were times when Mather would feel himself irradiated by the divine presence in the course of intercessory prayer, and persuaded by this to entertain not just a "general faith" that his prayers would gain some response from God but a "particular faith" that the answers would be positive. Mather derived his early belief in particular faith directly from his father, but the concept seems to have been common in New England Puritanism from the founding of the Massachusetts Bay Colony. Experiences of this kind occurred in the lives of John Cotton,[170] Thomas

Hooker,[171] and John Wilson;[172] and Mather even speaks of whole congregations having such impressions.[173]

In his early years, and especially toward the turn of the century, Mather had a profusion of such ecstatic assurances in connection with his concern about a preaching journey (*Diary*, I, 272), the arrival of a ship from Europe (I, 280), the publication of one of his books in London (I, 282), the growth of his congregation (I, 317), and many instances involving the birth or health of children (I, 294, 303, 307, 340, 345, 376). Of course, Mather might easily mistake his own enthusiasm for the assurance of God in such matters. He himself began to suspect that something on this order might have occurred after a few of his assurances failed to come to pass, especially his conviction that his father would make a second diplomatic journey to England (I, 303, 328, 353-356, 400), and a subsequent persuasion that his second wife would recover from an illness (I, 434, 435, 437, 453-454). In March of 1705 (6) Mather noted that he was still experiencing particular faiths, though the miscarriage in 1700 of his strong assurance about his father's trip made him now "rather shy . . . of any thing having such a Tendency" (I, 555). In 1707 he was still, almost against his will, being invaded by particular faiths, and he comments:

> On the one side, the Defeat I have once had in Particular Faith, has long rendered me afraid of ill-founded Enthusiasms; and it may bee, too ready, even to shake off some Impressions and Influences from the angelical Quarter, on my Mind. On the other Side, it is possible, that my great Sinfulness, and Sloth-fulness, and Filthiness, and my forward Indisposition to attend unto such Things, may deprive me, of many Communications from the heavenly World with which I might otherwise be favoured (I, 594).

After this point, however, there are no more *Diary* entries on the subject, and Mather seems to have adopted a studied caution with regard to it, at least in his personal life. Although he had formerly recommended that the laity seek after such assurances,[174] he cautioned in 1709 that "It is a *Jewel* so easily *Counterfeited*, (they who have thought they have had it, have sometimes been imposed upon)."[175] The warning about counterfeits is reminiscent of Edwards, who explicitly counsels against particular faiths and other forms of supernatural direction that can easily be fabricated by the flesh and the devil. In a later sermon Mather returns cautiously to the subject, trying to define certain signs that an assurance is genuine:

> Sometimes much and long *Importunity* in *Prayer;* This is a *Good Sign,* that the Prayer shall not be lost. . . . Is there enkindled such a *Warmth* in the Soul of the Supplicant, as distils the *Tears* of an Expanding and a Dissolving Heart? Is this *Warmth* kept alive, after many Damps cast thereupon; so that it is *Incessant,* it holds on, it holds out; Tho' the Lord seem in His Providence to rate it off like a *Dog,* yet it still pleads for Mercy? This is a *Good Sign.* . . . Again, Sometimes a Profound *Resignation* in *Prayer.* . . . The *Prayer* is *Answered,* if the *Soul* be *Strengthened.* [176]

The distinctive tests here are reminiscent of Thomas Goodwin's treatise on *The Returne of Prayers,* which is rather circumspect about subjective experiences of this sort, although it does credit their reality.[177] Shortly after his second wife's death and the disappointment of his assurance about her recovery, he preached a sermon with these remarks:

> Sometimes we ask for *temporal Blessings,* or, for such as are not particularly promised in the *Covenant of Grace.* The Holy Spirit of God favours us with so much of a *Particular Faith,* as to say, *the Lord hath heard the Voice of my Weeping; the Lord hath heard my Supplication; the Lord will receive my Prayer.* We may be too ready to *limit* the Sense of the Holy Spirit, by our own strong Affections to the *temporal Blessings,* and conclude, *the Thing must be done in just such or such a manner.* No; the Sense of the Holy Spirit, is no more than this . . . *I'l carry the matter, unto another Channel, wherein thou shalt have all thy Desires more than answered.* The bravest Effort of a True and a strong *Faith,* is, To leave all entirely unto the Lord, and be satisfied with the infinite Wisdom of His Conduct.[178]

But despite such warnings, in his latest writings Mather still felt that it is as dangerous wholly to deride such assurances as it is wholly to trust them, since he was concerned not to despise prophesyings and thus quench the Spirit.[179] In this conclusion Mather apparently spoke for one strand within New England Puritanism, which was unwilling to rule out all supernatural acts of the Holy Spirit, although it cautioned against antinomian enthusiasm.

Besides particular faiths, there were several extraordinary operations of the Spirit that were recognized among American Puritans. Mather records in the *Magnalia* instances of actual prophecy (in the sense of premonitions of coming events) in the ministries of Thomas Hooker, Samuel Stone, Francis Higginson, Thomas Parker, and John Eliot (*Magnalia*, I, 342, 436, 361, 486, 534-535); several instances of supernatural guidance by means of "sudden impressions" or "impulses" (I, 167-168, 489); and even a case of a vision given in a dream (I, 316). Mather also records a number of instances in the *Diary* when he felt himself directly guided under the Spirit's impulse (*Diary*, I, 195). He also had premonitions concerning the future fate of an Indian slave (I, 22), the emergence of scandals in his congregation (I, 213), and certain additions to his library (I, 214). Most of these instances, notably, were from his early years, before his partial disillusionment with particular faiths. However, he also records that in 1721 he foretold the coming great plague of smallpox in which he was signally involved (II, 621).

In all these cases Mather seems to have assumed as common belief the fact that revelations of this sort are the supernatural gifts that God often gives those who are marked out as spiritual leaders within Puritan Christendom. He remarks that his father experienced "those *Presagious Impressions* about *Future Events*, which are often Produced in Minds, which by *Piety* and *Purity* and *Contemplation*, and a Prayerful and Careful Walk with GOD, are made more Susceptible of them. . . ."[180] Kenneth Murdock comments that while most New England ministers experienced preternatural guidance and other supernatural phenomena, few had the courage to admit this and deal openly with the problems involved, as Mather did.[181] It is interesting that Mather's belief in the possibility of visions and direct guidance by the Holy Spirit was shared by Spener, and also by Francke, who was intensely aware of divine direction in the founding and building of Halle.[182] Edwards' later rejection of extraordinary gifts and operations of the Spirit may reflect an objectivist strand of New England thinking that came to prevail over Mather's position, or it may simply have been an understandable reversion to the anti-enthusiastic stance of the magisterial Reformers, brought on by the excesses of the Awakening and the scandal of Whitefield's claims to divine direction.

Like Edwards, however, and like the more famous medieval and Counter Reformation mystics, Mather came to deprecate the seeking of mystical states and extraordinary gifts as in any way preferable to the common walk of sanctification, which Catholics would call "the normal ascetic way."[183] "It is best not being too fond of *Enthusiasms,* that may carry you beyond the *Dispensation of the Day,*" Mather remarks.[184] "A Soul Sanctified with the *Love* of GOD, and of CHRIST, and of our Neighbor, is altogether to be preferred before all the *Extraordinary Gifts* of the Holy SPIRIT." Mather echoes Ignatius Loyola in his observation that too great an interest in such gifts can lead to delusion through the deception of evil spirits, and speaks of the necessity to discern the spirits:

> *Extraordinary Gifts* of the Holy SPIRIT bestowed upon Men are to be Examined by the Rules of PIETY, and if the Operations that look *Miraculous* do lead us into anything which is contrary to PIETY, they are to be rejected, among the *Wiles* of the *Prince of Darkness transforming himself into an Angel of Light.* I also Grant, and always Think, that there can be nothing more wholesome to be inculcated, than that Advice of our *Franckius, It is not safe to affect Extraordinary Gifts: For they may be at least accidentally, attended with Mighty Dangers to them that are not very deeply rooted in Humility. But who dare engage for himself his being so?*[185]

Still Mather insists that it is lawful to ask for "angelical operations" to assist in eminent ministries like his own, and even to seek them with repeated fasting and prayer.[186]

The presumption that Mather's accounts of his ecstasies and other extraordinary states are true to life, and not mere stagecraft aimed at the future reader of his diaries, is confirmed by the fact that he records honestly several occasions when his labors in prayer produced "nothing extraordinary" (*Diary,* I, 210, 296), and several in which he felt positively deserted by God, with "Much deadness . . . upon my sinful, slothful, woful Heart, in all the Exercises of the Day" (I, 206,

210, 296, 430). In explaining these experiences, Mather seeks to be consistently and tough-mindedly Augustinian. The desertions may be real withdrawals of God's grace, in which he humbles us simply by permitting our fallen nature to have its way. "How often have we a *Deserted* Soul; which is like the Heath in the Desert, that sees *no Good coming from* Heaven up on it! . . . How often . . . we are left without *Vigour* in the ways of God."[187] In *The Grand Point of Solicitude,* a treatise on "divine desertions," Mather states that these may extend to major declensions in which we become deaf to the thunders of warning providence, set in ruinous courses, and utterly careless about our spiritual welfare. On the other hand, there are minor states of darkness that do not involve God's abandonment; for we "sometimes mistake those Things for *Desertions,* which are not really so. . . . You may Enjoy *much of God,* when you imagine your selves to be *much Forsaken* of God" (pp. 23-24).[188]

> 'Tis possible, That God may Suspend those *Quickening Influences* on your Souls, wherewith He does often Actuate, Regulate, Corroborate, the souls of the Faithful. Or else, God may withdraw from your soul, the Peaceful, *Hopeful, Joyful Influences,* with which the Souls of the Faithful are sometimes Irradiated. Perhaps, you find, that tho' you come to the *Ordinances* of God, yet the Ordinances have *Little Force* upon you. . . . When you set about the Exercises of Devotion, you have no *Assistances* for those Exercises . . . When the *Devil* sets upon you, you are not able to *Resist him, stedfast in the Faith;* but are left unto your selves under this unhappiness. . . . Your *Conscience* is wounded, and bleeding under Sins that have wasted it; and Horror takes hold of you; It is the *Hour and Power of Darkness* with you . . . Your *Evidences for Heaven* are not clear. . . . At this Time the *Spirit of God Seals you not,* with any Comfortable, Powerful, Triumphant Perswasions, of your Heirship to the Kingdom of God; but leaves you in *Suspense* about your Title to Blessedness. . . . At the same Time, your *Cries* to Heaven are not answered (pp. 24-26).

Under these conditions Mather counsels believers to examine themselves for provoking causes; but above all he counsels them not to desert God, though deserted by him.[189] And in another tract on the subject, *The Case of a Troubled Mind* (1715), he admits that "*Very good people* have Cause for a very sad Complaint, that the glorious GOD hides his Face from them."[190] The conditions Mather describes are identical to those indicated by John of the Cross under the names of "the Night of the Senses" and "the Night of the Soul," in which God withdraws from the soul first all sensible consolations and then any sense of security in his love. But Mather did not venture to assert that God sends such states of relative desertion to advance the soul in its growth, as did Counter Reformation mysticism. Interestingly enough, Spener and Francke agreed with John of the Cross and Teresa on this matter. Francke held that God may withdraw at times from those who are very dear to him, "as if the Heavens were brass," in order to destroy self-will and to test and strengthen faith. He felt that experiencing the immediate help of God is a work for children and beginners in the faith, and that it is in a walk of faith—without the "sight" of direct experience of God—that maturity consists. This is essentially the same position on extraordinary consolations of the Spirit that Mather held, theoretically. But the Puritan tradition, from its beginning through Edwards, gravitated toward an insistence on the necessity of sensible awareness of the Holy Spirit which contrasts both with the views of the Pietists and those of Catholic mysticism, probably because of its doctrine of assurance.[191]

Despite all we have said about Mather's cultivation of mystical experience in isolated periods of prayer and meditation, his experience of God was not limited to these insular moments. Puritan "heavenly-mindedness," despite modern jests to the contrary, was a practical mysticism that sought communion with God among the common events of daily living. Its summary phrase for the godly life was "walking with God," moving from task to task under the direction of the Word and the illumination of the Spirit. Mather can say with satisfaction that "My Life is almost a continual Conversation with Heaven, and more particularly, in my Attendance on the divine Institutions, my Intentions of Piety, and my Applications to Heaven, are so many and so various—it becomes impossible for me to keep Records of thousands of them" (*Diary*, II, 267). In another place he says, "Therefore do's a Man *Walk with God,* when he *lives* in multiply'd Acts of *Respect* and *Homage* unto the Lord."[192] Elsewhere he defines a walk with God as one in which the mind occupies itself a great deal with "Multiplied and Operative *Thoughts* of GOD,"[193] so as "to be perpetually expressing some *Respect unto God,* wherever we come, and whatever we do."[194] The concept of being "filled with the Spirit" is defined merely in terms of a vigorous activity of the soul's faculties: "*Be filled with all the fulness of God.* Let us be *filled* with many Thoughts on God, and for God; be *fill'd* with apprehension of God, and with resolutions for God; be *filled* with Meditations upon the Fulness and Beauty that is in the Almighty God."[195] Walking with God is elsewhere defined as maintaining "a sense of God alwayes upon the Soul,"[196] "a Sense of GOD kept alive in every part of our *Walk,*"[197] "in which we not only Realize the *Being* of an Infinite GOD, but we also Remember His *Presence* in every Place, and therefore His Knowledge of every Thing. Yea, The Remembrance of this must be *Frequent* with us; the Remembrance of this must be *Awful* to us; and it must have a *Constant Efficacy* on us."[198] Thus conscientious obedience to divine laws is also a part of "walking with God": "Whatever purposes thou art pursuing in thy *Walk* . . . Be Inquisitive, *What would the Word of GOD now lead me to? So walk in all the Commandments & Ordinances of the Lord,* that thou mayest be Blameless."[199] Mather insists that there is an element of the experience of contact with God involved in the daily walk, since "*Walking* with God cannot be without an *having* of God: God and Man do mutually *possess* each other in this blessed thing."[200]

The mystical dimension of Mather's thought and experience involved another form of contact with the supernatural world that has exposed him to the charge of eccentricity. Mather felt that vital spiritual experience involved not only the sensible awareness of contact with God himself through the ministry of the indwelling Spirit but also the apprehension of other spirits, both good and evil, through the perception of help given us by some and conflict mounted against us by others.

Awareness of good and evil angels has not been part of

the central stream of piety since the eighteenth century, but it was commonplace in other times and traditions. Bernard of Clairvaux had prescribed meditation on the good angels as a means of sanctification, and had especially recommended devotion to the believer's "guardian angel" as an important mediator between man and God.[201] Bernard had also maintained against the pseudo-Dionysian school that knowledge of God in mystical experience was not a matter of direct contact with him, but a mediate knowledge through sensible images conveyed by angels.[202] The devotion to angels became a mark of Counter Reformation piety among the Jesuits and in Francis de Sales, and especially characteristic of the Italian school of the sixteenth century.[203] The same preoccupation is found among mystics and enthusiasts along the boundaries of Protestantism, including Jacob Boehme and his successors.[204] Spener expressed a cautious interest in angelology, admitting the possibility of revelatory dreams and miracles wrought through such agencies, and the subsequent Pietist movement operated within an aura of supernatural expectation that welcomed rumors of angelic visitations.[205] The Puritan background in angelology is hard to trace historically, but it is clear that Cotton Mather derived his interest in angels immediately from his father,[206] and that it was intimately connected with his expectation of premillennial revival.

The foundation of Mather's angelology is his concept of Jesus as Jehovah, the Lord of Hosts, surrounded and worshipped by a heavenly court containing innumerable gatherings both of natural and supernatural creatures.[207] The good angels among these are incorporeal creatures whose number and order are not revealed, but they are intellectual and invisible beings of a rank superior to humans.[208] The unfallen angelic hosts are charged with the fulfillment of a variety of tasks in the administration of God's providence, like cosmic engineers controlling the machinery of destiny, the "wheels" of the world's "Continual Revolution."[209] Among the offices and actions that Mather in the *Diary* attributes to the good angels are: afflicting men with diseases or healing them (I, 8, 140, 167; II, 8); ordering even the lesser daily providences of our lives (I, 201); defending or strengthening people in answer to prayer (II, 248-249); assisting in preaching (I, 396); imparting guidance through impulses, or even through the control of random bibliomancy (I, 377-378); and even the production of the spiritual ecstasy of the mystical relationship.[210] It is remarkable here that operations that later Protestantism would attribute principally to God's general providence, or else to the interior agency of the Holy Spirit, are here spoken of as controlled by angels. Benz comments that for Mather all the activity of the Holy Spirit is mediated by angels, who are to him "the direct effective organs of the Holy Spirit, Servants who fulfill God's commands and bring about purposes of the Spirit in history and in the human heart."[211] Mather even attributes the tongues of Pentecost to angels, rather than to the Holy Spirit.[212] Perhaps his motive in doing so is a caution about enthusiasm, a hesitancy about asserting too directly the indwelling of the Holy Spirit, tracing back through New England history to the Hutchinson case.

Mather believed firmly in the possibility of angelic apparitions. He was in contact with individuals who claimed to have seen "shining Spirits," such as the woman at Salem who predicted to him further storms of witchcraft, and Margaret Rule, the energoumen with whom Mather attempted exorcism, who was directed by an angel to regard Mather as her earthly father (*Diary*, I, 172, 175). But Mather himself experienced such visions, as recorded in the *Diary*. The most important of these occurred when he was twenty-three: an angelic figure appeared to him at the close of a time of prayer, assuring him that in the rest of his life he would fully express what was best in him, that he would publish many books and have a powerful influence both in America and Europe, and that he would have an important role in certain revolutionary developments in the church of Christ (I, 86-87). At thirty-five he had another vision of the support of his ministry by angelic legions, rather similar to Jacob's in the desert (I, 263-264); and around 1693 an angel even appeared to him with the express purpose of requesting him to preach on Acts 9:5 (II, 190). In his *Diary* references he Latinized two of the accounts of these visitations, including prayers to be delivered from satanic illusions, and he simply omitted mention of the third until a much later date; but by the end of his life he boldly asserted the possibility of communion with angels and intimated that he and his father had enjoyed such experiences.[213]

A great part of his interest in such occurrences—apart from the understandable surprise produced by their invading his own experience—was his gradually developing conviction that the new millennial age would be preceded not only by an outpouring of the Holy Spirit but by a remarkable descent of angels empowering certain spokesmen of revival who would bring in the reformation, "*Men* Qualified like, and Influenced by, the *Angels* of God . . . who shall fly thro' the *midst of Heaven,* having *this* EVERLASTING GOSPEL, *to Preach unto the Inhabitants of the Earth.*"[214] Even before his millennial enthusiasm was fully awakened, Mather was asking God for "the Enjoyment of all those *angelical Kindnesses*" common to his chosen servants, to be enjoyed "in a Manner and Measure more *Transcendent,* than what the great *Corruption* in the Generality of *good Men,* permitted them to bee made Partakers of" (*Diary,* I, 162-163). He early came to an assurance that because of Christ the angels would "*love* mee, *help* mee, *teach* mee, bee *nigh* mee, bee *with* mee, fetch mee to bee with *Them* forever" (I, 255; cf. I, 479). His goal in seeking such experience was not entirely limited to his usual ambition for spiritual greatness; he also hungered after this communion for its own sake (I, 281).

It is difficult not to sense in all of this a trace of what T. E. Hulme, referring to Romanticism, calls "spilt religion," a displacement of affections from God to creatures. Mather devotes sessions in his days of prayer to consideration of, and thanksgiving for, the angels' ministry (*Diary,* I, 267; II, 40, 520-522); and he feels guilty of insufficient devotion to angels and resolves to publicize their activities more widely among people by preaching on them or making a collection of biblical accounts on them (II, 200, 577-579, 659, 680). He is also involved in devotion to his guardian angel and concerned about his having often grieved this companion (I,

188). He does warn against thanking the angels themselves for their ministry, stating that we are simply to thank the Lord for his employment of them.[215] But the modern reader cannot help feeling that an inordinate amount of attention, and perhaps affection, is being directed away from God and toward religious beings about which the Bible is rather reticent. And yet the evidence indicates that Mather's interest in this realm was not unusual among Catholics and Protestants of his time, and that a remarkable quantity of medieval holdovers remain within Puritan piety.

The same is true of Mather's treatment of spiritual conflict and the whole realm of fallen angels which has deep roots in a variety of Christian traditions, beginning with the accounts of Anthony and the desert fathers. Anthony taught that those especially close to Christ were particularly subject to satanic assault, which might take the form of temptation to sin, obsessive thoughts, hallucinatory visions, doubts, suggestions of pride, goading toward extreme asceticism, and actual physical manhandling by demons. He felt that satanic revelations could be distinguished from the illumination of the Holy Spirit by the temper of calmness which the latter left on the soul, and he recommended repelling the attack of evil spirits by prayer, meditation, fasting, the practice of virtue, and even making the sign of the cross.[216] This basic picture of spiritual combat was reflected in one form or another by most of those involved in Christian spirituality during the patristic and medieval periods. In the pre-Reformation period, Gerson and others seeking to combat false mysticism placed a great deal of emphasis on the methods of "discerning the spirits" to weed out false visions and cast off oppression. *The Imitation of Christ* lists sixteen rules for discerning demonic onslaughts of the mind. Ignatius Loyola gave considerable attention to this problem,[217] and so did other main leaders of the Counter Reformation (and, we might note, Catholic writers on spiritual matters even to the present day).[218]

The same emphasis on spiritual conflict is carried over into the Puritan tradition as an essential part of the developed life of godliness. John Downame's *The Christian's*

Warfare against the Devill, the World, and the Flesh[219] and William Gurnall's *The Christian in Complete Armour*[220] were two immensely popular works on the warfare with hostile spirits circulating during the seventeenth century, testifying to the practicality of the subject for the common Puritan believer. Gurnall's battle manual continued to sell through many editions until the middle of the nineteenth century, and it is one of the most popular works ever published by a Puritan. A condition of fairly continuous spiritual combat was regarded by the Puritans as the normal milieu for the healthy Christian, who should consider himself Christ's soldier.[221] The roots of this concept of spiritual warfare in the Reformation are apparent both in Luther's teaching and experience and in Calvin's theology.[222]

Mather was characteristically uninterested in speculations about the nature of devils. He simply accepted them as fallen spirits, according to the common teaching of patristic, medieval, and Reformation doctrine, and then concentrated his attention on the ways in which they may affect our lives practically. The fallen angels are confined at present by God to a part of this invisible world; they are the "powers of the air" (Eph. 2:2). "The *Sovereign* GOD hath, with infinite *Wisdom & Justice*, confined the *Fallen Spirits* unto this *Atmosphere*. . . . Our *Air* is fill'd with them, as with *Flies* in *Mid-summer*."[223] These are the occupying powers holding secret control over the nations and mobilizing their visible and invisible forces to destroy the kingdom of God or impede its progress by counterattack. Thus the ministry is particularly subject to satanic attack, either through external persecutions or internal pressures,[224] especially in the early years of a pastorate.[225] We begin to sense at this point that Mather is speaking from his own experience, and the suspicion is confirmed: he remarks that "those Men who have least of the Devil *dwelling* in them, have most of the Devil *Striking* at them,"[226] and elsewhere he says that those who attempt especially great works for God are bound to undergo severe conflict:[227]

> You shall be *Especially* sensible of a *Blast from the Terrible*, when you are Engaging in any *Special Services* for your Glorious

> LORD: Perhaps, In some Ill Turn, some hard Shock, upon your
> *Health;* perhaps, In some Hours of *Distressing Darkness* upon
> your Mind; or, if not so, then in some *Storm of Obloquy* from
> the People, unaccountably running away with Base and False
> Representations of you.[228]

But though this fits the case of Mather himself rather exactly,
it was common lore among New England Puritan ministers,
"Who commonly have their spirits *buffeted* with strong *temptations* and sore *dejections,* before their performing any special service of their ministry."[229] Mather was convinced that
he would have to endure special retaliations when he spoke
or wrote to expose the devices of the devil (*Diary,* I, 330-331,
396), just as he experienced special angelic help in speaking
about the good angels; and two of his books along these
lines begin by expressing an expectation of such counterattack.[230] He also observes that any work that is powerfully
effective in reviving the kingdom of God will encounter
human and demonic resistance, as did the work of the
Pietists on the Continent:

> The World begins to feel a Warmth from the *Fire of God,* which
> thus flames in the Heart of *Germany,* beginning to extend into
> many Regions; the whole World will e're long be sensible of it!
> . . . These Performances, notwithstanding the evident Sanctity
> and laudable Tendency of them, have encountered with
> *Enemies, & Obloquies.* And indeed while what we have in the
> *Third Chapter of Genesis* is where it is, or while a *Lifeless Reli-
> gion,* with a Dread of all Disturbance given to it, so much suits
> the corrupt Nature of Man, we must not wonder at it.[231]

This analysis is identical to that of the Pietist leaders themselves, who found their efforts constantly attacked by Lutheran orthodoxy. Mather comments that the devil is particularly active in causing divisions within churches, and attacking the proponents of ecumenical unity.[232]

The devices used by the devil in retaliatory conflict are
much more various and subtle than those few that popular
folk-religion has retained. Temptation to sin is one such
stratagem, but it is only one of many, and perhaps not the
most important one in Mather's eyes.[233] The devil may also
thrust into the mind persuasive chains of argument leading
to doubt or heresy, or else injections of blasphemous
thoughts masquerading as the subject's own thinking. Prob-

lems like these, according to Mather, were a fairly common syndrome among New England ministers.[234] Like John Bunyan, who records his own early struggles with such mental assaults in *Grace Abounding to the Chief of Sinners*,[235] Mather knew about such devices from personal experience:

> Was ever man more tempted, than the miserable *Mather!* Should I tell, in how many Forms the Divel has assaulted me, and with what Subtilty and Energy, his Assaults have been carried on, it would strike my Friends with Horrour. Sometimes, Temptations to *Impurities;* and sometimes to Blasphemy, and Atheism, and the Abandonment of all Religion as a meer Delusion; and sometimes, to self-Destruction itself (*Diary,* I, 475).

Mather felt that there was a satanic energy behind false teaching which sought to overmaster and seduce the mind and make it into an instrument for the utterance of lies that would dishonor the Creator.

> Suggestions of *Infidelity* are very frequently such, as have plainly some Immediate *Energy* of *Evil Spirits* in them. . . . The *Thoughts* which carry *Blasphemies* against a *Risen Saviour,* and His *Glorious Gospel* in them, are frequently, Shot into the Minds of Men, at *such Seasons,* and with such impetuous *Envy,* and into Minds with such a mighty *Aversion* for them, and so Exquisitely, so Dolorously, so Intolerably *wounded,* when these *Fiery Darts* are stuck into them, that some *External Cause,* and yet a *Rational* One, must needs be active in the Inflicting of them. They can be no other than some *Evil Spirits,* the way of which *Serpents on the Rock,* is unknown unto us, that infest and harass our Minds, with the *Thoughts* which blaspheme the *Gospel* of a *Risen Saviour.*[236]

Even if there is no response to such temptation in the soul under attack—and in the heat of the assault it is hard to test this—the devil, in accordance with his character as an accuser, will endeavor to discourage and oppress the soul with the fear that it is guilty, for "it is often with Godly men, as it was with *Josephs* Brethren; a *Vile Thought* is laid in the *Soul* of these, as the *Lost Cup* was in their *Sack* of old. The Devil then Charges them with it; And such is the *Tenderness* of their *Conscience,* that they own; 'Tis indeed so; I have been a Blasphemer.' "[237] The soul under such affliction should endeavor to discern the hidden strategy in this assault, and contradict it by crying to God in prayer:

> Don't give way to *Despondencies*, because of these grievous and hideous Exercises. They are *Common to man*; Yea, to *Good* men; They are such as may befall the *Best* of Men. God will not Lay them to *your* Charge, if like a Chaste *Soul* under a Rape, you Cry *out* unto Him.[238]

> If the Devil fall to Barking in your Ears, any Ill thing of the God whom you Fear and Love, drown the Noise of that Cerberus, with a Cry to the LORD Himself, that shall have in it some *Acknowledgement* of His Glorious Excellencies.[239]

The fears and anxieties to which modern thought would assign a psychological cause were, for Mather, all part of the invisible conflict. He did admit that somatic factors had some part in spiritual depression, as he experienced in his own case: "My Health is overthrown, and my *Spleen* especially so disordered, that *Satan* getts into it: And now my Mind, is horribly buffeted with *Temptations*, which tell mee, that being unable to do any further Service, and unworthy that God should help mee to do any, I shall fall into an *unserviceable old-Age*, before I am forty years old" (*Diary*, I, 235-236). On the other hand, he felt that demonic attacks could sometimes come in the form of physical illness such as a migraine (*Diary*, II, 99),[240] and he believed that actual satanic possession was responsible for much mental illness,[241] which might therefore be cured by exorcism accomplished through prolonged prayer.[242] He observes that it was common knowledge that the devil attacked people especially in their dying hour, when they were physically most susceptible and spiritually closest to ultimate victory.[243] This kind of analysis of the negative factors in Christian experience, which allowed for somatic, psychological, and demonic forces interacting with the problem of indwelling sin to create spiritual difficulty for the believer, was common among Puritan pastors and was much more complex and sophisticated than the vestigial satanology of modern folk-religion.

In his early years Mather expressed a great many sentiments on spiritual combat that he later altered. As Calef correctly pointed out, he and the other Puritan ministers allowed far too much autonomy to the powers of darkness, assuming that God's providence was so permissive as to allow enchantments and counterfeit miracles, and even the ratification by demons of curses casually uttered by human beings.[244] But Mather rather readily outgrew much of this, admitting even in 1693 that the real strategy of the devil in the witchcraft scandal had been to precipitate all parties into passions, mistakes, and "enormous disorders"; and he remarked that "we have been in an *Egyptian Darkness,* buffeted by *Evil Angels,* and buffeting one another upon the Impulse of those *Angels.*"[245] He retained his faith in demonic agency but grew more sophisticated in his interpretation of its strategy.

Even at its most restrained, Mather's demonology has seemed eccentric to most observers in the nineteenth and twentieth centuries. It is difficult for us to realize the extent of the revolution in this area of thought accomplished by the eighteenth-century Enlightenment.

In reaction to the residue of medieval superstition in the seventeenth-century mind, the Enlightenment used Occam's razor to remove all created beings intermediate between God and man, sweeping away belief in angels along with the fear of ghosts and functioning witches. Mather had the misfortune to live exactly at that juncture in history where this shift was about to occur. In the Salem affair he played a minor part in precipitating the flight of Western civilization from superstition, and his own career was dragged painfully over the ridge of this ideological watershed. But his beliefs were not at all unusual among his contemporaries. His few visionary experiences and the numerous occasions when he felt himself involved in spiritual conflict are not at all unusual in the history of Christian experience, particularly among Puritans and Catholic mystics. For example, Luther, Bunyan, and Whitefield all had similar experiences of satanic oppression and obsession.[246] It is interesting that some recent theologians have reasserted the angelic dimension of creation, rejecting the Enlightenment simplification as an irrational and unimaginative overreaction. And, of course, the reemergence of the occult tradition that has been running underground since the eighteenth century has made Mather's response to witchcraft much more intelligible.

CHAPTER SIX

The Ministry of Doing Good

THE MISSION STRATEGY OF THE FIRST AND SECOND generations of Puritans in America was based on a theocratic model of the church taken directly from Geneva and ultimately from the Old Testament. Though they were held up as paragons of spirituality by their descendents, the founders responded to spiritual dullness and cultural decline with a nervous effort to secure the rule of the saints; and this did not lead to revival but only to deeper stagnation. The relentless lament of the jeremiad has a deadening as well as a saddening impact, because its analysis of spiritual decline does not issue in calm and vigorous assertion of the gospel combined with an exhortation to repentance but only in a tired recourse to the machinery of legal enforcement of religion. Roger Williams saw clearly to the root of theological failure in the first generation's misinterpretation of the relationship between the church under the Old Covenant and under the New, and he called for a new strategy; but the New England fathers were unable to hear the wisdom in his message through the static of his eccentricities.[1]

But in the mission strategy of nineteenth-century revivalism, a wholly new pattern supplanted the old theocratic mold. Disestablished and thrust back on "gospel weapons" instead of the instruments of civil compulsion, the churches (now transformed into "denominations") returned to the leavening strategy of the church in Acts.[2] They saw themselves as active cells within the whole society, seeking to reach and change both its members and its structures through the vigorous witness and influence of whole bodies of lay believers, instead of relying only on the fiat of leaders. The mood of the jeremiad was replaced by the mood of Pentecost, or at least by prayerful waiting for the movement of the Spirit in the new Pentecost of revival. The response to cultural decline or social evil was not direct reform by the magistrate but moral crusade conducted by voluntary reforming societies assembled across denominational lines. In this chapter we shall observe that there is not one of these emphases that is not clearly articulated by Cotton Mather, who was the John the Baptist of the coming revivalism.

It is obvious that this understanding of Mather as a prerevivalist can only be defended if we can separate the concept of "revivalism" from the methodology of mass meetings, with which it is too often almost exclusively identified. Large meetings to reach the alienated and the unchurched were an almost accidental invention of John Wesley and Whitefield, who were forced out of the local church into the fields by a fortunate burst of clerical resistance. The Great Awakening in Edwards' church and in the Middle Colonies of America took place with little resort to mass meetings, though Whitefield's visits consolidated, made visible, and augmented its fruits. The "Second Awakening" at the time of Timothy Dwight was closely identified with charismatic figures in whom a modified Puritan experientialism had become deeply operative, but it was not anchored to any single type of meeting. While the growing urban crisis in the nineteenth century pointed increasingly to the mass meeting as a major remedy for the loss of parish contact with city masses, revivals also took place in the parish ministry under leaders like Chalmers in Scotland, and even where there was initially no itinerant charismatic leadership (as in the Prayer Revival of 1858, where the focal centers were ecumenical lay prayer meetings). In every one of the periods that we designate as "awakenings" there was some use—at times and in certain places—of mass meetings. But as Joachim

Wach points out, revivalism is essentially a pietistic phenomena which is not anchored as to any specific techniques and which does not necessarily produce organizational residues, but which transforms the spirit of existing organizations.[3] Trinterud notes that the Middle Colonies Awakening was "a very different sort of revivalism": there were no protracted meetings or even extended periods of services; the work was confined to stated services; there was no anxious bench or its equivalent; personal counselling at some depth, and systematic home visitation, were emphasized; home nurture was strongly emphasized; and sudden conversions were rare. It appears that the first Awakening, in America at least, was essentially a pastoral revival, in which new life was breathed into the old message and methods.[4]

But if the common denominator of all "revivalism" is not the "revival meeting," or even the charismatic revivalist, what are the core characteristics of the genus that can be found in all its species? Are there any essential factors in all revivals of religion that would make it possible for a participant in one awakening—Edwards, for example—to detect a family likeness in other leaders and their movements, even where these are as far from Edwardsian Puritanism as Finney and D. L. Moody? One way of answering this question is to point to the evidence that every movement commonly designated as a spiritual awakening is radically related either to the Pietist or Puritan traditions, and often to both. Actually, all of the subsequent branches in the revivalist family tree meet in a fitful but quite real harmony at the time of the Great Awakening, like relatives who are uncomfortable with one another's eccentricities but aware of common kinship and responsibility to one another: Calvinist Puritans such as Whitefield and Edwards and the Tennents, Arminians such as Wesley, and Pietists such as the Moravians. In other periods, when the awakened church had returned to slumber, these may have been at each other's throats; but in every subsequent awakening they have been roused to a sometimes uneasy and reluctant awareness of kinship and the need to cooperate in the work of spiritual renewal.

But what are the characteristics that all members of the genus share? I suggest that the common factors are present in a biblical prototype to which every revivalist sooner or later refers as the model for his experience: the birth of the church described in the early chapters of the Acts of the Apostles. While the Reformation in its Calvinist form was primarily an adaptation of the pattern of revival demonstrated in the Old Testament accounts of theocratic kings such as Hezekiah and Josiah, the re-establishment and civil enforcement of sound doctrinal teaching and pure ordinances, the later revivalism shifted to a nontheocratic strategy which can be drawn from the prototypical "awakening" of the church described in Acts 2. The essential elements of revivalism contained in this chapter and its context are as follows:

1. The proclamation within and beyond the church of a message combining emphasis on divine grace (specifically on the provision of justification through faith in Jesus Christ) and on man's response (faith, repentance, conversion, sanctification).

2. A conception of the church's task as that of leavening society by witness and action within it rather than by dominating it in the Judaic or post-Constantinian fashion, with the continuous improvisation of appropriate methods through which to accomplish this.

3. The presence of a strong and widespread sense of need for the Holy Spirit's empowering in order to revitalize the church to equip it for this mission, over and above what can be achieved by the mere dissemination of a theological message, or the use of improved methods; and the implementation of this concern in prayer.[5]

Employing this definition, we can discern a nascent revivalism developing in the early English Puritanism and in the pre-Pietistic stream from Bucer and Arndt onwards. We can understand outbreaks of spiritual awakening under Baxter at Kidderminster, Stoddard at Northampton, and the Pietists in Germany, as all part of the revivalist stream; and we can see that the Great Awakening itself is not an entirely new phenomenon, but simply a damming up of this stream so that its extensive penetration into history was greater. The same Puritan/Pietist current underlay the Second Evangelical Awakening in England and America and the *Reveil* on the continent in the early nineteenth century, although important doctrinal shifts were present in these movements. It is true that in the subsequent course of revivalism in America some of the features of this model were obscured: the message proclaimed was weakened by a shallow understanding of sin, the scope of mission was reduced by the elimination of social action, and the meaning of "revival" was narrowed to bypass the renewal of the church and seize directly on the goal of church extension through mass evangelism. Post-Finneyan revivalism is at times so different from the movements involved in the first and second Evangelical Awakenings that we may be tempted to substitute a different word to replace the one that has been debased in our linguistic coinage, and call the earlier phenomenon "renewalism." But modern revivalism is only a mutation in a genetic line that leads directly back to the Puritan/Pietist reformulation of the Reformation's message and strategy. This is confirmed by the fact that the Evangelicalism that has recently emerged from revivalist roots in America has recognized the renewalists as its spiritual ancestry and is seeking to restore the dimensions of ministry eroded from their tradition. In the rest of this chapter we shall endeavor to place Mather within this tradition. We have already shown that Mather fulfills the first of the three criteria listed above, since his message was essentially identical to the thrust of earlier Puritan and Pietist awakenings, and to the common elements in the various strands combining in the later Great Awakening. It remains to be proved that he satisfies the second and third conditions.

A large part of Mather's response to New England's spiritual crisis involved, as usual, the adaptation of methods and ministries already in use, or simply the effort to deepen, refine, and energize those through the application of "methods of piety." This is completely natural, considering that Mather's innately conservative temperament operated in a tradition in which he was anchored to a rather steady, if confining, divine-right scriptural outline of what the ordinary methods of the church should be. Unlike modern theologians, facing a comparable spiritual problem in the culture but unsupported by any conviction of a fixed ministerial order laid down in the New Testament, he was not about to dismantle the old machinery of the church to meet new occasions.

Consequently, Mather's solution to the problem of renewal still centered around the basic stated meetings of the church, conducted for worship (as on the sabbath) or purely for biblical edification (as in the weekly lecture). In both instances he assumed that the principal agent in spiritual nourishment and awakening is the ministry of the Word of God, and thus he still used long bouts of preaching and teaching as the basic protein of his ministry. A great percentage of the energies of his pastoral work was invested in preparation for these. While earlier Puritan worship had included literally hours of preaching and pastoral prayer at a given service, it was Mather's custom (or at least his counsel) to hold a sermon to one hour in length, or a little over.[6] Even this length seems incredible to the modern imagination; but apart from such usually mentioned factors as the lack of other entertainment, the congregation could put up with sermons that long simply because Mather and other Puritans conscientiously put a great deal of time into studying for them during the week, and the result was a lot of meat combined with a masterful sauce.

Compared to the modern pastor's schedule, Mather's resembled that of an eremite living in a kind of utopia for Christian humanists. "Our *Time* is to be by far the most of it, *Spent Alone*," he says, "Separating our selves that we may *intermeddle with all Wisdom*."[7] "God will Curse that Man's Labors who Lumbers up and down in the World all the Week, and then upon Saturday, in the Afternoon, goes to his Study; whereas GOD knows, that Time were little enough to Pray and Weep in, and get his Heart into a fit Frame for the Duties of the approaching Sabbath."[8] His father's weekly regimen, which he lists in the *Parentator*, had been almost entirely consumed in the reading of commentaries, biblical study for the sermon, and other types of reading—"only allowance must be given for visitations and necessary avocations, which cannot be foreseen."[9] Cotton's own schedule is deducible from a specimen account from his twentieth year. There he describes a typical day in which he began by reading Scripture and praying, examined his children, read Descartes and commentaries, breakfasted, worked on his sermon, engaged in family prayer, heard his pupils recite, read Salmon on medicine, dined, visited friends, read some more in various books, worked more on the sermon, heard pupils recite again, meditated and prayed, supped, worked again on the sermon, and took part in family prayer.[10] This amount of preparatory labor is not surprising when we consider that Mather rarely preached less than twice a week, and at times as often as four times.[11] His standards for solid preaching were also extremely high. He recommended that the pastor carefully study in advance to preach to all varieties and ages in his congregation, especially the young, applying the content of the sermon to each spiritual condition present and not resting simply in a detailed doctrinal exposition.[12] The sermon should also be furnished with appropriate anecdotes if these could be delivered with a "deliberate, expressive, unstumbling brevity."[13] However, he felt that the construction of the sermon was only a part of the time-consuming labor that was required; a considerable part of its success would depend on how the minister worked its material into his own heart and experience through prayer and porismatic meditation.[14]

In the actual delivery of the sermon, Mather favored a very free and limited use of notes, rather than the reading of a manuscript or its delivery from memory.[15] Ideally, preaching was to be accompanied by a constant ejaculatory prayer for its penetration into the hearts of its hearers, and it was to be embedded in an immense background of pastoral prayer led publicly during the service. Mather's own pastoral prayer had a way of extending itself to remarkable lengths at times—once to two hours, which necessitated a public apology from the pastor to the numbed congregation.[16]

Regarding the material content of the sermon, Mather

was in favor of a planned curriculum of preaching flavored with some intermingling of topical subjects from time to time; but this curriculum was to be doctrinally determined rather than set by the consecutive exposition of large bodies of Scripture. "The whole *body of Divinity* should be in the Course of our Ministry, be gone through; And the more in Order, the better. So we shall *Declare the whole Counsel of GOD*."[17] Evidently Mather did frequently preach short series of sermons on texts lying together in a limited passage of Scripture. But he remarks in the *Diary* that he still preserved "a Liberty, usually every other Lord's Day, to discourse on *occasional Subjects;* and for my Direction in these, I consider the particular Condition, Occurrences, Temptations, of the Flock; and endeavour as well as I can to suit them with the Word of God" (I, 539). At times he would consult the members of the congregation or his deacons to determine what subjects they would like him to preach on (I, 547, 576). But in all this his effort was to keep to the central themes that he felt were vital to the nurture of Christian experience in his people.

Most of Mather's time was thus occupied in study, either in connection with his sermons or to fill out his erudition for his literary labors. We have already seen that he spent considerable time also in personal and private devotions. It also occurred to him, however, to pray specifically over the needs of his congregation. At the outset of his ministry, he noted that he kept "a *Catalogue* of all the *Communicants* belonging unto our church, and in my secret Prayers, I would sometimes go over this Catalogue, by Parcels at a Time, upon my knees; praying for the most *suitable* Blessings I can think of, to bee bestow'd on each Person, by Name distinctly mentioned" (*Diary*, I, 108). Some twenty-five years later he refers to this practice as if it had long fallen by the wayside: "I would renew my ancient Care of the Flock in this one Point" (II, 43).

Since Puritan evangelism employed a "waiting period" of supplication to effect conversion, instead of the immediate decision of Arminian Revivalism, Mather did not use any evangelistic machinery in the course of his preaching services. He did, however, suggest on many occasions another tool that the prospective convert could use privately to conclude his process of conversion: the written covenant. This was no innovation, but a settled part of Puritan tradition,[18] and Mather made particular use of it at the beginning of his ministry. Here is the earliest example in his writings:

> I Renounce all the *Vanities* and *Idols* of this World. I engage that I will cleave unto the Lord *Jehovah,* as my *Best Good,* and my *Last End;* promising to live *upon* Him, and *unto* Him, hoping to live ere long *with* Him for ever. I Engage, That I will cling unto the Lord *Jesus,* as my *Prophet,* and my *Priest,* and my *King;* Promising to acknowledge Him as the Author of all my Salvation. I Engage, That I will first study what is my *Duty* in these things; and wherein I find myself to fall short, I will ever count it my *Grief,* my *Shame,* and for pardon betake my self to the Blood of the Everlasting Covenant. All this I Engage, humbly imploring the Grace of the Mediator to be sufficient for me.
>
> It would hurt no Godly man, to *set* his *Name,* with Hand and Heart to such an Instrument; afterwards frequently Reflecting on it, frequently Renewing of it.[19]

By the second decade of the new century, however, Mather was experiencing second thoughts about the use of covenant forms.

> *Forms* have been used by Thousands, with honest minds, and have been of great use unto them. Yet, I verily think, a Glorious CHRIST, *as the Head of His People in the Covenant of God,* has not always been duly considered in these *Forms.* And hence, though the persons that used them have been *Real Converts,* yet God has often left them unto sad *Falls,* after they have entered into *Covenant.* It has been to show them, how *feeble* they are, how *nothing* they are; how displeased He is, to see the least Air of the *Covenant of Works,* in our Transactions with Him; and to chase us away unto our only Saviour.[20]

Mather is bold enough to object to the received Puritan teaching on this subject.

> The *Form* used by those Men of God, is hardly quite *Evangelical* enough. I would propose, that the *Nature* of the *New Covenant,* which is all over, *Grace, Grace;* be thoroughly considered by them who do this Action; and that the Terms of, *I Confess,* and, *I Consent,* and, *I Desire,* be preferred, unto, *I Will;* as Language best Suiting the Nature & the Tenour of a *Covenant,* in which, tis not by Doing, but by *Receiving,* that we arrive unto Blessed-

ness, and that our Holy *Resolutions* be form'd, as points of *Thankfulness* to the Lord from whom we *Receive* the Gift of *Righteousness,* and as parts of our Promised Blessedness; and the style thereof be, *O my God, I ask of thee, that thou wilt give me the Grace to do such and such things:*[21]

Thus, by the end of his life, Mather's suggested covenant was very brief and thoroughly evangelical in its hyper-Calvinist way: "So set thy *Hand,* (even that *Withered Hand*) with thy *Heart,* unto this acknowledgment. *O my Great SAVIOUR, I consent by thy Help, I consent unto it, That thou bring me into the Peace of GOD, and that thou fill me with the Love of GOD, that thou save me to the Uttermost.*"[22] Nevertheless, in his final great summary of the New England Way, Mather goes on record in favor not only of this practice but also the recurrent renewal of personal, church, and national covenants, those heavily theocratic "sacraments" which New England had developed.[23]

A very similar judgment might be given on Mather's understanding and practice of pastoral care. His father had no regular time during the week scheduled for pastoral visits, only undertaking these as occasions arose which demanded them; and he had been criticized for neglecting these in favor of his studies.[24] The younger Mather, however, set out at the beginning of his ministry as he records in the *Diary,* to reserve one afternoon per week (generally Thursday) for such visits by appointment (I, 55). He was able to visit anywhere from one to four families per week in this manner, talking to the adults with "as handsome and pungent *Addresses* as I was able . . . particularly about their everlasting Interests; and the young People I still asked some *Questions* of the *Catechism,* from the Answers whereof I made as lively Applications unto them as I could" (I, 114). This itinerant catechetical ministry had been the heart of Baxter's surprising success in the parish at Kidderminster, and Mather indicates that this and other elements in *The Reformed Pastor* had a profound effect on his own ministry (II, 498). He also justifies the practice from patristic examples—Augustine and Clement of Alexandria—and from the practice in the time of the Reformation, noting that even Rome and the Jews

have adopted the technique.[25] In his later writings for
ministerial candidates he unhesitatingly advises catechizing
as a vital part of an awakening ministry, and one that was in
common use among Puritan pastors:

> Your *Sermons*, tho' never so well-composed *Meat-Offerings* for
> the House of your God, will be very much lost, upon an
> *Uncatechized* People: Or, as our *Flavel* Expresses it; *All your*
> *Excellent Sermons, will be dashed to pieces on the Rock of your*
> *People's Ignorance*. . . . There have been Thousands, who have
> used very *Great Labors in Catechizing*, and have given very
> *Great Praises* unto God, for the *Successes* that have attended
> them.[26]

In many instances Mather evidently felt the catechetical
framework for the visit more suitable for the children and
simply endeavored to engage the adults directly in conversation about their spiritual interests, or sound them out to
determine their current condition.[27] In one of his late writings Mather gives a very full list of subjects to be inquired
after on such visits: the regeneration of family members;
special temptations interfering with godliness; financial
well-being; vocational direction; duties to relatives; family
devotions; warning against wicked company; the conversion
of servants; exhortation of those neglecting the Lord's Table;
and general encouragement to adhere to the church. It was
Mather's practice to leave a Scripture passage for the man of
the house if he was not present; the indication seems to be
that Mather did not regularly deal with the heads of households but with the women and children.[28]

Very frequently Mather distributed tracts on the subject
of regeneration or spiritual growth, usually copies of his own
writings, during these visits. He remarks, "Usually I give
away half a dozen Books, more or less, every Day that I make
them" (Diary, I, 518), and he distributed "I suppose, at least
six hundred Books in a Year" (I, 548). We have already commented on the flowering of devotional literature in the first
great period of Puritanism. From the beginning a large proportion of this material was used for pastoral distribution and
aimed largely at the unconverted. Like Francke,[29] Mather
was very eager to reinforce his visits by leaving a continuing
literary echo of piety in the household. Usually the echo was

that of his own voice, since a large part of his literary production was designed for this use. In his earlier career Mather recommended to the laity the distribution of such tracts;[30] his later works on the office of the pastorate do not mention the subject, probably out of a nervous modesty in the face of those critics who accused him of a mania for scribbling. But the practice was apparently widespread among ministers, and it is interesting that in the Great Awakening it became one of the more popular instruments for bringing revival.[31]

There is every evidence that Mather found his pastoral visits extremely rewarding. It is also clear that he found them uniquely difficult to keep up, "a Service wherein I enjoy a strange Presence and Conduct of Heaven, but go thro' very spending Labour" (*Diary*, I, 368). The diaries are littered with admissions of slackness in visitation and resolutions of reform (I, 168, 201, 304, 319; II, 24, 86, 230, 334, 352). As his ministry went on, he seems to have had a deepening sense of the importance of this work, and of his own difficulty in doing it. There was clearly a struggle taking place in his mind between the demands of the pastoral ministry and the delights of study and literary labor. Though it was his counsel and practice to make every conversation serviceable to the interests of piety, he still observes:

> I am afraid, lest while I am conversing with my Neighbors, (tho' it be alwayes with the Intentions of doing some Good unto them) I may, ere I am aware, be betray'd into some Degree of Slothfulness, when I am abroad among my Neighbours, I would often putt that Question to myself, *Would it not be more pleasing unto my glorious Lord, that I should be in my Study at this Time?* If I find myself in a Temper and Vigour to be carrying on greater Services in my Study, I would break off the most agreeable Conversation, and fly thither, with a Zeal of redeeming the Time, upon me (II, 48).

Considering Mather's mammoth appetite for scholarship and his desire for literary fame, it is unlikely that he often felt himself in any other "Temper and Vigour" when he posed this question. It was not only that he hesitated to pursue "cold contacts" and preferred to have those really desirous of spiritual counseling contact him at his home, as was the case with Edwards; even in his study the visitor was admonished by a sign to "Be Short." Perhaps Mather lacked a vivid understanding of what could be achieved in the way of spiritual growth through pastoral counseling on a deep and extended personal level, and thus aimed too low in his nurture of the life of the congregation while aiming very high at a more distant sort of outreach through literature—one which had attached to it the rewards of notoriety. In this connection we should note again that the original awakening that produced the Puritan movement in England was primarily moved by the experience of pastors like Greenham and Rogers in personal spiritual counseling,[32] and that an important factor in the Great Awakening in the Middle Colonies was an increase in such conferences and in systematic home visitation.[33] If we were to single out a single factor to explain the lack of continual and widespread awakening under Mather's ministry, it might well be this lack of personal spiritual counseling, which may also be part of the explanation for the miscarriage of the revival under Edwards' later ministry.

Along with his use of older methods and patterns of ministry, Mather adopted a number of new approaches in his work as a pastor. He was in no sense a creative inaugurator of strategies and theological emphases which would shape the future and meet the spiritual crisis in New England, but he did have an uncanny responsiveness to the new ideas of others that were in the main line of future church development. He was a condenser, not a generator. By a process of collection, he assembled piecemeal from more original minds in England and Germany a blueprint of post-theocratic strategy that would forecast with remarkable accuracy the program the American churches were to adopt a century later. He was not solely responsible for the shape of that future program; but he did import and plant in America all the seminal motifs which were already operating in Western Christendom and would combine to produce nineteenth-century evangelicalism.

One of the salient differences between the Protestantism of the nineteenth century and that of earlier periods was the growing role of the laity in personal witness, culminating in the lay revival of 1858 and the ultimate success of the great lay evangelist, D. L. Moody. Despite the theoretical groundwork for this development laid in Luther's concept of the priesthood of all believers, neither the Lutheran nor the Reformed branches of Christendom really developed a practical ministry of the laity during most of the sixteenth and seventeenth centuries. English Puritanism did concentrate quite seriously on the spiritual nurture of the individual believer, but it usually represented this as a process to be supervised by spiritual experts, principally the clergy. Charles and Katherine George insist that in both Anglican and Puritan circles laymen did not write from a consistently Protestant viewpoint in the early seventeenth century, and that the failure to convert laymen to a deeply felt Protestant view of life resulted in the tragically rapid disintegration of the Protestant outlook.[34] Edmund S. Morgan contends that the spiritual concern of the colonizing Puritan fathers in America was concentrated on dynastic sanctification rather than evangelization of the unchurched in noncovenant lines, so that the Puritan adult felt that his sphere of witnessing responsibility was essentially limited to his family, servants, and fellow churchmen.[35] Perhaps these theories overstate the case—they are not accurate for such eminent Puritans as Thomas Hooker[36] and Lewis Bayly.[37] At any rate, there does seem to be a greater appearance of concern for lay ministry toward the end of the seventeenth century. John McNeill notes that Spener's *The Spiritual Priesthood Briefly Set Forth* (1677) was publicly attacked by the clergy-centered Lutheran orthodoxy for encouraging the full implementation of Luther's doctrine of the general priesthood.[38] McNeill also finds a stronger emphasis in this direction in the Mathers and later in Edwards.[39]

At first glance, it appears that in many respects Cotton Mather was still deeply embedded in a theocratic understanding of the parish structure, which did not necessitate the training of any lay "fishers of men" because most of the fish in the community were directly under the care of pastoral experts. In urging his people to be fruitful, for instance,

Mather does not define the bearing of fruit in terms of the winning of souls, as the nineteenth century would, but in terms of personal godliness, acts of piety, loving God and one's neighbor,[40] the careful use of time,[41] and obedience to God.[42] This concept of fruitfulness is remarkably centered on the growth of sanctification in order to live to the greater glory of God. It is undoubtedly a good balance to the shallow emphasis on an oververbalized concept of "witness" which practically supplants sanctification in later revivalist models of the Christian life, but it is spiritually self-centered in the familiar ascetic pattern.

The absence of the concept of lay witness in most of Mather's sermons suggests that the older pattern of ministerial expertise dominated his thinking much of the time. In *A Family Sacrifice* (1703) and *Benedictus* (1715) he tells the Christian to do good to others but mentions no evangelistic thrust.[43] In *Desiderius* (1719) Mather advises his people to pity the unbeliever but abhor him,[44] and in *Ecclesiae Monilia* (1726) he urges them to shrink from contact with the ungodly;[45] in neither case is there any encouragement to attempt a conversion. A number of sermons encourage the practice of "brotherly love" among Christians and church members, and even the mutual spiritual awakening of one another, and yet they do not accompany this with any dynamic of evangelism outside the fold.[46] In *The Fisherman's Calling* (1712) he rings every conceivable change on the occasional reflections involved in a life of fishing but completely ignores the biblical injunctions to disciples to become "fishers of men."[47]

A relatively small number of Mather's works do give a clear-cut call to lay witness, however, and these range over every period in his ministry. In *Small Offers* (1689) he throws off a few phrases about this subject, embedded in a vast background of other concerns: "The *Living* here may be *praising* of God, by Bearing many a *Witness* to the *Truths,* and *Ways* of the Lord Jesus Christ. . . . In this life, we may be instrumental to Convince and to Convert *Unregenerate* Sinners, to build up the *Church* of the Lord Jesus, and to Do good among the ignorant by an *Exemplary Conversation.*"[48] In *A Good*

Master Well Served (1696) he commands the owners of slaves to value as of first importance the spiritual state of their slaves, and seek their conversion.[49] And Mather observes that the early Christians "followed their Unconverted Neighbors with Importunate and Unwearied *Counsels:* They Instructed them, they Advised them, they *Persuaded* them, to be more than *Almost Christians.*"[50] And one work—a Boston lecture sermon directed, significantly, to a more select audience of leaders and willing hearers than the regular Lord's Day service would draw—deliberates fully on the subject of the witness of the laity. The doctrine of *The Nets of Salvation* (1704) is: *"Those that win Souls are wise."* Quite a bit of this sermon is still given over to the project of getting the souls of Mather's immediate hearers thoroughly won. Near the close of the sermon he does, however, suggest that the devil and heretics sometimes do more to win souls than Congregational laymen, and proposes the case: *"What can we do about winning Souls?"* Oddly enough for a Calvinist, Mather appeals to an anthropocentric motive, urging a pitying consideration of the lost sinner and a setting of a high value on his soul: "But if that Soul go Christless, and Graceless out of the world, it sinks down into such Miseries, that thy Heart is all Stone, O man, if thou art not struck with horror at them; if thou Cry not out. . . . Methinks, were we under the Influence of such Thoughts, our Compassion for Souls, would make us with some Anguish to groan after the *winning of Souls*" (*Nets of Salvation*, p. 39). Mather is probably correct in considering the main obstacle to an effective ministry among the Boston laity to be carelessness of their responsibility for mission (pp. 37-38).

Like later revivalists (even including Arminians like Finney), Mather feels that *"Praying for Souls* is a main stroke in the *winning* of *Souls*. If once the *Spirit of Grace* be poured out upon a *Soul*, that *Soul is won* immediately" (p. 40). From this step he goes on to recommend, first, uniformly good conduct in Christ as a silent foundation for verbal witness, and finally, open conversation about Christ as well as the distribution of tracts such as his own, which, he notes, many in the congregation have used profitably. Although all of this treatment of personal witness is framed strictly within the limits of Boston parish work—there is an intramural flavor to it and no great sense of reaching "outside the camp" to the really distant and "ungodly" elements of the urban society—it is still a remarkably exact foreshadowing of the typical emphases of the nineteenth century, including group prayer for the revival of religion among the rising generation and all nations.

> Who can tell, how far the Prayers of the *Saints,* & of a few *Saints,* may *prevail* with Heaven to obtain that *Grace,* that shall win whole *Peoples and Kingdoms to serve the Lord? A New Heart* shall one Day be given to the *Israelitish Nation.* . . . It may be, the Nations of the world, would quickly be *won* from the Idolatries of *Paganism,* and the Impostures of *Mahomet,* if a *Spirit of Prayer,* were at work among the People of God (p. 42).

Still, the emphasis on lay witness here is an extremely rare one, considering the vast body of Mather's writing. We must assume that although the notion the laity can reach others for Christ was present in the seventeenth-century Puritan matrix in which Mather operated, it was a very muted strain. There are a number of possible reasons for this. The pastors had been accustomed to seeing a larger proportion of their parish in church than later generations could expect, and hence felt that evangelism could best be done by ministerial experts at first hand. Perhaps the doctrine of the sovereignty of God led the ministers to put their main trust in God's awakening sinners and bringing the troubled seekers to them. And whereas for the Arminian evangelism of the later nineteenth century conversion was a relatively simple act of commitment that could be elicited by a moderately trained layman, for Puritanism it was a work of surgery that required a specialist. Above all, however, the concept of the homogeneous parish had not yet sufficiently moved toward an unanchored pluralism. The ministers still felt that they, personally, had a grip on the lives in the community, and it was not yet necessary for them to seek a wider purchase through the enlistment of the laity in the evangelistic task.

It has been suggested, however, that another strategy

that Mather helped propagate in New England, the use of voluntary religious societies for the spread of piety and the suppression of moral disorders, was just such an attempt to get a grip on a post-theocratic society sliding away from ministerial control.[51] But there were two different types of society involved: the "religious society," intended to build up the spiritual lives of the participants—and similar to the Pietist conventicles or Wesley's group meetings—and the "reforming society," aiming mainly at the "suppression of moral disorder" in the surrounding culture, the prototype of most of the voluntary societies of the Benevolent Empire in the nineteenth century.[52] The first kind of society considerably antedates the shift in cultural control in New England and seems to be directed toward goals that are not necessarily connected with that cultural control.

The idea of deepening the spirituality of the church by building up bands of trained disciples through "small group meetings," which is experiencing a revival of interest today, has a long tradition in Western Christianity. There are roots of the *collegia* method in pre-Reformation sources such as Gerard Groote and the Brethren of the Common Life, and the Catholic usage among the Quietists may actually have influenced the development of Pietist conventicles.[53] Dudley Bahlman comments on a similarity to the Jesuit retreats, and it is not inaccurate to say that both the retreats and the *collegia* were innerworldly adaptations of the old monastic strategy. Within Protestantism, Luther made some tentative suggestions about *ecclesiolae in ecclesia* in his preface to the *German Mass* (1526) but, unfortunately for subsequent Lutheran development, he did not develop this project. But similar methods were adopted by the itinerant radical, Caspar Schwenckfeld,[54] and by Reformed leaders like Zwingli, John a Lasco, and Martin Bucer in Strassburg.[55] Arndt made some use of such *collegia pietatis;* and Boehme was involved in house meetings of this type in Goerlitz in 1600.[56] A scattering of German pre-Pietists and an important group of Dutch Precisianists, numbering among them Voetius, Cocceius, Lodensteyn, and Labadie, made use of conventicles.[57] Spener, who adopted these in 1670, was influenced probably more by his awareness of Labadie's work than by German sources.[58] These meetings, which involved prayer and the reading of sermons, devotional works, and Scripture, were moved out of homes and into the church in 1682 at the request of apprehensive church authorities, but this seemed to dampen the spirit; and because of this—and Spener's own doubts about the separatist tendencies in the *collegia* methodology when it spread beyond his direct supervision—he tended to play them down in later years, though the technique continued to characterize eighteenth-century Pietism.[59]

While the Pietist *collegia* were focussed on spiritual nurture through objective study of Scripture and devotional works, the class meetings later developed by the Wesleys on the model of the English religious societies (with some influence from the Moravian band meetings) brought in a much greater degree of subjective exposure in their characteristic interchange of mutual confession and intercession, and also less clerical control due to the total participation of members.[60] The Continental Pietists used the *collegia* strictly for the edification and renewal of church members, and consequently these developed an introversive and esoteric character; whereas Wesley's intent was always to evangelize, to thrust beyond the borders of nominal Christianity, so that even the class meetings were exoteric. Thus German Pietism produced a limited "awakening" which has a genetic relationship with the later revival under the Wesleys,[61] but the continuity between the two movements is occasionally insufficiently stressed because of the narrower limits and lesser goals of the Pietists.

Apparently, however, there was a tradition of small group meetings within English and American Puritanism which was independent of the Dutch and German Pietist streams, and which also antedated the London religious societies that are often presented as the model for Mather's *collegia*. Cotton Mather states that he was himself involved in a young men's religious society in Boston around 1678, when he was eighteen;[62] and he attempted to start another such society in 1683 (*Diary*, I, 67-68). In 1685 he successfully initiated a regular day of prayer for ministers and their wives (I, 106, 125); and in 1686-87 he began family meetings in the various neighborhoods inhabited by church people (I, 135). In 1693, he records, a Society of Negroes formed itself and approached him for advice and assistance (I, 176-177). In the *Magnalia* Mather indicates that various types of *collegia* had been flourishing since the very founding of the Massachusetts Bay Colony:

> In the beginning of the country, the ministers had their frequent meetings, which were most usually after their publick and weekly or monthly lectures . . . and these *meetings* are maintained unto this day. The private Christians also had their private meetings, wherein they would seek the face, and sing the praise of God; and confer upon some questions of practical religion, for their mutual edification. And the country still is full of those little meetings; yet they have now mostly left off one circumstance, which those our *primitive times* was much maintained; namely, their concluding of their more sacred exercises with *suppers*. . . . Our private meetings of good people to pray and praise God, and hear sermons, either preached perhaps by the younger candidates for the ministry . . . or else repeated by exact writers of short hand after their pastors; and sometimes to spend whole days in fasting and prayer, especially when any of the neighborhood are in affliction, or when the communion of the Lord's table is approaching; those do still abound among us.[63]

It is improbable that these meetings among the first generation were entire innovations; it is much more likely that they were modelled on English counterparts rooted in the private meetings in the early years of the Puritan movement.[64] Mather does mention the London societies in the *Ratio Disciplinae* (1726), but he simply implies that these are an Anglican counterpart of the native New England variety.[65]

The various kinds of *collegia* mentioned by Mather include meetings for families, women, and young men; and ministerial meetings, which were unique in that they were not primarily for purposes of government or discipline but for the spiritual edification of the participants through preaching, sharing of concerns, and prayer. The family meetings were ideally composed of about a dozen households in a neighborhood, meeting in homes once a month or fortnight, with ministers and ministerial candidates occasionally attending and preaching. The agenda of the meetings included prayers, the singing of psalms, the reading or hearing of sermons or devotional works, and even some sharing of spiritual experiences and personal needs. Sometimes whole days were devoted to prayer. The families involved in the cell group were to regard each other as prayer concerns, and also to feel a responsibility to look after one another's material and physical welfare, as well as to seek methods of doing good in the neighborhood. The young men's meetings followed a similar pattern: they met for two hours usually on a Sunday evening, with prayers and psalms, preaching and reading, and also an exchange of confidential mutual confession of spiritual needs. There was to be a quarterly collection, discipline of lapsed members, and a careful check on regular attendance; each member was to seek to recruit one new member on a regular basis; and once a month there was to be a whole evening of prayer for the rising generation. The pattern here sounds very close to that of Wesley's class meetings. Mather does not give any detailed description of the women's meetings, but probably these followed a similar pattern.[66] In several places Mather takes note of variants on this pattern such as societies for students meeting at college, along the lines of the Wesleys' Holy Club, and "sodalities" formed by ministerial students.[67]

It thus appears that Mather's use of religious societies was in no sense an innovation, or even the adoption of a new method pioneered elsewhere. As a matter of fact, the Puritan *collegia* seem to antedate—and in their development and variety to dwarf by comparison—their Anglican and Pietist counterparts. Although the concept of the *collegia pietatis* has been mainly attached to German Pietism in the past, probably due to the controversy over them engendered by Lutheran orthodox critics of Spener and Francke, the strongest roots of the conventicle approach seem to be in the Reformed tradition, in its English Puritan and Dutch Precisianist extensions.

But though Mather did not in any sense adopt a new

method in throwing the societies into the breach left by the loss of theocratic control, he was influenced by another kind of *collegium* pioneered in England in the 1690s, the "reforming society." This was a different species from the Anglican religious societies, as we have noted: it was composed of Nonconformists as well as Anglican churchmen, and it aimed mainly at the suppression of moral disorders which had begun to spread during the reign of James II and had reached a pitch of public decadence during the 1690s, with outbursts of drunkenness, prostitution, sodomy, and an unusually licentious theater. Suspecting in this a Roman Catholic plot to undermine English Protestantism, and widely moved by the familiar Puritan idea that such national sins would soon call down a national judgment from God, English Protestants banded together in societies for the suppression of disorders, supported in this by King William and particularly by his pious wife, and also by their successor, Queen Anne. These societies were initiated immediately following the revolution,[68] and their purpose was principally to implement on a popular level the laws against disorders that were rapidly being enacted or revived by the new administration. The reforming societies simply endeavored to get these laws enforced, mainly by the use of voluntary or paid informers who would bear witness against violators before the magistrate.

The first reforming society was begun in the East End of London in 1690 by a small group of men in the established church, meeting monthly, with the main goal of suppressing houses of prostitution. A second society was started in the Strand in 1691 by Edward Stephens, and it attempted to influence lax justices and magistrates with signed warrants; it ran into a certain amount of predictable controversy. By 1699 there were eight such groups operating in London and counterparts in six English towns, but there was little apparent success, and the original impulse was beginning to die. In that year, however, a letter of Archbishop Tenison endorsing the societies set off a second wave of enthusiasm for them, and by 1703 there were twenty societies, more or less organically related. The goals of some of these societies sound suspiciously Puritanical. The unpleasant figure of the informer soon became synonymous with the societies in the public imagination, so that by 1704 even advocates were admitting the insufficiency of this approach. In 1711, Swift complained of the factionalism and general ineffectiveness of the societies, which tended to become centers of controversy rather than peaceful reform. They were strongly (and probably accurately) suspected of Puritan and seditious tendencies because of the membership of dissenters, and they wakened a resentment among the common people at the infringement of their privacy which ultimately may have contributed to the downfall of the Whigs.

In the early 1700s the established church began to place more emphasis on the curative powers of moral and religious education through the Charity Schools being forwarded by the Society for the Propagation of Christian Knowledge, and the reforming societies died a lingering death which finally culminated in the late 1730s. John Wesley, who reestablished them later, commented that the original impetus in these and other attempted projects of reformation was lost because of the decay in evangelical religion in the successors of the founders. It is fairly evident, however, that nothing as intrinsically legal and theocratic as the reforming societies could have brought any vital renewal to English society. They were a final and unsuccessful echo of Geneva in English Protestant life.[69]

The idea of using *collegia* as instruments of moral reformation, however, did have some appeal in the early 1700s to leaders who had already found cell groups useful in supporting piety; and both Francke in Halle and Mather in Boston sought to blend an element of moral reformation into their practice. Even before the appearance of the reforming societies, Spener, in 1678, had been aware of the religious societies in England, and had prepared a Latin translation of the *Pia Desideria* to reach such groups. But around the turn of the century, Francke learned of the new reforming societies through the diplomat H. W. Ludolf, wrote an account of his own work for the S.P.C.K., and became a corresponding member of that organization.[70] In 1709, Francke told the

London groups that societies of reformation were in existence on the Continent in Nuremberg, Augsburg, Ratisbon, Schaffhausen,[71] and Brussels.[72]

Meanwhile, by 1702, Mather in Boston had heard of the London societies, probably through his friend Edward Bromfield, and had established two societies in his own area, one in imitation of the British Society for the Propagation of the Christian Religion (formed in London in 1699), and the other a society for the suppression of disorders, comprised of fourteen civic leaders and lesser magistrates (*Diary*, I, 412). In 1703 he published his own popularization of the work of the English Reformation societies, *Methods and Motives, for a Society to Suppress Disorders* (I, 500). By June 1705 the reforming society, composed of members from the three Congregational churches in town, had grown to the point where Mather had to split it into three societies, with one each for the north and south ends of town (I, 516-517). In 1706 some forty people involved in the Society for Propagating Christian Knowledge and "the several Societies for the Suppressions of Disorders" met at Mather's house for a day of fasting and prayer for revival and reformation at home and abroad (I, 531). In 1710, Mather noted that a new society had been formed, and he determined to devote one day in each weekly cycle of "Good Devices" to meditation on how to serve and animate these societies (II, 27). Throughout most of the rest of his life Mather regularly encouraged the societies to bring legal sanctions to bear on problems ranging from profane language among school children (II, 206) to houses of prostitution (II, 229, 235, 283). He also did everything in his power to convince the existing religious societies to add a dimension of reformation of manners to their character (II, 156).[73]

Mather's first publications urging the formation of reforming societies are fairly candid about what these intend. *Methods and Motives* (1703), which notes the spread of this method in Ireland, Scotland, Holland, and Switzerland as well as England and Germany, states that the societies should number between seven and seventeen members (though they can operate with only three or four); that they should include a minister and a justice of the peace; and that they should discuss during each meeting the existing disorders and means of restraining them legally. But he adds that the society and its membership should be kept secret, so it is evident that he already recognized the existence of a certain risk of controversy.[74] *A Faithful Monitor* (1714) discusses the London societies and insists that reformation must be prosecuted both by magistrates and informers such as the Tything men; but the tract is at least moderate in urging that some secret abuses could be settled out of court if the informer felt that to be more discreet.[75] Gradually, however, Mather's public utterances on the societies take on a cautious and defensive attitude. *Private Meetings Animated and Regulated* (1706) does not list reforming societies in its typology of *collegia*, but notes that these are only attacked where "The savour of Experimental *Piety* has left People," compiles a lengthy scriptural warrant for them, and protests that the kinds of meetings listed are not seditious or otherwise objectionable.[76] *Pastoral Desires* (1712) seems to stress mainly the meetings for spiritual edification, but notes carefully that these should avoid gossip and meddling.[77] A late revision of the section on the societies in *Bonifacius* is careful to state that these should:

> be exceedingly Careful, that their *Discourse* while they are together . . . have nothing in it, that shall have any Taint of *Backbiting* or *Vanity*, or the least Relation to the Affairs of the *Government*, or to things which do not Concern them and do not serve the Interests of *Holiness* in Their own Conversation. But let their Discourse be wholly on *Matters of Religion*, and those also, not the *Disputable* and *Controversial* Matters, but the Points of *Practical Piety*.[78]

The *Ratio Disciplinae* of 1726 goes into detail about the religious societies but does not even mention societies of reformation.[79] In the meantime, Mather's *Diary* indicates that things were not going smoothly for the reforming impulse among the societies after their first flowering, for after 1710 some of these were disbanding and others reverting to pure religious edification (II, 42, 56). The "General *Society, for the Suppression of Disorders*" was "dissolved by the Calamities of

Winter" in 1714 and had to be restimulated (II, 275). By 1724 all the societies devoted specifically to reforming manners had disintegrated, victims doubtless of the apathy of their members, the overall fruitlessness of their efforts, and the criticism that can be heard faintly behind Mather's guarded public references to them. But privately Mather was still staunchly behind the idea: "I purpose, if I can, to draw a number of our Ministers, into a Combination, to erect and revive a *Society for the Suppression of Disorders;* which may go on upon such a Plan, as in this Town such a Society formerly went upon; and a World of Good was accomplished" (II, 767).

It is true that the strictly religious societies experienced difficulties along with their cousins devoted merely to reformation (II, 107). Part of the problem with both types of society may have been their loose relationship to ministerial authority and the consequent lack of experienced guidance. Mather was of two minds about this. On the one hand, he speaks with admiration of the powerful impression made on Giles Firmin by the prayers of "plain mechanicks,"[80] and of the occasional preaching of laymen. On the other hand, his regard for church order (or his awareness of others' regard for it) caused him to go on record against purely lay leadership.[81] Yet it seems clear that very often the religious and reforming societies had to proceed without ministerial leadership, for Mather was constantly complaining that he was out of touch with the multiplicity of societies operating in Boston (*Diary*, II, 44, 153, 439).

Whatever problems the religious and reforming societies encountered, Mather throughout his life regarded them as both a prime index of spiritual vitality in a community and a potent instrument for producing it.

> Experience tells us, That where they have been kept alive, and under a Prudent Conduct, the Christians that have composed them, have like so many *Living Coals* kept one another alive, and kept up the Life of Christianity in the Vicinity. But the Dying of these has been accompanied with a Visible Death upon the *Power of Godliness;* the less Love to them, the less *Use* of them, there has been in any Place, the less has all *Godliness* flourished there.[82]

He considered even the pure reforming societies part of the vanguard of the expected premillennial awakening:

> A *Spirit of Association* for Noble & Pious Purposes, has of late begun Strangely to Visit the World; it begins to do Wondrously. Some *Societies* perhaps are yet only laying *Foundations*, for purposes of a more Exact Regulation hereafter to be built upon. But as far off as in *Switzerland* they Prognosticate upon them; *They annunciate a more Illustrious State of the Church of God, that is Expected, in the Conversion of Jews & Gentiles.*[83]

The reforming societies may seem rather legalistic to be considered a harbinger of revival, but, as Samuel Mather points out, Cotton Mather's use of them was not confined to legal repression of non-Puritan behavior but also extended to the consideration of cases of oppression or fraudulence in the business life of the community and care for the needy and afflicted.[84] The societies were employed as socio-religious associations for the spiritual and corporal care of whole neighborhoods. Thus they not only predicted some of the features of the nineteenth-century voluntary societies that were their lineal descendants, but in some measure surpassed those as expressions of local spiritual and social concern (*Diary*, II, 102).

Mather's equal concern for the spiritual well-being of his community and for its material, social, and political needs makes him uniquely fascinating to modern Christians weary of the current unnatural separation between these realms, or the reduction of one into the other. We have already indicated that Mather's social activism was in no way peculiar to him. In breaking down the monastery walls and endeavoring to make the whole parish into an ideal community of love and mutual concern modeled on the church in Acts or the Old Testament tribal unit, the Puritans had added an even stronger social dynamic to the already developed unity of medieval society, which has structured almsgiving to the poor and charity to other needy situations into its piety of works. Puritan casuistry conceived of the individual's responsibility to society as an economy of radiating circles of concern, spreading out from his own and his family's needs to embrace his neighbors, his countrymen, and all mankind, with a slightly greater priority given to the needs of people's souls than to those of their bodies, and to believers over nonbelievers. Though the hierarchical concept of class structure was still taken for granted—and indeed carefully reinforced by religious sanctions—Puritanism had a certain implicit revolutionary dynamic due to its biblical emphasis on the excellence of the lowly. This was balanced, however, by another strong biblical vector enforcing respect for constituted authority. The Protestant concept of vocation introduced a new egalitarian note against the older medieval attitude that ranked clerks above mechanics, insisting that careful fulfillment of a "low" vocation is as valid and praiseworthy as the same achievement in a calling of "higher status." While it was assumed (again, on biblical grounds from the prevalent teaching in the Old Testament) that normally the godly will prosper, there was no blanket endorsement of the wealthy as a class or capitalism as a system, but rather the emphasis was on restraint of usury and sinfully motivated economic endeavor.

For this reason the profit motive was universally condemned, competition was discouraged, a *via media* with respect to prosperity was endorsed as probably most healthy, and most forms of economic behavior were intrinsically suspect as either visionary or exploitative. The result was a thoroughly social-minded ethical consciousness that was the polar opposite of the rugged individualism attributed to nineteenth-century evangelicalism. The governmental theory that resulted involved an approach to the relief of social need which approximated that of the modern welfare state, with a concern even for "preventive charity," and for the maintenance of public institutions such as colleges, hospitals, libraries, and free schools. This, of course, was only in the theoretical basis of the ministers' consciousness: how their parishioners followed through on this ideal was, as always, another matter.[85] But in the favorable circumstances of New England Puritanism, the community which developed from the first generation of founders actually was bound together with strong ties of mutual concern—Battis characterized Governor Winthrop's administration as a typi-

cal welfare state that was less than acceptable to the prosper-
ous merchant class already appearing in Boston[86]—and, as
Murdock says, there was a long tradition in New England of
"public spirit" and social consciousness, culminating very
signally in Increase and Cotton Mather.[87]

I have already observed that, contrary to popular
stereotypes, Continental Pietism in its strongest period was
just as conscious and active as Puritanism in the remedy of
social need. Erich Beyreuther attributes this in part to a
general broadening in social outlook at the close of the seventeenth century, common to both religious and pre-
Enlightenment circles in Europe, as people reacted to a century of hatred and strife and sought constructive cultural
alternatives, producing a new and active leadership which
Beyreuther calls *homo societatis*.[88] But the same activism and
social concern were present virtually at the beginning of
Pietism in Germany. Arndt's *True Christianity*, for instance,
has a strong ethical impulse and stresses equally the love of
God and concern for neighbors, although it has usually been
pilloried as an expression of world-forsaking mysticism.[89]
J. V. Andreae, one of Arndt's friends, wrote a utopia, the
Christianopolis, which projects the distinctive Pietist approach to live orthodoxy, and also presents an advanced set
of suggestions for Christian social reform. Influenced
perhaps by Calvin's work in Geneva, Andreae has much to
say about associations for civic welfare, education and the
support of impoverished students, and government-directed
relief for the poor and sick.[90]

Essentially the same concern for social need is carried
over in Spener's *Pia Desideria* and in his whole ministry;[91]
but Spener (unlike the Puritans) agreed with Lutheran orthodoxy in advising against direct political action on the part
of churchmen,[92] and he did not project any practical solu-
tions to social problems.[93] It is with Francke, however, that
the full impact of Pietism for social transformation was first
historically demonstrated. Beginning in the parish at
Glaucha by feeding and simultaneously catechizing the orphaned and impoverished survivors of the Thirty Years'

War, in several decades he transformed the town into a social and cultural center in which the large cluster of institutions he began, including an orphanage, hospital, library, and missionary center, testified to the social impact of his approach to Christian experience.[94] Although most historians have represented Halle Pietism as essentially conservative and apolitical in Spener's fashion,[95] Beyreuther maintains that a systematic remedy for poverty—and even a levelling of social classes—were implicit in Francke's thought, and that not only the nobility but the state itself was to be mobilized toward these goals.[96] However, all these social ideals were grounded in Francke's expectation of spiritual awakening on a broad scale. In Francke's vision of the future, as in that of Comenius, churches and schools would not merely transmit knowledge but transform lives, and the result would be a new social and political order.[97]

Since there is so great an affinity between Mather's own tradition and Francke's, it is not surprising that Mather should respond eagerly to the news of the latter's charitable work at Glaucha, specifically to the accounts of his labors with orphans. In April 1711 he notes in the *Diary*: "Which of the Tribes of Israel, have I left yett unserved? The *Orphans.* They are numerous and afflicted. . . . I have an opportunity to publish a Book for *Orphans*" (II, 57). In May of that year he sent his *Orphanotrophium* and a gift of four pounds in gold to the orphanage at Halle (II, 73-74, 150), and some months later he wrote again to Halle with another gift, urging the translation of Puritan works on piety into German (II, 563). He continued to support the work in Halle during the rest of his life, and also on several occasions he took orphans into his own home for a season (II, 344, 349, 495, 518, 522, 570). Some years earlier, Mather had been active through the religious societies in the founding of a charity school for poor children and orphans, and he gave a good deal of subsequent attention to the preservation and improvement of this work (II, 24, 27, 214, 341, 344, 370). A second school, for the education of blacks, was begun in 1716 and maintained for years solely at Mather's expense (II, 379, 500, 663).

Most of Mather's social thought and charitable action

evolved from his own tradition, and not through Pietist
influence. Like Glaucha, Boston during Mather's lifetime
was an appropriate laboratory for the development of Christian social action. It was the wealthiest city among the colonies, and following Winthrop's original intent, it took better care of the poor than most others, and so attracted more
vagrants. There were many orphans and widows left from
the intermittent wars—Mather said in 1718 that a fifth of his
congregation consisted of widows[98]—and fires and plagues
combined to increase this problem during the early part of
the eighteenth century. Carl Bridenbaugh notes that the
churches, and particularly Mather, through his "animation"
of the religious societies, took an eminent part in meeting
these problems: "No family of colonial times ever demanded,
or deserved, more respect than the Mathers; in religious,
political and public concerns, they exerted an enormous influence. . . . Cotton Mather was without question the most
public spirited colonial before Benjamin Franklin, who drew
much of his inspiration from the Boston minister."[99]

There are two main presuppositions that motivated
Mather's social concern, both directly rooted in his tradition.
The first is drawn more or less from the light of reason,
although Mather could find a theocratic text for it in Esther
4:14: it is "the duty of a public spirit, that every Christian
should venture all for God's People," for the commonwealth
of which he is a member.[100] The second is derived from the
teaching of Christ in the parable of the Good Samaritan, that
every Christian has an obligation to his neighbors, including
a responsibility to give material aid to them when needed.[101]
"It would be the unspeakable Joy of a Good man, to See all
his Neighbours about Him, *Happy.* If he can't see all that he
would see of that, he will do all he can however to make
them, *Easy.* A minister should Study to be a *Barnabas;* and to
Cheer as well as to *Save,* the Souls of them that Hear him."[102]
The mixture of physical sympathy and spiritual concern here
is echoed in other sermons: "Christians, Let your *Hearts*
Bleed with *Compassion,* when you see the *Spiritual* . . . and
the *Temporal Miseries* of other men."[103] "And *agreeably,* while
we satisfy not our selves with saying, *Be you Warmed and*

Filled; but help you to such *Things as are needful to the Body,* there are some Things, relating to your *Soul,* which we judge it proper at the same time to mind you of."[104]

Perry Miller has criticized Mather's handling of the relationships between poverty and wealth, asserting that he was a semiconscious instrument of the preservation of the establishment and that his addresses to the poor "are among the most brutal" of all the religious apologists for privilege.[105] This appears to be a seriously mistaken evaluation of Mather when it is analyzed within the whole scope of Mather's statements on the issues. Mather is typical of classical Puritanism in his mistrust of wealth: *"Great Estates,* like to *great Rivers,* often are swelled by Muddy Streams running into them. Some of the *Wealth* is *Ill gotten Wealth. Dishonest Gain* has increased it. *Unfair* and *unjust* Things have been done in the amassing of it."[106] This is not a simple moralistic attack on overt robbery. Mather considers the covetousness of the rich evil not only because it breaks commandments but because it destroys the fabric of society:

> Men grow more *Dangerous Criminals,* and are so sharp with the *Cursed Hunger of Riches,* that they do things wherein *Humane Society* shall be considerably Damnified. Our Gracious GOD has a Wondrous Tenderness for *Humane Society;* And when men grow so Outrageous in the Ways of *Dishonesty,* that *Humane Society* suffers Insupportable Damages from them; Now there goes up that Cry to Heaven, *'Tis Time, Lord, for thee to work!* And GOD comes down, GOD steps in, GOD in Compassion to *Humane Society,* fulfils that word upon the man who *trusted in the abundance of his Riches.*[107]

There is abundant evidence that Mather was extremely disturbed by the prevalence of dishonest business practices in Boston, and he was not afraid to rebuke these before congregations which numbered wealthy tradesmen among the supporters of the church. The techniques of this malpractice are described principally in two sermons devoted to business ethics, *Lex Mercatoria* (1705) and *Theopolis Americana* (1710). In the first of these, while protesting that Boston's business habits were better than average, Mather attacks the prevalence of open theft, misrepresentation of defective merchandise, false measures, financial exploitation of the poor and ignorant, inordinate and uncompensated borrowing, the dishonesty of lawyers, cheats on the public treasury, and trades that are socially destructive (such as prostitution, gaming, fortune-telling, and tavern-keeping improperly managed). As partial answers to these problems, Mather recommends the practice of the Golden Rule, and he urges a real consideration of the benefit of the commonwealth on the part of merchants. Both of these sermons urge as the ultimate answer, however, the repentance and regeneration of more of the merchant population.[108] But it is not just dishonest practice among employers that Mather attacks here, but all oppression of the working class, or even a coldly businesslike attitude that leaves them to their fate. In *The Fisherman's Calling* Mather includes a preface directed to the employers of fishermen, encouraging them to regard their employees as a kind of family for which they are responsible:

> [I] Entreat of *You,* That you would not only be always very *Just;* but also be very *Kind* unto them. And that you would not cause *The Fishes Life,* (a very Ancient Proverb, for a Life Obnoxious to continual Difficulties, and Depredations,) to be the *Fisherman's* . . . That you do not use any Unfair *Oppression* or *Extortion* upon them; That you do not improve the Opportunities which their *Necessities* and *Entanglements* may give you, to Exact Severely upon them; That in your Dealings with them, you manifest your selves to be *Full of Goodness;* Very Tenderhearted and Compassionate; Very Averse to the doing of any thing which will not square well with the *Conscience* of that *Golden Rule, To do as you would be done unto* . . . That you would be very *Fathers* to them; and fore-cast for them, to make a better Provision for them, and for their Families, than they would themselves make, if they were left unto themselves, and their own Unhappy Conduct. Estates Raised by a cruel scruing upon Poor *Fisher-men,* may feel, and have often felt, an Observable Blast from God upon them.[109]

It is true that at other points in this tract, as in certain other writings, Mather endeavors to allay social unrest by persuading the poor to accept their position as providentially ordained.

> There is one thing more, against which I will warn my *Fisherman,* and then I will add no more: That is, A Sinful Discontent, with his own *Low, & Small, & Hard* Circumstances in the

World. . . . Tis true, you may *fare hardly*, and you can't enjoy many possessions & enjoyments, wherein you may see some other People flourishing. But it is a Wise GOD, who has made this Condition, *The thing appointed for you;* And a *Contentment* with your Condition, is no little part of that Obedience, wherewith you are to Glorify Him. . . . It will be but a *little while* that you shall Continue in any of your Uneasy Circumstances. Know CHRIST, and Serve Him, and Live Religiously & Contentedly, and you will quickly be taken into that Heavenly World, where you shall be with *Peter* and *James* and *John*, and see things beyond what they saw, when they were with our Saviour. . . . Pious, and Prayerful, and Patient Fisher-men, will be some of them who shall *Shine, in the Kingdom* of our Saviour.[110]

Another tract devoted exclusively to this line of thought make a cheerful submission to poverty one of the marks of regeneration, and goes on to say:

Tis the GOD of Heaven who has Ordered your being found among the *Poor of the Earth. O potsherd of the Earth,* Since 'tis the *work of His Hands,* which has made you to be what you are, and will have you to be a Vessel not guilded with some of the shining Dust that He has allowed unto others, Glorify Him with a Submission to His Holy *Sovereignty.* . . . All your present *Poverty,* is but the Inconvenience of an *Inn,* where you are but *as a wayfaring Man, which turns aside but for a Night. . . .* And if you carry it well under your *Poverty,* it will be but a *Short Moment* before you come to that *Glad Moment,* when you shall at once find yourself invested with what will render you Richer, than if you should light on a Rock of Diamonds, or a Mountain of Gold. . . . You must be *Poor in Spirit,* if you would have a part in the *Kingdom of Heaven.* The *Poor in Spirit,* are they that bear to be Poor, and have a *Spirit* reconciled unto *Poverty,* if it please the Sovereign Disposer of all things, to bring them unto it. What? Can't you bear to be *Beholden unto Friends,* when GOD will have you to be so? This *Heighth* of *Spirit* looks ill. . . . It may seem an *Hard Saying,* but it must be said; If you can't bring your *Spirit* unto this, *To be willing to go to Heaven by the way of an Alms-house, when God shall assign you such a Lodging,* you may justly question, whether you shall ever come thither.[111]

It should be noted here that Mather did not assume in nineteenth-century fashion that poverty was the inevitable punishment for slothfulness, or for any other kind of sin. On the contrary, like Job's misfortunes, it may be just part of the

life one has been dealt by providence, simply one kind of
obstacle course whose completion can lead to our sanctification. Mather occasionally remarks that God may bless piety
in this life with an increase in riches or status,[112] and he even
uses this as a bait to encourage piety.[113] His answer to the
Weber-Tawney thesis is that God does bless Protestant nations with material goods: "The *Protestant Religion* hath not
been set up scarce in *any Nation*, but it has made them, even
in Temporals, within a very little while, twice as *Rich* and as
Great as they were before; And one, somewhat curious in his
Calculations, has demonstrated, That the Abolishing of *Pop-
ery* in the *English Nation*, is worth at least Eight Millions of
Pounds Sterling, yearly profit unto it.[114]

On the other hand, he held that the Old Testament promises of prosperity accompanying piety were never absolutely
universal, and were less certain than ever in the New Testament era. In discussing the proposals of the Reforming
Synod, Mather even went so far as to question the prevailing
theory of providence and the national covenant, although he
asserts elsewhere that there is still value in testing ourselves
when our circumstances decay too far: "Its true, In the Dayes
of the *Old Testament*, there was more of a *Temporal Advantage*
usually Rewarding the Service of God. A more Carnal &
Childish Temper, was then prevailing. The Lord hired His
People, to learn His Lessons, with the fine Apples of *Temporal Advantage*. . . . But now the Dealings of God with His
People are more Mysterious."[115] "Indeed . . . our SAVIOUR
has no where Promised a *Temporal Prosperity*, unto a Life of
Piety; but bid us look for the Discipline of the *Cross*."[116]
Actually, for Mather, both prosperity and poverty were only
diverse kinds of trials sent to test the sincerity of piety,[117]
and the only assured promise we have as a reward for piety is
that God will give us the desires of our heart if we delight
ourselves in him, even if he must change those desires in the
process.[118] Mather was evidently quite accustomed to finding a disproportion between wealth and piety within his
own congregation: "You are my Witnesses, that when a *con-
spicuous Piety* has distinguished [men], I have not fail'd of
taking a due Public Notice of them. Tho' they may have been

Persons of a *Low Degree* in *Poverty*, yet if they have had an *High Degree* of *Piety*, to render them observable Blessings to the Neighborhood, I have endeavored, that *GOD may be Glorified in them.*"[119]

Mather clearly felt that there was a public as well as a private dimension in our responsibility for the relief of the poor, for he was one of the most active agents in forwarding civic care in this direction, specifically in the improvement of the Boston Alms House.[120] It is true, however, that much of his treatment of the subject falls back on private means as institutionalized in medieval almsgiving. "Is not *Alms-giving* a considerable Article of *Righteousness?* 'Tis all over the Bible call'd so, and for weighty and obvious Reasons. 'Tis opposite here, to the spirit and conduct of the *Men of this World*, who what they don't spend on their own bellies, are studious to leave all the rest unto their Children."[121] Both Increase Mather and his son were themselves extraordinarily generous in almsgiving, even in times of personal poverty.[122] The Mathers attached no connotation of superiority to the donor of alms, at least in theory; he was merely an instrument of providence:

> GOD your SAVIOUR saw your *Necessities*, and made *Impressions* on the Mind of your *Benefactor*. When your *Benefactor* was *Considering the Poor*, and *Considering* whom to *do Good* unto, it was GOD, who brought *You*, rather than *Another*, into his *Consideration*. And no doubt, He employed His *Good Angel*, in the Matter; and sent one of those *Ministering Spirits . . . Ministering to your Necessities.* Your *Benefactor* is but the *Instrument* of Heaven in what is done for you.[123]

This concept of charity permits the recipient of help to ignore the donor rather than to grovel before him, and it allows an honorable posture to the man whom God has chosen to place in poverty.[124] It is a posture that may mortify his sinful pride, but, as any monastic saint under the twofold surgery of vows of obedience and poverty would have recognized— and as Mather clearly emphasizes—this cannot be anything but beneficial. The comparison is appropriate, for Mather actually viewed class structures as though the world were simply a gigantic monastery without walls, a school of obedience to God, to be learned by careful subservice to superiors or responsible management of inferiors. Of course, he felt that the hierarchy of classes was clearly taught in Scripture, especially in the practical portions of Paul's letters.

This assumption of the divine right and origin of class distinctions helps to explain Mather's attitude toward slavery, which in typical Matherian fashion attempted to ameliorate the abuses and harmful side effects of the institution without radically changing it. The Puritan tradition in general dealt sparsely and rather ambiguously with this subject. William Perkins merely tolerated the institution, hedging it about with a number of imperatives dealing with the duties of masters, and preferring the use of hired servants; but he held that the practice could be considered ethically valid if carefully used and established by positive law in a country, basing this on Paul's toleration of it. He qualified this, however, by a number of precepts from the Old Testament, which effectively removed slavery from its Aristotelian basis in natural inferiority and made it a result of the Fall and not inherent in the natural order.[125]

Baxter, in his *Christian Directory*, condemned the slave trade as "One of the worst kinds of Thievery in the World,"[126] but did not object to Christians owning slaves if they took pains to bring the gospel to them; and this is substantially the position that Mather adopted. He was fairly enlightened for a man who frequently admitted the dependence of his own household on slave labor.[127] *A Good Master Well Served* (1696), his tract adjudicating both sides of the slave-master relationship, is a reasonably balanced account of his position. After first stating that his relation is one of three social orders within "the Domestical Society"—the Conjugal, Parental, and Herile—Mather goes on to exhort the owners to assign only good work and in moderation; to provide adequate food, clothing, and medicine; to keep appropriate discipline among them; and most importantly, to care for their slaves' souls. In the second half of the tract, Mather first advises the slaves how to be subject first to Christ and only secondarily to men, and then instructs them in obedience, diligence, fidelity, and serviceableness to their masters, and the duty to avoid spiritually and economically injurious pastimes such as reading idle romances and gaming. Mather seems genuinely to have the spiritual interests of the slaves at heart and not simply their pacification; he urges slaves to witness to their masters about Christ, showing by their obedience to them their obedience to God, and even advises occasional civil disobedience.[128]

Mather was moved to compassion by the physical indignities suffered by slaves, as he makes clear in a letter to A. W. Boehm: "Our Islands are indeed inhabited by such as are called Christians. But, alas, how dissolute are their Manners! And how inhumane the way of their Subsistence, on the sweat and Blood of Slaves treated with infinite Barbarities!" (*Diary,* II, 412). Most of his concern, however, was channeled toward the conversion of slaves under Christian masters. In July 1700 he projected a tract exhorting slavemasters to seek the conversion of their servants (I, 356). In a September 1706 entry he records that he wrote letters to persons of eminence in the West Indies urging the same cause, and sought through Sir William Ashurst to procure an act of Parliament to forward that purpose (I, 570). E. S. Morgan states that most evidence compels the conclusion that not many Negro slaves in New England actually became devoted Puritans,[129] but Mather intimates the conversion of those in his own household (*Diary,* II, 663), and the presence of a fair number of them in his congregation (I, 278): "I have a Number of black Sheep in my Flock, which it is time for me again, to send for; and pray with them, and preach to them, and enquire into their Conduct, and encourage them, in the ways of Piety: a Religious Society of Negros" (II, 532). Thus the Negro religious society formed in 1693 was still functioning successfully in 1718.

Mather himself evidently felt that he had an outstanding record as a proponent of slave rights and welfare. His activities on their behalf ranged from widescale public efforts, such as his activation and support of the Charity School (II, 478, 663), to innumerable small acts of charity. He states that he had often done "Good Offices . . . for oppressed and afflicted Slaves . . . without my making in these Records any Mention of them" (II, 769). It is, nevertheless, unavoidably evident that in today's social context Mather would be attacked as a typical "white liberal," since even his defense of blacks is patronizing and riddled with ethnic prejudice. He states magnanimously that all will gather in Heaven at Abraham's Table, "even, the *Indians,* and the *Negro's*—Hear this, ye *dark-hued Ones,* & under your Despised Complexion, let these News wondrously encourage you to become the *Seekers of GOD.*"[130] The adjectives "poor" and "miserable" invariably accompany the mention of blacks, although this may simply be a reflex of Mather's compassion and not a value judgment. Mather preaches the equality of the races, but seems to use it to tear down the pride of masters rather than to exalt the status of the slaves: "All . . . Rational Beings . . . are the *Off-spring* of the *First Adam.* . . . The Difference of *Complexion* . . . is no Objection. . . . We may value our selves on this Account; But, *Wilt thou know, O vain Man?* Thy *Negro* is thy *Brother.*"[131] Mather himself was not able to see it quite this objectively, however, when enemies named their slaves after him. "*What has a gracious Lord given me to do,* for the Instruction, and Salvation, and Comfort, of the poor *Negro's?* AND YETT, some, on purpose to affront me, call their *Negro's,* by the Name of *Cotton Mather,* that so they may with some Shadow of Truth, assert Crimes as committed by one of that Name, which the Hearers take to be *me*" (*Diary,* II, 706).

The Mathers, like all their contemporaries, failed to see the corporate basis of the problems which they sought to solve by individual acts of charity, and they did not often suggest remedies involving changes in the social organism. It is easy for hindsight to criticize the insufficiency of their remedies for poverty and other social ills without remembering the costliness of these remedies and the dogged moral courage which drove them into something relatively more difficult than holding and voting correct political opinions and paying taxes cheerfully: the daily struggle to become aware of local need and the hourly challenge to relinquish varying amounts of money and goods in order to rectify the problems. It can safely be said that there were no more socially concerned individuals in America than the Mathers during their era. The fine criteria for this concern in Mather's portrait of the ideal minister are simply a mirror of his own life—or at the least, of the goals he set himself:

> HAS he a tender sense of the *Temptations* and *Afflictions*, in which many of the People are Languishing? Is he as ready to visit the Poor, as the Rich? Will he hazard his own Health, to visit the *Sick*? Does he keep with him a *Catalogue* of such as are in want? Is he always *devising Liberal Things* for them? Scattering his own *Alms* like the Showers of Heaven; Exciting those of *others* when his own are Exhausted? Making it a common Subject of Conversation where he comes, *What shall be done for such or such a Distressed Object?* [132]

Like the late nineteenth-century evangelicals and many of their descendants in this century, Mather was convinced of the priority of spiritual regeneration in the transformation of society; but unlike these, he was not content to hold that evangelistic proclamation was all that the church need worry about, and that it should leave the bodies of people untouched by its concern. Like Francke, he felt that spiritual revival on the basis of the existential core of Reformation Christianity was the key to unlocking the hearts of men to deal with social ills:

> Oh! if our *Prayers* may have any share, in obtaining a *Zeal of the Lord of Hosts* to be Enkindled in more of His People, for the Propagating of a *Religion* which Glorifies Him, and Recovers Mankind unto Felicity! Then should we see another face of the corners of *England*, the Highlands of *Scotland*, the boggy Recesses of *Ireland*, than there is yet appearing. *Then* should we see the *Africans* no longer so treated like meer *Beasts of Burden,* as they are in the Plantations of cruel *Americans:* and the Great Revenues left unto the Charitable Design of *Christianizing* the *Negro's,* would have some Good Account given to them. *Then* should we see the Noble *Essays to Save a Lost World,* carried as far as the Hunger of *Trade,* now makes Men run thro' *Sea* and *Land,* even to the *Indies.* [133]

Mather had only contempt for a docetic orthodoxy that would limit its response to spiritual well-wishing in the presence of human need. "How runs the Final Sentence of the *Righteous* but so? *Come, ye Blessed, Inherit the Kingdom; Inasmuch as you*

were Liberal to my Afflicted Members in the former World.
(Mark) He says not, *For you have been Orthodox in your
Opinions,* or, *You have been Eminent in your Professions,* or, *You
have been abundant in your Devotions;* No, *But you have been
Liberal to the Miserable."*[134]

What was the response of the city of Boston, and
Mather's own congregation, to all his labors and projections
of good will? There was a certain amount of gratitude toward
Mather among the fairly large group of his friends, and there
were steady accessions to church membership and several
larger ingatherings of converts; but there were rarely any
signs of widespread spiritual awakening. Mather occasionally had a good word for his congregation, at least in public.
In his father's funeral sermon he tells them, "He ever look'd
on you, and spoke of you, as a very *Loving* People: And he
very much ascribed the Prolongation of his Life unto your
praying for it."[135] He was grateful even in private for the
collection taken up by a group of his people to relieve him of
the debt incurred in his settlement of his wife's husband's
estate *(Diary,* II, 739). On the other hand, most of Mather's
private ruminations have to do with the shortcomings of his
people. Late in his career he lamented that so little of what he
had preached had got through to them and become real in
their lives. "I am astonished, I am astonished at the prodigious
Ignorance of our People in Matters of Religion, after all the
Instruction bestow'd upon them. Among other instances, their
foolish Talk, about the *Decrees of* GOD, is notorious" (II, 664).
The abuse he complains of here is probably the same one he
commented on fifteen years earlier:

> In my continual Addresses unto People of all sorts, to sett upon
> the Practice of serious Religion, I am still answered by them,
> *that they can't.* They fearfully abuse the Doctrine of Man's
> Inability to turn to God and walk with Him, until supernatural
> Grace enable him, as if it were a very pretty Apology for their
> Continuance in their Slothfulness and Wickedness (I, 573).

Mather's accommodations in presenting this doctrine were
evidently not enough to eliminate the problem. I have already commented on the concern he expressed in his sermons regarding those who neglect the Lord's Supper, and

this is also a refrain in the diaries (II, 251, 462, 783). The problem in the congregation he remarked on most, however, was its response to affluence: "Worldly-mindedness, the *Praecipuum crimen humani Generis;* there is nothing my Flock is more in danger of" (II, 79). A concomitant to the congregation's preoccupation with wealth was its indifference to spiritual mission: "We have religious People, whose nearest Relatives are poor, vain, carnal Creatures, utterly destitute of the Symptomes of Regeneration. And yett they seem very easy and thoughtless about them. While they are in this World well provided for, and carry it well towards them, they seem to take no further Thought about them" (II, 120).

Mather's use of the jeremiad form in responding to these problems is considerably less frequent and strident than is usually thought. [136] It is significant that the largest block of utterances of this sort was produced within a single decade, 1690-1700, when Mather was still digesting his father's chiliastic philosophy of history and was also most under the influence of the sermonic models of the previous generation. Five of these are full-length essays in the jeremiad form, counting the *Magnalia,* which may be considered its apotheosis. [137] A number of other works allude to New England's spiritual decline in small passages of lament. [138] The tone and the type of analyses in these works is indeed that of the traditional jeremiad: "The Lord our God, seems to have a peculiar Controversy with the *Rising Generation* of *New England.*" [139] The evils touched on by Mather include those of contention, ingratitude, [140] neglect of education, sloth in re-pastoring churches, contempt of public servants, [141] and violation of the seventh commandment. [142] But the principal roots of the problem appeared to him to lie in the worldliness of the older generation, which had made them spiritually impotent, and the consequent unregeneracy of so many in the rising generation: "The chief *hazard* and symptom of degeneracy, is in the verification of that old observation, . . . 'Religion brought forth Prosperity, and the *daughter* destroyed the *mother.*' " [143]

> Men are so taken up with *secular* and *sensual* matters, that they have no leisure to acquaint themselves with a precious Jesus.

> . . . But among all the *deadly Symptoms* which threaten us with
> a speedy Ruine, there is none more ghastly, than the igno-
> rance, the wildness, the lewdness found in so great a part of
> the *Rising Generation*. . . . It was the last and worst of all the
> *Egyptian* plagues, That a *Child* was *dead* in every house.[144]

But it is highly significant that the remedies proposed for
spiritual degeneration in these sermons are strictly evangelical and not legal, as in the case of some of the recommendations of the Reforming Synod; and it is especially
noteworthy that over half the documents conclude by urging
prayer for the outpouring of God's Spirit as the answer.[145] It
was natural even at this point for Mather to turn to revival as
the ultimate answer to decline, since his father had voiced
hopes for this as early as 1678.[146] It is also interesting that all
but two of the jeremiads in this first decade of Mather's
published works appear before 1696, when he expected the
imminence of a new and unprecedented spiritual awakening.

In the next twenty years of Mather's ministry, from
1700-1720, there are fewer instances of the jeremiad style
than we can find in all his writings prior to 1696. There are
only two real jeremiads published during the period, although others may have been preached.[147] A number of
other sermons strike the jeremiad note, probing a number of
signs of decline, chiefly religious apathy.[148] But in half these
sermons there is either an encouragement to prayer for revival or else an outright statement of Mather's expectancy for
revival. In the final seven years of Mather's life, from 1720-
1727, the jeremiad note begins to sound again with comparative frequency. Mather composed three full-scale jeremiads
during this period which are of significance. The first of
these, *The Ambassadors Tears* (1721), subtitled "An unsuccessful ministry bewailed," is conventional in its analysis of the
problem, but sounds an unusual note of tired self-accusation
against the Puritan ministry as partially responsible for the
decline.[149] *Suspiria Vinctorum* (1726) is remarkable in that it is
a jeremiad for the entire Christian world, not just for the
covenant nation of New England, surveying principally the
martyrdom of Protestants under persecution by Rome and
the loss of Protestant territory, but issuing in a treatment

of world-wide spiritual decline among the Reformed churches.[150]

And yet, in the face of his discouraging experience with his own congregation and the city of Boston, and his wide knowledge of the presence of spiritual decline elsewhere in the Christian world, it is remarkable that Mather's basic mood over the years is one of militant optimism. Apart from his own temperament, three theological factors contributed to this outlook.

The first factor was an assumption about the history of the church. Mather's philosophy of history, like that of most Puritans and the later Pietists, assumed that the Reformation of the sixteenth century had been only a partial restoration of the New Testament form of the church, as the Anabaptists had insisted.[151] Martin Schmidt points out that the goal of Continental Pietism was always the re-establishment of first-century Christianity, and the finishing of the first and incomplete Reformation.[152] Thus the main theme of Spener's *Pia Desideria* is, as Stoeffler indicates, the incomplete reformation, lamented by Luther himself, in which an original concern for internal piety was smothered by Caesaropapism, an almost magical interpretation of the Word and sacraments, an over-emphasis on forensic justification, and an unbalanced emphasis on purity of doctrine combined with a rationalistic extrapolation of biblical truth into unbiblical systems.[153]

Later Pietists did not hesitate to charge Luther himself with retrogression from the main work of interior reform. Spener himself compared the church of the sixteenth century to the children of Israel after they had left Babylon but had not yet rebuilt the temple or the city of Jerusalem, and he considered himself one who fulfilled Luther rather than simply reiterating his teaching.[154] In his first utterances on the need to perfect this "half-Reformation," Mather seems to lean heavily on the necessity to bring the discipline and government of the church into line with biblical prescriptions: "It must be acknowledged that, in the Protestant Reformation, there has been a great *neglect* and *defect* as to what concerns the discipline and government of Christ in his church. As the *apostacy* was gradual, so has the *Reformation* been."[155] Mather agrees with Owen that this was providential, since he admits that if the Protestants had sought to change all the things initially which the Puritans felt like changing, they would have unchurched the world. He seems at this point still to have conceived of the necessary new Reformation entirely in terms of "the religion of the second commandment," that is, in the establishment of biblically instituted worship, discipline, membership requirements, and polity.[156] There is no mention here of the revitalization of interior godliness, but in the early 1700s this came to be an increasing concern with Mather, and he began to define the new Reformation in slightly different terms.

In *An Advice to the Churches of the Faithful, Briefly Reporting the Present State of the World, and Bespeaking That Fervent Prayer for the Church Which This Time Calleth for . . .* (1702), Mather observes that "the faithful *Reformers* have sometimes bewayled it, That the *Protestants* have *Reformed* nothing but their *Doctrines*," but describes what is lacking as the reformation of lives and manners, to be remedied by prayer for "a wondrous Effusion of the Holy Spirit."[157] By 1715 he had come to define the problem as a neglect of emphasis on sanctification and the preaching of "cheap grace," echoing the analysis of Continental Pietism:

> It is too just an Observation of Late Learned and Famous Writer, That the Zeal of the *Reformed Churches*, hath mostly run out, in declaring that *Path of Faith*, which respects mainly our *Justification* by the *Righteousness* of our Lord Jesus Christ Imputed unto us. But that the notorious and scandalous want of *Godliness* that so disparages the Protestant World, very much arises from their so little Studying and Applying another Doctrine. Even that of *Faith in the Spirit of our Lord Jesus Christ*, which He has promised unto Believers, that by His Assistance we may become *Full of Goodness*, and in the conquest of our Corruptions, and carry on Holiness to *Perfection in the Fear of God*.[158]

A part of Mather's mind had thus come round to a position on the *semper reformanda* that was counter to his old approach: he was now an ecumenist who was partly willing to overlook structural differences and even embrace an Arminian as a brother in Christ, and what he wanted reformed was basically the human heart. We have noted that he was conventional in his defense of the Congregational polity to the very end of his life; but in the face of the decline of the Congregational churches both in New England and the mother country, contrasting to the rebirth of Lutheranism in Pietism, he simply could not locate the deepest need of the churches in the areas of polity and discipline. So in his world jeremiad he returns to the theme of cheap grace:

> The Churches of the *Reformation,* it has long been complained of them, that when they have *Reformed* their *Doctrines,* they have not proportionably *Reformed* their *Manners.* It was the Complaint of *Luther* in his Day . . . People are as *immoral* in their Lives *now,* as they were while they were under the *Slavery* of *Popery.* . . . Among the *Protestants,* how frequent, how common, how Epidemical, is that most offensive Spectacle, *The Truth held in Unrighteousness!* . . . And where Immoralities are less conspicuous, even *There* also, [there is a] *General Decay of Real and Vital PIETY.*[159]

The second theological factor contributing to Mather's lifelong mood of revivalist expectation was a logical extension of Calvin's emphasis on divine sovereignty, and especially his unique accent on the work of the Holy Spirit in redemption. In Mather's ultimate spiritualization of the Puritan concept of the "completed Reformation," in which this tends to become identified with inner transformation rather than exterior reform, there is an unprecedented emphasis on the necessity of the reviving and illuminating power of the Holy Spirit. Mather was first of all convinced that the vitality of Christians was fundamentally dependent neither on the purity of the ministry they were under nor on the willingness of their hearts to respond, but ultimately on the sovereign action of God himself, making the Word fruitful and penetrating the darkened human mind: "The *Success* of the *Ministry* depends on the Gracious Influences of the Holy Spirit; that *South-Wind* blowing on the *Garden.*"[160]

> 'Tis no rare Thing, for the *Great Things* of the *Gospel,* to remain *Strange Things* unto those that have the Revelation brought unto them. The *Mystery of CHRIST* may be preached unto

> People for many Years together, and yet that *Great Mystery of Godliness* be little apprehended with them; they can give but a very poor and mean Account of it. The people who *sat in Darkness*, may see a *great Light*, and yet be so Stupid and Sottish and Unattentive, as to continue in a most unaccountable Darkness after all.[161]

Since the quality of Christianity in an era is thus dependent not on the excellence of the seed, nor the quality of the soil, but on the "weather" of the Spirit's sovereign operation in people's hearts, Mather was led to emphasize continually—as the most important practical answer to the problem of spiritual decline—the concerted prayer of Christians for the charismatic empowering of their ministers and the rising generation.

> *Praying for Souls* is a main stroke in the winning of Souls. If once the *Spirit of Grace* be poured out upon a *Soul*, that *Soul is won* immediately. . . . Yea, who can tell, how far the Prayers of the *Saints*, & of a few *Saints*, may *prevail* with Heaven to obtain that Grace, that shall win whole Peoples and Kingdoms to serve the Lord? . . . It may be, the Nations of the world, would quickly be *won* from the Idolatries of *Paganism*, and the Impostures of *Mahomet*, if a *Spirit of Prayer*, were at work among the People of God.[162]

I have already commented on the fact that from the very beginning of his ministry Mather was calling on Christians to pray privately and corporately for revival, especially for the conversion of the rising generation.[163] He refers to this as a new practice in 1692, so that it probably arose among his father's generation;[164] but he complains even in 1704 that it is a remedy more discussed than practiced.[165] In *Private Meetings Animated* (1706) and the *Essays to Do Good* (1710), Mather urges such corporate prayer meetings to be conducted on a regular bimonthly basis in the young men's societies;[166] and in *Suspiria Vinctorum* (1726), he proposes regular and synchronized ecumenical days of prayer for revival, to be conducted among all evangelical Protestants—a proposal later taken up by Edwards—and he proposes a monthly midweek meeting, which was the origin of the weekly prayer meetings typical in the nineteenth century.[167] This emphasis on prayer for the "moving of the Spirit" became so foundational in the development of American revivalism that even Charles Finney, who had abandoned the Augustinian rationale for such dependence, still emphasized the necessity of group prayer in his *Lectures on Revivals of Religion*.[168]

The third theological factor prompting Mather toward the expectation of revival, his eschatology, has already been discussed. The remarkable practical effect of this millennialism on his own spiritual experience is revealed in a long series of diary entries spanning his lifetime.

Mather's own prayers began to yield a series of particular faiths concerning the coming premillennial revival of Christendom in 1696, and the entries in his *Diary* for the period 1696-1702 are filled with references to these, which varyingly define the coming event as the Second Coming, a reformation of manners, a political "shaking" among the nations, and an outpouring of the Spirit. In February 1696, he began to pray for a revival of the interests of evangelical Christianity in England, Scotland, and Ireland (I, 184). In April he found himself, while in the midst of a sermon, uttering "under a marvellous Impression upon my Spirit" a prophecy about the "shaking" of these countries (I, 191). These are, of course, the three nations, or national stocks, which were to be most affected by the coming awakening, either in the same countries or among American immigrants. About the same time he began to be persuaded of an imminent "Revolution" in another nation important in the interests of Reformed Christianity, France (I, 198, 202-203). He continued to pray particularly for the British Isles and France, and later in the year added a premonitory concern for a "Revolution upon the Turkish Empire" (I, 207, 212-213). Entries about these international concerns continued during the ensuing months (I, 214, 222-223, 233, 241-242, 259), and in February 1697 Mather started to gather around him a select group of Christian leaders to study "the great *Reformation* at hand" and "the *Characters* and Approaches of the Kingdome of our Lord Jesus Christ" (I, 224-226). In December 1697, Mather was discoursing to this group on I Thessalonians 5:3, noting that a concern for peace among the nations would precede "*the second Coming of the Lord Jesus Christ . . . with a sudden Destruction on the Kingdome of Antichrist,*" when news arrived from England of the Peace of Reswyck and of "such an Overthrow given to the *Turk,* as looks like the *second wo passing away*" (I, 243). In May 1698, Mather felt his premonitions about the British Isles and France partially fulfilled through a suppression of moral disorders, by parliamentary proclamation, in Scotland, and a resurgence of Protestantism in Orange (I, 262). However, he continued to have further premonitions of revival (I, 301-302, 321, 347, 365, 397-398, 403).

From this point onward in the *Diary* the references to the coming renovation grow sparse during a period lasting until 1716. In June 1711, Mather examines the "late strange Extasies and Prophecies" in southern France and Britain rather suspiciously to determine whether these are signs of awakening (II, 83). An entry in August 1716 seems to mark a decided rebirth of his particular faith about the future, together with a clearer definition of its spiritual nature:

> We can do very Little. Our Encumbrances are insuperable; our Difficulties are infinite. If He would please, to fulfill the ancient Prophecy, of *pouring out the Spirit on all Flesh,* and revive the extraordinary and supernatural Operations with which He planted His Religion in the primitive Times of Christianity, and order a Descent of His holy *Angels* to enter and possess His Ministers, and cause them to speak with the Tongues of Men under the Energy of *Angels,* and fly thro' the World with the *everlasting Gospel* to preach unto the Nations, wonderful Things would be done immediately; His Kingdome would make those Advances in a Day, which under our present and fruitless Labours, are scarce made in an Age. I pleaded, that His Word had given us Reason to hope for a Return of these Powers, and for the making bare the Arm of the Lord before the Nations; and He has promised His holy Spirit unto them that ask Him. I pleaded, that His diligent Servants, having preferred the *sanctifying Influences* of His holy Spirit, above any *miraculous Powers,* and been humbly willing to undergo any Fatigues for the Service of His Kingdome, seem'd somewhat prepared for these Favours of Heaven. And having made this Representation, that Orders may be given by the glorious Lord, for a Descent of His mighty Angels, to give wonderful Shakes unto the World, and so seize upon the Ministers of His

Kingdome, as to do Things which will give an irresistible Efficacy unto their Ministry; I concluded with a strong Impression on my Mind; *They are coming! They are coming! They are coming! They will quickly be upon us; and the World shall be shaken wonderfully!* (II, 365-366).

Subsequent passages repeat this strong conviction, emphasizing the imminent descent of angels and particularly the prophecy of the outpouring of the Spirit in Joel (II, 371, 376, 387, 396, 449, 453, 460, 469). This whole series of particular faiths is centered on the concept of the coming revival as a new Pentecost to reinvigorate the churches with life and the power for missionary propagation, "a Return of the Showers which first introduced and propagated Christianity in the World" (II, 469).

During the course of his life Mather discerned a number of harbingers of the coming millennial revival. Some of these involved the early conversion and spiritual precocity of children, which had been a focus of interest among the first generations in New England, and which Edwards was later to mark as one of the signs of the Great Awakening.[169] In 1693 he remarks on the production of scholars and ministers in the young men's societies as a good sign for the future.[170] He also speaks of a revival in a Scottish church following a night of corporate prayer, in which 500 were converted,[171] and of several miracles occurring in London.[172] But there is no doubt that during the decades from 1690 to 1710 Mather found the main support for his hopes, and perhaps the impetus for their genesis, in the contagious enthusiasm of the British reforming societies (and even Francke felt these to be "comfortable signs that the Spirit of God is now about a great work to put a new face on the whole Christian Church").[173] This perhaps explains the fact that Mather's early references to the coming reformation, in his first burst of enthusiasm for it between 1696 and 1702, define it more externally—with reference to manners and institutions—than do his later statements.

These later comments, on the other hand, reflect a more internalized conception of "completing the Reformation," under the influence of Continental Pietism. In 1710, Mather refers again to early childhood conversions, but this time among the Pietists.[174] Two years later he speaks of "a most surprising revival of good things amid the world," citing the publication of "a collection of observable things, wherein the Kingdom of God has been more sensibly opening itself in the heart of Germany." He notes also the diminution of the papal authority and "the spirit of persecution, which wherever it is found is the spirit of Antichrist," and the appearance of a great number of solid ministerial candidates.[175] He considered Pietism simply one evidence of a spiritual stirring throughout the Western world, however, including Britain and America; for he found the hymns of Watts and other contemporaneous poets a harbinger of *"the time of the Singing of Birds coming on,"*[176] and he mentions a revival connected with a young man's society at Harvard.[177] In *A New Offer* (1714) he commends his own *Biblia Americana* to the public and the publishers with the implication that he is one of those in the vanguard of international Pietism:

> An Age of *Light* comes on; *Explications* and Discoveries are continually growing; which all that will but *show themselves Men* cannot but imbibe with Satisfaction. The *Path of the Just One*, in His gracious Approaches towards us, causes the *Light* which opens His Oracles unto us, to *shine more and more towards the perfect Day.* . . . The Instruments by whom this *Light* is brought down unto us, have of late been greatly Multiplied: *God has given His Word* for it, and *Great has been the Army of those that have published it.*[178]

But he points to Halle as the most eminent example of spiritual awakening in that era, citing with particular interest the social impact of Francke's work in the orphanage, the schools and colleges, where "still Piety is the main Concern," the widow house and the *"Englische Haus,"* and the distribution of Bibles and Christian literature.

> Dr. *Franckius* is a Person truly Wonderful for his vast *Erudition*; but much more so for his most shining *Piety*; and yet more so for his most peerless *Industry*; and most of all so, for the Astonishing *Blessings of God* upon his Undertakings to advance His Kingdom in the World.
>
> . . . .
>
> That which lies at the bottom of all this Great Man's Designs, is, to advance *True, Real, Vital Piety*; and such a *Knowledge* of a

Glorious Christ, as will bring the Children of Men into the *Service* of their only Saviour, and Such a *Love* of God, and of their Neighbour, as the Gospel calleth for: or in a word, *Right Christianity,* and a Glorious Revival of the *Primitive.*

. . . .

The *Blessings* of God our Saviour upon these essays of this Great Man are altogether Astonishing. The Vast Numbers of Souls brought Home to God, and made Instances of *Serious Piety!*———The Vast Number of *Instruments* qualified here to do good abroad in the World! More than all *Europe* will soon feel, yea, has already felt, the precious Effects of the *Franckian Education. . . .* There the Printing-Presses have brought forth *Books,* which have had an Incredible Efficacy for the Producing of Piety, even in far distant Countrys. . . . But what appears to me very particularly entertaining, is, the Uncommon and Successful Care taken by this *Man of God,* for dispersing the *Book of God,* & Procuring the *Waters of Life* to run into all Parts of the Earth.

. . . .

The truly Amiable *Boehm* Writes . . . "Here is one of the *greatest Transactions* at this Day in the World, which if it Proceeds, as if has hitherto done, will in a very few Years come to have a much greater Influence on the *Publick Affairs of the World,* than all the Battels, and Sieges, which our *Gazetts, Mercuries,* and *Registers* have been filled withal.

. . . .

Behold, A *Seed of Piety,* & of Pure Christianity, which is the *Kingdom of God* in the true Essence, and Glory of it, Quickened, & Expanding in the Bowels of *Germany.*[179]

Mather continued for several years to nourish his hopes of revival on the progress of "that PIETY, of which the Incomparable *Franckius* and his Collegues, have been such noble Propagators."[180] In his last public utterance of the imminent revival, however, an account in 1718 of the conversion of three Jewish children in Berlin, he seems to detect an ebb in the movement toward revival. He quotes an anonymous German author on the situation of world Christianity: "The various Motions observed in several parts of Europe, tending to a Revival of *Sound and Substantial Piety,* do presage the Approach of Better Times, and a fuller Measure of the Divine Spirit promised to the Latter Days. But then the Intervening Night of the Judgment of GOD, provoked by a long and continued Course of Sinning, will perhaps destroy again the Flowers, which appear up and down on the Earth."[181] Mather's public and private statements during the twenties reflect this same cautious—and somewhat disheartened—evaluation of the spiritual situation. This was the period, both in England and America, of extreme darkness before the dawn, from the evangelical point of view. Mather's last jeremiad, *Suspiria Vinctorum* (1726), sums up the mood of his last years. This work is remarkable in that it is a jeremiad for the entire Christian world, not just for the covenant nation of New England. It surveys principally the martyrdom of Protestants under persecution by Rome and the loss of Protestant territory, but issues in a treatment of world-wide spiritual decline among the reformed churches.

It is not surprising that Mather's eschatological shift in 1724 had cleared the way for the possibility of an immediate deliverance from these troubles through the return of Christ, without preliminary completion of the half-reformation and a national calling of the Jews. What is remarkable, however, is that *Suspiria Vinctorum* does not advise a passive waiting for this final deliverance, but instead continues to sound the call for revival prayer:

> Wherefore under a *Terror of GOD,* it becomes us to *Labour fervently in our Prayer* . . . That the Glorious *GOD of our Life,* would *Revive* Decay'd PIETY . . . and that His *Quickening Spirit* would not withdraw any further. . . . *Lord, Revive thy Work in the midst of the Nations.*[182]

Despite his premillennial eschatology, Mather's mind is still reverberating with the battle songs of the great positive amillennial leaders of his time, and some of his last utterances are consonant with the hopes of postmillennialists like Brightman, Whitby, and Edwards.

CHAPTER SEVEN

The Unity of the Godly

THERE IS NO AREA IN WHICH MATHER APPROACHED greatness so nearly—and offered so assured a lead toward the future—as in his ecumenism. But here again he was no innovator, for this ecumenism had a double root system in Pietist and Puritan sources. It is disconcerting for the modern churchman, braced against the "divisive" polemic stance of twentieth-century revivalism, to face the fact that the founders of the revivalist tradition were the first ecumenists after the period of the Reformers; of course, the fact may be equally unsettling to the modern revivalist.

The "unitive tendency of Pietism" which Ritschl noted[1] was necessarily rather carefully disguised in the writings of Arndt, who was under constant pressure from orthodoxy because of Reformed and mystical strands palpable in his thinking. His friend Andreae made his utopian city recognizably Lutheran, but cautiously spoke up against factions over small points, advancing the theory that Christ would prefer ignorant saints to contentious scholars if learning and piety could not be combined in one group of leaders.[2] Andreae and J. A. Comenius cooperated in stressing church unity and a number of other goals that would assume importance in later Pietism: educational reform, improved Bible study, practical piety, and scientific research.[3]

The most typical Lutheran ecumenist of this early period

was undoubtedly Georg Calixtus.[4] But there were also a number of ecumenical pre-Pietists stemming from Arndt, such as Müller, Quistorp, and Lütkemann, teaching in university centers with liberal Melanchthonian backgrounds or at Strassburg, where there was a Reformed influence.[5] At a later period, Spener was severely restrained by the need to preserve an appearance of Lutheran orthodoxy; but even so, his early suspicion of Calvinism yielded to a receptive charity (especially after the revocation of the Edict of Nantes and the attendant persecution).[6] He early concluded that unconditional freedom of conscience was necessary for the full vigor and extension of true Christianity, and that orthodoxy sins when it attempts to compel belief by force. Spener came to feel that all Evangelical and Reformed groups holding the Bible as the rule of faith could and should eventually unite, regardless of differences over Christology, the sacraments, and even the problematic doctrine of predestination. Eventually, he arrived at a broad base of tolerance embracing Arminians, Mennonites, disciples of Jacob Boehme, and even Quakers of the stamp of Robert Barclay.[7] Spener drew the line at Socinians, however; and though he admitted the presence of regenerate Christians within the Roman Church, he held that the papacy is Antichrist and thus beyond the reach of ecumenical cooperation.[8] Toward the end of his life he was involved in negotiations considering the union of Reformed and Lutheran churches, but he came to feel that organic unity would have to wait for a spiritual revival in both communions, and he adopted a strategy of disseminating Pietism in all branches of Christendom as a preparation for eventual structural union.[9]

Spener's basic outlook was adopted and put into action by Francke, who produced what Erich Beyreuther has called the greatest ecumenical and missionary network since the sixteenth century, linking Holland, England, America, the Scandinavian countries, South Africa, India, Poland, Russia, the Balkan states, Switzerland, France, and Italy. Part of the dynamic of this outreach was the burgeoning spirit of reform and the awakening consciousness of the possibility of world unity among nations in national leaders such as Ernest the

Pious.[10] Francke's remarkable linguistic genius, and his acquaintance with world leadership through correspondence and travel, made him the ideal representative of unitive evangelical mission,[11] and his educational involvement in the intellectual *Zeitgeist* of Europe during this period made him particularly open to ecumenism.[12] The attacks of a bitterly anti-Reformed orthodoxy within the Lutheran church,[13] compelled Francke to whisper about his ecumenical goals even while he was boldly proclaiming those of his missionary concern, so that his published writings do not much reflect what Beyreuther calls the "crypto-ecumenism" at Halle.[14]

However, this ecumenism was openly articulated in situations where it was advantageous. Halle's remarkable agent for the dissemination of the Pietist vision in London, A. W. Boehm, analyzed the problem of unity and division in the church in a way that left no doubt about Pietism's real ecumenical convictions. According to Boehm, division in the church issued mainly from dead confessional orthodoxy. "Faith as it is now in Vogue, signifieth no more than a stiff adhering to a certain Sect or Denomination of Men, and a zealous Defence of such particular Tenets as have been received and approved of by that Party. All the Ingredients of such a Faith, are nothing but humane Education, Custom, Traditional, Perswasion, Conversation, and the like. The Zeal which goeth along with it, is the product of Self-Love, and of corrupt Reason, the two great Framers of Sects and Party-Notions."[15] Because traditional orthodoxies neglected the central need for spiritual transformation in the church, Boehm felt, they placed a great emphasis on incidental matters and innovation, and even used these to mask their spiritual barrenness.

> [True Christianity] is principally concerned with the Essentials and Substantials of Religion: Such as is the great Work of Faith and of the New Birth, with the Rest of Christian Virtues that freely accompany it; as Resignation, Mortification, Imitation of Christ, Self-Abnegation, Contrition, and others relating to the inward Principle of GRACE, and its various Effects and Operations. But the False Christian is chiefly, if not only, busie about the ceremonious Part, and some accessory and circumstantial

> Points. He bringeth forth every Age, if not every Year, new
> Schemes, New Models, new Projects of Religion. He mouldeth
> it one Time into this, and again at other Times into another
> Form, according as the Humour of the Age, and the interest of
> Men worketh, which with him hath the greatest Influence in
> Affairs of Religion. And at this rate, alas! the Substance of
> Christianity lieth neglected, in the midst of so many Schemes,
> framed under pretense to support it![16]

Yesterday's modernism, therefore, is today's dead and divisive hand of tradition. But the church can look forward to a
period when the central principles of godliness that are
obscured by these peripheral concerns will be set forth
clearly and illuminated by the Holy Spirit.

> There will be a Time, when the Church of Christ will come up
> from the Wilderness of various Sects, Parties, Nations, Lan-
> guages, Forms, and Ways of Worship, nay of Crosses and
> Afflictions, leaning upon her Beloved, and in his Power bid-
> ding Defiance to all her Enemies. Then shall that Church,
> which now doth but look forth as the Morning in its Dawn,
> after a continual Growth in Strength and Beauty, appear Terri-
> ble as an Army with Banners; but terrible to those only that
> despised her whilst she was in her Minority, and would not
> have her Beloved to reign over them.[17]

This passage echoes many of Mather's convictions, and he
must have been familiar with it, since it was published in
1712 in the first edition of Boehm's translation of Arndt's *True
Christianity*. And Mather maintained a corresponding friendship with Boehm from 1715 until his death.

However, Mather did not need to import his ecumenism
from the Continent; he was himself part of a long tradition of
unitive thought in English and American Puritanism. While
we are accustomed to thinking of Puritanism as a disintegra-
tive force, considering the fragmentation of sects during the
Commonwealth period, it remains true that it was only those
rationalistic strands in the Puritan movement that insisted
on rigid structural or theological orthodoxy—or, at the opposite pole, those who opened their minds to the irrational
forces of enthusiasm—which were responsible for the divisive thrust among Puritans. Formalist Puritans like Thomas
Cartwright and Walter Travers were part of a dissident

minority whose extreme concern for structural purity was unrepresentative of the moderation of most early Puritans;[18] and the evidence clearly indicates that the main leaders of early Puritanism were moderate proponents of interior godliness who were simply pressing for freedom of conscience with respect to a few ceremonies. Perkins, for example, felt that the errors in the established church were such as weakened but did not destroy it, and he abhorred the practice of defining Christians by party, such as "Lutherans" or "Calvinists." Such other early Puritans as Richard Sibbes, Thomas Adams, and Robert Bolton were comparatively moderate.[19]

But particularly significant is the open reception later English Puritans gave John Dury in the 1630s, for he was a pioneer ecumenist and an earlier incarnation of the ecumenical Pietism represented by Francke, Boehm, and Mather almost a century later. Strongly influenced by Comenius' ideal of a pan-Christian union through the educational reform of culture, and persuaded that the promotion of practical piety was the key to accomplishing this goal, the Scotsman Dury held that Christian unity was necessary both for Protestant survival in the face of hostile Catholic powers and for effective mission in the unchristianized sectors of the world. He was supported in some measure in his activities in England both by such Anglicans as Usher, Gouge, Downame, Davenant, and Hall, and by such Puritans as Sibbes, John Cotton, Owen, Thomas Goodwin, Nye, Greenhill, Byfield, and John Goodwin. The degree to which Dury's program had captured the Puritan imagination is revealed by the fact that one of the charges brought by Parliament against Laud in 1643-44 was his indifference to Dury's efforts. Dury's only initial opposition, in fact, seems to have come from very high-church Anglicans such as Laud, and from Lutheran orthodoxy, though he was later suspected of an excessive latitudinarianism, as tensions rose between competing parties, and his impartial friendship with all of these became an embarrassment.

Dury's four-point program, offered in 1650, is amazingly prophetic of the concerns of Spener, Francke, and Mather.

He proposes that the ministers work with the magistrates to find how "the Knowledge, Practice, and Power of Godlinesse may be most effectually advanced throughout the nation, either by an impartiall settlement and regulating of Catecheticall Exercises, or Propheticall Conferences, and of a preaching ministery," the suppression of scandals and disorders, the healing of breaches between parties of Christians, and the establishment of effective Christian schools. As in Mather's case, his concern for ecumenical spiritual awakening was driven by millennial expectations and by a missionary concern that included the conversion of the Jews.[20]

As the divisions and conflicts of the Commonwealth period gradually demonstrated to the English Puritans the necessity of some kind of cooperative unity between Christians, proposals akin to Dury's were taken up by men of more established reputation in the English churches. While there were advocates of unity in all parties, notably in the growing latitudinarian stream within the established church—Jeremy Taylor's *Liberty of Prophesying* had appeared in 1647[21]—here again the central core of those receptive to ecumenical thought was among the Puritans, the moderate episcopal Noncomformists.[22]

The most famous English ecumenist of the late seventeenth century, Richard Baxter, who was influenced by Dury and by fellow churchmen like Davenant and Ussher, sought after 1652 to urge the goal of a loose ecclesiastical comprehension rather than mere toleration.[23] His pioneering espousal of an organic church unification, which would seek to fuse into one structure diverse elements of polity and worship, was based on a concern for the effectiveness of the church's spiritual mission. For, as he said to Owen and the Congregationalists, "PARISH REFORMATION TENDETH TO THE MAKING GODLINESS UNIVERSAL, and . . . your SEPARATION tendeth to dwindle it to nothing."[24] He considered such unity equally necessary to evangelism and foreign missions.[25] Baxter's passionate concern for structural church unity and his hatred of schism, together with his practice of "occasional conformity" and his piercing critical vision into the imbalances of Nonconformists, was intensely irritating to English Congregationalists.[26] But by the 1670s comprehension had become a dead issue and toleration was the only serious possibility, and Baxter was accepted by people of all parties for his godliness and passion as an ecumenical pioneer.[27] A pamphlet of this period notes that "there is not one party in England that holds it as a principle of their religion that it is lawful to persecute for mere religion."[28]

The unsuccessful attempt at organic union between English Congregationalists and Presbyterians, who joined together in 1690 as "United Brethren" but began a lingering dissolution in 1693 over unresolved issues of polity and supposed antinomianism, confirmed the majority opinion that toleration was the best that could be managed before the churches were more awakened spiritually. But it did not dampen the general ecumenical enthusiasm of the '90s, which was spurred on by the cooperation of the reforming societies.[29] With the close interaction between Halle and London after the founding of the S.P.C.K. in 1699—through correspondence, travelers, the immigration of German refugees, student interchanges, the English translations of Francke's *Pietas Hallensis*,[30] and the ambassadorial work of Boehm—ecumenism reached its peak in England after the turn of the century, and its vigor persisted until a new generation of leaders of cooler Enlightenment temperament appeared on the scene.[31]

The New England Puritans had lagged somewhat behind their English brethren in the growth of toleration and ecumenism, as we have seen. The first generation had been unable to stomach Roger Williams' blend of extremism and sophisticated theological understanding of the theocratic problem; and John Cotton had been unwilling to relinquish carnal weapons as a support for the gospel.[32] The founding fathers settled into an uneasy (and of course unacceptable) gentlemen's agreement to tolerate heresy if the "heretics" did not attempt to proselytize;[33] and at a time when the English Puritans were beginning to extol the virtues of toleration, American Puritans were reacting with the surprised insistence that the maintenance of religious purity by the exercise of theocratic force was part of their "errand into the wilderness."[34] Cotton Mather mentions a favorable response from a synod of forty ministers to a letter from "the famous John Dury" in 1633, by the pen of John Norton in the last year of his life, and a similar response to Dury from John Davenport.[35]

American Puritanism went through an uncomfortable battle between its growing ecumenical conscience and the logic of its theocratic presuppositions; but the more flexible minds of the second generation and the rising genius of the third were forced by the logic of events into a consistent ecumenism. Writing in 1724, Cotton Mather indicates that his father began to change his mind in the 1680s on the duty of the magistrate to punish heresy, and Increase came to conclude that the tares (other than blasphemers and atheists) had to be tolerated because the sacrifices of a forced conscience are an abomination to God. "He saw, that until *Persecution* be utterly Banished out of the World, and *Cain's* Club taken out of *Abel's* Hand, 'tis Impossible to rescue the World from Endless Confusions."[36] There was necessarily a shift in Increase's understanding of the biblical picture of the treatment of heresy; Cotton says he supported his change of views by the facts that there was no compulsion of sojourners in Israel to worship in the Israelitish manner, that ordinarily even heretics within Israel were not molested by the magistracy, and that New Testament weapons against heresy were not carnal.[37] Cotton Mather put himself firmly on record in favor of toleration in his earliest published sermons,[38] and in 1692 he remarks:

> I ran the Hazard of much Reproch by testifying . . . against the *Persecution* of erroneous and conscientious Dissenters, by the *civil Magistrate.* I feared, that the *Zeal* of my Countrey had formerly had in it more *Fire* than should have been; especially, when the mad *Quakers* were sent unto the *Gallowes*, that should have been kept rather in a *Bedlam.* . . . I think, I am the only *Minister* Living in the Land, that have testifyed against the *Suppression* of *Haeresey* by *Persecution.* And I hope, the Lord will own mee with a more singular Success, in the Suppression of Haeresy by Endeavours more *spiritual* and *evangelical.*[39]

Reinforced by contemporaneous English thought and later by Pietism, Mather continued to reiterate this position boldly, though he seems to have been considerably in the vanguard of the conservative leadership of the colony.[40] Occasionally he used his attacks on persecution as levers against the impositions of the Church of England,[41] and he could defend a reformed New England as if it had never acted in the role of persecutor.[42] But there is no doubt whatsoever that Mather was thoroughly—and theologically—convinced of the necessity to tolerate heretics. He seems to have absorbed Roger Williams' biblical critique of the New England position, for he acknowledges that while heresies were indeed to be punished in the Old Testament theocracy, it was because "they were an *High Treason* against the KING of the *Theocracy. . . . The Christian Religion* brings us not into a Temporal *Canaan*. It knows no *Designs*, it has no *Weapons*, but what are purely *Spiritual.*"[43] Therefore, the civil magistrate usurps the throne of God himself when he pretends to punish any offenses that do not directly break the peace of "humane society," and the sword is not to compel the observation of the first table of the Law, for "all the *Sacrifices* of Men unto GOD, not proceeding from a *Conscience* perswaded, that He does *command* them . . . All *Acts* of *Religion* produced merely by *External Violence*, are, Detestable Things."[44]

It is true, however, that Mather's theory of toleration operated within quite narrow limits when judged from our perspective. There were two forms of religion which the Mathers could not allow to be openly expressed within a Christian society: atheism and Roman Catholicism. In this they were simply in harmony with the most liberal insight of their time, for the most advanced Protestant ecumenism of this period still ruled out Rome.[45] Mather's own bitter distrust of the Roman church was determined by a strong combination of political fear and theological prejudice. "The Church of *Rome*, with the *Man of Sin* at the Head of it, entirely possessed by *Satan*, is resolved upon the Extermination of all the Christians upon Earth, who come not into a Combination with her, in her *Detestable Idolatries.*"[46] With a peculiar logical sleight of hand, Mather even managed to blame Rome for Protestant disunity:

> All true *Protestants* are Agreed, That it is a *Duty* to depart from the Church of *Rome:* And the DIVISIONS among *Protestants* proceed from the Weakness of many, who are not Agreed, about the *Degree* of Departure from that *Apostate Church.* Our *Divisions* are therefore to be counted but, *Remainders of the Church of Rome with us;* and are to be charged upon the *Roman Church,* and not upon the *Reformed.* And there are as Grievous *Divisions* in the Communion of the Church of *Rome,* as there are among us; whereof the *Dominicans & Franciscans,* the *Jansenists & Jesuites,* are notorious Instances.[47]

He was, of course, not blind to the presence of Christians within Rome, nor did he glamorize the Protestant decay of his day:

> The *Church of Rome* is an Example, of a *Golden Candlestick* Eternally Damn'd in *Haeresies.* And yet it is a thing to be spoken with Regret and Horrour, There are Hundreds of Thousands this day in the *Church of Rome,* who had the main Articles of the *Protestant Religion* (the *Jansenists,* I mean) better than multitudes of pretended *Protestants,* who are fallen into the *Haeretical Idolatries* of *Pelagianism.*[48]

The virulence of statements like these, and the unrelievedly dark picture of Rome given in the rest of Mather's work, can only be understood as we reflect on his memory of 1685 and his observation of the continuing plight of Protestants in France. Mather could pray with deep concern for "the replacement of the Candlestick" of the Greek churches, despite their share in many of the decadent features of Rome, partly because of the occasional interest of the Greeks themselves in union with Protestantism,[49] but mainly because the Greek churches did not share in what Mather considered a permanent mark of the Antichrist, the corporal persecution of true believers. It would seem that if a Puritan could hope for revival and reformation according to his standards in the Eastern church, he could hope for this also for Rome; but Mather was prevented from this consideration by the structure of his eschatology, which required that Rome remain a permanent villain in the drama of history.

There were other forms of religious expression which

Mather was prepared to tolerate, but never to embrace ecumenically. I have already examined his response to Enlightenment rationalism; he detected a linkage between it and another movement he considered equally unbiblical, Quakerism. In his early pastoral letter to the New England churches warning against the Quaker missionary, George Keith, he attacks the Friends' religion as a "great Choakweed of the Christian and Protestant Religion."

> I have seriously *Turned unto that Light,* and with best of my *light* as yet, I can see many damnable Heresies in *Quakerism; if* I have . . . one spark of *Light* in me, *Quakerism* is but a profound and a deadly *Pit of darkness.*
>
> . . . .
>
> There is hardly any one Fundamental Article of that Reformed Religion, whereby we look to be saved, that is not undermined by *Quakerism,* whatever professions it makes unto the contrary.[50]

Nevertheless, Mather declared himself in 1691 to be utterly against crippling the Quakers with punishments, and also open to reason about their doctrines, and hopeful of their recovery.[51] He was rather more severe with rationalist heresy, as we have seen:

> In very many Disputed Points of Religion, they who pull the Saw may by and by shake hands with one another, as *Brethren in Christ;* because the Piety which they both mean to support by their several different Positions is one and the same. Yea, even the Calvinists and the Lutherans may on this Account go on together, not falling out by the Way, for they are Brethren. Whereas the Arian and the Gentilist, obtruding upon us another Christ, than *He who is our Life,* this kills our Piety at once. Our greatest acts of Piety, must be to him, no other than so many Flaming Impieties; and anon, when he's got you well under, he'll tell you so! He brings in *another Gospel.* And what censure would an apostle Paul, writing to his Galatians, have passed on such an one? I don't find, that he would have said, *Hold Communion with him.* No, that is not the English of the Word, *Anathema!*[52]

It may at this point seem obscure to the reader why Mather should have been in any danger of being mistaken for a latitudinarian. But even in the 1690s the Mathers were moving beyond most of their New England colleagues in

beginning to urge the organizational union of churches holding the Reformed faith. While Increase Mather was in England helping to negotiate the merger of the United Brethren,
Cotton Mather's *Blessed Unions* (1692) placed a benediction
on the English venture and urged that New England had
come to the point of being equally open to the godly conversation of Presbyterian, Congregational, "and EPISCOPAL
too when Piety is otherwise visible . . . and I may add, the
Name of, ANTIPEDOBAPTIST."[53] The charge that the
Mathers' ecumenism at this point was only a cover for a plan
to consolidate the dissenters to preserve the Puritan establishment in New England[54] is effectively refuted by *Blessed
Unions;* it is too enthusiastically ecumenical to be merely part
of a political scheme. It states the case for union in a shower
of epigrams:

> Strife, 'tis a Sin that stirs up all other sorts of Distempers and
> Corruptions in us; the *Lusts* in our Souls, like so many chill'd
> *Snakes,* do horribly Crawl, and Hiss, and Sting, when this *Fire*
> has Envigorated 'em. The *Devil* has a Lodging, where men do
> not Ring a *Curfew Bell.* We are as *Bottles;* if we take and shake
> one another, a world of *dirty Stuff* will be Raised from the
> Bottom in us.
>
> . . . .
>
> We must first, *Forebear to Impose* one upon another. It is impos-
> sible for any but, *God who forms the Spirit of man within him,* to
> *form* the understandings of men, into a Beleef of every *Christian
> Doctrine.* If we shall Violently and Forceably *Compell* all about
> us, to take in our *Schemes,* we shall be as Unhumane as that
> *Giant,* who cut or stretch'd all his Lodgers, to the Exact Length
> of the Bed, he had provided for them. . . . Shall he bicker
> about *Black* and *White,* until God make us meet in *Red? . . .* We
> should make the fairest *constructions* of all Actions, and Lov-
> ingly take everything by the *Best Handle.* We should, if we
> knock with *Hard Reasons,* yet stroke them with *Soft Answers;*
> and let them find us of the *Tribe* which, giveth *Godly Words.* A
> *Samaritan* sort of crabbedness, churlishness, forwardness, to-
> wards all that are not in everything just jumping with us . . .
> 'Tis not the Spirit of the Gospel. . . . We must beware how we
> *Monopolize* all Godliness to our own *Little Party.* . . . Where-
> ever we can see, *Aliquid Christi,* any thing of Christ, let it be
> dear to us.
>
> . . . .
>
> Be Affected with *Mortality.* They say, *Dust* thrown on Fighting

Bees, will presently make 'em give over the Fight. If we are prone to Sting one another, Let us cast a little of our *Grave-Dust*, upon us by our Devout, Gracious Antedating Meditations. . . . Especially, when it comes to stabbing of one another with *Pens*, Let us remember our *Sand* runs faster than our *Ink*, and we are as Brittle as the *Glasses* which we now use instead of Inkhorns. How near are we to that State, *Ubi Luthero cum Zwinglio optime jam Convenit?* A *Luther* and a *Zwinglius* will be less eager one against another, if they think *How soon they are to meet!* . . . If every *Sheaf* must *alwayes* bow to Yours and Mine, when shall we be quiet?

. . . .

If we can't have but *One Mouth*, yet let us have but *One Heart*.[55]

The main body of this sermon asserts the basis of unity in the common engrafting of regenerate Christians in Christ, but hesitates to offer doctrinal or other bases of organic union, pressing instead a general union in goals and mutual love. It warns against compromising the purity of the church to obtain unity, but insists on the evils of schism and persecution, and the importance of peace. On the other hand, Mather does clearly indicate that a visible union of existing Christian organizations is the final goal of ecumenism: "Our Lord here says, *That they all may be ONE.* . . . It is not enough that we have *Invisible Union* with all the Saints of God; but we must have a *Visible Union,* too, or such an one as our context mentions, *That the World may Believe,* at the Contemplation and Invitation of it."[56] Mather's horizon did not extend beyond the limits of ecumenical Puritanism. He wanted to repair the breaches torn in the church by English history, but he did not hope for a mending of those made by the Reformation.

The emphases in this early document are very Baxterian. One very notable tone which Mather continued to sound until the end of his life, and which was also an obsession with Baxter, was the harmfulness of controversy and contention. In another 1692 publication Mather urges Dury's argument that dissension in Protestant circles has encouraged and aided Rome.[57] A few years later he reflects uneasily about the Hutchinson conflict, when "a Factious Distinction made between, *Men under a Covenant of Works,* and *Men*

under a Covenant of Grace, as it were by some *Enchantment,*
insinuated itself into all our Concernments, to the producing
of *Works* wherein there was little enough of *Grace* discovered."[58] To the end of his life Mather felt that one of the most
serious spiritual problems within Puritanism was its tendency toward schism and faction.

> 'Tis astonishing to think, how much the success of the Gospel
> is hindered, when a Spirit of Contention is got among a
> People. Satan knows what he does, when he throws in Bolts of
> Contention among a People, which embroil them and enrage
> them. . . . The house of *God* becomes as a House haunted with
> Evil Spirits. . . . Indeed, our *Saviour* once appeared in a
> Thorn-Bush. But, When a Church once becomes a Thorn-Bush,
> embarrassed with contention, our *Lord Jesus Christ* will grant
> little appearance of himself.[59]

In later sermons he presses this point with a sharp wit and
discernment.

> 'Tis by this project of the Devil, that Christianity is almost
> ruined in the world. Men are not concerned about the *Essentials,*
> the *Substantials,* the *Vitals* of Christianity; Why? Because the
> *Strength* of their Spirits is all spent in the Concerns of some
> *little Party.*
>
> To what purpose is it, for a man to be a Protestant, if he don't
> cast off the *Devil,* as well as the *Pope?* To what purpose is it, for
> a man to deny a *Freewill to Spiritual Good in the Unregenerate,* if
> the man remain himself *Unregenerate?* . . . What signifies it,
> whether a man be for the *Congregational* Church-discipline, or
> for the *Presbyterian,* if a man have not a Soul under the
> *Heavenly-discipline?*[60]

Mather also offers some illuminating insights into the
psychology of schism.

> The Zeal of many is but a meer Composition with Conscience,
> for some Favour unto some detestable Ungodliness. Hence tis,
> that the most odious and hideous Monsters in Wickedness,
> have been the fiercest Zealots, and the most Fiery Bigots for,
> The *CHURCH.* A Man does not *keep his heart with all Diligence;*
> does not *Walk in the Fear of God* continually; does not subdue
> his Natural and Culpable Inclinations; does not carry on a
> constant warfare, in Resisting of Daily Temptations; does not
> lead a Life of Communion with Heaven; does not Love his
> Neighbor, and seek his Wellbeing, and rejoyce in it. And now

he compounds with his Conscience, to make a mighty Noise about something or other, that is not Essential to Christianity. Oh! the Deceits, the Deceits, of Wretched *Hypocrisy!*[61]

A second emphasis common to Baxter and Mather throughout the latter's lifetime was the relative unimportance of nonfundamentals in doctrine and ceremony. In *Blessed Unions* (1692) Mather alludes to a favorite statement of Baxter and later ecumenists: "It is a Rule as Good as Old, *In Necessariis Unitas, in Adiaphoris Libertas, in Utrisque Charitas.*"[62] It is evident that from the outset of his ecumenical thinking he conceived of the future of Protestant churches in terms of a loosely tolerant plan of evangelical comprehension similar to Baxter's.

> In the Primitive Church, the *Christians* who were agreed in the *Essential* and *Substantial* points of our Holy Religion, yet had their different Perswasions about some *Circumstantial* Matters. To Compromise these *Differences,* the *Apostles* did not see cause to Exert any *Apostolical Authority,* that they might Exact a rigid and perfect *Uniformity.* . . . Nay, the HOLY SPIRIT of our SAVIOUR Himself did not see cause presently to put a period unto these *Differences.* He saw these *Differences,* to afford an Opportunity for the Exercise of His *Graces* in the Hearts of His People. He would have the *Union* among His People to lie in the *Unity of the Spirit;* and that work of His upon their Souls that lies in *Fearing of GOD, and Working of Righteousness.* The *Foundation* of their *Union,* He would have to be in those *Holy Mountains;* the MAXIMS of the EVERLASTING GOSPEL, wherein *All Good Men are United . . . Differences* must continue; But where PIETY has *United* People, they should pay Brotherly *Regards* to One another, notwithstanding their *Differences.*[63]

Mather comments elsewhere, "We may with more reason be angry, that two Persons do not look alike, than that they do not at all Think just alike."[64]

It becomes more and more clear, as Mather deals with the subject of unity, that its central *sine qua non* is, as with Comenius, Dury, Baxter, and the Pietists, the presence of true godliness shared by groups of Christians. As early as 1702, Mather reflected an analysis of schism and union which sounds as if it is derived directly from Spener's dissection of dead orthodoxy:

There are some of a *Sectarian Spirit,* that will be *Zealous* for the
particular and peculiar *Opinion* of their own *Parties* in Christianity; but they *omit the weightier matters in Christianity:* It will
be no matter with them, whether they be in *the Fear of the Lord
all the Day long,* and whether they *wash their Hearts* from all
wicked Lusts, and whether they *keep their Tongues* from Evil,
or, whether they walk as the *Lord* Jesus Christ *walked,* or no. By
this *Device of Satan* it is that *Christianity* is almost Ruined in the
world; Men are not concerned about the *Vitals* of Christianity;
but only about some *Notions* in it. Men are not Christians
because the chief of their *Christianity* lies, not in the *Imitation* of
Christ, but in being such or such a sort of *Christians. . . .*
Christianity turns upon higher points, than meer *Niceties* of
Opinion.[65]

The solvent for these carnal differences can be none other
than piety, or in its Puritan incarnation, "holiness," which,
as Mather comments in 1695, "lies not principally in *Parties,*
in *Garments,* or in the Rites of a Superstitious *Pharisee.* No,
but for a Man to be *filled with all the fulness of God,* for Man to
have God *possessing* of Him, to have God *influencing* of him;
this is true *Holiness.*"[66] By the middle years of the 1710-1720
decade, when Mather was under the strongest direct influence of European Pietism, his ecumenical vision had wid-
ened to embrace those on the Continent in whom he found
the seriousness of Puritan godliness operative under another
name. Now he flatly states that evangelical piety is the universal adhesive force for the building of a united church:

Among the diverse Colonies of *Bees,* fierce Wars are sometimes
carried on, in which they neither give, nor take any Quarter,
but make a very great Slaughter of one another. Of these
Opposing Armies, the Voice is the same; the *Aspect* is the
same; the *Armour* is the same; 'Tis only by their *Scent,* that
they distinguish themselves from one another. Wherefore if
any one throw among them a *Sweet-scented Liquour,* which may
impart the *same Scent* to all the Contenders, presently the *Fight*
is over; the *Strife* is at an end; there is a Cessation of all
Hostilities. Most certainly, the *Maxims* of the *Everlasting Gospel*
exhibit such a *Sweet-scented Liquour,* which being poured, and
cast upon the Church-Militant (Alas! too *Militant!*) All the
Faithful Servants of God, of whose *Union* the *Blood* of their
Saviour is the Eternal *Cement,* will presently be sensible, that

they all have the *same Scent* upon them; and they will without any more ado, give over wounding one another. *God put an End unto their doing so!*[67]

Mather thus became increasingly occupied with the question of the creedal "lowest common denominator" which could serve as the noetic foundation, or the discriminating test, for that genuine piety that was to be at the center of the united church. Earlier ecumenists in the Puritan/Pietist tradition had already considered the matter. In his early years, John Dury had projected a new confession of faith derived from the Bible, the ecumenical creeds, and the catechisms, perhaps with the Lutheran *Augustana* as the basis, but he left certain issues indefinite (such as the three that destroyed the Colloquy of Leipzig).[68] In 1652 he joined with a caucus of Puritan divines to produce a list of fifteen fundamentals worded so as to exclude Quakers, Unitarians, Anglicans, and Roman Catholics.[69] Richard Baxter was understandably dissatisfied with this, proposing instead a much broader base consisting of the Apostles' Creed, the Lord's Prayer, and the Ten Commandments. In his four subsequent books on church union he broadened this base to include explicit faith in the Trinity, Jesus Christ as mediator, the divinity of the Holy Spirit, the validity of baptism, and the Lord's Supper as seals of faith, along with a commitment to godly life and a general acknowledgment of the authority of Scripture. He included a carefully designed list of "True and Easie terms of Unity and Concord" designed to harmonize conforming and dissenting habits of polity and worship.[70]

On the Continent, Spener was necessarily guarded in his utterances on this subject, but he openly held that there were doctrinal articles of secondary importance as well as a core of faith that was vital to piety. He felt that *"Alte Simplizität"* (apostolic simplicity) could reduce the whole content of faith to a curriculum which might be rehearsed in an hour. Calixtus had reduced the basis of faith to the Apostles' Creed; Spener felt that it was reducible beyond this simply to a confession of sin and of faith in Christ, a kind of anteroom of regenerate Christianity beyond which the convert could be led for advanced doctrinal enlightenment. Beyond this point, the more developed doctrinal corpus was to contain only credenda that were vital for piety and overwhelmingly clear scripturally.[71]

Mather referred to the problem of the creedal basis of a united church in *Blessed Unions* (1692) but did not elaborate. "As far as we can, we should be of the same Opinion, and hold the same *Doctrine* of Christianity; be sure we must concur in all the *Fundamental* Ones, or else we cut off ourselves from the *Communion of Saints*; and as he that had the *Plague in his head*, we are shut out from the Camp and Church of God."[72] He did not develop this any further until his contact with Pietism went into its most active stage after 1710, probably because he was satisfied that the English Heads of Agreement were adequate as a basis for the union of the Reformed and Puritan types of Protestant. When he became fully aware of the awakening among Lutherans, however, he became interested in finding a doctrinal base that would go beyond the Puritan sphere to encompass others whom he now recognized as very vital believers. Early in the year 1713, Mather recorded in the *Diary* a new concern to arrive at a theological base for ecumenical unity.

> 'Tis hardly possible for me to do a greater Service than to publish unto the World, the Maxims, which are to unite the People that the glorious God will form for Himself, and that will quickly be the Stone growing into a great Mountain, which the whole Earth shall be filled withal. There is a mighty Tendency to Reformation, which has been long working in the Minds of Multitudes and Millions of People, both among the Romanists and Protestants. The Efforts made by this Inclination in the Souls of Men, have hitherto, thro' the Temptations of the Day, been generally encumbered with Errors, and Follies, and with naughty Superfluities. But when the pure Maxims of Truth, and of real, vital, spiritual Religion, and manly Christianity, are set before the People of God, who can tell, what may be done in some new, and the next Essayes, to bring on the Kingdome of God? (II, 196-197).

Later that year he set the "Maxims" before the public in a list of fourteen points, about which I have already commented. In 1717, Mather recorded his intent to "make a fresh essay, to draw up in a plain and brief manner the Points of Religion and Liberty, which the several Parties . . . may and should unite upon" (II, 467); and in August of that year he stated that he had drawn up an "*Instrument* of Union" based on the revised list of maxims, which he proposed to publish and send abroad. This document was *Malachi* (1717). As we have seen, it offers a condensed list of credenda, mentioned almost as an afterthought in the application: a Trinitarian view of God as Creator and Lord; Jesus Christ as divine redeemer; and the Golden Rule as the norm and test of sanctification.[73] The body of the work, however, deals with piety as the sole qualification of membership in the kingdom of God, and it emphasizes that the entrance to this piety is through Christ. It is clear that Mather was intent on finding the absolute minimum of creedal substance which would define and identify live Christians, so that the terms of communion would equal those of regeneration. He wanted to draw the broadest circle practicable:

> It is not proposed, That we should make such a, *Quicunque vult,* upon every clause in the INSTRUMENT, as absolutely and positively to pronounce a Sentence of *Damnation* upon every one who does not subscribe unto it. It is enough, that we *Leave them unto GOD!* All we have to say, is, that we do not see our selves under Obligations, (nor will they ask us,) to *Unite* with them, as our *Brethren,* in the Affairs of His Kingdom. It may be proposed, That there should be formed *SOCIETIES* of Good Men, who can own some such Instrument of PIETY.[74]

Piety and Equity of the same year (1717) focuses on Christology as the central issue in ecumenical affairs:

> Now 'tis in a Glorious CHRIST, that all Good men are *United.* 'Tis a Recourse to a Glorious CHRIST as, the *Ensign of the People,* and Looking for a *Glorious Rest* in and from Him, that Unites them all. Wherein soever they vary from one another, yet here all the *Good men* in the World are, *One man,* and with *One mouth* declare, CHRIST is our All.
>
> . . . .
>
> The *Rule of Fellowship* in the Churches of GOD, is that *Golden* One; Rom. XV.7., *Receive ye one another, as CHRIST also has Received us unto the Glory of GOD.* Those of whom we ought for to Judge, that our *SAVIOUR* will Receive them to His *Glory* in the Heavenly World, we ought now to Receive into our Fellow-

ship; and none of the Brotherly Respects due to *Brethren in CHRIST,* are to be withheld from them.[75]

Mather goes on to remark that such a union can only be propagated spiritually, by means of a revival organically uniting the fragments of Christ's church:

> Here, Here is the proper *Basis* for an *Union* among the People of GOD. Attempt any other *Basis,* and it is not *Zion,* but *Babel* that is built upon it; and it will prosper accordingly. Yea, Would you Learn, what is to be done for the *Uniting* of *Differing Parties?* Don't Combate so much those which you take to be their *particular Errors;* But Labour to *Draw* them to CHRIST, *Win* them to CHRIST: Render their SAVIOUR dear unto them. They will then drop their *Zeal* for their little *Particularities,* as far as may be necessary to leave Room for your Union with them.[76]

The accomplishment of the ecumenical task is assumed to be part of the premillennial revival, and the full flower of Mather's ecumenical thought precisely coincides with the second long period of revivalist expectation occurring in his lifespan, beginning in 1713:

> There has been awakened of late Years, in the Minds of Men, a vehement Inclination, to shake off those *Religious Formalities,* by which they do not find themselves brought nearer to GOD; and to get more into a *Real, Vital, Spiritual Religion,* and such as will have the *Life of God in the Soul of Man,* with a more transforming Energy operating in it. Multitudes and Millions of People, are at this Day, both among the *Romanists,* and among the *Protestants,* thus disposed; and the Disposition which is now too much *imprisoned in Unrighteousness,* will one Day break forth with an astonishing Revolution upon the World. At present, they that are under these Impressions, continue in many *Mistakes* and *Errors,* thro' the fatal Encumbrances that are upon them. . . . The Continuance of which *Darkness in their Paths* will be, until the Term allotted by the Great *Lord of Time* not far off, Christian Apostacy be expired. But there is a Time not far off, and probably tremendous Concussions, and Convulsions, and Confusions upon the Nations, will be felt in the Approaches of it, when these *Impressions from God* on the Spirits of Men, will be under a more *Effectual Direction,* disentangling and disengaging them from the *Follies* which many Sectaries have been left unto; and this Panting and Heaving *Tendency to Reformation* will bear down

all before it; and nothing shall obstruct the KINGDOM OF GOD, from appearing in an universal Reign of *Holiness* and *Righteousness* among the Nations.[77]

Thus for Mather there can be no revival, and no millennium, unless ecumenical unity is achieved:

> GOD will one day bring His People to Embrace One another upon these Generous MAXIMS; and to keep the *Lesser Points* in a due *Subordination* to them; and manage their controversy on the *Lesser Points* with *another Spirit*, than what has been too frequent among the Disputers of this world. . . . The World will not presently come to *This; One Year* won't bring them to it. But it may be infallibly foretold unto you, God will go on to *Shake all Nations*, until they come to *This*. God will *Overturn, Overturn, Overturn!* And O Unrighteous *Nations*, O *Foolish People & Unwise;* You shall never see *Rest* until you come to This.[78]

There will be no revival unless there is unity, and the converse is equally true.

Mather was not content, however, to rest in a merely passive "spiritual" expectation of ecumenism. As usual, he made the matter a project, and the project produced a new society. Shortly after he conceived the idea of the maxims, he reflected on the idea of forming groups of Christians united on this basis, and began "studying of Methods to draw Mankind into their Association" (*Diary*, II, 202). The idea was dropped until 1718. A letter of that year to Sir William Ashurst indicates that he could not now be satisfied only with a union of Reformed Christians (II, 511). His son records that he succeeded in founding a "Society of Peacemakers" in 1719.[79]

Mather's ecumenism was certainly imperfect enough when it is viewed from some angles. For one thing, he had a great deal of trouble being civil with Anglican prospects during periods when the English established church was dealing roughly with dissenters. It is not true that he merely used the concept of toleration as a lever to pry concessions from the government; but he did use it constantly as a club to punish Anglican aggression, and this prejudice can always be distinctly heard when Mather speaks of truly pious Chris-

tians as above petty concerns over ceremonial matters.[80]
Mather was quick to indicate that his ecumenical charity was
not meant to encourage the younger generation in Boston to
go back to the abominations of the Anglican faith.[81] His real
allergy, of course, was only to the High Church wing, the
"Party in the Church of *England*, which *hates to be Reformed.*"[82] It is ironic that while Francke was enthusiastically
doing business with the Society for the Propagation of the
Gospel, Mather was privately and publicly fed up with that
organization, which he correctly felt to be a High Church
invasion intent on recapturing lost ground in New England.[83]
He wrote to Thomas Hollis in 1723:

> The Truth is, if all the Remonstrances that we make about a
> Charity so abominably prostituted as that of the *Society*, will
> only produce a care of our Diocesan to send over better Mis-
> sionaries we are best as we are. For the Missionaries they have
> hitherto sent, have generally been such Ignorant Wretches, and
> such Debauched and Finished Villains, that Like the Rattle
> snakes in our Country they carry with 'em what warns and
> arms our People against being poisoned with them (*Diary*,
> II, 691-692).

Toward Baptists Mather is uniformly more charitable. In 1696
he sent money "unto a poor Man, a Preacher in my
Neighbourhood, who, I hope, is a good Man, however hee
see not of my Perswasion, but a froward Anabaptist" (I, 209).
In 1718 he found a good opportunity to forward the purpose
of the maxims in an invitation to act and preach in the
ordination of a Baptist minister in the neighborhood. The
instance shows both the reputation of Mather for ecumenic-
ity, and the degree to which he was ahead of his compatriots,
for he comments: "My Action will cause much Discourse and
Wonder; but . . . I see the Kingdome of God opening in what
is now adoing" (I, 530-531). Mather's dialogue on baptism,
published in 1724, attempts to handle the matter "moderately
but successfully," and charitably hopes that "God will preserve his People, on both sides in this Controversy, from all
foolish Passions; for the *Wrath of Man* hurts the Truth, spoils
the Cause."[84] On the other hand, Mather was disturbed
about the pew-hunters from his congregation who had de-
fected to a local Baptist meetinghouse, where "they never see

the Baptism of the Lord administered, nor hear the pathetical and affectionate Prayers made on that Occasion"; and he resolved to see "proper and prudent Wayes" to reclaim the strayed sheep.[85] Mather's ecumenism was most successful when it was directed toward those who did not have the drawback of being his neighbors, such as the German Lutherans.

On the other hand, the progressive balance of Mather's ecumenism considerably outweighs its defects. Modern ecumenists are tempted either to unite the church before an adequate doctrinal and spiritual unity has been established, or else to fold the hands and wait passively until the church automatically and organically grows into unity through the renewal of its parts. Mather steered a clear course between these extremes, insisting on the primacy of spiritual renewal but making every effort to establish doctrinal and organizational unity. While Mather at his widest seems narrow to modern vision, anyone familiar with Puritan Calvinism will have to acknowledge the immense maturation of his viewpoint under the impact of Pietism. In later years he wrote to an Arminian:

> Being myself a *Calvinist*, I must needs differ pretty much from a Gentleman who professes himself an *Arminian*. But I consider what those *Maxims of Piety* are, which engage the Arminian to maintain his Distinguishing Positions. Those Maxims are, *That* the holy and sin-hating Lord must not be reproach'd as the Impeller of the Sin, whereof he is the *Revenger; that* our Merciful Father is not to be blasphemed, as if He dealt after an illusory manner with Men, when He invites them to His Mercy; *That* none among the Fallen Race of the *First Adam,* are to be shut out from the Hopes of Life in the Death of the *Second Adam;* That impenitent Unbelievers must not cast on God the Blame of their Unbelief, but the Wicked must lay wholly on themselves the Fault of their own Destruction; and *That* Men must work out their own Salvation with as much Industry, and Agony, and Vigilancy, as if all turned upon their own Will and Care, whether they shall be saved or no. Now these are *Maxims* which every pious *Calvinist* will most heartily consent unto. And if I should repeat the *Maxims of Piety* which make me fall in with the Position of a *Calvinist,* prerequisite unto the supporting of them, I am confident the pious Mr. *de la Pilloniere* would most heartily subscribe unto them. And we shall both

> have the Modesty to confess that we have to do with Matters
> which are to us incomprehensible. Now if good Men are so
> united in the *Maxims* which are the END, for the serving
> whereof they declare that they pursue their Controversies, why
> should not this *Uniting Piety* put an End unto their Controver-
> sies? and beat *their Swords into Ploughshares, and their Spears
> into Pruning-Hooks?*[86]

This statement demonstrates that Mather felt himself on a
kind of high ground, possessing biblical piety, from which
all the theological Gordian knots created in former conten-
tions could be untied. He felt that the key of a vitalized
Christian experience was sufficient to unlock all the doors
built up between genuine Christians through misunderstanding. In this conviction the most significant leaders
in the Puritan and Pietist movements, and those who would
come in the period of the Great Awakening, were agreed.
Samuel Davies and the Tennents were concerned for the
ecumenical effect of the first Awakening; Wesley was in
agreement with Spener that church union would eventually
come as the outgrowth of revival; and Zinzendorf's plan for
world revival and missionary extension was based on an
informal union of all those in every denomination (even
including Rome) who were followers of the Lamb and had
experienced "the death of Christ upon the heart."[87] Cotton
Mather was unable to transcend his Puritan background to
reach the thorough catholicity of Zinzendorf, who recognized every denominational expression of Christianity as a
tropos paideia, a tradition preserving a particular jewel of
truth and self-expression without which the wholeness of
Christendom could not be achieved.[88] But within his limitations Mather is one of the most vigorous spokesmen for the
ecumenical tradition.[89]

Mather's theory of premillennial awakening and his ecumenical interests are closely connected with another feature
in which he foreshadows the future of Protestantism: his
concern for world missions. This same mixture of components may have existed in some Continental Pietists and
even in the "crypto-ecumenism" at Halle. There was cer-

tainly an open connection in European Pietism between the ecumenical and missionary ideals, since Francke enlisted support from all Protestant communities for the Danish mission at Malabar.[90] The same connection had been operative earlier—during the seventeenth century in England. Dury had been moved partly by an urgency for world mission in his ecumenical concern,[91] and he had been active in promoting Eliot's mission to the Indians. Baxter had observed, "No part of my prayers are so deeply serious as that for the conversion of the infidel and ungodly world."[92]

Cotton Mather imbibed his own early interest in Christian mission throughout the world from Puritan sources. Edmund Morgan has speculated that by the time of the Mathers the New England clergy had gained sufficient control of the situation that they were looking out at one another with thoughts of consociation and out at the world with a concern for mission that had leisure to expand beyond their own particular parish, on which earlier generations of Congregational clergy had been perhaps too concentrated. But there was a definite turning point in Cotton Mather's life, a time at which he felt himself called to effect a revolution in his own sensibility which would direct his concern more generally toward the state of the gospel enterprise in other churches and the world at large. This occurred exactly at the time of his first burst of enthusiasm for the outpouring of the Spirit, in February 1696.[93] In July of that same year he writes:

> I sett myself to consider, That, altho' in my Devotions I had still remembered the *Churches* and *Interests* of my Lord Jesus Christ, abroad in the World, yett I had not arrived unto a due *Enlargement* of Soul, in my doing so. Wherefore I now lamented before the Lord, the *Privateness* and *Selfishness* of Spirit, which in my former Devotion had attended mee; and I resolved, that I, as poor and as vile, as I am, would now become a *Remembrancer* unto the Lord, for no less whole *Peoples,* Nations, and Kingdomes. I apprehended with myself that if I would thus lay to Heart the *Concerns* of the Lord Jesus Christ, and the State of whole *Peoples,* and Continue, with extraordinary Supplications crying to Heaven, for mercy to them, I should bee more Angelically disposed and employed, than I have been heretofore (*Diary*, I, 199-200).

From this burst of curiously self-centered altruism onward, Mather set himself to become one of the great spiritual statesmen of his time, one of those watchmen on the walls of Christendom who plant and pluck up kingdoms. During the rest of his career, in his prayers for world revival, he felt himself dwelling in the actuality of this role, with every promise in his first intimation of such a calling fulfilled. From this point on the entries in the *Diary* are filled with prayerful reflections on the news from Europe, viewed against a background of concern for the progress of world Protestantism, at first centering on the interests of Puritanism and then broadening to include evangelicals of every kind. The concept of the "gapman," the solitary individual of eminent piety who takes on the world as his parish and stands in the gap in times of decline to avert the wrath of God, continued to preoccupy him until his death. In 1717 he observes:

> Among the people of GOD, there are some, who are *Conspicuously Favoured* of Him, in His *Answers of the Prayers,* which they make unto Him. There are some, whose *Prayer availeth much;* Some who have the *Golden Key* to the Treasures of Mercy, under a skillful, powerful, successful management; Some who have their Petitions to Heaven so granted, that *all they who see them, acknowledge them* to be the *Favorites* of Heaven. It may be said unto them, as in Gen. XXXII:28, *As a Prince thou hast power with God.*[94]

Such individuals are blessings to their environs because they pray for them and, like Abraham and Lot, turn back God's judgment, and because they contrive to do good by their advice, their examples, and their various projections to reform and retard evil.

But Mather did not limit his zeal for missionary concern to exceptional men such as he felt himself to be; he urged it upon his own parishioners and upon laymen and ministers everywhere. In 1695 he had urged Christians to take pity on the world, two-thirds of which was still pagan and lying in the control of the devil, and had urged them to offer prayer in missionary concern. "By being much in Prayer, we may like *Noah*, like *Job*, like *Daniel*, we may our selves be *Publick Blessings;* we may be the gapmen of the places in which we live; we may *deliver Islands,* and be the Saviours of our Country."[95] A particularly powerful and moving example of this is *Advice to the Churches of the Faithful* of 1702. This work begins with a prayer for world revival, "A Few Sighs for a Distressed Church, For the Dispersed *Israelites,*" which includes petitions for the ailing Puritan heart-line of Christendom, the Greek churches, those under Muslim and Roman oppression, the American churches, and the parts of the earth that had not received the gospel: "Lord, *Let the Sun of Righeousness at last Shine upon the Dark Recesses in these goings down of the Sun; and let the Son of God, have these Ends of the Earth for His Possession.* In fine; Come, Lord JESUS, come quickly!"[96] Mather goes on to charge his readers with the duty of prayer, and to re-emphasize the revivalist elements that should inspire this prayer:

> Every *Christian,* who is any more than a *Rotten* or a *Wooden* Member, in this *Mystical Body* of our Lord, will be still sensibly touched with its uneasy circumstances, and be heartily *sollicitious* about it. . . . There is much of Omen . . . of Mighty and Happy *Changes* nigh unto the *Church,* when God stirs up the Hearts of His Praying People, to be much in *Prayer* for them. . . . Wherefor it appears one of the worst Symptoms upon our *Evil Time,* That there is no more *Striving* and *Wrestling* in *Prayer* among the People of God, for His Mercy to His Distressed People. *O Lord, be merciful! What a Dead Sleep are thy People, and even the Watchmen of thy People fallen into!* Nevertheless, there are some so much *Awake,* as to be Inquisitive after the Condition of the *Church* at this Day. . . .[97]

The peculiar blending of optimistic urgency and pessimism here is echoed again in *Another Tongue,* a tract for the Indians which Mather published in Iroquois, Latin, English, and German, aiming at a maximum audience (and perhaps at maximum public notice). Mather was considerably upset by the zeal of Catholic missionaries, who had newly penetrated to the Iroquois in America.

> Certainly, The zeal of *Protestants,* to Propagate our Holy Religion, well Purified from the *Popish Mixtures,* ought to be more Flaming, more Lively, than any thing that we can see in the Church of *Rome.* . . . Verily, Did we Love our Glorious CHRIST, or had we any agreeable Sense of the Vast Obligation which He has laid upon us, how Studious, how Vigorous

> would be our Endeavors to bring all men to Know Him, and
> Serve Him, and have Him Glorified among all Nations of Men!
> Oh! That a *Spirit for the Propagation of Christianity*, were more
> Operative among those, *Who say they are Christians!* The want
> of it, makes it sadly questionable, How far we *are*, from what
> we *Say!* Had not the *Spirit of God* very dreadfully abandoned
> *Christendom*, there would be seen a Thousand Times more of it,
> than there is. *Blessed* SPIRIT, Oh! *Return, and Visit, this Misera-
> ble World; and let marvellous things be done by thy Operations!*[98]

Mather's resources and energies were mainly employed
in supporting already existing mission works, by prayer,
gifts, and publicity, rather than in organizing new ministries. By far the majority of his references to mission relate to
the work already established among the Indians in
America.[99] The detailed description of Eliot's work in the
Magnalia[100] shows Mather's interest in those "Hedious creatures" for whom he displayed a lifelong compassion mingled
with the element of fear and vindictiveness which emerges
in his writings on the Indian wars.[101] In 1699 he began work
on a tract "to make the Knowledge of Christ, and Christianity, more effectually apprehended among the Indians"
(*Diary*, I, 304), and this was published in 1700. Its style is an
interesting effort to get close to the Indian milieu:

> The English have been your great Friends; you must be for
> them . . . if you be their enemies, or help their enemies, you
> will *Requite Evil for Good,* and you will be, as if an Indian
> should bring to the fireside a Snake frozen and starved, and the
> Snake after he is comforted should sting the kind Indian, and
> kill him.
>
> . . . .
>
> You shall be blessed with the Lord Jesus Christ, infinitely more
> years than you see stars in the Sky, or stones on the Earth, or
> Drops of water in the Rivers.[102]

The unconscious colonialism here is borne out in the body of
the work, which after a brief statement of Reformed essentials gives the Decalogue in detail and concludes with a
warning against drunkenness, the inflammatory sin to which
the Indians were especially susceptible. Samuel Mather notes
that in 1708 his father took the trouble to learn Iroquois so
that he could reach this tribe.[103]

There are a large number of references in the *Diary* to Mather's concern for the Indians in his later years, beginning around 1711. He was concerned about the discipline in the Indian churches and the report of oppressions practiced by the English on them (II, 48); and later in that year he "animates" the commissioners of Indian affairs to investigate these matters (II, 78). In October he remarks:

> By a prudent and faithful Visitation of the Indians, we are furnished with very punctual account of . . . their Circumstances; and we have something on which we may proceed unto numberless Actions for the Kingdome of our Saviour, and the Welfare of that miserable People. I propose, that the Commissioners of the Indian-affayrs, may now have their very frequent Meetings (II, 120-121).

In November he notes the number of proposals for Indian welfare he has made to the commissioners, including sending missionaries to the Mohicans in Connecticut and rewarding sober Indians with gifts of hats which he procured for them (II, 132-133); and several subsequent references reflect a fairly single-hearted concern for the spiritual and physical welfare of the Christian Indians in a number of different locations (II, 143, 182). In 1717 he is concerned to procure an attorney for the congregation on Martha's Vineyard (II, 396).

Entering the melancholy decade of the 1720s, Mather found the same decline in the Indian mission work that was evident to him in the rest of world Christendom. *India Christiana* (1721), commenting on the glory of the past work among the Indians, admits that at present "'Tis a Day of Small things. . . . Religion . . . is under a Decay among them."[104] And yet Mather urges the continuance of the mission, and especially the instruction of the Indians in the English tongue: "If but a *Few* of them, should be brought into a Sincere *Love* of GOD and of their *Neighbour*, and a Living *Faith* in our only *Saviour*, it will be richly worth all the Time and Cost that has been laid out upon them all."[105] A letter to Lieutenant Governor Dummer, the head of the Commission, in 1725, laments the condition of "dying Religion among these miserable objects," and urges the appointment of a "Visitor" to inquire into the "Languishing State of many things" (*Diary*, II, 807-809).

In the succession of Mather's writings dealing with the Indian missions, there is a perceptible shift away from the pragmatic motive of protecting the colonists through spiritual pacification of the Indians toward a pure and outspoken concern for their spiritual welfare as they became less of an immediate threat. This may have been Mather's principal concern all along, but in his earlier attempts to rouse public support for this mission he correctly judged that the most sensitive nerves in New Englanders were involved in their sense of self-preservation.

The *India Christiana* reflects the fact that Mather's missionary concern embraced the "Indians" of all sectors of the globe, including the islands of the West Indies to the South, and the East Indian mission at Malabar. In May of 1706 he mentions a concern for "the distressed Condition of the American Islands" (*Diary*, I, 563), and in 1718 he was involved in the "Settlement of the evangelical Affairs at *Barmudas*" (I, 532). There is more widespread mention of the East Indian missions, especially the Pietist mission, which he directly supported (II, 348, 365, 516, 517, 520, 544).

The concern to be a watchman on the walls of world Christendom involved Mather in other missionary projects besides the Indians, in which he grappled tentatively with the missionary's task of identifying with the culture he seeks to reach. His concerns included, first, the winning of souls in civilized countries which he regarded as oppressed by the Islamic or Roman Catholic systems of Antichrist.[106] In 1699 he learned the elements of Spanish in a matter of two weeks in order to satisfy an urgent concern to produce a tract for the conversion of South Americans from Catholicism. The resulting work is highly theological in tone and covertly polemical, and it shows less ability to empathize with the subjects of his mission than some of his other tracts.[107] In keeping with his millennial interest, he produced a tract to reach the Jews around this time, which is even more pugnacious and inclined to scare the fish he sought to catch, but it is carefully couched in Old Testament language.[108]

From 1696 onward he was also very concerned with the progress of the gospel in home missions for English-speaking peoples. The condition of religion in the outlying plantations was a burden of concern to him throughout his life. In February of 1697 he mentions that he and his congregation made "a liberal *Contribution* for the *Propagation of the Gospel* unto the dark Places in our Borders" (*Diary*, I, 217), and this remained a persistent concern, as his *Letter to Ungospellized Plantations* (1702) and a number of diary entries indicate (I, 426, 554, 574, 593; II, 78, 471-472). He was interested also in "evangelical missions"—that is, Puritan ones—to the other colonies, and particularly in Jamaica, Long Island, and New Amsterdam (II, 132). In April 1713 he secured and financed a young man as an itinerant missionary in "the southern Colonies" (II, 353). He was also continuously involved in the vital interests of churches closer to home, in Massachusetts and Connecticut (II, 46, 105, 112, 160, 226, 750). And, of course, he was regularly involved in the care of other churches in Boston (I, 316-317; II, 460, 505). In 1725 he proposed the establishment of what amounts to a denominational—or even ecumenical—fund for domestic and foreign missions.[109]

It is easy to discern that a part of Mather's urgency in embracing such a wide scope of concerns was his desire to be a great man. But while this may have been part of his initial motivation, we cannot say that something more did not develop in him as he continued in a lifetime of prayer for world mission. To some of his contemporaries he doubtless seemed the very incarnation of prying interference. To some modern viewers who see him mainly in a political dimension, even this altruism is only a stalking horse for political strategy. He did not, like Francke or Wesley, initiate missionary structures, but only prayed for and worked through the ones already created by others. Still, perhaps, he deserves a niche close to these men who adopted the world as their parish; for we know of no more vigilant watchman on the walls of Zion among the ministry of America, one who had so much at heart the afflictions of Joseph throughout the entire world.

Epilogue

COTTON MATHER IS AN IMPORTANT LINK IN A LONG chain of witnesses within the Christian church who have pursued the development and full expression of "the spiritual life." This tradition includes as its most authentic exponents the principal fathers of the early church, certain of the medieval and pre-Reformation mystics, the Puritans and Pietists of the sixteenth and seventeenth centuries, and the eighteenth- and nineteenth-century Protestant Evangelicals. Development over the last five centuries within this tradition has addressed itself to the solution of two main problems. The first has been the purification of Catholic piety through the elimination of Judaistic and other extra-Christian components, with the restructuring of the Christian life on an authentic Pauline basis, combining in biblical tension the elements of justification and sanctification. The second has been the formulation of a post-Constantinian and non-theocratic missionary strategy, containing in proper balance the concerns for individual redemption and those for physical and social healing. It is my conclusion that Cotton Mather is a uniquely important "condenser" within this theological and spiritual current, recapitulating in his own piety much of the spiritual practice of the early church, but also remarkably charging it with potential for the future. For this line of development, he is the most important man of his generation in America, with only a handful of contemporary peers in the rest of Western Christendom.

As Sidney Mead has commented, Mather's work "unknowingly was fanning the spark in New England that eight years later would burst into flames in Jonathan Edwards' Northampton church."[1] This perception of Mather correctly indicates the Puritan roots of the American phase of the Great Awakening, and it suggests also that Edwards' approach to revival was not a novel invention constructed out of Lockean philosophy and the rhetoric of sensation but a redaction of the experiential tradition going back through Mather to such diverse exponents of Puritan spirituality as John Cotton and Thomas Shepard. Mather was the initial important figure in the transition Mead traces from the "sacerdotal" to the evangelical ministerial style in American church history. This study has underscored the fact that the Evangelical tradition was neither originated nor entirely shaped in the American context, although it has perhaps enjoyed the greatest freedom to develop its essential identity in the American denominational system.

Evangelical spirituality arose simultaneously and spontaneously at the end of the sixteenth century in English Puritanism and the pre-Pietism of Johann Arndt, as the descendants of the Reformation sought for a piety to express their new theological synthesis. During the seventeenth century the Puritan and Pietist evangelical strains noted, admired, and cross-pollinated one another; Mather's correspondence with Boehm and Halle was only a late instance of this communication. The interrelationships during the Great Awakening between Zinzendorf's Lutheran Pietism, Wesleyan Arminianism, and the Puritan Calvinism of Whitefield, Edwards, and the Tennents was a later instance of the same sort. The Second Awakening in America in the early nineteenth century, and the simultaneous evangelical renaissance in England, were expressions of the same impulse, which realized in amazing detail the hopes and plans of Cotton Mather for ecumenical cooperation in evangelism and social and cultural renewal. The vitality of the Evangelical Movement ebbed during the late nineteenth and early twentieth centuries, as its center declined into Fundamentalism, relinquishing the ecumenical and social initiatives cherished by Mather and Francke, and magnifying their tendencies toward confessionalism and legalism. But fortunately the ideals of biblical doctrine, godly living, unity, evangelistic mission, and social compassion held by these men have constantly been upheld in one segment of the church or another, even when those segments have been at odds with one another.

Currently, the international and ecumenical fellowship of Christians which Mather so urgently sought appears to be taking shape despite these divisions, in what Kenneth Latourette has called "the emergence of a world Christian community."[2] Mather would undoubtedly be surprised to discover that his own concerns and the labors of Dury and Zinzendorf have led to the emergency of at least *two* international ecumenical movements, somewhat at odds with one another, the one represented by the World Council of Churches and the other by the informal network of agencies and voluntary societies that is contemporary Evangelicalism. But it is possible that he would be encouraged by the occasional signs that these organizations are listening to one another and learning, and perhaps making progress toward the recovery of wholeness of vision.

Mead suggests that the temporary decline of the Evangelical tradition into post-Finneyan revivalism was the inevitable result of irrationalist and anti-intellectual currents that were components of Pietism.[3] This judgment would be difficult to defend in the light of current scholarship on Spener and Francke, which underscores the fact that the early Pietists, like the mainstream Puritans and the magisterial Reformers, were Christian humanists with a balanced appreciation of intellectual culture. Most of the factors that produced Fundamentalism arose considerably later than Mather and Edwards, although it may be true that Timothy Dwight was the last major representative in America of the strain of Evangelicalism that sought both spiritual renewal and a thorough intellectual command of its cultural milieu. But it is certainly possible that some of the weaker features of

American Fundamentalism were latent in Mather's Puritanism, and most of these have been discussed above. American Evangelicalism is still struggling to divest itself of some of the features it has inherited from its Puritan origins. In this connection, it must be admitted that Cotton Mather was not only an example of the Evangelical tradition at its best but also, in some features of his personality, an exhibit of Puritan Evangelicalism at its worst.

This is not, however, because his character lacked integrity. We have seen that while Mather's critics (and some of his friends) have generally described his thought and his personality as a composition of opposites, his theology was thoroughly self-consistent, and his character was equally coherent. Most of his reputed inconsistencies are the result of either the uncritical attempts by later critics to fuse together the testimonies of his friends and his enemies, or of the attempt to judge him without a thorough acquaintance with Puritan spirituality in the context of the history of Christian experience. What appears abnormal and grotesque in a secular context takes on a different light when it is set against the background of the normal practice of desert saints, the early fathers, medieval mystics, and many other Puritans. Seen in this setting, Mather was merely an ordinary contemplative ascetic with literary ambitions and a bent for activism. But he did have a few major and distinctive spiritual problems.

How many of these problems are psychological in origin? Long-distance psychoanalysis of Mather is a difficult, risky, and probably fruitless task, even for those with more professional training than the average historian. It cannot be definitely proved from historical evidence that Mather was "neurotic," paranoid, masochistic, sexually maladjusted, or even hypochondriacal; and several of these conditions are in fact contraindicated. Mather's friends speak of him as a balanced and urbane gentleman, and his enemies do not accuse him of insanity but of credulity and meddlesomeness, qualities that were programmed into every Puritan of his generation, not the result of psychological stress. Mather's relationship with his father seems grounded in mutual respect and love, with few hints of domination and rebellion. His life with his first two wives was evidently full of real tenderness and affection. As for Mather's persecution complex: he was, in fact, persecuted; he was a main leader on one side of a religio-political war and quite naturally drew fire. The fact that he interpreted all of this in terms of a spiritual conflict for the prevailing of the gospel in New England does not necessarily imply megalomania. From his own doctrinal position he could come to no other conclusion; and he was supported by biblical examples that would today show many of the psalmists to be paranoid. The occasional expressions of rage and vindictiveness in his diary undoubtedly reveal moral weakness under pressure. Either he was honest enough to leave these in, assuming that any future readers would understand the crushing injustices he felt himself to be suffering, or he found theological support for them in the imprecatory psalms.

The major charge against Mather that must be sustained by the evidence is that of egocentricity. This defect was particularly thrust upon him by his precocity, his gifts, his position of leadership, and, above all, by his theology. Puritan conversion was rooted in a fearful search for ultimate self-preservation, aggravated by an insistence on interior evidences of acceptance by God. The resulting crisis of introspection left a centripetal bias on the souls of Puritans for the rest of their lives. Thus the foci of attention in much of Mather's life were these: not God, but his experience of God; not man, but the fruitfulness of his ministry toward man. We do not often gaze outward through the *Diary* into the grandeur of the face of God, or into the drama of the lives of his people, or the events of his age; we look down into the close confines of Mather's ego, which is aching with conviction or exulting in ecstasy. Whether he is berating his own depravity, lamenting his pride, or projecting a great work for God, there is the endless, monotonous, and quite unconscious self-reference, probing the state of his destiny and taking the temperature of his soul. It might be understandable if this were confined to the *Diary*. The diary form was the Puritan equivalent of the confessional, and it is thus not surprising that it is egocentric and exhibits pathological

material. Few Christians would fare better if they were unwise enough to transcribe their inner experience honestly for
subsequent public reading. But in scores of Mather's sermons we can observe the same compulsive side-glances at
his career and reputation, as if a mirror were continually
being inserted between himself and his audience. This self-
consciousness might have been hidden by a thousand people
of greater basic egotism but sharper worldly and literary
prudence. But Mather's egocentricity is so innocently displayed precisely because he almost felt it to be a virtue. It
was, after all, ordinary Puritan heroic saintliness, a "normal"
product of his theological assumptions.

What was the theological ingredient that caused this
pathology? Within the Puritan/Pietist stream, it is mainly
concentrated on the Puritan side; for example, it does not
seem to be present in the Pietism of Arndt, Spener, Francke,
or Zinzendorf. This suggests that the stronger emphasis on
justification by faith in the Lutheran tradition neutralized to
some extent the danger of overemphasis on sanctification
which prevailed in Puritanized Calvinism. The Puritan experiential synthesis, particularly in New England after the
Hutchinson trial, was always fairly "nomistic" compared to
the "antinomianism" of John Cotton. When we juxtapose the
thrust of Luther's *Commentary on Galatians* with the diaries of
Michael Wigglesworth and Cotton Mather, we cannot avoid
the conclusion that the Reformer would diagnose the Puritans as mired in scrupulous introspection induced by an
imperfect balancing of Law and Gospel, justification and
sanctification. Thus the movement of nineteenth-century
Evangelicalism from a Calvinistic to an Arminian theological
base was not the developed extension of crypto-Arminian
tendencies in Puritans like Mather; it was rather an understandable reaction against Puritan hyper-Calvinism, offering
once again salvation by faith rather than by experience.

P. T. Forsyth, in an incisive attack on "Pietism" (seen
through the distorting mirror of Ritschl's analysis), describes
the central problem of the Puritan style of Christian experience as a divergence from faith into introspection. "It is a
fatal mistake to think of holiness as a possession which we

have distinct from our faith. . . . Every Christian experience is an experience of faith; that is, it is an experience of what we have not." Thus the goal of mature Christian experience is extrospective, looking outward toward God and man in receptive faith and love, not inward at the experience which is generated by the outward gaze and cannot survive inspection.

> Faith is always in opposition to seeing, possessing, experiencing. A faith wholly experimental has its perils. It varies too much with our subjectivity. It is not our experience of holiness that makes us believe in the Holy Ghost. It is a matter of faith that we are God's children; there is plenty of experience in us against it. . . . That is to say, *perfection is not sanctity but faith.* . . . We are not saved by the love we exercise, but by the Love we trust.

Forsyth's description of what happens when this is overlooked sounds very much like the weaker side of Cotton Mather's character.

> A Church of sanctified egoisms would be no Church. Its essence would not be faith but moral or spiritual achievement. . . . There are certain forms of self-edification which run out into self-absorbtion, and leave men . . . working at goodness rather than at duty. . . . There is an absence of true humility. In its stead there may be either a laboured counterfeit, as painfully sincere as it is unsimple; or there is a precise self-righteousness which cannot veil a quiet air of superiority. . . . In its choicer forms this pietism is devoted to love and prayer; but it seldom escapes the tinge of self-consciousness in their culture.[4]

This is surely not true of all Puritans; many were able to move past the sloughs of self-consciousness into a broad central awareness of God and other people as the main foci of consciousness, as the experience of Edwards shows. But in the case of others, introspection, the training-ground of Puritan sanctity, produced a spiritual adolescence from which they never matured.

Compounding this weakness in Mather is the problem of his style, which is exactly the worst vehicle for a person with the problem of unconscious vanity, although for this reason it is perhaps the most natural. With its departure from the plain style and cold serious logic of his father into an opulent and humorous floridity—its puns, tropes, allusions, and encrustations of literary jewelry—Mather's style is constantly in danger of sounding ridiculous, whenever his taste, or ear, fails. And this failure is all too frequent, except in the handful of works which he really labored to edit and revise. The result is that Mather often sounds insincere even when he is basically serious, and so he is thoroughly vulnerable to casual misreading by his critics.

Nevertheless, when we look past these weaknesses and try to determine the stature of Cotton Mather, we must find him to be a far greater man in his generation, both by intrinsic merit and in terms of his far-reaching influence, than he is usually portrayed to be. If his voice lacks the depth and timbre of Edwards, a man who was in reality many of the things Mather was only trying to be, he was still involved in breaking ground for the movement Edwards came to represent. If he was unable to achieve spiritual greatness, he did approve the things that are excellent. He had the sensitivity to appreciate spiritual genius wherever he saw it in his world and the wisdom to recognize and applaud some of the forces that were to mold the future church. When we consider the immense body of published material that flowed from his pen—and the large number of persons eager to subsidize these works or publish them—we must conclude that he was the greatest single intellectual influence on his generation in America. Mather's influence did not end with his death, but it persisted in the great microcosm of the *Magnalia*, which relays in its saga the condensed world-picture of the early Puritans; in the *Manuductio ad Ministerium*, which was still being used as a ministerial guidebook in the nineteenth century; and in *Bonifacius*, which contained the seeds of the Benevolent Empire.

APPENDIX

Mather's Changing Image: a Bibliographical Inquiry

MOST OF COTTON MATHER'S CONTEMPORARIES DEEPLY
admired him and dismissed Robert Calef's attack on him, and
even his enemies seem to have concluded that he was basically a good man, if at times an irritating political opponent.
In the public memory, however, he personifies the worst elements of Puritanism. Even among scholars he has until recently been perceived as a disconcerting mixture of scarcely
reconcilable opposing qualities, good and bad. A brief analysis of the secondary literature dealing with Mather will help
clarify the sources of these problems. A bibliography of
Mather's own works currently in print is provided at the close
of this appendix.

Most previous accounts of Mather have been negative or
ambivalent either because they were generated in an atmosphere of religious warfare directed against Mather's theological position and tradition, in the struggles between orthodoxy
and rationalism, or because they have sought to comprehend
Mather without careful analysis of his theology and his role
in the development of the international Protestant consensus
which came together at the time of the Great Awakening to

form the Evangelical Movement. These two ways of misunderstanding Mather, reacting against his theology and overlooking its importance and significance, are easily illustrated in a brief review of the history of his reputation, which has some of the interest of a criminal investigation in a libel suit. A great part of the difficulty in evaluating Mather today is due to polemic stereotypes which earlier historians have built on a relatively small basis of evidence, which have an odd way of persisting and coloring the judgments of later historians even when that basis has been destroyed.

Calef's *More Wonders of the Invisible World* (London, 1700) intimated that both the Mathers were credulous and perhaps salacious, and accused them of trying to drum up another witchcraft scare in Boston.[1] The same charges are repeated in Francis Hutchinson's *Historical Essay Concerning Witchcraft* (London, 1718), but Hutchinson states more bluntly that the circulation of the works of Baxter and the Mathers on witchcraft fomented the delusion, and that the ministers, and particularly the younger Mather, whipped it on to enhance their own reputation as exorcists.[2] These allegations were recirculated by Dr. William Douglass and other opponents of inoculation during the smallpox epidemic of 1721 in Boston, but they do not appear in print again for the duration of the eighteenth century. Governor Thomas Hutchinson, in *The History of Massachusetts* (Boston, 1764), examines the two streams of testimony carefully and accepts the reasoning of Calef and Hutchinson on the nature of the delusion involved in the trials, but rejects their treatment of the ministers, placing the principal blame on the magistrates.[3]

Cotton Mather felt that the main motive behind Calef's attack on him and on the Puritan approach to witchcraft was theological in character. In his *Diary*, he spoke of Calef as a "Sadducee."[4] Calef cannot be convicted of total antisupernaturalism, since he acknowledged in his book the existence of angels, devils, and self-styled witches. Moreover, he used a deeply Protestant argument to attack the Puritan treatment of witches: he asserted that the whole error lay in building up an extra-biblical casuistry on the opinions of men in order to handle instances of supposed witchcraft. Although the appeal from tradition to scripture is classically Reformed, it was also one of the trademarks of the party in England which desired at this time to push on to a more radical reformation, and which would ultimately discard both creeds and orthodox Christology at Salter's Hall in 1719. It is not surprising, then, that when the case of Cotton Mather is again taken up by historians critical of his person and work, it is by men who represent a historical extension of the theological position implicit in Calef and Hutchinson and who rely for evidence on the witness given by these men.

In 1821, Henry Ware, Jr., the current heir to Mather's pulpit and the son of the first avowed Unitarian on the Harvard faculty, published *Two Discourses* (Boston, 1821) incorporating an historical review of the Mather dynasty and of later leaders in the church. Ware is reasonably moderate in his estimate of Mather's part in the witchcraft scandal, though he does assert that Cotton Mather must have been more involved in the affair than his father, because of his supposed want of judgment and credulity. Ware reads Calef and Mather with little historical perspective, concluding that the latter provides an exceptionally vivid instance of superstition, while actually Mather represented the norm, and Calef was the exception. Ware's estimate of Mather breathes the most refined essence of the later Bostonian Enlightenment:

> His original powers of mind were doubtless equal to those of his father, and his industry and learning far superior; but he was deficient in judgment and good taste, and therefore, with all his attainments, became rather an extraordinary than a great man. His character was a very mixed one. You would regard him with wonder and admiration, but hardly with a feeling of entire confidence. His religious sense was as strong as his father's, but it was mingled with more superstition, and was perpetually bordering on fanaticism, and running into the unprofitable observances of the ascetics.[5]

Ware's main evidence for the deficiency in Cotton Mather's judgment is the persistent failure of Harvard College to elect him President. He does not suspect that part of the underlying reason for the hesitation of the directors, especially in the 1720's, was the same distaste for Puritan Calvinism which Ware himself reveals.[6]

It is impossible to read the accounts of Mather by Ware and certain of his successors without being aware that they are viewing him not only through the glasses of the Enlightenment, but also in the wake of the controversy at the time of the Great Awakening—Ware has some shuddering words about that period of "religious excitement" and the active part played in it by Joshua Gee, Mather's successor and spiritual godchild[7]—and that the historians themselves are in the thick of the Unitarian controversy, in which the ideological successors of the Mathers are vigorously attacking them. Considering these conditions, it is surprising and praiseworthy that most of them are as careful, objective, and gracious as Ware seeks to be. Others, like the staunch anti-Calvinist apologist, C. W. Upham, were less restrained. Upham, who even more than Calef is responsible for the dark side of Mather's reputation, came to the study of the witchcraft affair with a respect for Mather's character and industry, but was led by his examination of newly available evidence (the *Diary* and certain letters) to formulate the image of Mather as a scheming, bloodthirsty hypocrite. In Upham's *Lectures on Witchcraft* (Boston, 1831) we find the elements of nineteenth-century anti-Puritanism in America fully emerging into an iconoclastic stereotype: the reactionary ministers (and chiefly the Mathers) scheming to hold power in the colony by fomenting the Salem affair and trying to rekindle it in Boston, their total loss of face among the populace after the scandal had broken, and their hypocritical attempts to cover up by maintaining that they had been against the trials all along. Upham accuses Mather of blatant lying and many other forms of corruption and dishonesty, and rings the changes at length upon the superstition of the minister.[8]

It is not surprising that W. B. O. Peabody, another Boston Unitarian, theologically trained by the younger Henry Ware,[9] who published a fairly moderate and careful *Life of Cotton Mather* (Boston, 1844), expresses difficulty in fitting this picture of Mather into the rest of the man's character as revealed in his work and through other witnesses. Peabody's solution is to make him out as a schizoid personality, not consciously scheming for power but driven by subterranean pride, and equipped with the weaknesses earlier critics described plus a few new ones: impulsiveness, indiscretion, refusal to repent his mistakes in the Salem incident, a "strangely perverted" moral sense, and a vicious temper. Peabody suspects that Mather was seeking to drum up a "religious revival" in his attempts to exorcise Margaret Rule, and he holds up for ridicule Mather's sense of divine guidance and his struggles and ecstasies in prayer. Peabody's inability to sympathize with Mather's spirituality clearly connects that religious temper with nineteenth-century revivalism. But Peabody is fair in citing Mather's virtues and his pioneering labors for social causes which flowered in the Benevolent Empire, such as temperance and slavery; and he does correctly state that Mather's enemies did not include the general public, but only the members of one religious party in Boston.[10]

Unfortunately Peabody's treatment, which at least attempted to balance off the conflicting accounts of Mather, and often achieves brilliant insights into his character, was less heeded during the rest of the century than was Upham's. Josiah Quincy's account, in his *History of Harvard University* (Cambridge, Mass., 1840), was written while the author's administration as president of the college was under attack by Trinitarian Congregationalists; and Samuel Eliot Morison observes that his book is a conscious retaliation against the conservatives in his own time through an attack on their ancestry.[11] It endorses all of Upham's conclusions, but goes beyond them in vituperation, depicting Mather as a headstrong fool who joined disloyalty to his usual poor judgment in his later preference for Yale over Harvard.[12] Few subsequent accounts of the Mathers are quite as unrelievedly vitriolic as Quincy's. The earlier *History of Harvard University* by Benjamin Pierce (Cambridge, Mass., 1883) portrays Mather as a great man with a few blemishes of judgment and taste, and passes over the witchcraft incident with favorable words for both Mathers.[13]

But according to W. F. Poole the majority of lesser histories and textbooks in the nineteenth century continued to reflect Upham's account, which was reprinted in 1859 in an enlarged edition.[14] More important works to follow Upham's interpretation were W. B. Sprague's *Annals of the American Pulpit* (New York, 1857) and J. L. Sibley's *Biographical Sketches of the Graduates of Harvard College* (Cambridge, Mass., 1885).[15] At the end of the line of Mather antagonists in the nineteenth century is Charles Francis Adams, whose metaphor of the "glacial age" of Puritan ascendency in New England, in *Massachusetts: Its Historians and Its History* (Boston, 1893), perfectly sums up this school of interpretation.[16] In *The Emancipation of Massachusetts* (Boston, 1919) Brooks Adams yokes the names of Cotton Mather and Jonathan Edwards, described as two great, awkward, abhorrent boulders left on the ground of history by the Puritan glacier.[17]

By the middle of the nineteenth century, Mather had begun to accumulate a few friends among historians, some of them in unlikely places. Chandler Robbins, a moderate Unitarian who occupied the pulpit of the Second Church after Emerson had succeeded Ware in that position in a brief tenure from 1829-32, was chairman of the committee which published the Mather papers, and subsequently wrote a much fuller account of the history of the Second Church than Ware's. In his *History of the Second Church, or Old North, in Boston* (Boston, 1852) Robbins not only defends the Mathers from the more serious charges of the Upham school, but also stands up for Cotton Mather's character with some passion:

> I am convinced that few historical characters are less understood than COTTON MATHER. He has paid the penalty always attached to singularity. The protuberance of a few eccentricities has thrown all the elements of his character into false perspective. His oddities stand in the light of his virtues. They give a grotesqueness to his whole image. . . . His virtues are in nature far more prominent and striking than his faults. The latter are more accidental and occasional; the former, more constant and permanent. The one seem to have been rather temporary waverings from the real point of his life's aim, like the oscillations of the disturbed needle; while the other evidently mark the true line of his earlier and later aspirations, principles, and efforts.[18]

Robbins praises Mather's transparent honesty even in revealing his faults, and his industry and his zeal to do good, and follows Pond and Peabody in observing that "most of the reformatory and benevolent movements which have signal-

ized the last quarter of a century were anticipated by him."
Robbins goes on to reject most of the charges against Mather
in the witchcraft affair, criticizing the Upham school for failure
to understand Mather's "credulity" in terms of his historical
context, misreading his *Diary* utterances, and mistakenly
transferring the blame for the witchcraft affair from the magistrates to the clergy. Robbins does not attempt to deal very
thoroughly with negative testimony like Calef's; he seems so
charmed with Mather's character as revealed in his writings
that he is simply willing to throw out contrary witnesses.[19]

Two full-length biographies of Mather appeared almost
simultaneously at the end of the nineteenth century: A. P.
Marvin's *The Life and Times of Cotton Mather* (Boston, 1892)
and Barrett Wendell's *Cotton Mather, the Puritan Priest* (New
York, 1891). Marvin was an orthodox defender of the Puritan
tradition, while Wendell's book reflects that *fin-de-siècle* Bostonian "devout free thought" which was one of the ultimate
mutations of the tradition of Ware and Robbins. Both are
largely positive in their evaluation, and both present what is
more or less an enlarged and historically broadened version
of Mather-as-seen-by-the-Mathers, largely derived from Cotton Mather's *Diary*. Wendell, whose biography has until recently remained the best and most balanced account of
Mather's life, is out to prove that "it was a good man they
buried on Copp's Hill one February day in the year 1728."[20]
He accepts most of Mather's account of his motives and actions in the Salem affair, and forgives what he cannot accept.
It would appear that by the end of the nineteenth century the
dust of theological warfare had settled enough so that Cotton
Mather could be understood and critically received both by
friends and opponents of his religious tradition.

The rehabilitation of Mather's reputation continued during the early decades of this century. Thomas J. Holmes, in
Cotton Mather: A Bibliography of His Works (Cambridge, Mass.,
1940), wrote in 1924 that most of the nineteenth-century literature on the witchcraft scandal was out of harmony with the
truth because the historians had "turned their fiddles to Calef's
key." Homes claimed that the very size of the Mather bibliography is graphic and unanswerable proof against the charge
that Mather lost his popularity because of the Salem affair,

and that on the contrary Mather continued to the end to be almost a matinee idol of the pulpit, in demand as a speaker in outlying districts and preaching to a congregation of 1500 on Sundays. Holmes judges Mather's religious ecstasies to be no sign of neurosis, but rather a genuine expression of mystical piety accompanied by a deep sense of sin.[21]

In *Witchcraft in Old and New England* (Cambridge, Mass., 1929) and a series of carefully documented papers, George Lyman Kittredge set out to defend Mather's scientific judgment and intellectual eminence against the charges of weakness and credulity, concluding that "It is easy to be wise after the fact,—especially when the fact is two hundred years old."[22] In "The New England Clergy of the Glacial Age," Clifford Shipton attacked the whole theory of the Puritan era as an intellectual glacial age, maintaining that the Puritan establishment operated on a wide base of popular support, and that anti-Mather sentiment was localized to a small clerical party in Boston, since "Calef himself seems to have comprised a very large part of his minority party, and . . . he did not have the same standards of intellectual honesty that his opponents showed. . . . The picture, which is built up of logic, a dislike of New England, and Calef's statements, is not supported by contemporary records."[23] Shipton documents the moderating efforts of the Mathers in the witchcraft affair, and presents Cotton Mather as a religious liberal who had to smuggle in progressive ideas carefully under the glares of conservative laymen. The picture of the younger Mather as an intellectual pioneer is enlarged in further detail in *Cotton Mather, First Significant Figure in American Medicine* (Baltimore, 1954), by Otho Beall and Richard Shryock, which takes his scientific judgment with utter seriousness and recognizes him as the most significant figure in American medical history before the nineteenth century.[24]

One might suppose that the waning of religious controversy and this considerable amount of careful and objective historiography would have altered the public image of Mather by this time. But the negative stream of testimony has persisted up to the present writing—partly because anti-Puritan bias has continued to inform the comment of some twentieth-century historians maintaining a secular standpoint, but also because others who have tried to give a balanced evaluation of Mather have approached him without a full appreciation of his theological context and have consequently misread certain areas of his character even while exonerating him from the worst caricatures of his critics. One kind of treatment subject to this weakness is the psychohistorical analysis of Mather, which began with Barrett Wendell's biography. Although Wendell is remarkably tolerant of Mather's weaknesses, much of his charity springs from his conviction that the inconsistent areas in Mather's character spring from neurotic traits which he could not help: a sensitive and passionate emotionalism, driven activism, and megalomaniac pride, either inflamed or expressed through Mather's abnormal religious practices. "Cotton Mather had for years been a religious enthusiast whose constant ecstasies brought him into such direct communication with Heaven as he believed the witches to maintain with Hell; in other words, he had for years been, what he remained all his life, a constant victim of a mental or moral disorder whose normal tendency is towards the growth of unwitting credulity and fraud."[25] While the effect of Wendell's book was to reinforce the refutation of the Upham school and to exonerate Mather from much of what nineteenth-century criticism said about him, Wendell's failure to comprehend Puritan mysticism led him to retain some questionable features from the older histories.

Another psychoanalysis-at-a-distance, the popular account of Ralph and Louise Boas in 1928, is somewhat more sympathetic, but finds in Mather a morbid preoccupation with death, a persecution complex, tendencies to hypochondria, and a compulsive urgency which drove him to live in a constant state of feverish excitement. According to *Cotton Mather, Keeper of the Puritan Conscience* (New York, 1928), the madness of Mather's third wife was the effect of sexual frustration induced when Mather devoted all his energies to mystical experience, only to produce a singularly boring life "curiously lacking in historical charm," unable to "see into the heart of things" through critical analysis—a life which "could never leave a mark on succeeding generations," and which bequeathed us nothing more valuable than an account of its spiritual interests.[26] Kenneth Murdock, in *Increase Mather: the Foremost American Puritan* (Cambridge, 1926) and in several subsequent studies, extricates the Mathers from guilt in the Salem trials but judges Cotton to be less stable than his father, "the apotheosis of intense Puritan character,"[27] a mixture of obvious nervous and moral failings,[28] "given to those transports of religious feeling which have seemed to some to be evidence of an unsound mental constitution."[29] Vernon Parrington's analysis of Mather in *Main Currents in American Thought* (New York, 1927, 1930), a work which has virtually programmed the attitude toward Puritanism of several generations of American schoolteachers, continued to develop and intensify the psychohistorical critique. Mather is portrayed as a petulant, irritable, sulking, garrulous, meddlesome, scolding sexual psychopath, whose *Diary* is "the produce of a crooked and diseased mind, a treasure-trove for the abnormal psychologist which would be inconceivable if it were not in print." Mather was a bourgeois soul who loved respectability and refused to fraternize with the poor; "a morbid New England flagellant, a Puritan Brother of the Cross," to be compared only to that other abnormality, the elder Edwards.[30]

Most of the negative treatments of Mather during this century have absolved him of extraordinary guilt in the witchcraft scandal and have concentrated on analyzing psychological and moral problems along the lines of Wendell's biography, but less sympathetically. Some of this criticism is very insightful as far as it goes, and yet much of it is strangely rooted in the assumptions of the witchcraft literature of the Calef/Upham School, as if the critics could not shake off these conclusions even when they have discarded their premises. In some instances they may be the result of reading Mather through the lens of older secondary works. It is also the natural result of an approach which attempts to psychoanalyze Mather without placing him in the context of the tradition of Puritan spirituality.

In addition to the psychoanalytic approach, one other set of conceptual tools has been applied in the twentieth century to understanding Cotton Mather, the tools of cultural and intellectual history. These are instruments which penetrate much more readily to the theological heart of Mather, and their use is steadily demythologizing his reputation among scholars, although one of the less satisfactory attempts in this direction, that of Perry Miller, may continue to perpetuate a distorted image of Mather because of the brilliance and deserved eminence of its author. *The New England Mind: From Colony to Province* (Cambridge, Mass., 1953), in which Mather figures as one of the major actors, combines serious flaws with some telling insights. Miller continues to picture Mather as a "frenetic genius" filled with egotism and false unction, whose schizophrenic admixture of intelligence and virtue with Pharisaism is almost more annoying than sheer depravity. He absolves the Mathers of trying to retain and defend the theocratic tenure of Puritanism, in the sense of brute power, but instead pictures their struggle as an effort to preserve the intellectual substance of Puritanism, the theology of the Covenant. He sees Cotton Mather as ultimately diluting and transforming the older Calvinism in a gradual capitulation to the Enlightment, and finds Mather's increasing stress on Christian experience to be simply a "pietism of the disinherited"—in this case, of the ruling aristocracy which has been displaced from the place of political and intellectual command.

> The forces that wrought this transformation can be summarized: the growth of a capitalist economy, imperial interference, and enforced yielding to toleration, class struggles. The result can be given a name: Pietism. What had happened here was that under the impact of the blows, mild as they may seem, of the repeal of the charter, of fragmentation in ecclesiastical and political theory, the human spirit sought for surcease. It found that life might yet be worth living if piety could still pervade society.[31]

All of this is true; all the forces described did combine to help transform New England Christianity from a theocratic to a pietistic organism, from a rigid structure with a hard exoskeleton of creed and polity to a leavening movement. But there is a curious wrongness about the end result of this analysis, true as are its particulars. The Pietism Mather was advocating, like that which was germinating at a number of points in Europe—and under differing historical conditions—was not the tired, last-ditch effort of an evaporating superstition:

it was a vital force for spiritual, social, and cultural transformation, the first of many related waves of energy which were to sweep across Christendom in the next two centuries. We do not understand this movement correctly if we see it as a mere intellectual epiphenomenon, the creature of the "real" social and economic forces in its environment. Its ideology and its spirit must be considered elements in a living organism, adapting itself in slightly different ways to differing historical circumstances, pressed and shaped by these, and yet essentially independent of them in its growth.

Since Miller's analysis, a number of new treatments of Cotton Mather have emerged. Some have perpetuated the negative or confused images of his character. Peter Gay, a magisterial interpreter of the Enlightenment and committed to its values, is predictably hard on Mather. His chapter of Mather in *A Loss of Mastery: Puritan Historians in Colonial America* (Berkeley, 1966) presents him as "a pathetic Plutarch," disposed to liberal sentiments but distorting history to provide his party with mythology and hagiography.[32] (On the other hand, Sacvan Bercovitch, in *The Puritan Origins of the American Self* [New Haven, 1975], values the interpretive imagination which offends Gay, and views Mather's treatment of history as a source of important symbols and themes in later American literature.) Kenneth Silverman's *Selected Letters of Cotton Mather* (Baton Rouge, 1971) seeks to expose both Mather's strengths and weaknesses, and furnishes a massive amount of new documentation indicating his role in church history. Silverman's introduction commends Mather's "staggering energy issuing in specific acts of kindness: money for the poor, firewood for the sick, consolation for the grief-stricken, care for the orphaned, letters of recommendation or encouragement for the young, visits to the languishing, uplift for the degraded." It also mocks Mather's identification of his own labors and reputation with the cause of Christ, and finds him "very devious" in advancing the publication of his own work. Silverman suggests that from one perspective Mather is "a fascistic super-prig bloated with the kind of self-regard that results from filiopiety," and concludes that "his letters show him by turns peevish, loving, dishonest, devout, spiteful, witty, unctuous, self-sacrificing, petty, ambitious, courtly, and brilliant—by and large a charitable and holy man tainted with an overreaching pride, fearful of antagonizing his elders, and temperamentally unsuited for the worldly affairs in which he felt he must play a part."[33] W. R. Manierre, approaching Mather from a literary perspective, offers a perceptive explanation of the rationale behind Mather's style in his unpublished doctoral dissertation, "Cotton Mather and the Plain Style" (University of Michigan, 1958), but reverts to brilliant yet one-sided analysis of Mather's "neurosis" in his introduction to the *Diary* for the year 1712 (Charlottesville, 1964), confirming the fact that the *Diaries* are the main stone of stumbling for Mather students.

Still, it is significant that most recent Mather scholarship along the lines of intellectual historiography has been positive in tone, paralleling the trend in Puritan scholarship which has rehabilitated the reputation of Jonathan Edwards. Alan Heimert's introduction to the second republication of Barrett Wendell's biography of Mather (New York, 1963) concurs with Wendell's favorable treatment. Heimert finds in Mather a consistent development of his father's values, goals, and methods of piety, and notes that "far from being forsaken of mankind, [he had] attained by the end of his career an influence in many respects greater than at any time since the new charter." Heimert agrees with my own conclusions: "He ended his days as something of a John the Baptist to Jonathan Edwards."[34] Joyce Ransome's unpublished dissertation on "Cotton Mather and the Catholic Spirit" (Berkeley, 1966) effectively traces the balance between conservative and progressive elements in Mather's evangelical synthesis, and minimizes the effect of rationalism on his thinking. Robert Middlekauff's careful analysis of *The Mathers: Three Generations of Puritan Intellectuals, 1596-1728* (New York, 1971) deals extensively with Cotton Mather's theology and quietly contests the thesis that there was a decay of piety and an accommodation to rationalism in the succeeding generations of the dynasty, although it does not attempt to explore fully the international context of Mather's pietism or his relationship to the subsequent evangelical tradition. Finally, after publishing several short studies vigorously contesting all the conventional stereotypes of Mather,[35] David Levin has provided in *Cotton Mather: The Young Life of the Lord's Remembrancer, 1663-1703* (Cambridge, Mass., 1978) the first half of a definitive biography of Mather which is both thorough and fair. While maintaining a carefully objective tone, Levin enters so thoroughly and sympathetically into the presuppositions and the milieu of New England Puritanism that he virtually recreates the events of Mather's early life as Mather himself experienced them. The result is a positive and coherent portrait of a gifted scholar who was also in many respects simply a normal and typical Puritan minister, a religious leader who was also a man of extraordinary good will. We can hope that the impact of this new scholarship will eventually reach the high school classroom and rebalance the stereotypes of Mather still presented there, although our experience with the Edwards renaissance is not very encouraging in this respect.

With the rising interest in Mather among scholars, reprints and new editions of his works are becoming available. Kenneth Murdock's *Selections from Cotton Mather* (Riverside, N.J.: Hafner Press, 1960), the *Magnalia Christi Americana*, ed. Raymond J. Cunningham (New York: Frederick Ungar, 1971), and *The Wonders of the Invisible World* (Amherst, Wis.: Amherst Press, n.d.) are available in paperback. The *Magnalia* is also available in two other editions, one edited by Kenneth B. Murdock (Cambridge, Mass.: Harvard University Press, 1976) and the other a reprint of the 1702 edition (New York: Arno Press, 1971). David Levin has provided a new edition of *Bonifacius* (Cambridge, Mass.: Harvard University Press, 1966), which can also be obtained in a reprint of the 1710 edition (Delmar, N.Y.: Scholars' Facsimiles, 1967). The *Manuductio ad Ministerium* is available in a reprint of the 1938 edition (New York: AMS Press, 1976). Other works currently in print are *Agricola*, reprinted from the 1727 edition (St. Clair Shores, Mich.: Somerset Pub., n.d.); *The Angel of Bethesda*, ed. Gordon W. Jones (Charlottesville, Va.: University Press of Virginia, 1972); *The Christian Philosopher* (Delmar, N.Y.: Scholars' Facsimiles, 1968), a reprint of the 1721 edition; *Christianus per Ignem*, a reprint of the 1702 edition (St. Clair Shores, Mich.:

Somerset Pub., n.d.); *A Companion for Communicants,* a reprint of the 1690 edition (St. Clair Shores, Mich.: Somerset Pub., n.d.); *Days of Humiliation* (Delmar, N.Y.: Scholars' Facsimiles, 1970); *The Life of Sir William Phips,* a reprint of the 1929 edition (New York: AMS Press, 1971; also, St. Clair Shores, Mich.: Somerset Pub., n.d.); *Ornaments for the Daughters of Zion* (Delmar, N.Y.: Scholars' Facsimiles, 1978); *Parentator* (St. Clair Shores, Mich.: Somerset Pub., n.d.); *Paterna,* ed. Ronald A. Bosco (Delmar, N.Y.: Scholars' Facsimiles, 1976); *The Present State of New England,* a reprint of the 1690 edition (Brooklyn, N.Y.: Haskell House, 1969); and *Ratio Disciplinae Fratrum Novanglorum,* a reprint of the 1726 edition (New York: Arno Press, 1971). Substantial deposits of Mather's writings are available at many major libraries in the United States; perhaps the best guide to these is the massive annotated bibliography by Thomas Holmes.

Notes

CHAPTER ONE

1. W. F. Poole, "Cotton Mather and Salem Witchcraft," *North American Review*, CVIII (1869), 338.
2. Perry Miller, *The New England Mind: From Colony to Province* (Cambridge, Mass., 1953), p. 476.
3. Henry Ware, *Two Discourses Containing the History of the Old North and New Brick Churches* (Boston, 1821), pp. 14, 19-20.
4. Kenneth B. Murdock, "Cotton Mather," *Dictionary of American Biography* 12:387.
5. David Levin, "The Hazing of Cotton Mather," *New England Quarterly*, XXXVI (1963), 148, 169.
6. G. L. Kittredge, "Cotton Mather's Election into the Royal Society," *Publications of the Colonial Society of Massachusetts*, XIV (1911), 81-114.
7. Ernst Benz, "Pietist and Puritan Sources of Early Protestant World Missions," *Church History*, XX (1951), 50.
8. T. J. Holmes, *Cotton Mather: A Bibliography of his Works* (Cambridge, Mass., 1940), p. xii.
9. Williston Walker, "The Services of the Mathers in New England Religious Development," *Papers of the American Society of Church History*, V (1893), 62-67.
10. Increase Mather, *The Mystery of Israel's Salvation* (London, 1669).
11. Kenneth B. Murdock, *Increase Mather* (Cambridge, Mass., 1926), pp. 86-124.
12. C. M., *Diary*, I (New York, 1957), 20 [June 1681].
13. Barrett Wendell, *Cotton Mather, the Puritan Priest* (New York, 1891), p. 28.
14. *Ibid.*, pp. 33-34 (quoting the unpublished "Paterna" of C. M.).

15. Not, as usually recorded, at age twelve; see David Levin, "The Hazing of Cotton Mather," *New England Quarterly*, XXXVI (1963), 158.
16. Wendell, p. 36.
17. Samuel Eliot Morison, *Harvard College in the Seventeenth Century*, I (Cambridge, Mass., 1936), p. 417.
18. Levin, "Hazing of Cotton Mather," p. 157.
19. Wendell, pp. 37-38.
20. *Religious Societies* (Boston, 1724), which C. M. revised and published late in his life.
21. C. M., *Diary*, I, 86-87.
22. Samuel Mather, *Life of Cotton Mather* (Boston, 1729).
23. Clifford Shipton, "The New England Clergy of the 'Glacial Age,' " *Publications of the Colonial Society of Massachusetts*, XXXII (1933), 24-54.
24. Kittredge notes publications defending the existence of witchcraft within the two decades before the Mather works, by the Cambridge Platonist Henry More and the otherwise rather skeptical Joseph Glanvil (author of *The Vanity of Dogmatizing*), the physicist Robert Boyle, Newton's master Isaac Barrow, Méric Casaubon, and Baxter, among others. See *Witchcraft in Old and New England* (Cambridge, Mass., 1929), pp. 329-338.
25. Wendell, p. 107.
26. Murdock, p. 294.
27. C. M., *Diary*, I, 142-143.
28. Murdock, pp. 287-316; Wendell, *Cotton Mather*, pp. 88-123.
29. C. M., *Diary*, I, 216.
30. *Ibid.*, p. 215.
31. C. M., *Diary*, II, 200.
32. Morison, I, 505-506.
33. Wendell, pp. 130-153; Murdock, pp. 337-374.
34. Murdock, pp. 354, 358.
35. J. L. Sibley, *Biographical Sketches of Graduates of Harvard University*, III (Cambridge, Mass., 1885), pp. 17-18.
36. C. M., *Diary*, I, 264 [June 1698].
37. Sibley, p. 17.
38. J. H. Tuttle, "The Libraries of the Mathers," *Proceedings of the American Society*, New Series, XX (1911), 302.
39. Kittredge has shown that the election was actually intended in 1718 and omitted through a blunder, but carried through in 1723 when the mistake had been discovered. See "Cotton Mather's Election into the Royal Society."
40. John Wise, *The Churches' Quarrel Espoused* (New York, 1713).
41. Benjamin Colman, *The Holy Walk of Blessed Enoch* (Boston, 1728), pp. 23-24.
42. Thomas Prince, *The Departure of Elijah Lamented* (Boston, 1728), pp. 19-21.

43. Joshua Gee, *Israel's Mourning for Aaron's Death* (Boston, 1728), pp. 13-19.
44. W. B. O. Peabody, *Life of Cotton Mather* (Boston, 1836), p. 342.
45. Quoted in Ware, *Two Discourses*, p. 20.
46. Moses Coit Tyler, *A History of American Literature* (New York, 1879), I, 88.
47. *Ibid.*, p. 83.
48. Edward Farley, *Requiem for a Lost Piety* (Philadelphia, 1966).

CHAPTER TWO

1. Joyce Olson Ransome, "Cotton Mather and the Catholic Spirit" (Ph.D. diss., University of California, 1966), pp. 75-78.
2. Ernst Benz, "Pietist and Puritan Sources of Early Protestant World Missions," *Church History*, XX (1951), 32.
3. See C. M., *Diary*, 2 vols. (New York, 1957), II, 406, 411, 563; Kenneth Silverman, ed., *Selected Letters of Cotton Mather* (Baton Rouge, La., 1971), pp. 92, 215, 260.
4. See Silverman, p. 89.
5. C. M., *Diary*, II, 23.
6. For other published correspondence between C. M. and Halle, see Kuno Francke, "The Beginning of Cotton Mather's Correspondence with August Hermann Francke," *Philological Quarterly*, V (1926), 193-195; Francke, "Cotton Mather and August Hermann Francke," *Harvard Studies and Notes in Philosophy and Literature*, V (1896), 57-67; "Further Documents Concerning Cotton Mather and August Hermann Francke," *Americana Germanica*, I (1897), 31-66.
7. C. M., *Diary*, II, 411.
8. MS in Archiv der Franckeschen Stiftungen, Universitäts-und-Landesbibliothek Sachsen-Anhalt, in Halle, Germany.
9. MS in Archiv der Franckeschen Stiftungen.
10. Microfilms of the letters cited above and of other correspondence between Mather and Francke from the Franckeschen Stiftungen in Halle and the Staatsbibliothek Preussischer Kulturbesitz in West Berlin are available at the Gordon-Conwell Seminary Library, South Hamilton, Mass. J. P. Hoskins agrees with this analysis that the influence of German Pietism on Mather was a matter of indirect stimulation, the resonance of two sympathetic traditions, rather than a direct transfer of content between the two Pietisms. In his tendency to assert the European origin of the later Awakening, however, Hoskins is inclined to exaggerate the difference between the Puritan and Pietist traditions, and is led to conclude that Mather saw more unity in the two streams than actually existed. See "German Influence on Religious Life and Thought in America During

the Colonial Period," *Princeton Theological Review,* V (1907), 225-227.

11. Miller, *The New England Mind,* p. 213.
12. *Ibid.,* p. 214.
13. Perry Miller, "The *Manuductio ad Ministerium,*" in T. J. Holmes, *Cotton Mather: A Bibliography,* II, 632.
14. Cf. Jerald Brauer, "The Nature of English Puritanism," *Church History,* XXIII (1954), 99-108; Alan Simpson, *Puritanism in Old and New England* (Chicago, 1955).
15. See F. E. Stoeffler, *The Rise of Evangelical Pietism* (Leiden, 1965); Stoeffler, *German Pietism During the Eighteenth Century* (Leiden, 1973).
16. II Tim. 3:5.
17. See Dietrich Bonhoeffer, *The Cost of Discipleship* (London, 1959), Ch. 1.
18. Cf. Benz, "Pietist and Puritan Sources," p. 51; Erhard Peschke, *Studien zur Theologie August Hermann Franckes,* I (Berlin, 1964), 16.
19. Cf. Peschke, *Studien,* I, 16.
20. Klaus Deppermann, *Der Hallesche Pietismus und der preussische Staat unter Friedrich III* (Göttingen, 1961), p. 177.
21. James Hastings Nichols, *History of Christianity, 1650-1950* (New York, 1956), pp. 81-82.
22. The typology here is a variation on that of Lang; cf. Stoeffler, *Rise of Pietism,* p. 27.
23. Gisbert Voetius, "Selectae Disputationes Theologicae," in *Reformed Dogmatics,* ed. and trans. John W. Beardslee, III (New York, 1965), 317.
24. For an analysis of Spener's approach, see Dale Weaver Brown, "The Problem of Subjectivism in Pietism" (Ph.D. diss., Northwestern University, 1962), p. 183.
25. Cf. Stoeffler, *Rise of Pietism,* pp. 78-101.
26. *Ibid.,* p. 28.
27. Heinrich Bornkamm, in *Mystik, Spiritualismus und die Anfange des Pietismus im Luthertum* (Giessen, 1926), p. 16, notes the same fusion of mystical piety and Lutheran scholastic orthodoxy in the formation of German Pietism.
28. Stoeffler, *Rise of Pietism,* pp. 134-137.
29. Hugo Visscher, "William Ames, His Life and Works," *William Ames,* ed. and trans. Douglas Horton (Cambridge, Mass., 1965), p. 70.
30. *Ibid.,* pp. 14-15.
31. Ralph Bronkema and others have supposed that the practical flavor of Puritanism comes from some special bias in the British national character (see R. Bronkema, *The Essence of Puritanism* [Goes, Holland, 1929], pp. 3, 17). But Puritan legal precision really springs from a Zwinglian stream on the Conti-

nent, and the Dutch and German pietists were just as susceptible to the experiential approach to theology as the English. It
is much more satisfactory to explain all of these experiential
movements as basic products of grass-roots pastoral concern,
later articulated by theologians produced by that pastoring.

32. C. M., *Malachi* (Boston, 1717), p. 62.
33. C. M., *Ratio Disciplinae* (Boston, 1726), p. 194.
34. C. M., *Parentator* (Boston, 1726), p. 194.
35. Carl Bridenbaugh, *Cities in the Wilderness* (New York, 1938),
    p. 289; cf. Otho Beall and Richard Shryock, *Cotton Mather, First
    Significant Figure in American Medicine* (Baltimore, 1954), p. 34;
    K. B. Murdock, ed., *Selections from Cotton Mather* (New York,
    1926), Introduction.
36. Miller, "The *Manuductio ad Ministerium*," in Holmes, *Cotton
    Mather: A Bibliography*, II, 634-635.
37. C. M., *Diary*, I, 312.
38. C. M., *A Letter of Advice to the Churches* (London, 1701),
    pp. 11-12.
39. C. M., *A Pillar of Gratitude* (Boston, 1700), pp. 21, 24.
40. C. M., *American Tears upon the Ruins of the Greek Churches*
    (Boston, 1701), p. 46.
41. C. M., *Diary*, I, 429.
42. *Ibid.*, II, 416.
43. *Ibid.*, II, 60; cf. pp. 64, 120, 327, 412, 692, 702, 797.
44. C. M., *The Marrow of the Gospel* (Boston, 1727), p. 25.
45. C. M., *Free-Grace* (Boston, 1706), p. 23.
46. C. M., *A Conquest over the Grand Excuse* (Boston, 1706), p. 21.
47. C. M., *The Man of God Furnished* (Boston, 1708); cf. *Diary*, I,
    572.
48. C. M., *A Letter to the University of Glasgow* (Boston, 1710),
    p. 11.
49. C. M., *Diary*, II, 106.
50. *Ibid.*, II, 107, 109.
51. *Ibid.*, II, 186; Cotton Mather, *Things to be More Thought Upon*
    (Boston, 1713).
52. C. M., *Diary*, II, 205.
53. C. M., "A Letter to Thomas Bradbury," in Thomas Bradbury,
    The Necessity of Contending for Revealed Religion (Boston, 1720),
    pp. 20-23.
54. C. M., *Parentator*, p. 201.
55. Cf. Increase Mather, *The Mystery of Christ* (Boston, 1686),
    Foreword, p. 46; Increase Mather, *A Discourse Proving That the
    Christian Religion is the Only True Religion* (Boston, 1702).
56. C. M., *Manuductio ad Ministerium* (Boston, 1726), pp. 97-98.
57. C. M., *Baptismal Piety* (Boston, 1727), p. 9; note the allusion to
    Locke.
58. C. M., *Diary*, II, 625-626.

59. *Ibid.*, II, 296-297.
60. *Ibid.*, II, 816-817.
61. C. M., *Parentator*, p. 178.
62. C. M., *Manuductio*, pp. 93-94.
63. Cf. C. M., *The Minister* (Boston, 1722), p. 28.
64. C. M., *Meat Out of the Eater* (Boston, 1703), p. 81.
65. C. M., *Manuductio*, pp. 94-95.
66. The same Christocentric thrust is quite evident in the early and classical periods of German Pietism, and especially in Francke: Cf. Johann Arndt, *Of True Christianity*, trans. A. W. Boehm (2nd English ed.), 2 vols. (London, 1720), I, iv; Peschke, *Studien*, I, 24-25; Erich Beyreuther, *Der Geschichtliche Auftrag des Pietismus in der Gegenwart* (Stuttgart, 1963), pp. 24-34.
67. C. M., *A Seasonable Testimony to the Glorious Doctrines* (Boston, 1702).
68. C. M., *Free-Grace* (Boston, 1706), p. 2.
69. C. M., *Small Offers* (Boston, 1689), p. 106.
70. C. M., *Meat Out of the Eater* (Boston, 1703), p. 119.
71. C. M., *The Right Way to Shake Off a Viper* (Boston, 1720), p. 3.
72. C. M., *A Short Life* (Boston, 1714), p. 18.
73. See below, Ch. 6.
74. C. M., *Little Flocks Guarded* (Boston, 1691), p. 20.
75. *C. M.*, *The Everlasting Gospel* (Boston, 1700), pp. 22-23.
76. *Ibid.*, p. 40.
77. C. M., *The Marrow of the Gospel* (Boston, 1727).
78. *Westminster Confession of Faith*, I, 1.
79. John Calvin, *Institutes of the Christian Religion* I, v, 1; cf. Heinrich Heppe, *Reformed Dogmatics*, trans. G. T. Thomson, ed. Ernst Bizer (London, 1950), pp. 1-2.
80. C. M., *A Man of Reason* (Boston, 1718), pp. 1, 3-4.
81. *Ibid.*, p. 7; cf. Mather, *Diary*, II, 144.
82. C. M., *The Christian Philosopher* (London, 1721), p. 114.
83. C. M., *Utilia* (Boston, 1716), pp. 260-261.
84. C. M., *Iconoclastes* (Boston, 1717), pp. 18-19.
85. Miller, *The New England Mind*, p. 345.
86. Holmes, *Cotton Mather: A Bibliography*, pp. 614, 889.
87. C. M., *Reasonable Religion* (Boston, 1713), p. 40.
88. C. M., "Biblia Americana" (MS in Massachusetts Historical Society) on Rom. 1:18.
89. C. M., *Utilia* (Boston, 1716), p. 115; cf. Heppe, *Reformed Dogmatics*, p. 7.
90. Cf. Harvey G. Townsend, ed., *The Philosophy of Jonathan Edwards from His Private Notebooks* (Eugene, Ore., 1955).
91. C. M., *Manuductio*, p. 83.
92. *Ibid.*, p. 49.
93. *Ibid.*, pp. 35-36.
94. *Ibid.*, p. 50.

95. Miller, *The New England Mind*, pp. 406-416.
96. E. g., Erich Seeberg, who calls them "inimical brethren"; and Karl Barth, who refers to them as two forms of one nature, both based on the spirit of life improvement and thus anthropocentric in nature. Emil Brunner feels that both orthodoxy and Pietism were involved in the generation of Enlightenment rationalism. See Dale Weaver Brown, "The Problem of Subjectivism in Pietism," pp. 129, 156, 171.
97. C. M., *Manuductio*, p. 83.
98. *Ibid.*, p. 84.
99. *Ibid.*, pp. 80-89. Particular concentrations of the works of individual theologians in the Mather libraries included five titles of Ames, six of Alsted, four of Baxter, six of Owen, five of William Prynne, three of Ramus, three of Maccovius, and eight volumes of Jonathan Edwards given to C. M. by the author. Pietist works included a copy of Johann Arndt's *De Vero Christianismo* (London, 1708) and J. A. Comenius' *De Bono Unitatis* (London, 1710), gifts to the author by A. W. Boehm; two other works of Comenius; a tract by Francke; and Spener's *De Natura et Gratia* (Frankfort, 1715).
100. Miller, *The New England Mind*, pp. 406-407.
101. C. M., *The Man of God Furnished* (Boston, 1708), p. 32.
102. *Ibid.*
103. "The Shortest Catechism," in *Maschil*; repeated in *The Instructor* (1726), together with "The Shortest of All Catechisms."
104. C. M., *Le Vrai Patron des Saines Paroles* (Boston, 1704), pp. 1-8; cf. *Une Grande Voix de Ciel* (Boston, 1725), where this is repeated.
105. *Manuductio*, pp. 107-108.
106. C. M., *Things to Be More Thought Upon* (Boston, 1713), pp. 86 ff.
107. C. M., *Malachi* (Boston, 1717).
108. *The Tryed Professor* (Boston, 1719), p. 16.
109. *India Christiana* (Boston, 1721), p. 53.
110. *Manuductio*, pp. 118-119.
111. *A Christian Conversing* (Boston, 1709), pp. 8-9.
112. C. M., *The Serviceable Man* (Boston, 1690), p. 10; cf. Heppe, *Reformed Dogmatics*, pp. 53-57. The definition of God as *actus purissimus et simplicissimus* is common in Reformed orthodoxy.
113. Cf. C. M., *The Wonderful Works of God* (Boston, 1690) and *Christian Loyalty* (Boston, 1727).
114. C. M., *The Principle of the Protestant Religion Maintained* (Boston, 1690), p. 76.
115. C. M., *Little Flocks Guarded* (Boston, 1691), p. 69.
116. Cf. *Utilia* (Boston, 1716), p. 263; *Free-Grace* (Boston, 1706), p. 39.
117. *Utilia*, p. 263.

118. C. M., *A Conquest over the Grand Excuse* (Boston, 1706), pp. 13-14.
119. C. M., *The Converted Sinner* (Boston, 1724), p. 27.
120. C. M., *The Duty of Children* (Boston, 1703), passim; also C. M., *The Converted Sinner* (Boston, 1724), pp. 27-31. Cf. C. M.'s treatment of the Covenant of Grace in *The Wonderful Works of God* (Boston, 1690); *Unum Necessarium* (Boston, 1693); *Free-Grace* (Boston, 1706); *The Temple Opened* (Boston, 1709); *Man Eating the Food of Angels* (Boston, 1710); *Winter Piety* (Boston, 1712); *Thoughts for the Day of Rain* (Boston, 1712); *The Tribe of Asher* (Boston, 1717); *The Quickened Soul* (Boston, 1720); *The Marrow of the Gospel* (Boston, 1727); and *Hor-Hagidgad* (Boston, 1727).
121. C. M., *Renatus* (Boston, 1725), pp. 10-11. The unpublished "Biblia Americana" refers to federal guilt in its commentary on Rom. 5:12 ff.
122. Heppe, *Reformed Dogmatics,* pp. 105-108.
123. C. M., *Blessed Unions* (Boston, 1692), p. 47.
124. Cf. Benz, "Pietist and Puritan Sources of Early Protestant World Mission," p. 51.
125. C. M., *Military Duties* (Boston, 1687), p. 2.
126. C. M., *A Midnight Cry* (Boston, 1692), pp. 62-64; *Things to Be Look'd For* (Boston, 1692), pp. 26-34, 62-64.
127. C. M., "Problema Theologicum" (MS in the American Antiquarian Society, ca. 1703-1704), sect. III.
128. C. M., "Biblica Americana" (MS in Massachusetts Historical Society, ca. 1706-1713), "Revelation," "Coronis."
129. C. M., *Diary,* II, 733.
130. "Tri-Paradisus" (MS in the American Antiquarian Society), sect. XI.
131. Cf. *American Tears* (Boston, 1701), p. 9; *Faith Encouraged* (Boston, 1718), p. 13; *India Christiana* (Boston, 1721), p. 46; *Columbanus* (Boston, 1722), p. 2.
132. "Tri-Paradisus," sect. XII.
133. Cf. Iain Murray, *The Puritan Hope* (London, 1971).
134. Stoeffler, *Rise of Pietism,* p. 241.
135. Cf. J. A. de Jong, *As The Waters Cover The Sea: Millennial Expectations in the Rise of Anglo-American Missions, 1640-1810* (Kampen, 1970), pp. 6-11; Murray, *The Puritan Hope,* pp. 38-55; cf. Sidney H. Rooy, *The Theology of Missions in the Puritan Tradition* (Grand Rapids, 1965), pp. 242-284.
136. C. M., *Vigilantius* (Boston, 1706), pp. 9, 12.
137. *A Midnight Cry* (Boston, 1692), p. 63. Robert Middlekauf assumes that Mather was expecting Christ's return both in 1697 and 1716 (*The Mathers* [New York, 1971], pp. 339-341, 343-346). Mather was tentative enough about the events in the final countdown of history not to have ruled this out, but he was

also careful enough not to have gone out on a limb in predicting it; and a review of Middlekauf's evidence does not compel me to agree with him on this point.
138. *Things to Be Look'd For* (Boston, 1692), pp. 48-64.
139. "Tri-Paradisus," sect. XI.

CHAPTER THREE

1. Cf. Alan Simpson, *Puritanism in Old and New England*, p. 2; H. C. Porter, *Reformation and Reaction in Tudor Cambridge* (Cambridge, Eng., 1958), p. 289; Gordon Wakefield, *Puritan Devotion* (London, 1957), pp. 160-161.
2. C. M., *Unum Necessarium* (Boston, 1693); cf. Luke 10:42.
3. Cf. Edmund S. Morgan, *Visible Saints* (New York, 1963), p. 66.
4. Cf. G. G. Coulton, "The High Ancestry of Puritanism," in *Ten Medieval Studies* (Boston, 1959 [1906]), pp. 59-60.
5. Cf. Stoeffler, *The Rise of Evangelical Pietism* (Leiden, 1965), pp. 16-17.
6. Johann Arndt, *Of True Christianity*, I, xlvi.
7. See Peschke, *Studien zur Theologie August Hermann Franckes*, vol. I.
8. Morgan, *Visible Saints*, p. 68.
9. Norman Pettit, *The Heart Prepared* (New Haven, Conn., 1966), pp. 62-78.
10. Cf. Geoffrey F. Nuttall, *Visible Saints* (Oxford, 1957), pp. 158-159, on Baxter's disgust with the English Antinomian controversy.
11. C. M., *Menachem* (Boston, 1716), pp. 14, 15. Erich Beyreuther, in *August Hermann Francke, 1663-1727, Zeuge des Lebendigen Gottes*, 2nd ed. (Marburg, 1961), p. 51, relates Francke's reply from his deathbed to a student who asked if he should know the date of his conversion: "We do not have to ask, are you converted? When were you converted? But rather: What does Christ mean to you? What have you personally experienced with God? Is Christ important to you in your daily life?"
12. C. M., *The Christian Cynick* (Boston, 1716), p. 33.
13. C. M., *Batteries upon the Kingdom of the Devil* (London, 1695), pp. 112-114.
14. C. M., *The Greatest Concern in the World* (Boston, 1765, 1707), p. 13.
15. C. M., *Grace Defended* (Boston, 1712), pp. 30, 32.
16. C. M., *Christodulus* (Boston, 1725), p. 27.
17. C. M., *Vita Brevis* (Boston, 1714), p. 28.
18. C. M., *Speedy Repentance Urged* (Boston, 1690), p. 62.
19. C. M., *Unum Necessarium*, p. 45.
20. C. M., *The Everlasting Gospel* (Boston, 1700), p. 52.

21. C. M., *Restitutus* (Boston, 1727), pp. 35-36.
22. C. M., *Agricola* (Boston, 1727), p. 13.
23. C. M., *Free-Grace* (Boston, 1706), p. 51.
24. *Agricola*, p. 11.
25. C. M., *Tremenda* (Boston, 1721), pp. 37-39.
26. Cf. Phil. 2:12, 13.
27. Cf. Frank H. Foster, *A Genetic History of the New England Theology* (New York, 1963 [1907]), pp. 29, 43.
28. His *Monitor for Communicants* (Boston, 1714), p. 4, states that less than half of the congregation engaged in the Lord's Supper. The same problem persisted from the beginning of his ministry to its end; cf. his *Several Sermons Concerning Walking with God* (Boston, 1689), p. 21; *Winter Piety* (Boston, 1712), p. 22; *Virtue in its Verdure* (Boston, 1725), p. 16.
29. See his *Agreeable Admonitions* (Boston, 1703); *The Spirit of Life Entering into the Spiritually Dead* (Boston, 1707); *Pastoral Desires* (Boston, 1712); *The Converted Sinner* (Boston, 1724); *Nails Fastened* (Boston, 1726); *Signatus* (Boston, 1727).
30. Miller, *The New England Mind*, pp. 66-67, 214-215.
31. The motif is present quite early in his ministry; cf. his *Unum Necessarium*, p. 89.
32. C. M., *Hades Look'd Into* (Boston, 1717), pp. 28-29; *The Marrow of the Gospel* (Boston, 1727), p. 24.
33. C. M., *The True Riches* (Boston, 1724), p. 24; *The Mystical Marriage* (Boston, 1728), p. 7.
34. C. M., *Batteries upon the Kingdom*, pp. 36-37.
35. *Ibid.*, p. 108.
36. C. M., *Converted Sinner*, p. 14.
37. C. M., *The Quickened Soul* (Boston, 1720), *passim*.
38. C. M., *Spirit of Life*, p. 35.
39. *Unum Necessarium*, p. 41.
40. C. M., *Free-Grace*, p. 37.
41. *Ibid.*, p. 66.
42. If encouraging people to "make a tryal" is indeed a movement toward theoretical Arminianism, then Increase Mather is involved in the same shift, for his *Soul-Saving Gospel Truths* (Boston, 1703) incorporates most of his son's emphases. Probably the Mathers worked together in developing a corrective to the hyper-Calvinist component in the spiritual decline.
43. C. M., *A Conquest Over the Grand Excuse* (Boston, 1706), p. 29.
44. C. M., *The Armour of Christianity* (Boston, 1704), p. 142.
45. C. M., *The Man of God Furnished* (Boston, 1708), p. 27.
46. Porter, *Reformation and Reaction*, pp. 218, 227.
47. C. M., *Magnalia Christi Americana*, I, 389-390.
48. *Free-Grace*, pp. 1-2.
49. *Ibid.*, p. 33.
50. *Ibid.*, p. 37.

51. *Ibid.*, p. 35.
52. *Ibid.*, pp. 34-35.
53. *Ibid.*, p. 41.
54. *Ibid.*, p. 41. The same approach is employed in Increase Mather's *Soul-Saving Gospel Truths* (Boston, 1703), p. 20.
55. *Ibid.*, p. 43.
56. C. M., *Instructions to the Living* (Boston, 1717), p. 11.
57. C. M., *Agreeable Admonitions*, pp. 19-20; *Nails Fastened*, pp. 9-10. This peculiar medieval doctrinal remnant was also used by Spener and Francke; see A. W. Nagler, *Pietism and Methodism* (Nashville, 1918), pp. 37-38.
58. *Unum Necessarium*, p. 158.
59. *Utilia* (Boston, 1716), pp. 13, 51.
60. C. M., *Zalmonah* (Boston, 1725), pp. 72-106.
61. C. M., *The Duty of Children* (Boston, 1703), pp. 20-21.
62. *Greatest Concern*, pp. 10-11.
63. *Everlasting Gospel*, p. 16.
64. *Unum Necessarium*, p. 122.
65. Ralph Bronkema, *The Essence of Puritanism* (Goes, Holland, 1929), pp. 107-108, 120, 122, 124.
66. *Unum Necessarium*, pp. 19-22.
67. Peter De Jong, *The Covenant Idea in New England Theology* (Grand Rapids, 1945), pp. 90, 107, 217.
68. C. M., *Winter Piety*, p. 29; cf. idem, *The Curbed Sinner* (Boston, 1713), p. 15.
69. *Greatest Concern*, p. 19.
70. *Unum Necessarium*, pp. 7-8.
71. C. M., *What the Pious Parent Wishes for* (Boston, 1721), p. 18.
72. C. M., *Vigilius* (Boston, 1719), pp. 10-11.
73. *Everlasting Gospel*, p. 41.
74. C. M., *Desiderius* (Boston, 1719), p. 7.
75. C. M., *Spirit of Life*, pp. 14-16.
76. C. M., *A Letter to Ungospellized Plantations* (Boston, 1702), p. 12.
77. C. M., *Meat Out of the Eater* (Boston, 1703), p. 98.
78. C. M., *Baptistes* (Boston, 1705), p. 17.
79. C. M., *Baptismal Piety* (Boston, 1727), p. 46. Mather observes, however, that most of those baptized were called to awakened faith between the ages of 15 and 30; see *Magnalia*, II, 374.
80. This inconsistency was noted by Giles Firmin in *The Real Christian* (1670); see Pettit, *The Heart Prepared*, p. 187.
81. Cf. Morgan, *Visible Saints*, pp. 67, 72.
82. Larzer Ziff, *The Career of John Cotton* (Princeton, N. J., 1962), pp. 119, 153-154; cf. Emery Battis, *Saints and Sectaries* (Williamsburg, Va., 1962), pp. 20, 35.
83. Ziff, *Career of John Cotton*, p. 110; Battis, *Saints and Sectaries*, p. 30.

84. Cf. Calvin S. Malefyt, "The Changing Concept of Pneumatology in New England Trinitarianism, 1635-1755" (Ph.D. diss., Harvard University, 1966). Malefyt develops a threefold typology to cover the two extremes and the central synthesis: he speaks of Enthusiasts, Formalists, and Evangelicals, and speculates that the Unitarian stream in the eighteenth century developed out of the Formalist party, which insisted that assurance could only be indirect and ruled out the personal indwelling of the Spirit and the possibility of direct communion with him. Both Mathers were "Evangelicals," in Malefyt's terminology, and "enthusiasts" in the literal sense of the word; see Increase Mather, *Pray for the Rising Generation* (Boston, 1678), p. 7. Malefyt calls John Cotton an "Evangelical Spiritualist," and this label is not inappropriate for the Mathers.

85. C. M., *Sincere Piety Described* (Boston, 1719), p. 18.

86. C. M., *The Marrow of the Gospel* (Boston, 1727), p. 14.

87. C. M., *The Right Way to Shake Off a Viper* (Boston, 1711), p. 11.

88. C. M., *Nunc Dimittis* (Boston, 1709), p. 17.

89. C. M., *Speedy Repentance,* p. 27.

90. *Magnalia,* pp. 175, 334, 346, 415, 451.

91. *Magnalia,* II, 508.

92. C. M., *Adversus Libertinos* (Boston, 1713), p. 40.

93. *Magnalia,* I, 432.

94. C. M., *Signatus, passim.*

95. *Ibid.,* pp. 16-17.

96. *Ibid.,* p. 23.

97. *Ibid.,* p. 25.

98. C. M., *Menachem,* pp. 16-22.

99. C. M., *Sincere Piety,* p. 6.

100. *Free-Grace,* p. 9.

101. C. M., *The Retired Christian* (Boston, 1703), pp. 24-26.

102. C. M., *The Accomplished Singer* (Boston, 1721), p. 12.

103. C. M., *Seasonable Advice to the Poor* (Boston, 1712), p. 9.

104. *The Tryed Professor* (Boston, 1719), pp. 9-10.

105. C. M., *Parentator* (Boston, 1724), p. 223.

106. C. M., *A Companion for Communicants* (Boston, 1690), p. 129.

107. *Ibid.,* p. 130.

108. *Ibid.,* pp. 131-132. But the hair's breadth of difference from Stoddard is significant. As Perry Miller has pointed out, Stoddard refused to lower his conception of the requirements for assurance, but he was compelled by pastoral concern to bring the congregation to the Lord's Supper so that they might be lifted to meet his standard. Mather elects instead to lower the standard of assurance required, so that many may come. As a matter of fact, it has not been noted how nearly identical *in practice* are the approaches of Mather and Stoddard, despite

their strife over converting ordinances; for in theory Mather could not turn any applicant away who was not outwardly scandalous, since it was his conviction that no person could be sure of his own reprobation, as we have said before. But this amounts to saying that all were invited to partake of the Supper! The controversy between the Mathers and Stoddard was then mainly about a technical point in theology, whether we should invite the hypothetically unregenerate *as unregenerate* to partake of the Supper; but the two approaches in practice must have worked out the same. Between the two, however, we must give the palm to Mather for greater logical and biblical consistency; Stoddard's thinking was a little crooked, though his practice was intuitively straight. (See Perry Miller, "Solomon Stoddard," *Harvard Theological Review*, XXXIV [1941], 277-300.)

109. C. M., *An Heavenly Life* (Boston, 1719), p. 10.
110. *Utilia*, pp. 171-172, 174, 175.
111. C. M., *The City of Refuge* (Boston, 1716), p. 33.
112. Charles H. and Katherine George, *The Protestant Mind of the English Reformation* (Princeton, N. J., 1961), p. 42.
113. *Everlasting Gospel*, p. 30.
114. C. M., *Armour of Christianity*, pp. 103, 105.
115. *Tryed Professor*, p. 5.
116. *Christianity Demonstrated* (Boston, 1710), p. 33.
117. The original of this species was, of course, Horace Bushnell's *Christian Nurture* (New York, 1863); see Sanford Fleming, *Children and Puritanism* (New Haven, Conn., 1933).
118. Peter De Jong, in *The Covenant Idea in New England Theology*, suggests that this straining for effect provoked an Arminian counteremphasis. Some other critics have defended the Puritans on this account: Ola E. Winslow feels that the emphasis on hell was not unbalanced, nor was it unnatural considering the ministers' biblical literalism (Winslow, *Meetinghouse Hill, 1630-1783* [New York, 1952], p. 96), and Leonard Trinterud holds that the "terrors of the Law were used not to scare people into heaven but to humble them under divine sovereignty" (*The Forming of an American Tradition* [Philadelphia, 1949], p. 96).
119. C. M., *Nicetas*, p. 42.
120. C. M., *Seasonable Thoughts Upon Mortality* (Boston, 1712), p. 15.
121. C. M., *The Fisherman's Calling* (Boston, 1712), p. 38.
122. C. M., *Life Swiftly Passing and Quickly Ending* (Boston, 1715), p. 16.
123. C. M., *Corderius Americanus* (Boston, 1708), p. 18.
124. *Winter Meditations* (Boston, 1693), pp. 81-82.
125. C. M., *The Soul Upon the Wing* (Boston, 1722), pp. 16-17.

126. C. M., *Durable Riches* (Boston, 1695), p. 32.
127. *Corderius Americanus*, p. 18.
128. C. M., *Early Religion Urged* (Boston, 1694), pp. 63-64.
129. C. M., *Perswasions from the Terror of the Lord* (Boston, 1711), p. 36.
130. Cf. Bronkema, *Essence of Puritanism*, p. 180; De Jong, *Covenant Idea*, pp. 107, 198, 218.
131. Søren Kierkegaard, *The Attack upon Christendom*, trans. Walter Lowrie (Boston, 1956 [1944]), p. 108.
132. Cf. Pierre Pourrat, *Christian Spirituality*, trans. W. H. Mitchell and S. P. Jacques, 4 vols. (London, 1922-1927), III, 209; IV, 510. See Adolphe Tanqueray, *The Spiritual Life*, trans. Herman Branderis, 2nd ed. (Tournai, Bel., 1930), pp. 605-606: "Acquired contemplation is nothing more than a simplified affective prayer, and may be defined as contemplation in which the simplification of our intellectual and affective acts is the result of our own activity aided by grace. . . . Infused or passive contemplation is necessarily a free gift; we cannot obtain it by our efforts even with the help of ordinary grace. It is a kind of contemplation in which the acts of the mind and of the will have become simplified under the influence of a special grace which takes hold of us and causes us to receive lights and affections which God produces in us with our consent."
133. In this connection it is interesting to compare the conversion theory of Puritanism with the approach of the Jansenists, whom Mather much admired. Here also there was a rationalistic overdevelopment of double predestination (the Jansenists were in express accord with the Canons of the Synod of Dort); here again there was an insistence on assurance of salvation to avoid the *tentatio praedestinationis*, and again it must be obtained through a process of repentance (or rather, of penance) rather than solely by faith; and again the assurance approaches the level of infused contemplation. Another parallel morphology is present in the later development of Quietism, with its doctrine of resigned waiting on God for assurance. See Pourrat, *Christian Spirituality*, IV, 15-23.
134. Alan Simpson, *Puritanism in Old and New England*, p. 24.
135. Porter, *Reformation and Reaction*, pp. 281, 285-286, 310.
136. Simpson, *Puritanism*, p. 3.
137. Cf. Hugh Martin, *Puritanism and Richard Baxter* (London, 1954), p. 186; Nuttall, *Visible Saints*, pp. 158-159.
138. Nuttall, *Philip Doddridge* (London, 1951), p. 3.
139. C. J. Stranks, *Anglican Devotion* (London, 1961), p. 147.
140. Lyman Beecher, *The Autobiography of Lyman Beecher*, ed. Barbara M. Cross, 2 vols. (Cambridge, Mass., 1961), I, 29-30.
141. Cf. Jonathan Edwards, *A Faithful Narrative of the Surprising Work of God*, in *The Great Awakening*, ed. C. C. Goen (New Haven, Conn., 1972), pp. 167-168.

CHAPTER FOUR

1. C. M., *Diary*, I, 60.
2. Harold A. Perluck, "Puritan Expression and the Decline of Piety" (Ph.D. diss., Brown University, 1955), p. 6.
3. C. M., *Diary*, I, 458.
4. Beall and Shryock, *Cotton Mather, First Significant Figure in American Medicine*, p. 64.
5. Pierre Pourrat, *Christian Spirituality*, II, 2; III, 4.
6. Pourrat, *Christian Spirituality*, III, 285.
7. C. M., *Diary*, II, 87-88. The proposed collection never seems to have been finished.
8. Pourrat, *Christian Spirituality*, III, 5.
9. *Ibid.*, II, 34.
10. *Ibid.*
11. *Ibid.*, III, 13.
12. Gordon S. Wakefield, *Puritan Devotion* (London, 1957), pp. 85 ff.
13. Pourrat, *Christian Spirituality*, III, 33-39.
14. *Ibid.*, III, 13.
15. Samuel Mather, *Life of Cotton Mather*, p. 7.
16. C. M., *Man Eating the Food of Angels* (Boston, 1729), p. 7; *The Sailours Companion* (Boston, 1709), p. ii.
17. *Diary*, I, 303.
18. *Diary*, II, 479. "Porismatic" is presumably derived from the Greek *porizo*, to produce or provide food for oneself.
19. A. H. Francke, *A Guide to the Reading and Study of the Holy Scriptures*, trans. William Jacques (Philadelphia, 1823), pp. 123, 129, 131, 147. Francke gives here a schema of tests to determine if affections are truly gracious and issue from the Spirit and not from the old nature, quite reminiscent of Edwards' later work.
20. C. M., *Psalterium Americanum* (Boston, 1718), p. xxiv.
21. C. M., *The Accomplished Singer* (Boston, 1721), p. 12.
22. *Psalterium Americanum*, p. xxiv.
23. *Magnalia*, II, 110.
24. C. M., *Batteries upon the Kingdom of the Devil* (London, 1695), p. 177.
25. C. M., *The Christian Philosopher* (London, 1721), pp. 298, 300-301.
26. Pourrat, *Christian Spirituality*, II, 107-128.
27. C. J. Stranks, *Anglican Devotion* (London, SCM Press, 1961), pp. 23, 45. Of course, the concept is not so obscure or original that it needs such a channel of influence to spring up anew in the context of ordinary Christian intercourse between the Bible and the world. The last book of Arndt's *True Christianity* (1606) is entirely composed of typological meditation of this sort.
28. Wakefield, *Puritan Devotion*, p. 85.

29. Cf. the testimonial preface to *Agricola* (Boston, 1727).
30. *Military Duties* (Boston, 1687), Preface.
31. *Agricola* (Boston, 1727).
32. *The Fisherman's Calling* (Boston, 1712); *The Religious Marriner* (Boston, 1700); *Elizabeth* (Boston, 1710).
33. *Diary*, I, 357.
34. *Ibid.*, II, 69.
35. Cf. Increase Mather, *The Doctrine of Divine Providence* (Boston, 1684), p. 65.
36. C. M., *Advice from Taberah* (Boston, 1711), p. 23.
37. C. M., *Vigilius* (Boston, 1719), p. 8.
38. *Diary*, I, 24.
39. C. M., *The Retired Christian* (Boston, 1703), p. 2.
40. C. M., *The Day, and the Work of the Day* (Boston, 1693), p. 48.
41. *Military Duties*, p. 76.
42. C. M., *What the Pious Parent Wishes for* (Boston, 1721), p. 19.
43. C. M., *Several Sermons Concerning Walking with God* (Boston, 1689), p. 5.
44. C. M., *Shaking Dispensations* (Boston, 1715), p. 32.
45. *Utilia* (Boston, 1716), p. 198.
46. Cf. Thomas Goodwin, *The Returne of Prayers* (London, 1636).
47. *Utilia*, pp. 216-217.
48. *Ibid.*, pp. 212, 209.
49. *The Day*, p. 26.
50. C. M., *The Cure of Sorrow* (Boston, 1709), p. 12.
51. *Ibid.*, p. 14.
52. *The Day*, pp. 36-37.
53. C. M., *Family-Religion Urged* (Boston, 1709), pp. 14 ff.
54. *Sailours Companion*, p. 42.
55. C. M., *Instructions to the Living* (Boston, 1717), p. 22.
56. *Family-Religion Urged*, pp. 14 ff.
57. Stranks, *Anglican Devotion*, p. 26.
58. *Diary*, II, 769; cf. Samuel Mather, *Life of Cotton Mather*, p. 19.
59. *Manuductio ad Ministerium*, p. 108.
60. C. M., *Reasonable Religion* (Boston, 1713), p. 94.
61. *Diary*, I, 337; II, 5, 169.
62. Wakefield, *Puritan Devotion*, p. 68.
63. C. M., *Parentator* (Boston, 1724), pp. 145-147, 182.
64. *Several Sermons*, p. 6.
65. *Parentator*, pp. 145-147.
66. C. M., *Grata Brevitas* (Boston, 1712), p. 14.
67. Ralph and Louise Boas, *Cotton Mather, Keeper of the Puritan Conscience* (New York, 1928), p. 258.
68. *Parentator*, p. 41.
69. Cf. Irvonwy Morgan, *The Godly Preachers of the Elizabethan Church* (London, 1965), p. 167; Gerald R. Cragg, *Puritanism in the Period of the Great Persecution* (Cambridge, Eng., 1957), pp. 152-153.

70. Samuel Mather, *Life of Cotton Mather*, p. 8.
71. C. M., *The Good Old Way* (Boston, 1706), p. 86.
72. *Manuductio*, p. 109.
73. C. M., *Bonifacius* (Boston, 1710), p. 47; cf. C. M., *Pastoral Desires* (Boston, 1712), p. 76.
74. C. M., *The Religion of the Closet* (Boston, 1705), pp. 16 ff.; the directions are identical to his own practices as recorded in the *Diary*.
75. *Utilia*, p. 87.
76. Irvonwy Morgan, *The Godly Preachers*, p. 214.
77. Charles H. and Katherine George, *The Protestant Mind of the English Reformation*, p. 275.
78. John T. McNeill, *A History of the Cure of Souls* (New York, 1951), p. 266.
79. A. W. Nagler, *Pietism and Methodism* (Nashville, 1918), p. 63.
80. C. M., *A Good Master Well Served* (Boston, 1696), p. 5.
81. *Family-Religion Urged*, p. 3.
82. Horton Davies, *The Worship of the English Puritans* (London, 1948), p. 278.
83. C. M., *Pastoral Desires* (Boston, 1712), p. 79.
84. *Ibid.*
85. C. M., *Small Offers* (Boston, 1689).
86. *Family-Religion Urged*, pp. 14 ff.; C. M., *A Family Sacrifice* (Boston, 1703), pp. 23-24.
87. F. E. Stoeffler, *The Rise of Evangelical Pietism*, p. 39.
88. R. Bronkema, *The Essence of Puritanism*, p. 163.
89. Stoeffler, *Rise of Pietism*, pp. 39-41. Hooper was influenced by Bullinger, Bradford by Bucer.
90. Stoeffler, *Rise of Pietism*, p. 65; Bronkema, *Essence of Puritanism*, p. 164.
91. Stranks, *Anglican Devotion*, pp. 49, 163.
92. Cf. Pourrat, *Christian Spirituality*, III, 42; IV, 95 ff.
93. The public days of prayer in Massachusetts might be considered a form of retreat and a separate method of revitalization in themselves. I have not given them lengthy separate consideration here mainly because they are treated by C. M. more or less as a transferred sabbath, and because their basic contribution to spiritual renewal does not seem to differ from that of the Lord's Day.
94. This pragmatic use of the sabbath went far beyond Calvin, whose original position on the sabbath, expressed in the *Institutes*, was rather loose. Although his later commentary on Genesis is somewhat more strict, even here he regards the day not as an engine of piety but as a time for worship, for thoughtful celebration of the resurrection, and gratitude to God.
95. *Several Sermons*, p. 80.
96. C. M., *A Town in its Truest Glory* (Boston, 1712), pp. 38-39.

97. C. M., *The Day Which the Lord Hath Made* (Boston, 1707), p. 29.

98. Increase Mather, "To the Reader," in C. M., *A Good Evening for the Best of Dayes* (Boston, 1708).

99. *Man Eating the Food of Angels*, p. 25.

100. *Good Evening*, p. 18.

101. *Ibid.*, p. 19.

102. *Ratio Disciplinae* (Boston, 1726), p. 187.

103. Cf. Bronkema, *Essence of Puritanism*, p. 174.

104. Hugh Martin, *Puritanism and Richard Baxter* (London, 1954), p. 109.

105. J. O. Bemesdorfer, *Pietism and Its Influence on The Evangelical United Brethren Church* (Annville, Pa., 1966), p. 43.

106. Nagler, *Pietism and Methodism*, p. 54; Peschke, *Studien Zur Theologie August Hermann Franckes*, I, 101.

107. Nagler, *Pietism and Methodism*, p. 140.

108. Cf. J. H. Nichols, *Romanticism in American Theology* (Chicago, 1961), pp. 84 ff.

109. On the Puritan approach to the Lord's Supper, cf. Wakefield, *Puritan Devotion*, pp. 42-46; Davies, *Worship of the English Puritans*, p. 182; W. W. Biggs, "Preparation for Communion: A Puritan Manual," *Congregational Quarterly*, XXXII (1954), 17-27. C. J. Stranks, in *Anglican Devotion*, p. 53, notes that the longest single chapter in Lewis Bayly's phenomenally popular *Practice of Piety* is on the subject of preparation for communion.

110. E. g., *Diary*, I, 64-65, on Mather's meditations at the Lord's table.

111. C. M., *Winter Piety* (Boston, 1712), p. 22; cf. the almost identical passage in *A Monitor for Communicants* (Boston, 1714), pp. 2-3, and *Pastoral Desires*, p. 45.

112. Wakefield, *Puritan Devotion*, pp. 51-52.

113. *Monitor for Communicants*, pp. 7-11.

114. *Winter Piety*, p. 24.

115. Leonard Trinterud, in *The Forming of an American Tradition* (Philadelphia, 1949), p. 181, notes the same modified Stoddardism in the Log College men during the Great Awakening. John Wesley moved beyond this to a fully Stoddardean position; see Irvonwy Morgan, *The Nonconformity of Richard Baxter* (London: Epworth Press, 1946), p. 173.

116. *Monitor for Communicants*, p. 18.

117. *Pastoral Desires*, pp. 57-58.

118. C. M., *The Minister* (Boston, 1722), p. 34.

119. *Good Old Way*, p. 90.

120. C. M., *A Tree Planted by the Rivers of Water* (Boston, 1704), pp. 46-47.

121. Norman Pettit, *The Heart Prepared* (New Haven, Conn., 1966), p. 123.

122. C. M., *Baptistes* (Boston, 1705), p. 15.
123. C. M., *A Soul Well Anchored* (Boston, 1712), p. 10.
124. Morgan, *The Godly Preachers*, p. 170.
125. *Parentator*, p. 12.
126. Stoeffler, *Rise of Pietism*, p. 74.
127. *Tryed Professor, passim*.
128. Cf. *Several Sermons*, p. 9; C. M., *The High Attainment* (Boston, 1703), p. 26; C. M., *The Christian Temple* (Boston, 1706), p. 25; C. M., *Malachi* (Boston, 1717), p. 13; C. M., *Signatus* (Boston, 1727), p. 38.
129. C. M., *Several Sermons Concerning Walking with God* (Boston, 1689), p. 9.
130. C. M., *The Rules of a Visit* (Boston, 1705).
131. Stoeffler, *Rise of Pietism*, p. 18.
132. C. M., *Honesta Parsimonia* (Boston, 1721), p. 23.
133. C. M., *Nuncia Bona e Terra Longinqua* (Boston, 1715), p. 7.

CHAPTER FIVE

1. Cf. Harold A. Perluck, "Puritan Expression and the Decline of Piety" (Ph.D. diss., Brown University, 1955), pp. 84, 88, 92, 95, 108, 121.
2. Leonard J. Trinterud, *The Forming of an American Tradition*, pp. 176, 180.
3. Thus the Log College men sought both for experiential examination of candidates and for subscription to the Westminster standards; cf. Trinterud, pp. 62, 66, 170.
4. From another perspective, Emil Brunner clearly differentiates the Puritan/Pietist approach from that of scholastic orthodoxy, and vindicates its basic "existentialism," though he intends to go beyond its limitations; see *The Divine-Human Encounter*, trans. A. W. Loos (Philadelphia, 1943), p. 39.
5. *Several Sermons Concerning Walking with God*, p. 8.
6. C. M., *The Wayes and Joyes of Early Piety* (Boston, 1712), pp. 9-11, 13.
7. Brunner, *Divine-Human Encounter*, p. 153.
8. C. M., *Christianity Demonstrated* (Boston, 1710), p. 23.
9. C. M., *Reason Satisfied* (Boston, 1712), p. 27; *The Man of God Furnished*, p. 52; *Christianity Demonstrated*, p. 22.
10. *Man of God*, pp. 52-53.
11. *Pastoral Desires* (Boston, 1712), pp. 5-6.
12. C. M., *The Greatest Concern in the World* (Boston, 1765 [1707]), pp. 5, 8.
13. C. M., *Utilia* (Boston, 1716), p. 36.
14. C. M., *The Spirit of Life Entering into the Spiritually Dead* (Boston, 1707), pp. 14-16.

15. C. M., *Three Letters from New England* (London, 1721), p. 11.
16. *Ibid.*, p. 20.
17. Pierre Pourrat, *Christian Spirituality*, I, chs. 2-8.
18. John Calvin, *Institutes of the Christian Religion,* trans. John Allen, 2 vols. (Grand Rapids, 1949), I, 656-658 [III, iii, 8-9]).
19. John Owen, "The Mortification of Sin in Believers," in *Temptation and Sin* (Grand Rapids, 1958), pp. 5-33.
20. Pourrat, *Christian Spirituality*, III, chs. 12-15.
21. Cf. Owen's statement: "The vigour, and power, and comfort of our spiritual life depends on the mortification of the deeds of the flesh" (*Temptation and Sin*, p. 9).
22. Francis de Sales and later Salesians are perhaps the main exemplars of the *via positiva*. Adherents to this approach tend to be sub-Augustinian in general theological outlook.
23. Calvin, *Institutes*, I, 657; Owen, *Temptation and Sin*, pp. 83-86; Pourrat, *Christian Spirituality*, III, 342, 364-365.
24. C. M., *A Good Character* (Boston, 1723), p. 10.
25. *Utilia*, p. 175.
26. C. M., *Desiderius* (Boston, 1719), p. 26.
27. C. M., *Tremenda* (Boston, 1721), p. 6.
28. *Good Character*, p. 12.
29. *Ibid.*, p. 11.
30. C. M., *The Curbed Sinner* (Boston, 1713), p. 16.
31. *Pastoral Desires*, p. 100.
32. Cf. Pourrat, *Christian Spirituality*, II, 146.
33. C. M., *Military Duties* (Boston, 1687), pp. 70-71.
34. C. M., *The Christian Temple* (Boston, 1706), p. 22.
35. C. M., *Icono-Clastes* (Boston, 1717), p. 2.
36. C. M., *Speedy Repentance Urged* (Boston, 1690), p. 11.
37. *Curbed Sinner*, p. 36.
38. Cf. Richard Sibbes, *The Returning Backslider* (Ann Arbor, 1957).
39. C. M., *Vigilius* (Boston, 1719), p. 10.
40. Cf. C. M., *Agricola* (Boston, 1727), pp. 47-48.
41. Cf. Trinterud, *Forming of an American Tradition*, p. 185.
42. C. M., *The Armour of Christianity* (Boston, 1704), p. 125.
43. C. M., *Blessed Unions* (Boston, 1692), pp. 11-20.
44. C. M., *Baptismal Piety* (Boston, 1727), pp. 5-7.
45. *Military Duties*, p. 69.
46. *Ibid.*, pp. 72, 74.
47. *Magnalia*, I, 537-538.
48. *Diary*, II, 264.
49. C. M., *Triumphs over Troubles* (Boston, 1701), p. 21; cf. Arndt, *Of True Christianity*, II, 38; III, 23.
50. C. M., *Insanabilia* (Boston, 1714), p. 29.
51. C. M., *Silentiarius* (Boston, 1721), pp. 22-23.
52. C. M., *Meat Out of the Eater* (Boston, 1703), p. 41; cf. C. M., *The Cure of Sorrow* (Boston, 1709), p. 9; and C. M., *The Religion of the Cross* (Boston, 1714), pp. 16-17.

53. C. M., *Nunc Dimittis* (Boston, 1709), p. 14.
54. C. M., *The Right Way to Shake Off a Viper* (Boston, 1711), pp. 3-4.
55. *Utilia*, p. 103.
56. E. g., in Teresa of Avila and John of the Cross; see Pourrat, *Christian Spirituality*, III, 168, 182.
57. C. M., *Tela Praevisa* (Boston, 1724).
58. *Religion of the Cross*, p. 25.
59. C. M., *The High Attainment* (Boston, 1703), p. 27.
60. *Christian Temple*, p. 19.
61. *Agricola*, p. 150.
62. C. M., *The Nightingale* (Boston, 1724), p. 15.
63. C. M., *The True Riches* (Boston, 1724), p. iv.
64. Benjamin Colman, *The Holy Walk of Blessed Enoch* (Boston, 1728), p. 26.
65. Erich Beyreuther, *August Hermann Francke, 1663-1727, Zeuge des lebendigen Gottes*, 2nd ed. (Marburg, 1961), pp. 39, 53; Erhard Peschke, *Studien zur Theologie August Hermann Franckes*, I, 16, 150.
66. *Cure of Sorrow*, p. 32.
67. C. M., *The Christian Thank Offering* (Boston, 1696), p. 18.
68. C. M., *Signatus* (Boston, 1727), pp. 39-40.
69. *High Attainment*, p. 17.
70. C. M., *Sincere Piety Described* (Boston, 1719), p. 15.
71. *Diary*, II, 443.
72. C. M., *The Pure Nazarite* (Boston, 1723), p. 14.
73. C. M., *Nicetas* (Boston, 1705), p. 42.
74. *Sincere Piety*, p. 8.
75. Owen, *Temptation and Sin*, p. 83.
76. Samuel Mather, *Life of Cotton Mather*, p. 10.
77. *Diary*, I, 36.
78. Cf. Samuel Mather, *Life of Cotton Mather*, p. 10.
79. C. M., *The Serviceable Man* (Boston, 1690).
80. C. M., *The Minister* (Boston, 1722), p. 14.
81. *Good Character*, p. 3.
82. Kenneth B. Murdock, *Increase Mather*, p. 85.
83. Hugh Martin, *Puritanism and Richard Baxter*, p. 84.
84. Charles H. and Katherine George, *The Protestant Mind of the English Reformation*, pp. 153 ff.
85. Cf. *ibid.*, p. 30.
86. Erich Beyreuther, *August Hermann Francke und die Anfänge der Ökumenischen Bewegung* (Hamburg-Bergstedt, 1957), pp. 37, 82.
87. Rezeau Brown, *Memoirs of A. H. Francke* (Philadelphia, 1831), pp. 40, 178-179.
88. Mather, *Diary*, II, 24-28.
89. Perry Miller, *The New England Mind*, p. 413.
90. *Bonifacius*, pp. 24 ff.

91. C. M., *Piety and Equity United* (Boston, 1717), pp. 3, 17-18.
92. C. M., *Several Sermons Concerning Walking with God* (Boston, 1689), p. 15.
93. *Utilia*, p. 153.
94. C. M., *Christianity to the Life* (Boston, 1702), pp. 6-11.
95. Horton Davies, *Worship and Theology in England, 1690-1850* (Princeton, N. J., 1961).
96. Dudley Ward Rhodes Bahlman, *The Moral Revolution of 1688* (New Haven, Conn., 1957), p. 78.
97. C. M., *Malachi* (Boston, 1717), p. 63.
98. C. M., *Benedictus* (Boston, 1715), p. 1.
99. *Ibid.*, pp. 5-6, 16.
100. *Bonifacius*, p. 19.
101. Cf. Dale Weaver Brown, "The Problem of Subjectivism in Pietism," p. 234.
102. Cf. Bahlman, *Moral Revolution*, pp. 10, 42, 59.
103. *Speedy Repentance*, p. 19.
104. C. M., *Adversus Libertinos* (Boston, 1713), pp. 37-39. One summary of English antinomianism as seen by its critics identifies its distinctive doctrines as follows: 1) that God never inflicts punishment for sins upon the elect; 2) that God is never angry with his children; 3) that he sees no sin in them; 4) that the elect are at all times beloved by God, even in the act of sin; 5) that sanctification, in duties of piety, is little esteemed by God. See Gertrude Huehns, *Antinomianism in English History* (London, 1951).
105. Mather, *Adversus Libertinos*, p. 46.
106. *Ibid.*, pp. 48-49.
107. *Agricola*, p. 16.
108. *Magnalia*, II, 398.
109. *Ibid.*, II, 494.
110. C. M., *Seasonable Thoughts Upon Mortality* (Boston, 1712), p. 12. The distinction between mortal and venial sins was redefined and retained by Perkins, and even Baxter considered it quite important; see Gordon Wakefield, *Puritan Devotion*, p. 113.
111. *Magnalia*, II, 383.
112. C. M., *Menachem* (Boston, 1716), p. 10.
113. C. M., *Hezekiah* (Boston, 1713), p. 7.
114. *Meat out of the Eater*, p. 117.
115. *Ibid.*, p. 126.
116. C. M., *An Heavenly Life* (Boston, 1719), p. 9.
117. *Ibid.*, pp. 19-21.
118. See Irvonwy Morgan, *The Nonconformity of Richard Baxter* (London, 1946), p. 97.
119. August Hermann Francke, *A Letter Concerning the Most Useful Way of Preaching*, trans. David Jennings (London, 1725), p. 71.

120. F. E. Stoeffler, *The Rise of Evangelical Pietism*, p. 34.
121. Cf. Wakefield, *Puritan Devotion*, p. 114.
122. Thomas Wood, *English Casuistical Divinity during the Seventeenth Century* (London, 1952), p. 64.
123. Matthew Nethenus, "Introductory Preface," in *William Ames*, ed. and trans. Douglas Horton (Cambridge, 1965), p. 15.
124. C. M., *Addresses to Old Men, and Young Men, and Little Children* (Boston, 1690), pp. 32-33.
125. *Christianity to the Life*, p. 12.
126. C. M., *Tabitha Rediviva*, pp. 6, 8.
127. George, *The Protestant Mind*, p. 53; William P. Holden, *Anti-Puritan Satire, 1572-1642* (New Haven, Conn., 1954).
128. Larzer Ziff, *The Career of John Cotton* (Princeton, N. J., 1962), p. 162.
129. Hugh Martin, *Puritanism and Richard Baxter*, pp. 95-98; G. F. Nuttall, *Philip Doddridge, 1702-1751*, p. 111.
130. Stoeffler, *Rise of Pietism*, p. 141.
131. *Ibid.*, p. 58.
132. Brown, "The Problem of Subjectivism," pp. 269-273.
133. Peschke, *Studien*, pp. 92, 121-122, 138.
134. John T. McNeill, *Modern Christian Movements*, p. 69.
135. Cf. Stoeffler, *Rise of Pietism*, pp. 22, 77; Klaus Deppermann, *Der Hallesche Pietismus und der Preussische Staat Unter Friedrich III*, p. 56.
136. *Good Character*, p. 15.
137. *Wayes and Joyes*, p. 44.
138. C. M., *The Pourtraiture of a Good Man* (Boston, 1702), pp. 12-13.
139. C. M., *Grace Defended* (Boston, 1712), pp. 12-13.
140. C. M., *A Cloud of Witnesses* (Boston, 1700), *passim;* and *Ornaments for the Daughters of Zion* (Cambridge, Mass., 1694), pp. 18 ff.
141. C. M., *The Good Old Way* (Boston, 1706), p. 17.
142. C. M., *A Good Master Well Served* (Boston, 1696), p. 50.
143. Ola Elizabeth Winslow, *Meetinghouse Hill, 1630-1783*, p. 109.
144. *Ornaments*, pp. 20-21.
145. C. M., *Man Eating the Food of Angels* (Boston, 1710), pp. 27-28.
146. *Good Master*, p. 48.
147. *Wayes and Joyes*, p. 48.
148. *Nunc Dimittis*, pp. 34-35.
149. *Manuductio*, p. 134.
150. C. M., *The Good Old Way* (Boston, 1706), p. 13.
151. C. M., *Sober Considerations* (Boston, 1708), pp. 5-6.
152. *Magnalia*, I, 128.
153. *Good Old Way*, p. 12.
154. *Sober Considerations*, p. 17.
155. C. M., *Lex Mercatoria* (Boston, 1705), p. 20.

156. C. M., *A Monitory and Hortatory Letter* (Boston, 1700), pp. 8, 10.
157. Wakefield, *Puritan Devotion*, p. 102.
158. R. Newton Flew, *The Idea of Perfection in Christian Theology* (London, 1934), p. 277.
159. Peschke, *Studien*, p. 113.
160. Pourrat, *Christian Spirituality*, I, 209; II, 177.
161. Cf. Wakefield, *Puritan Devotion*, pp. 102-160.
162. *Agricola*, p. 206.
163. Pourrat, *Christian Spirituality*, II, 91; cf. Mather, *Diary*, I, 278, 483.
164. *Diary*, I, 214; cf. I, 278, 483, II, 578.
165. C. M., *Batteries upon the Kingdom of the Devil* (London, 1695), pp. 175-176.
166. C. M., *Nehemiah* (Boston, 1710), pp. 3, 5.
167. *Utilia*, p. 67.
168. *Diary*, I, 178, 207.
169. *Ibid.*, I, 426, 411; cf. I, 222, 278, 471, 483, 501.
170. *Magnalia*, I, 258.
171. Emory Battis, *Saints and Sectaries*, p. 61.
172. *Magnalia*, I, 247.
173. *Ibid.*, I, 192.
174. C. M., *Help for Distressed Parents* (Boston, 1695), p. 33; *A Family Well-Ordered* (Boston, 1699), p. 34.
175. *Cure of Sorrow*, pp. 25-26.
176. *Menachem*, pp. 25-26.
177. Thomas Goodwin, *The Returne of Prayers* (London, 1636).
178. *Diary*, I, 453-454.
179. *Parentator*, p. 195.
180. *Ibid.*, pp. 79-80.
181. Kenneth B. Murdock, *Literature and Theology in Colonial New England* (Cambridge, Mass., 1949), p. 110.
182. A. W. Nagler, *Pietism and Methodism*, p. 39; J. T. McNeill, *Modern Christian Movements*, p. 63; Beyreuther, *August Hermann Francke, 1663-1727, Zeuge des lebendigen Gottes*, p. 81.
183. Pourrat, *Christian Spirituality*, II, 38; III, 171, 198.
184. *Parentator*, p. 195.
185. C. M., *India Christiana* (Boston, 1721), p. 72.
186. *Ibid.*, p. 73.
187. *Utilia*, p. 239.
188. C. M., *The Grand Point of Solicitude* (Boston, 1715), pp. 23-24.
189. The same counsel was given by John of the Cross; see Pourrat, *Christian Spirituality*, III, 198.
190. C. M., *The Case of a Troubled Mind* (Boston, 1715), p. 5.
191. Cf. Stoeffler, *Rise of Pietism*, p. 14.
192. *Several Sermons*, p. 4.
193. C. M., *A Life of Piety Resolv'd upon* (Boston, 1714), p. 9.

194. *Christian Temple*, p. 31.
195. *Batteries upon the Kingdom*, p. 41.
196. *Several Sermons*, p. 6.
197. *Good Character*, p. 4.
198. *Life of Piety*, p. 9.
199. *Good Character*, p. 7.
200. *Several Sermons*, p. 10.
201. Pourrat, *Christian Spirituality*, II, 60.
202. *Ibid.*, II, 36, 70-71.
203. *Ibid.*, II, 46-47, 244.
204. Nils Thune, *The Behmenists and the Philadelphians* (Uppsala, Sweden, 1948), p. 15.
205. F. F. Walrond, *Philipp Jacob Spener* (London, 1893), p. 93.
206. Cf. Increase Mather, *Angelographia* (Boston, 1696).
207. C. M., *A Vision in the Temple* (Boston, 1721), *passim*.
208. C. M., *Coelestinus* (Boston, 1703), pp. 12-13, 91.
209. C. M., *Observanda* (Boston, 1695), pp. 15 ff.
210. C. M., *Memorials of Early Piety* (Boston, 1711), p. 50.
211. Ernst Benz, "Pietist and Puritan Sources of Early Protestant World Missions," *Church History*, XX (1951), 46.
212. C. M., *Things to be More Thought Upon* (Boston, 1713), p. 26.
213. *Parentator*, pp. 79, 199; C. M., *The Palm Bearers* (Boston, 1725); cf. Increase Mather, *Essay for the Recording of Illustrious Providences* (Boston, 1684), p. 202.
214. C. M., *Shaking Dispensations* (Boston, 1715), p. 28.
215. *Magnalia*, I, 96.
216. Pourrat, *Christian Spirituality*, I, 130-134.
217. Ignatius Loyola, *Spiritual Exercises* (Baltimore, 1959), pp. 141-153.
218. Pourrat, *Christian Spirituality*, II, 274, 300; III, 25 ff.; cf. Adolphe Tanqueray, *The Spiritual Life*, pp. 450, 718-724.
219. John Downame, *The Christians Warfare Against the Devill, the World, and Flesh* (London, 1604).
220. W. Gurnall, *The Christian in Compleat Armour* (London, 1655-1662).
221. Murdock, *Increase Mather*, p. 101.
222. E.g., Martin Luther, *Commentary on Galatians* (1535), in *Luther's Works*, ed. Jaroslav Pelikan, vol. XXVI (St. Louis, 1963), pp. 5, 18-19, 35-39; John Calvin, *Institutes of the Christian Religion* (Grand Rapids, 1949), I, xiv.
223. C. M., *Armour of Christianity* (Boston, 1704), *passim*.
224. *Manuductio*, p. 79.
225. *Parentator*, p. 26.
226. *Batteries upon the Kingdom*, p. 24.
227. *The Minister*, p. 41.
228. *Icono-Clastes*, preface.
229. *Magnalia*, I, 491.

230. C. M., *Wonders of the Invisible World* (Boston, 1693), p. iii.
231. C. M., *Nuncia Bona e Terra Longinqua* (Boston, 1715), p. 9.
232. *Wonders*, p. 26; cf. C. M., *Zalmonah* (Boston, 1725), p. 47.
233. C. M., *Armour of Christianity* (Boston, 1704), *passim*.
234. *Parentator*, p. 26.
235. John Bunyan, *Grace Abounding To The Chief of Sinners*, in *The Works of John Bunyan*, ed. George Offor, 3 vols. (London, 1855), I, 6, 13, 17-20.
236. C. M., *Reason Satisfied*, pp. 28-29; cf. *Batteries upon the Kingdom; Manuductio*, p. 49; *Zalmonah*, p. 47.
237. *Armour of Christianity*, p. 204.
238. *Reason Satisfied*, p. 29.
239. *Armour of Christianity*, p. 208.
240. Cf. Mather, *Wonders*, p. 52.
241. *Batteries Upon the Kingdom*, p. 11.
242. Cf. *Several Sermons*.
243. C. M., *Memorials of Early Piety*, pp. 40 ff.; *Nunc Dimittis*, p. 14. Pourrat notes this as a common element in traditional understanding of spiritual conflict (see *Christian Spirituality*, III, 368).
244. Mather, *Wonders*, pp. 49-57.
245. C. M., *The Day, and the Work of the Day* (Boston, 1693), p. 65.
246. Cf. Luther, *Galatians: 1535*, p. 36; Bunyan, *Grace Abounding;* George Whitefield, *Journals* (London, 1960), pp. 52-56.

CHAPTER SIX

1. Cf. Mauro Calamandrei, "Neglected Aspects of Roger Williams' Thought," *Church History*, XXI (1952), 239-258.
2. Cf. Sidney E. Mead, "From Coercion to Persuasion," *Church History*, XXIV (1956), 317-337.
3. Joachim Wach, *Sociology of Religion* (Chicago, 1944), p. 159.
4. Leonard J. Trinterud, *The Forming of an American Tradition*, p. 76.
5. Luke 24:49; Acts 1:7, 8 (cf. Luke 13:18-20); Acts 1:14; Acts 2:1, 4, 5, 8, 14-40; Acts 4:24 ff.; Acts 13:2.
6. C. M., *Ratio Disciplinae* (Boston, 1726), p. 58.
7. C. M., *The Minister* (Boston, 1722), p. 37.
8. *Ibid.*, p. 33.
9. C. M., *Parentator* (Boston, 1724), p. 38.
10. *Diary*, I, 72; cf. Barrett Wendell, *Cotton Mather, The Puritan Priest*, p. 54n.
11. R. and L. Boas, *Cotton Mather, Keeper of the Puritan Conscience*, p. 161.
12. *Bonifacius*, pp. 92-93; *Diary*, II, 88.
13. *Manuductio*, pp. 104-145.

14. *Ibid.*, pp. 91, 104-105; cf. C. M., *The Minister*, p. 39.
15. *The Minister*, p. 34.
16. *Diary*, I, 531.
17. *The Minister*, pp. 27-28.
18. C. M., *Memorials of Early Piety* (Boston, 1711), p. 11.
19. C. M., *Small Offers* (Boston, 1689), p. 25.
20. C. M., *Pastoral Desires* (Boston, 1712), p. 22.
21. *Memorials of Early Piety*, pp. 11-12.
22. C. M., *The Quickened Soul* (Boston, 1720), p. 30.
23. *Ratio Disciplinae*, pp. 178-179.
24. *Parentator*, p. 182.
25. C. M., *The Man of God Furnished* (Boston, 1708), pp. 1-3.
26. *Ibid.*, pp. 14-15. Francke was an equally dedicated proponent of catechizing; see A. H. Guericke, *The Life of A. H. Francke*, trans. Samuel Jackson (London, 1847), pp. 85-87.
27. C. M., *The Rules of a Visit* (Boston, 1705), p. 14.
28. C. M., *A Brief Memorial of Matters and Methods for Pastoral Visits* (Boston, 1723), *passim*.
29. Rezeau Brown, *Memoirs of A. H. Francke*, p. 65.
30. *The Nets of Salvation* (Boston, 1704), pp. 47-48.
31. Trinterud, *Forming of an American Tradition*, p. 182.
32. Irvonwy Morgan, *The Godly Preachers of the Elizabethan Church*, pp. 119-120.
33. Trinterud, *Forming of an American Tradition*, p. 76.
34. Charles H. and Katherine George, *The Protestant Mind of the English Reformation*, p. 5.
35. Edmund S. Morgan, *The Puritan Family* (Boston, 1944), pp. 90 ff.
36. *Ibid.*, p. 97.
37. Cf. F. E. Stoeffler, *The Rise of Evangelical Pietism*, p. 73.
38. E. Beyreuther, *August Hermann Francke und die Anfänge der Ökumenischen Bewegung*, p. 42.
39. John T. McNeill, *A History of the Cure of Souls* (New York, 1951), p. 276.
40. C. M., *Agricola* (Boston, 1727), pp. 154, 175, 192.
41. C. M., *A Good Old Age* (Boston, 1726), p. 25.
42. C. M., *Virtue in its Verdure* (Boston, 1725), pp. 10, 14.
43. C. M., *A Family Sacrifice* (Boston, 1703), pp. 45-46; C. M., *Benedictus* (Boston, 1715), pp. 30 ff.
44. C. M., *Desiderius* (Boston, 1719), p. 5.
45. C. M., *Ecclesiae Monilia* (Boston, 1726), p. 17.
46. C. M., *A Faithful Monitor* (Boston, 1704); *Vigilius* (Boston, 1719); *Love Triumphant* (Boston, 1722).
47. C. M., *The Fisherman's Calling* (Boston, 1712), *passim*.
48. *Small Offers*, p. 111.
49. C. M., *A Good Master Well Served* (Boston, 1696), pp. 6ff.
50. C. M., *The Good Old Way* (Boston, 1706), p. 47.

51. Miller, *The New England Mind*, p. 411.
52. See D. W. R. Bahlman, *The Moral Revolution of 1688*, p. 92.
53. Wach, *Sociology of Religion*, p. 174.
54. Beyreuther, *Francke und die Anfänge*, p. 41.
55. Stoeffler, *Rise of Pietism*, p. 19; John T. McNeill, *A History of the Cure of Souls*, p. 180.
56. Nagler, *Pietism and Methodism*, p. 50; Beyreuther, *Francke und die Anfänge*, p. 41.
57. Stoeffler, *Rise of Pietism*, pp. 142, 160, 162.
58. *Ibid.*, p. 230.
59. Nagler, *Pietism and Methodism*, p. 51.
60. G. V. Portus, *Caritas Anglicana* (London, 1912), pp. 197, 219; and F. F. Walrond, *Philipp Jacob Spener*, pp. 32-35.
61. Nagler, *Pietism and Methodism*, p. 135.
62. C. M., *Addresses to Old Men, and Young Men, and Little Children* (Boston, 1690), p. 46.
63. *Magnalia*, II, 145.
64. Cf. H. C. Porter, *Reformation and Reaction in Tudor Cambridge* (Cambridge, Eng., 1958), p. 197; I. Morgan, *Godly Preachers*, pp. 68-100, 158, 170.
65. *Ratio Disciplinae*, pp. 93, 96.
66. C. M., *Private Meetings Regulated and Animated* (Boston, 1706); C. M., *Religious Societies* (Boston, 1724).
67. C. M., *Golgotha* (Boston, 1713), p. 43; *Hor-Hagidgad* (Boston, 1727), p. 22; *Manuductio*, p. 72.
68. J. Wickham Legg, *English Church Life from the Restoration to the Tractarian Movement* (London, 1914), p. 301.
69. Bahlman, *Moral Revolution*, pp. 1-22, 31-37, 60-66, 77-80, 101.
70. Martin Schmidt, "Der Ökumenische Zinn des deutschen Pietismus und seine Auswirkungen in der Bibelverbreitung," in Oskar Söhngen, ed., *Die Bleibende Bedeutung des Pietismus* (Wittenberg, 1960), p. 63.
71. J. S. Simon, *John Wesley and the Religious Societies* (London, 1921), p. 26.
72. Portus, *Caritas Anglicana*, p. 112.
73. C. M., *Pastoral Desires* (Boston, 1712), p. 87.
74. C. M., *Methods and Motives for Societies to Suppress Disorders* (Boston, 1703), p. 1.
75. *Faithful Monitor*, pp. 49-52.
76. *Private Meetings Animated*, p. 21.
77. *Pastoral Desires*, p. 89.
78. *Religious Societies*, p. 7.
79. *Ratio Disciplinae*, pp. 93-104, 102-103.
80. *Magnalia*, p. 242.
81. *Ratio Disciplinae*, pp. 192-193.
82. *Pastoral Desires*, p. 88.
83. C. M., *Thoughts for the Day of Rain* (Boston, 1712), p. 61.

84. Samuel Mather, *Life of Cotton Mather*, pp. 55-56.
85. C. and K. George, *The Protestant Mind of the English Reformation*, pp. 83-85, 89-90, 104, 131-139, 156-158, 162-169.
86. Emery Battis, *Saints and Sectaries*, pp. 103, 117.
87. Kenneth B. Murdock, *Literature and Theology in Colonial New England*, p. 131.
88. Beyreuther, *Francke und die Anfänge*, pp. 30-31.
89. *Ibid.*, pp. 26, 36-37.
90. Johann Valentine Andreae, *Christianopolis*, trans. and ed. F. E. Held (New York, 1916), pp. 242-243, 272 ff.
91. *Francke und die Anfänge*, pp. 39-40; Klaus Deppermann, *Der Hallesche Pietismus und der preussische Staat unter Friedrich III*, pp. 51-55.
92. McNeill, *Modern Christian Movements*, p. 72.
93. Nagler, *Pietism and Methodism*, p. 54.
94. Beyreuther, *August Hermann Francke, 1663-1727*, pp. 148-162.
95. E. g., Deppermann, *Hallesche Pietismus*, pp. 173-174.
96. Beyreuther, *August Hermann Francke, 1663-1727*, p. 181.
97. Beyreuther, *Francke und die Anfänge*, p. 50.
98. C. M., *Marah Spoken to* (Boston, 1718), p. 1.
99. Carl Bridenbaugh, *Cities in the Wilderness*, pp. 233-234, 252.
100. C. M., *The Present State of New England* (Boston, 1690), pp. 16 ff.
101. *Pastoral Desires*, p. 72.
102. C. M., *Mare Pacificum* (Boston, 1700), p. 2.
103. C. M., *Christianity to the Life* (Boston, 1702), pp. 50-51.
104. C. M., *Seasonable Advice to the Poor* (Boston, 1726), pp. 1-2.
105. Miller, *The New England Mind*, pp. 399-402.
106. *Agricola*, p. 63.
107. C. M., *Instructions to the Living* (Boston, 1717), pp. 58-59.
108. C. M., *Lex Mercatoria* (Boston, 1705), *passim*; C. M., *Theopolis Americana* (Boston, 1710), *passim*.
109. *Fisherman's Calling*, pp. ii-iii.
110. *Ibid.*, pp. 47-49.
111. *Seasonable Advice*, pp. 7 9.
112. C. M., *The Best Ornaments of Youth* (Boston, 1707), p. 6; *Agricola*, p. 198.
113. C. M., *The Tribe of Asher* (Boston, 1717), p. 24; *The Sailours Companion* (Boston, 1709), preface; *Euthanasia* (Boston, 1723), pp. 25-27; *Durable Riches* (Boston, 1695).
114. C. M., *A Pillar of Gratitude* (Boston, 1700), p. 19.
115. C. M., *The Armour of Christianity* (Boston, 1704), pp. 158-159.
116. *Parentator*, p. 83.
117. C. M., *Meat Out of the Eater* (Boston, 1703), p. 41.
118. *Utilia*, pp. 82-83.
119. C. M., *The Soul Upon the Wing* (Boston, 1722), pp. 23-24.
120. Bridenbaugh, *Cities in the Wilderness*, pp. 234-235.

121. C. M., *Psalterium Americanum* (Boston, 1718), p. 33.
122. C. M., *A Father Departing* (Boston, 1723), p. 24; cf. *Parentator,* p. 185.
123. *Seasonable Advice,* p. 3.
124. Cf. Miller, *The New England Mind,* p. 401.
125. C. and K. George, *The Protestant Mind,* pp. 300-302.
126. Quoted in *Theopolis Americana,* p. 22.
127. *Diary,* I, 22, 579; II, 383, 663.
128. *A Good Master,* p. 40.
129. E. S. Morgan, *The Puritan Family,* p. 73.
130. C. M., *Terra Beata* (Boston, 1726), p. 35.
131. C. M., *Renatus* (Boston, 1725), p. 9.
132. *Love Triumphant,* pp. 9-10.
133. C. M., *India Christiana* (Boston, 1721), p. 47.
134. *Ibid.,* pp. 27-28.
135. *A Father Departing,* p. 28.
136. Miller, *The New England Mind,* pp. 179, 183-184, 203-204, 206, 305-309, 330, 332-333, 338, 366.
137. C. M., *The Serviceable Man* (Boston, 1690); *Present State of New England; a Midnight Cry* (Boston, 1692); *The Short History of New England* (Boston, 1694); *Magnalia.*
138. Mather, *Small Offers; The Wonderful Works of God* (Boston, 1690); *Addresses to Old Men, Unum Necessarium* (Boston, 1693); *The Day, and the Work of the Day* (Boston, 1693); *Early Religion Urged* (Boston, 1694); *Observanda* (Boston, 1695).
139. *A Midnight Cry,* p. 49.
140. *Ibid.,* p. 62.
141. *Unum Necessarium,* pp. i-ii.
142. *Early Religion Urged,* p. 8.
143. *Magnalia,* I, 63.
144. *Addresses to Old Men,* pp. 17, 90.
145. *The Wonderful Works of God,* pp. 35-36; *Addresses to Old Men,* p. 37; *Serviceable Man,* p. 55; *Midnight Cry,* p. 51; *Magnalia,* II, 355.
146. Increase Mather, *Pray for the Rising Generation* (Boston, 1678).
147. C. M., *Testimony Against Evil Customs* (Boston, 1718); *The Good Old Way.*
148. *The Rules of a Visit,* p. 31; cf. *Private Meetings Animated,* p. 1; *The Wayes and Joyes of Early Piety* (Boston, 1712), pp. 38-41; *Zelotes* (Boston, 1717), *passim; A Voice from Heaven* (Boston, 1719), p. 11.
149. C. M., *The Ambassadors Tears* (Boston, 1721), pp. 15, 25.
150. C. M., *Suspiria Vinctorum* (Boston, 1726), *passim.*
151. Cf., e. g., Richard Smith, *Munition against Man's Miserie and Mortalitie* (London, 1634), pp. 89-90.
152. Martin Schmidt, "Der Ökumenische Zinn des deutschen Pietismus und seine Auswirkungen in der Bibelverbreitung," p. 71.

153. F. E. Stoeffler, *The Rise of Evangelical Pietism,* p. 235.
154. Dale Weaver Brown, "The Problem of Subjectivism in Pietism," p. 23.
155. *Magnalia,* II, 74.
156. C. M., *Eleutheria* (London, 1698), p. 38.
157. C. M., *An Advice to the Churches* (Boston, 1702), p. 9.
158. *Benedictus,* p. 38.
159. *Suspiria Vinctorum,* p. 18.
160. *Ambassadors Tears,* p. 13.
161. *Ibid.,* p. 6.
162. *Nets of Salvation,* pp. 40-42.
163. Cf. *Wonderful Works,* pp. 35-36; *Addresses to Old Men,* p. 37; *Serviceable Man,* p. 55; *Midnight Cry,* p. 51; *Early Religion Urged; Short History of New England; Nets of Salvation,* pp. 40-42; *Faithful Monitor; Private Meetings Animated; Bonifacius; Successive Generations* (Boston, 1715), p. 28; *The Duty of Children* (Boston, 1703), p. 43; *American Tears upon the Ruins of the Greek Churches* (Boston, 1701), p. 25; *Religious Societies,* pp. 3-4; *Suspiria Vinctorum,* pp. 20-21.
164. *Midnight Cry,* p. 51.
165. *Nets of Salvation,* p. 41.
166. *Private Meetings Animated,* p. 19; *Bonifacius,* p. 87.
167. *Suspiria Vinctorum,* p. 11.
168. Charles G. Finney, *Lectures on Revivals of Religion,* William G. McLoughlin, ed. (Cambridge, Mass., n.d.), chs. 4-6, 8.
169. *Addresses to Old Men,* pp. 109-111; Sanford Fleming, *Children and Puritanism* (New Haven, Conn., 1933), p. 127.
170. *The Day, and the Work of the Day,* pp. 69, 71.
171. C. M., *Help for Distressed Parents* (Boston, 1695), p. 31.
172. *Eleutheria,* p. 109.
173. J. S. Simon, *John Wesley and the Religious Societies,* p. 26.
174. C. M., *Man Eating the Food of Angels* (Boston, 1710), pp. 63 ff.
175. *Thoughts for the Day of Rain,* pp. 60-64.
176. *Wayes and Joyes,* appendix.
177. *Golgotha,* p. 46.
178. C. M., *A New Offer* (Boston, 1714), pp. 2-3.
179. C. M., *Nuncia Bona e Terra Longinqua* (Boston, 1715), pp. 2, 7-8, 11.
180. *Utilia,* author's preface; cf. C. M., *Menachem* (Boston, 1716), p. 39.
181. C. M., *Faith Encouraged* (Boston, 1718), p. 14.
182. *Suspiria Vinctorum,* pp. 20-21.

CHAPTER SEVEN

1. Hans Martin Rotermund, *Orthodoxie und Pietismus* (Berlin, 1959), p. 113.

2. J. V. Andreae, *Christianopolis*, p. 241.
3. J. M. Batten, *John Dury: Advocate of Christian Reunion* (Chicago, 1944), p. 17; Martin Schmidt, "Der Ökumenische Zinn des deutschen Pietismus und seine Auswirkungen in der Bibelverbreitung," p. 60.
4. F. E. Stoeffler, *The Rise of Evangelical Pietism*, p. 182.
5. Dale Weaver Brown, "The Problem of Subjectivism in Pietism," p. 49.
6. F. F. Walrond, *Philipp Jacob Spener*, p. 51.
7. Brown, "The Problem of Subjectivism," p. 57.
8. Klaus Deppermann, *Der Hallesche Pietismus und der preussische Staat unter Friedrich III*, pp. 40-44.
9. A. W. Nagler, *Pietism and Methodism*, p. 41.
10. See Erich Beyreuther, *August Hermann Francke und die Anfänge der Ökumenischen Bewegung*, pp. viii-ix, 27-28.
11. *Ibid.*, p. 33.
12. Cf. *ibid.*, pp. 55-56.
13. Rotermund, *Orthodoxie und Pietismus*, p. 22.
14. Beyreuther, *Francke und die Anfänge*, p. 82.
15. A. W. Boehm, in Johann Arndt's *Of True Christianity*, I.
16. *Ibid.*
17. *Ibid.*
18. I. Morgan, *The Godly Preachers of the Elizabethan Church*, pp. 186-189, 210.
19. C. and K. George, *The Protestant Mind of the English Reformation*, pp. 376-378, 414-416; cf. Stoeffler, *Rise of Pietism*, p. 49.
20. Batten, *John Dury*, pp. 16, 18, 26, 32, 45, 51-52, 57, 67, 110-111, 121, 123-129, 139-140, 197-198.
21. Paul Elmer More and F. L. Cross, eds., *Anglicanism* (London, 1957), p. 187.
22. Harry Grant Plum, *Restoration Puritanism* (Chapel Hill, N. C., 1943), pp. 10-11.
23. Hugh Martin, *Puritanism and Richard Baxter*, p. 159. Baxter corresponded with Dury, and his Association Plan was identical with one earlier proposed by the Scotsman (Batten, *John Dury*, p. 174).
24. See A. Harold Wood, *Church Unity without Uniformity* (London, 1963), p. 243.
25. Martin, *Puritanism and Richard Baxter*, p. 164.
26. *Ibid.*, pp. 68-71; Wood, *Church Unity*, p. 242.
27. Plum, *Restoration Puritanism*, p. 55.
28. *Ibid.*
29. Carl Bridenbaugh, *Mitre and Sceptre* (New York, 1962), pp. 32-35; cf. F. Tudor Jones, *Congregationalism in England, 1662-1962* (London, 1962), pp. 114-119; D. W. R. Bahlman, *The Moral Revolution of 1688*, p. 80.
30. London, 1706; 2nd ed., 1709.
31. Martin Schmidt, "Der Ökumenische Zinn des deutschen Pietis-

mus und seine Auswirkungen in der Bibelverbreitung," p. 60; Beyreuther, *Francke und die Anfänge,* pp. 111, 129, 134, 151, 159, 184.

32. Larzer Ziff, *The Career of John Cotton,* pp. 89, 215-216.

33. Emery Battis, *Saints and Sectaries,* p. 157.

34. Cf. Perry Miller, *Errand into the Wilderness* (New York, 1956).

35. *Magnalia,* I, 299-301, 326-327.

36. C. M., *Parentator* (Boston, 1724), p. 60.

37. Perry Miller refuses to believe this account, and conjectures that the shift occurred in 1690 for political reasons, since Increase could not take advantage of the Act of Toleration, to salvage liberty for New England's churches, without somehow inventing' a rationale to swallow toleration itself (*The New England Mind: From Colony to Province,* p. 165). Considering Increase's close connection with English Puritans and moderates like Baxter during the '70s and '80s, however, it is more likely that Cotton gives an accurate representation of the evolution of his father's views and his own.

38. C. M., *The Serviceable Man* (Boston, 1690), pp. 34-35; *Optanda* (Boston, 1692), p. 43.

39. *Diary,* I, 149.

40. Cf. C. M., *Observanda* (Boston, 1695), p. 44; *Magnalia,* I, 35, 62, 113, 250, 259, 298, 327, 499; II, 536; *Theopolis Americana* (Boston, 1710), p. 29; *A Town in its Truest Glory* (Boston, 1712), p. 53; *Thoughts for the Day of Rain* (Boston, 1712), p. 62; *Things to be More Thought Upon* (Boston, 1713), p. 61; *Utilia* (Boston, 1716), p. 229; *Piety and Equity* (Boston, 1717), p. 27; *Malachi* (Boston, 1717), p. 68; *Three Letters from New England* (London, 1721), p. 24; *Ratio Disciplinae* (Boston, 1726), p. 172.

41. *Magnalia,* I, 35, 250, 327; *Piety and Equity,* p. 27.

42. *Ratio Disciplinae,* p. 172.

43. *Malachi,* p. 71.

44. *Ibid.,* p. 72.

45. The Puritan founding theologians had been willing to admit the presence of regenerate believers within the Roman system, but they felt that since Trent the papacy itself was more than ever clearly identifiable with the Antichrist, and not to be tolerated (George, *Protestant Mind,* pp. 379-389). Even Baxter agreed to this, and the political situation in England in the late seventeenth and early eighteenth centuries made a hard line against Rome seem a life and death necessity to English Protestants (Martin, *Puritanism and Richard Baxter,* p. 120). The attitude of Spener and Francke toward Rome was precisely in line with the typical Puritan view, admitting the presence of believers within the church but considering toleration of such a dangerous political entity as the Roman system unwise (Nagler, *Pietism and Methodism,* p. 41).

46. C. M., *Suspiria Vinctorum* (Boston, 1726), p. 3.

47. C. M., *The Fall of Babylon* (Boston, 1707), p. 19.
48. C. M., *American Tears upon the Ruins of the Greek Churches* (Boston, 1701), p. 50.
49. *Ibid.*, p. 43.
50. C. M., *Little Flocks Guarded Against Grievous Wolves* (Boston, 1691), pp. 3-4.
51. *Ibid.*, p. 10; C. M., *A Town in its Truest Glory* (Boston, 1712), p. 53.
52. *Three Letters*, p. 12.
53. C. M., *Blessed Unions* (Boston, 1692), dedication.
54. Miller, *The New England Mind*, p. 217.
55. *Blessed Unions*, pp. 52, 72-79.
56. *Ibid.*, p. 41.
57. C. M., *A Midnight Cry* (Boston, 1692), p. 7.
58. C. M., *The Short History of New England* (Boston, 1694), p. 13.
59. C. M., *Agricola* (Boston, 1727), p. 66.
60. C. M., *The Armour of Christianity* (Boston, 1704), pp. 168-170.
61. C. M., *The Tryed Professor* (Boston, 1719), p. 13.
62. *Blessed Unions*, p. 44.
63. C. M., *Genuine Christianity* (Boston, 1721), p. 1-2.
64. C. M., *A Vindication of the Ministers* (Boston, 1722), p. 14.
65. C. M., *Christianity to the Life* (Boston, 1702), p. 15.
66. C. M., *Batteries upon the Kingdom of the Devil* (London, 1695), p. 185.
67. C. M., *The Stone Cut Out of the Mountain* (Boston, 1716), p. 6.
68. Batten, *John Dury*, p. 74.
69. *Ibid.*, pp. 129-130.
70. Martin, *Puritanism and Richard Baxter*, p. 165; Irvonwy Morgan, *The Nonconformity of Richard Baxter*, pp. 206-207.
71. Brown, "The Problem of Subjectivism," pp. 182-184.
72. *Blessed Unions*, p. 42.
73. *Malachi*, pp. 33-36.
74. *Ibid.*, p. 92.
75. *Piety and Equity*, pp. 26-28.
76. *Ibid.*, pp. 28-29.
77. *Things to be More Thought Upon*, pp. 86-87.
78. C. M., *Shaking Dispensations* (Boston, 1715), pp. 27-28.
79. Samuel Mather, *Life of Cotton Mather*, p. 48.
80. *The Stone*, p. 7.
81. C. M., *The Wayes and Joyes of Early Piety* (Boston, 1712).
82. C. M., *Eleutheria* (London, 1698), p. 76.
83. Bridenbaugh (*Mitre and Sceptre*, pp. 26, 55-60) shows rather conclusively that the message and strategy of the S.P.G. in America was less than exclusively evangelical, and that it represented "British imperialism in ecclesiastical guise." He notes that after the Anglican victory at Yale in 1722, with the conversion of Timothy Cutler, the Mathers began to emphasize strongly that there were really two churches involved in the

English church, the "Low," with which they maintained communion, and the "High," which they considered simply a remainder of the apostate and persecuting Roman church.

84. C. M., *Baptistes* (Boston, 1724), p. 21.
85. *Diary*, II, 53.
86. C. M., *Letter to F. de La Pilloniere* (Boston, 1717), pp. 3-4.
87. A. J. Lewis, *Zinzendorf The Ecumenical Pioneer* (London, 1962), pp. 12-18.
88. *Ibid.*, pp. 139-141.
89. Ernst Benz, "Ecumenical Relations between Boston Puritanism and German Pietism: Cotton Mather and August Hermann Francke," *Harvard Theological Review*, LIV (1961), 159-193.
90. Erich Beyreuther, *August Hermann Francke, 1663-1727, Zeuge des Lebendigen Gottes*, pp. 192-198; cf. Erich Beyreuther, *Bartholomaeus Ziegenbalg*, trans. S. G. Land and H. W. Gensichen, 1st Eng. ed. (Madras, India, 1955).
91. Batten, *John Dury*, pp. 11-12, 139.
92. Martin, *Puritanism and Richard Baxter*, p. 187.
93. Barrett Wendell, *Cotton Mather*, p. 155.
94. C. M., *The Tribe of Asher* (Boston, 1717), p. 11.
95. *Batteries upon the Kingdom*, p. 57.
96. C. M., *An Advice to the Churches* (Boston, 1702), p. 2.
97. *Ibid.*, pp. 3-4.
98. C. M., *Another Tongue* (Boston, 1707), pp. 2-3.
99. For a more extensive handling of this subject, which is, however, confined principally to the *Magnalia*, see Sidney H. Rooy, *The Theology of Missions in the Puritan Tradition*, pp. 242-328.
100. *Magnalia*, I, 556-575.
101. *Ibid.*, II, 552-644.
102. C. M., *Epistle to the Christian Indians* (Boston, 1700), pp. 3, 14.
103. Samuel Mather, *Life of Cotton Mather*, p. 49.
104. C. M., *India Christiana* (Boston, 1721), p. 40.
105. *Ibid.*, p. 44.
106. *American Tears*, p. 35; *Diary*, I, 402; II, 80.
107. C. M., *La Fe del Christiano* (Boston, 1699).
108. C. M., *The Faith of the Fathers* (Boston, 1699); cf. *Diary*, I, 298, where Mather indicates that his authorship of the tract is due to an urgent desire to help precipitate the millennium.
109. C. M., *A Proposal for an Evangelical Treasury* (Boston, 1725), p. 2.

EPILOGUE

1. Sydney E. Mead, "The Rise of the Evangelical Conception of the Ministry in America (1607-1850)," in *The Ministry in Historical Perspectives*, H. Richard Niebuhr and Daniel D. Williams,

eds. (New York, 1956), p. 238. Cf. David Hall's analysis of Mather's place in the spectrum between "sacramental" and "prophetic" forms of ministry, in *The Faithful Shepherd: a History of the New England Ministry in the Seventeenth Century* (Chapel Hill, N. C., 1972), pp. 202-211, 221-225, 245-267, 275-277.

2. Kenneth Scott Latourette, *The Emergence of a World Christian Community* (New Haven, Conn., 1949).
3. Mead, "Rise of the Evanglical Conception," p. 240.
4. P. T. Forsyth, *Christian Perfection* (London, 1899), pp. 7, 9, 16, 54, 71, 81.

APPENDIX

1. Robert Calef, *More Wonders of the Invisible World*, in *Narratives of the Witchcraft in Massachusetts*, ed. by George Lincoln Burr (New York, 1914), pp. 299-334, 392-93.
2. Francis Hutchinson, *Historical Essay Concerning Witchcraft* (London, 1718), pp. 73, 77, 93.
3. Thomas Hutchinson, *The History of Massachusetts*, 2 vols. (Boston, 1764), 2:24-63.
4. C. M., *Diary*, I, 264.
5. Henry Ware, *Two Discourses* (Boston, 1821), p. 18.
6. *Ibid.*, pp. 16-17, 19, 36.
7. *Ibid.*, pp. 22-29.
8. C. W. Upham, *Lectures on Witchcraft*, 2nd ed. (Boston: Carter and Hendee, 1832), pp. 283ff. Otho Beall and Richard Shryock are thus mistaken in their contention that the main blow to Mather's reputation came after the publication of the Mather papers by the Massachusetts Historical Society in 1868 (Cotton Mather, First Significant Figure in American Medicine [Baltimore: Johns Hopkins Press, 1954], p. 1).
9. *Dictionary of American Biography*, s.v. "Peabody, William Bourn Oliver."
10. W. B. O. Peabody, *Life of Cotton Mather* (Boston, 1844).
11. *Dictionary of American Biography*, s.v. "Quincy, Josiah."
12. Josiah Quincy, *The History of Harvard University* (Cambridge, Mass., 1840), pp. 55-72, 132-53, 201-29, 330-46, 482-88, 558-60.
13. Benjamin Pierce, *History of Harvard University* (Cambridge, Mass., 1833), pp. 49-71, 136-39.
14. W. F. Poole, "Cotton Mather and Salem Witchcraft," *North American Review* 108 (1869), 337-38.
15. W. B. Sprague, ed., *Annals of the American Pulpit* (New York, 1857), 1:189-95 (the sketch is by a later and considerably different Joshua Gee); J. L. Sibley, *Biographical Sketches of Graduates of Harvard University* (Cambridge, Mass., 1885), 3:156-58.

16. Charles Francis Adams, *Massachusetts, Its Historians and Its History* (Boston, 1893), pp. 65-89.
17. Brooks Adams, *The Emancipation of Massachusetts,* 2nd and rev. ed. (Boston, 1919), pp. 417-39.
18. Chandler Robbins, *A History of the Second Church, or Old North, in Boston* (Boston, 1852), pp. 68, 71.
19. *Ibid.,* pp. 75-77. This connection is noted also by an orthodox mid-century defender of Mather, Enoch Pond, in *The Mather Family* (Boston, 1844), pp. 98-138. Another kind of defense of Mather appeared some years after Pond and Robbins' works, the *New England Tragedies* of Longfellow (Boston, 1868). Influenced by the original sources—the poet incorporates some of Mather's phrases into his work—and probably also by Robbins and Pond, Longfellow presents Mather as a courageous man of God attempting to dampen the zeal of the judges at Salem. The new edition of Upham in 1869 took occasion to throw dust at Longfellow's treatment (*Salem Witchcraft* [New York, 1969]), but W. F. Poole in turn attacked Upham in the same year, in a lucid dissection of the latter's historiography ("Cotton Mather and Salem Witchcraft," *North American Review* 108 [1869]:337-97). Poole accuses Upham of jumping to conclusions from meagre evidence and reading Mather's mind beyond the limits of possibility, putting him on trial by the scientific standards of the nineteenth century, neglect of important evidence and apparent misinterpretation or concealment of other data, and too much regard for Calef's "unreliable" personal judgments on the Mathers. Poole's article seems to have Upham's work in a shambles. The latter draws some blood on minor issues in his rebuttal ("Salem Witchcraft and Cotton Mather," *The Historical Magazine,* Second Series, 6 [1869]:129-219), but Poole held grimly to his conclusions in his later article on the Salem tragedy in Justin Winsor's *Memorial History of Boston* (Boston, 1881), 2:130-72.
20. Barrett Wendell, *Cotton Mather, the Puritan Priest* (New York, 1891), p. 109.
21. Thomas J. Holmes, "Cotton Mather and His Writings on Witchcraft," *Papers of the Bibliographical Society of America,* 18:31-59.
22. George Lyman Kittredge, *Witchcraft in Old and New England* (Cambridge: Harvard University Press, 1929), p. 372; and cf. idem, "Cotton Mather's Election into the Royal Society," *Publications of the Colonial Society of Massachusetts,* 14 (1911):81-114; idem, "Some Lost Works of Cotton Mather," *Proceedings of the American Antiquarian Society* 45 (1912):418-79; idem, "Cotton Mather's Scientific Communications to the Royal Society," *Proceedings of the American Antiquarian Society* 26 (1916), 3:18-57.
23. Clifford K. Shipton, "The New England Clergy of the 'Glacial Age'," *Publications of the Colonial Society of Massachusetts* 32 (1933):24-54.

24. Otho T. Beall and Richard H. Shryock, *Cotton Mather, First Significant Figure in American Medicine* (Baltimore, 1954).
25. Wendell, *Cotton Mather*, p. 109.
26. Ralph and Louise Boas, *Cotton Mather, Keeper of the Puritan Conscience* (New York, 1928), pp. 256-70.
27. Kenneth B. Murdock, *Increase Mather: the Foremost American Puritan* (Cambridge, Mass., 1926), p. 3.
28. Kenneth B. Murdock, "Cotton Mather," DAB, pp. 386-89.
29. Kenneth B. Murdock, *Selections from Cotton Mather* (New York, 1926), p. xxiii.
30. Vernon L. Parrington, *Main Currents in American Thought* (New York, 1927, 1930), pp. 93-117.
31. Perry Miller, *The New England Mind: from Colony to Province* (Cambridge, Mass., 1953), p. 408.
32. Peter Gay, *A Loss of Mastery: Puritan Historians in Colonial America* (Berkeley, 1966), pp. 53-87.
33. Kenneth Silverman, *Selected Letters of Cotton Mather* (Baton Rouge, 1971), pp. xi, xiii, xv.
34. Wendell, *Cotton Mather*, ed. Alan Heimert (New York, 1963), p. xxi.
35. David Levin, ed., *What Happened in Salem?* (New York, 1960), "Introduction"; "The Hazing of Cotton Mather," *New England Quarterly* 36 (1963); "Piety and Intellect in Puritanism," *William and Mary Quarterly* 20 (1965), 457-70; ed., *Bonifacius* (New Haven, 1966).

Index